Cornerstone Curriculum

Cornerstone Curriculum Student Workbook

© 2021. The Urban Ministry Institute. All Rights Reserved.

Copying, redistribution, and/or sale of these materials, or any unauthorized transmission, except as may be expressly permitted by the 1976 Copyright Act or in writing from the publisher is prohibited. Requests for permission should be addressed in writing to:

The Urban Ministry Institute
3701 East 13th Street North
Suite 100
Wichita, KS 67208

ISBN: 978-1-62932-060-1

Published by TUMI Press
A division of World Impact, Inc.

The Urban Ministry Institute is a ministry of World Impact, Inc.

All Scripture quotations, unless otherwise noted, are from The Holy Bible, English Standard Version, copyright © 2001 by Crossway Bible. A division of Good News Publishers. Used by permission. All Rights Reserved.

STUDENT WORKBOOK

The
Urban
Ministry
Institute
a ministry of
World
Impact,
Inc.

Cornerstone Curriculum

Rev. Dr. Don L. Davis
and *Rev. Terry G. Cornett*
with *Rev. Ryan Carter*

So then you are no longer strangers and aliens, but you are fellow citizens with the saints and members of the household of God, built on the foundation of the apostles and prophets, Christ Jesus himself being the **cornerstone**, *in whom the whole structure, being joined together, grows into a holy temple in the Lord. In him you also are being built together into a dwelling place for God by the Spirit.*

~ Ephesians 2.19-22

TUMI Press
3701 East 13th Street North
Suite 100
Wichita, Kansas 67208

Table of Contents

Overview

9   About the Instructors

11 Introduction to the Cornerstone Curriculum

13 Course Requirements

Part One: Biblical Studies & Theology and Ethics

Unit One: Biblical Studies

25 Introduction to Biblical Studies Unit

29 **Lesson 1**
    Conversion and Calling: The Word That Creates

47 **Lesson 2**
    Bible Interpretation: The Three-Step Model

77 **Lesson 3**
    The Old Testament Witness to Christ and His Kingdom:
    The Promise Given

101 **Lesson 4**
    The New Testament Witness to Christ and His Kingdom:
    The Messiah Opposed

Unit Two: Theology and Ethics

123 Introduction to Theology and Ethics Unit

127 **Lesson 1**
    The Kingdom of God: God's Reign Inaugurated

145 **Lesson 2**
    God the Father: The Triune God – The Greatness of God

167 **Lesson 3**
    God the Son: Jesus, the Messiah and Lord of All – He Died

189 **Lesson 4**
God the Holy Spirit: The Person of the Holy Spirit

Part Two: Christian Ministry & Urban Mission

Unit Three: Christian Ministry

211 Introduction to Christian Ministry Unit

215 **Lesson 1**
Theology of the Church: The Church at Worship

239 **Lesson 2**
Foundations of Christian Leadership:
The Christian Leader as Pastor – *Poimenes*

263 **Lesson 3**
Practicing Christian Leadership:
Effective Worship Leading – Worship, Word, and Sacrament

283 **Lesson 4**
The Equipping Ministry:
The Ministry of Proclamation – *Kerygma*

Unit Four: Urban Mission

311 Introduction to Urban Mission Unit

315 **Lesson 1**
Foundations for Christian Mission:
The Vision and Biblical Foundation for Christian Mission

349 **Lesson 2**
Evangelism and Spiritual Warfare:
Spiritual Warfare – Binding of the Strong Man

363 **Lesson 3**
Focus on Reproduction:
Church Growth – Reproducing in Number and Quality

389 **Lesson 4**
Doing Justice and Loving Mercy:
Let Justice Roll Down – The Vision and Theology of the Kingdom

Appendix

419 Appendix 1: The Nicene Creed

421 Appendix 2: List of Core Documents and Charts from *Picturing Theology*

Ministry Assessment Program

425 MAP Process: Diploma Students

427 C3-303 Ministry Assessment Project:
Agreement to Supervised Ministry Plan

428 Course Instruction Plan: C3-303 Ministry Assessment Project

441 Outline for First Interview with
Academic Advisor, Student, and Pastoral Supervisor

443 Outline for Final Interview with
Academic Advisor, Student, and Pastoral Supervisor

About the Instructors

Rev. Dr. Don L. Davis is the Executive Director of The Urban Ministry Institute and a Senior Vice President of World Impact. He attended Wheaton College and Wheaton Graduate School, and graduated summa cum laude in both his B.A. (1988) and M.A. (1989) degrees, in Biblical Studies and Systematic Theology, respectively. He earned his Ph.D. in Religion (Theology and Ethics) from the University of Iowa School of Religion.

As the Institute's Executive Director and World Impact's Senior Vice President, he oversees the training of urban missionaries, church planters, and city pastors, and facilitates training opportunities for urban Christian workers in evangelism, church growth, and pioneer missions. He also leads the Institute's extensive distance learning programs and facilitates leadership development efforts for organizations and denominations like Prison Fellowship, the Evangelical Free Church of America, and the Church of God in Christ.

A recipient of numerous teaching and academic awards, Dr. Davis has served as professor and faculty at a number of fine academic institutions, having lectured and taught courses in religion, theology, philosophy, and biblical studies at schools such as Wheaton College, St. Ambrose University, the Houston Graduate School of Theology, the University of Iowa School of Religion, the Robert E. Webber Institute of Worship Studies. He has authored a number of books, curricula, and study materials to equip urban leaders, including *The Capstone Curriculum*, TUMI's premiere sixteen-module distance education seminary instruction, *Sacred Roots: A Primer on Retrieving the Great Tradition*, which focuses on how urban churches can be renewed through a rediscovery of the historic orthodox faith, and *Black and Human: Rediscovering King as a Resource for Black Theology and Ethics*. Dr. Davis has participated in academic lectureships such as the Staley Lecture series, renewal conferences like the Promise Keepers rallies, and theological consortiums like the University of Virginia Lived Theology Project Series. He received the Distinguished Alumni Fellow Award from the University of Iowa College of Liberal Arts and Sciences in 2009. Dr. Davis is also a member of the Society of Biblical Literature, and the American Academy of Religion.

Rev. Terry Cornett (B.S., M. A., M.A.R.) is Academic Dean Emeritus of The Urban Ministry Institute in Wichita, Kansas. He holds degrees from The University of Texas at Austin, the Wheaton College Graduate School, and the C. P. Haggard School of Theology at Azusa Pacific University.

Terry ministered for 23 years as an urban missionary with World Impact before his retirement in 2005. During that time he served in Omaha, Los Angeles, and Wichita where he was involved in church-planting, education, and leadership-training ministries.

Rev. Ryan Carter is the Academic Dean of The Urban Ministry Institute. He is a native of Houston, Texas. Before joining the World Impact Wichita staff in 2008, he and his wife, Amber, served among the urban poor in Houston and Dallas. In September 2018, after ten years as a missionary in Wichita, Ryan joined TUMI Staff as our Resource Developer.

He is a graduate of the University of Houston (BA in Philosophy) and Dallas Theological Seminary (ThM in Old Testament Studies and Christian Education). His ministry experience includes missionary, children and youth ministries, associate pastor, church planter, and pastor.

The Carters have two sons, Benjamin (3/10/09) and Nathaniel (12/09/10).

Introduction to the Cornerstone Curriculum

Welcome to the *Cornerstone Curriculum*, your new opportunity to be equipped for effective ministry in the Church!

The Challenge: Great Need, No Time, Few Funds

The harsh reality faced by anyone equipping pastors and lay ministers serving in at-risk communities is that of scarcity. Money and time are too scarce and too short for these valiant leaders to engage in a long, structured study who serve God in poor communities. They do extraordinary work often while holding down a full-time job and growing ministry. Many thousands of urban Christian workers who would benefit from our premier, comprehensive, seminary-level curricula like the *Capstone Curriculum* don't have either the availability or the funds to complete it. (The average time for bi-vocational students to finish *Capstone's* sixteen modules is three to four years.)

Meeting the Challenge: The *Cornerstone Curriculum*

To meet this great need, we have designed this unique curriculum, the *Cornerstone Curriculum*. Selected from specific, targeted lessons taken from *Capstone*, we created this course of study for those who will never have the time or funds to complete our more extensive *Capstone* set. The time to complete *Cornerstone's* eight lessons, along with Dr. Sanders's *Redemptive Poverty Work* module, is the equivalent of only three *Capstone* modules. We created this resource to help these students access helpful resources without sacrificing quality or their ministry opportunities. *Cornerstone* will dramatically cut both the time and expense associated with typical Bible school or seminary studies or even the *Capstone Curriculum*, with no loss to either our fidelity to biblical truth or practical ministry training.

Be Equipped to Plant, Pastor, and Serve the Church!

We distilled the content of *Cornerstone's* lesson materials directly from *Capstone's* modules, drawing out its essential truths from its four department areas (Biblical Studies, Theology and Ethics, Christian Ministry, and Urban Mission). We put together *Cornerstone's* lessons to provide you with a timely, cost-effective, and solid training regimen. Our training will provide you with certification, enrich your knowledge of the Scripture, and outfit you to minister effectively as a pastor, lay leader, or a Christian worker where you live and work. God has called and gifted you, and we hope to see you fulfill his calling on your life, that you may honor our Savior in everything you do.

I challenge you, therefore, to fulfill the Lord's ministry for you, all in the spirit of Paul's admonition to Timothy, "Do your best to present yourself to God as one approved, a worker who has no need to be ashamed, rightly handling the word of truth" (2 Tim. 2.15, ESV). Know that if you do present yourself to God as one approved, you will fulfill his call and bear spiritual fruit that honors Christ and pleases God. May God richly bless you in your studies, your discipleship, and your ministry!

With bold confidence in God's eternal Word to heal and transform,

Dr. Don Davis
Wichita, Kansas
April 26, 2021

Course Requirements

Required Books and Materials

- Bible (for the purposes of this course, your Bible should be a translation [ex. NIV, NASB, RSV, KJV, NKJV, etc.], and not a paraphrase [ex. The Living Bible, The Message]).

- Each Cornerstone Curriculum unit has assigned textbooks which are read and discussed throughout the course. We encourage you to read, reflect upon, and respond to these with your professors, mentors, and fellow learners. Because of the fluid availability of the texts (e.g., books going out of print), we maintain our *official* Cornerstone Curriculum Required Textbook list on our website. Please visit *www.tumi.org/books* to obtain the current listing of this unit's texts and reading assignments.

- Paper and pen for taking notes and completing in-class assignments.

Suggested Readings

- Davis, Don L. with Terry Cornett and Don Allsman. *Picturing Theology: An A-Z Collection of TUMI's Key Diagrams, Charts, Graphics, and Articles*. Wichita, KS: TUMI Press, 2019.

Course Requirements

Summary of Grade Categories and Weights

Attendance and Class Participation	30%	90 pts
Memory Verses	20%	60 pts
Exegetical Project	20%	60 pts
Ministry Project	10%	30 pts
Readings and Homework Assignments	10%	30 pts
Final Exam	10%	30 pts
Total:	100%	300 pts

Grade Requirements

Attendance and Class Participation

Attendance at each class session is a course requirement. Absences will affect your grade. If an absence cannot be avoided, please let your Mentor know in advance. If you miss a class it is your responsibility to find out the assignments you missed, and to talk with your Mentor about turning in late work. Much of the learning associated with this course takes place through discussion. Therefore, your active involvement will be sought and expected in every class session.

Memory Verses

The memorized Word is a central priority for your life and ministry as a believer and leader in the Church of Jesus Christ. There are relatively few verses, but they are significant in their content. Each class session you will be expected to recite (orally or in writing) the assigned verses to your Mentor. (See page 16 for a sample Scripture Memory Grading Form. Your Mentor will provide this form for you.)

Exegetical Project

The Scriptures are God's potent instrument to equip the man or woman of God for every work of ministry he calls them to (2 Tim. 3.16-17). In order to complete the requirements for this course you must select a passage and do an inductive Bible study (i.e., an exegetical study) upon it. The study will have to be five pages in length (double-spaced, typed or neatly hand written) and deal with one of the four aspects of the Word of God covered in the four lessons of this course. Our desire and hope is that you will be deeply convinced of Scripture's ability to change and practically affect your life and the lives of those to whom you minister. As you go through the course, be open to finding an extended passage (roughly 4-9 verses) on a subject you would like to study more intensely. The details of the project are covered on page 17, and will be discussed in the introductory session of this course.

Ministry Project — Our expectation is that all students will apply their learning practically in their lives and in their ministry responsibilities. The student will be responsible for developing a ministry project that combines principles learned with practical ministry. The details of this project are covered on page 19, and will be discussed in the introductory session of the course.

Class and Homework Assignments — Classwork and homework of various types may be given during class by your Mentor or be written in your Student Workbook. If you have any question about what is required by these or when they are due, please ask your Mentor.

Readings — It is important that the student read the assigned readings from the text and from the Scriptures in order to be prepared for class discussion. Please turn in the "Reading Completion Sheet" on a weekly basis. There will be an option to receive extra credit for extended readings. (See page 20 for an example of the Reading Completion Sheet. Your Mentor will provide this form for you.)

Unit Exam — At the end of each unit, your Mentor will give you a unit exam (closed book) to be completed at home. You will be asked a question that helps you reflect on what you have learned in the unit and how it affects the way you think about or practice ministry. Your Mentor will give you due dates and other information when the Unit Exam is handed out.

Grading

The following grades will be given in this class at the end of the session, and placed on each student's record:

A – Superior work	D – Passing work
B – Excellent work	F – Unsatisfactory work
C – Satisfactory work	I – Incomplete

Letter grades with appropriate pluses and minuses will be given for each final grade, and grade points for your grade will be factored into your overall grade point average. Unexcused late work or failure to turn in assignments will affect your grade, so please plan ahead, and communicate conflicts with your instructor.

Scripture Memory Grading Form Sample

Name: _____ Credit: _____

Translation: _____ Passage Memorized: _____

It is the student's responsibility to grade his/her own Scripture Memory Work. As a reminder, please memorize Scripture only from a translation (ex. EXV, NIV, NASB, RSV, KJV, etc.) and not a paraphrase (ex. The Living Bible, The Message). Please follow the process below in order to grade your work:

1. Put away any helps you may have (including your Bible), and on a blank sheet of paper, write out your Scripture Memory passage in its entirety.

2. Write the translation on the top of your page along with your name.

3. Using your Bible, check your work, word for word, and put a line through any errors you may have.

4. Count up the number of errors and write them here: _____

5. How many verses were there in this memorized passage? _____

6. You are allowed the equivalent of one mistake per verse to receive full credit for your memory work. If your passage was three verses and you scored perfect on two of the verses and had three errors in the third verse, you will receive full credit for this passage.

7. You are allowed the equivalent of two mistakes per verse to receive half credit for the passage. If your passage was three verses and you made 4-6 mistakes you will receive half credit for this passage.

8. If you made more than the equivalent of two mistakes per verse, you will receive no credit for this passage.

9. Write "full credit," "half credit," or "no credit" at the top of this page, depending on how you scored, and give this page to your instructor.

The following ARE counted as errors:
- *A wrong word (each wrong word is an error)*
- *A missing word (each missing word is an error)*
- *A word or words out of order (each word out of order is an error)*

The following SHOULD NOT be counted as errors:
- *Missed or wrong punctuation*
- *A misspelled word*

Exegetical Project

Purpose

As a part of your participation in the Cornerstone Curriculum, you will be required to do an exegesis (inductive study) on a passage in the Word of God.

The purpose of this exegetical project is to give you an opportunity to do a detailed study of a major passage on the nature and function of the Word of God. As you study one of the texts listed under "Unit Assignments" at the beginning of each Unit, our hope is that you will be able to show how this passage illumines or makes plain the significance of the Word of God for our spirituality and for our lives together in the Church. We also desire that the Spirit will give you insight as to how you can relate its meaning directly to your own personal walk of discipleship, as well as to the leadership role God has given to you currently in your church and ministry.

Outline and Composition

This is a Bible study project, and, in order to do exegesis, you must be committed to understanding the meaning of the passage in its own setting. Once you know what it meant, you can then draw out principles that apply to all of us, and then relate those principles to life. A simple three-step process can guide you in your personal study of the Bible passage:

1. What was *God saying to the people in the text's original situation?*

2. What principle(s) does *the text teach that is true for all people everywhere*, including today?

3. What is *the Holy Spirit asking me to do with this principle here, today*, in my life and ministry?

Once you have answered these questions in your personal study, you are then ready to write out your insights for your *paper assignment*.

Here is a *sample outline* for your paper:

1. List out what you believe is *the main theme or idea* of the text you selected.

2. *Summarize the meaning* of the passage (you may do this in two or three paragraphs, or, if you prefer, by writing a short verse-by-verse commentary on the passage).

3. *Outline one to three key principles or insights* this text provides on the Word of God.

4. Tell how one, some, or all of the principles may relate to *one or more* of the following:

    a. Your personal spirituality and walk with Christ

    b. Your life and ministry in your local church

    c. Situations or challenges in your community and general society

As an aid or guide, please feel free to read the course texts and/or commentaries, and integrate insights from them into your work. Make sure that you give credit to whom credit is due if you borrow or build upon someone else's insights. Use in-the-text references, footnotes, or endnotes. Any way you choose to cite your references will be acceptable, as long as you 1) use only one way consistently throughout your paper, and 2) indicate where you are using someone else's ideas, and are giving them credit for it. (For more information, see *Documenting Your Work: A Guide to Help You Give Credit Where Credit Is Due* on page 81 in *Picturing Theology: An A-Z Collection of TUMI's Key Diagrams, Charts, Graphics, and Articles*.)

Make certain that your exegetical project, when turned in meets the following standards:

- It is legibly written or typed.

- Is a study of one of the passages listed under "Unit Assignments" at the beginning of each Unit.

- It is turned in on time (not late).

- It is 5 pages in length.

- It follows the outline given above, clearly laid out for the reader to follow.

- It shows how the passage relates to life and ministry today.

Do not let these instructions intimidate you; this is a Bible study project! All you need to show in this paper is that you *studied* the passage, *summarized* its meaning, *drew out* a few key principles from it, and *related* them to your own life and ministry.

Grading

The exegetical project is worth 60 points, and represents 20% of your overall grade, so make certain that you make your project an excellent and informative study of the Word.

Ministry Project

Purpose

The Word of God is living and active, and penetrates to the very heart of our lives and innermost thoughts (Heb. 4.12). James the Apostle emphasizes the need to be doers of the Word of God, not hearers only, deceiving ourselves. We are exhorted to apply the Word, to obey it. Neglecting this discipline, he suggests, is analogous to a person viewing our natural face in a mirror and then forgetting who we are, and are meant to be. In every case, the doer of the Word of God will be blessed in what he or she does (James 1.22-25).

Our sincere desire is that you will apply your learning practically, correlating your learning with real experiences and needs in your personal life, and in your ministry in and through your church. Therefore, a key part of completing the Cornerstone Curriculum will be for you to design a ministry project to help you share some of the insights you have learned from this course with others.

Planning and Summary

There are many ways that you can fulfill this requirement of your study. You may choose to conduct a brief study of your insights with an individual, or a Sunday School class, youth or adult group or Bible study, or even at some ministry opportunity. What you must do is discuss some of the insights you have learned from class with your audience. (Of course, you may choose to share insights from your Exegetical Project in this unit with them.)

Feel free to be flexible in your project. Make it creative and open-ended. At the beginning of the course, you should decide on a context in which you will share your insights, and share that with your instructor. Plan ahead and avoid the last minute rush in selecting and carrying out your project.

After you have carried out your plan, write and turn in to your Mentor a one-page summary or evaluation of your time of sharing. A sample outline of your Ministry Project summary is as follows:

1. Your name

2. The place where you shared, and the audience with whom you shared

3. A brief summary of how your time went, how you felt, and how they responded

4. What you learned from the time

Grading

The Ministry Project is worth 30 points and represents 10% of your overall grade, so make certain to share your insights with confidence and make your summary clear.

CORNERSTONE CURRICULUM
READING COMPLETION SHEET

Name _____

Date _____

For each assigned reading, write a brief summary (one or two paragraphs) of the author's main point. (For additional readings, use the back of this sheet.)

Reading 1

Title and Author: _____ Pages: _____

Reading 2

Title and Author: _____ Pages: _____

Part One

Biblical Studies

Theology and Ethics

Biblical Studies

**Conversion and Calling:
The Word That Creates**

**Bible Interpretation:
The Three-Step Model**

**The Old Testament Witness to Christ and His Kingdom:
The Promise Given**

**The New Testament Witness to Christ and His Kingdom:
The Messiah Opposed**

Introduction to Biblical Studies Unit

Greetings, dearest friends, in the strong name of Jesus Christ!

Welcome to the first unit of the Cornerstone Curriculum, *Biblical Studies*.

According to the clear testimony of the Scriptures themselves, God equips his representatives through the Spirit-breathed Word of God, the Scriptures. Everyone God calls into the ministry must determine to discipline themselves so as to master its contents, submit to its injunctions, and teach its truths. Like a workman (or work-woman!) they must strive to handle the Word of truth accurately, and so be approved of the Lord in their study (2 Tim. 2.15).

As disciples of Jesus Christ, we affirm our deep belief in the creative, convicting, converting, and calling power of the Word of God. To understand the wonderful blessing of conversion and calling, we will need to critically evaluate the place of the Word of God in the Church.

Our first lesson, *Conversion and Calling: The Word That Creates*, explores the nature of the Holy Scriptures as the Word of God as the means by which the Holy Spirit creates new life in those who believe. We prove to be disciples by abiding in Jesus' Word. As members of the Church we receive the Word together in community, the same which provides us with the ultimate purpose of the created universe, which is the glorification of Almighty God.

In our second lesson, *Biblical Interpretation: The Three-Step Model*, we will introduce an effective method of biblical interpretation designed to help you approach your study of Scripture so as to bridge the gap between our ancient and contemporary worlds. We call it the *Three-Step Model*: understand the original audience, discover general principles, and make applications to life. The Bible's own remarkable claim of its transforming power ought to be reason enough to challenge us to master the Word of God. "All Scripture is breathed out by God and profitable for teaching, for reproof, for correction, and for training in righteousness, that the man of God may be competent, equipped for every good work" (2 Tim. 3.16-17). The God-breathed Word of God in the words of humankind is sufficient to enrich us, delight us, and make us competent and equipped for every good work. Truly, the Word of God cannot be broken, will always accomplish its purpose, and will ensure the person of God enjoys good success in all they do to advance the Kingdom of God wherever they are (John 10.35; Isa. 55.8-11; Josh. 1.8).

The Spirit-breathed Scripture is anchored on the witness of Jesus of Nazareth. He and he alone provides unity, continuity, and coherence to both the Old and New Testaments, and no one can claim a holistic or accurate view of the Bible without him being central in all phases of exegesis. He is the Bible's theme (John 5.39-40).

In our third lesson, *The Old Testament Witness to Christ and His Kingdom: The Promise Given*, we will examine the relationship of the Old Testament to the New Testament through the idea of progressive revelation. We will look at the complimentary connections which exist in the OT and NT as they relate to the person of Christ and his Kingdom, and consider the unique motif of *promise and fulfillment*, and how this integrates and makes one the teaching of Scripture on the person of Jesus Christ. This unity of truth is seen in God's marvelous promise to send a redeemer to humanity through whom God's enemy would be destroyed, and humankind would be redeemed. In the *protoevangelium* (i.e., the first telling of the Gospel in Genesis 3.15), through the covenant promise of Abraham and its extensions we see how the Messianic hope is the unifying principle of the Old Testament and the joyous fulfillment of the New, all finding their climax in the person of Jesus Christ. He is both the seed of the woman and the seed of Abraham. May the Hebrew Scriptures unveil his glory to us, and transform us as we become diligent students of God's holy Word!

There can be no question that the most critical and important subject to master in the life of a Christian leader is the actual person and teachings of Jesus of Nazareth. No other subject is as significant or controversial as the meaning of his life and ministry.

In our fourth lesson, *The New Testament Witness to Christ and His Kingdom: The Messiah Opposed*, we will explore the Jewish concept of the Kingdom of God at the time of Jesus. We'll see how the nation of Israel, oppressed by political powers, believed that when the Messiah came, the Kingdom of God would come in power, restoring the material universe and saving humankind from the control of Satan. Of course, Jesus proclaimed the Kingdom present, and demonstrated its reality in his healings and exorcisms, revealing the Kingdom's presence in his own person and ministry. Again, there can be little doubt that the depth of our ministry and leadership can proceed no further than the depth of our knowledge of Jesus Christ, the Messiah of God and Lord of all.

Therefore, may our God and Father provide you with the hunger, passion, and discipline to master the life and ministry of Jesus. In so doing, you will be able to be his disciple and make disciples of Jesus in your church, in your ministry, and wherever else God may lead.

Take his yoke upon yourself, and learn of him – this is the key to godly servant leadership in Christ.

My sincere prayer is that all of these blessings and more become yours as the Holy Spirit enables you to explore the principles and practices of interpreting his holy and eternal Word!

Unit Assignments

Exegetical Project

As a part of your participation in the Cornerstone Curriculum, you will be required to do an exegesis (inductive study) on a passage in the Word of God:

a. Psalm 110.1-4

b. Isaiah 55.1-10

c. Luke 24.36-48

d. 2 Timothy 3.14-17

The purpose of this exegetical project is to give you an opportunity to do a detailed study of a major passage on the nature and function of the Word of God. As you study one of the above texts (or a text which you and your Mentor agree upon which may not be on the list), our hope is that you will be able to show how this passage illumines or makes plain the significance of the Word of God for our spirituality and for our lives together in the Church. We also desire that the Spirit will give you insight as to how you can relate its meaning directly to your own personal walk of discipleship, as well as to the leadership role God has given to you currently in your church and ministry.

Memory Verses

The memorized Word is a central priority for your life and ministry as a believer and leader in the Church of Jesus Christ. There are relatively few verses, but they are significant in their content. Each class session you will be expected to recite (orally or in writing) the assigned verses to your Mentor.

a. 2 Timothy 3.16-17

b. Psalm 1.1-3

c. Luke 24.44-48

d. John 15.18-20

Textbooks

Each Cornerstone Curriculum unit has assigned textbooks which are read and discussed throughout the course. We encourage you to read, reflect upon, and respond to these with your professors, mentors, and fellow learners. Because of the fluid availability of the texts (e.g., books going out of print), we maintain our *official* Cornerstone Curriculum Required Textbook list on our website. Please visit *www.tumi.org/books* to obtain the current listing of this unit's texts and reading assignments.

Ministry Project

Our sincere desire is that you will apply your learning practically, correlating your learning with real experiences and needs in your personal life, and in your ministry in and through your church. Therefore, a key part of completing the Cornerstone Curriculum will be for you to design a ministry project to help you share some of the insights you have learned from this course with others.

Unit Exam

At the end of each unit, your Mentor will give you a unit exam (closed book) to be completed at home. You will be asked a question that helps you reflect on what you have learned in the unit and how it affects the way you think about or practice ministry. Your Mentor will give you due dates and other information when the Unit Exam is handed out.

Conversion and Calling
The Word That Creates

Lesson Objectives

Welcome in the strong name of Jesus Christ! After your reading, study, discussion, and application of the materials in this lesson, you will be able to:

- Defend the idea that the Holy Scriptures are the Word of God, a written record of the Lord's own living and eternal Word.

- Discuss how continuing in and receiving this implanted Word of God is the true sign of discipleship and authentic adoption into the family of God. As saints of God, we receive the Word of God together in his covenant community.

- Demonstrate how the Word reveals the ultimate purpose of the created universe, which is the glorification of Almighty God.

- Recite from memory a passage relating to the creative power of the Word of God.

Devotion

The Desirability of the Living Word of God

Read Psalm 19.7-11. If our age is known for anything it is the age of passion. People give themselves to acquire things, to experience pleasures, to attain positions, and to accomplish goals, sometimes making great sacrifices for the things that they desire. Perhaps the saddest tragedy in the lives of millions of people is that they are giving themselves over to things that, in the long run, won't matter at all. They are living for fleeting pleasures, material possessions, and personal accomplishments that within a hundred years either won't exist or won't matter at all. To really live well we must not merely have great passion, but we must direct our passions and desires after the things that will last, and the things that really matter.

According to the Word of God, very few things really matter, and therefore, few things are to be desired and sought after. One of the most significant treasures spoken of in Scripture is the very Word of God itself. God declares that his Word, the written Word of the Holy Scriptures, is a treasure that is worthy of our most sincere and concentrated efforts to acquire. Nothing on earth lasts like it; nothing can provide us with the wisdom, insight, hope, and joy that it gives.

The Word of God is a profoundly rich asset, giving light to the eyes, joy to the heart, wisdom to the spirit, and hope to one's life. The psalmist here makes plain the remarkable desirability of the living Word of God to us. There is nothing that we own or could own that is as valuable and important as God's Word regarding his Son, his plan, and our hope. In keeping them we are warned, and in clinging to them there is great reward.

Are you seeking the Word of God like you seek money, or pleasure, or free time, or great opportunity? Nothing in this world is as valuable or as significant as a deep knowledge of God's Word. Where is the desire of your heart today?

Nicene Creed and Prayer

After reciting and/or singing the Nicene Creed (located in the Appendix), pray the following prayers:

> Eternal God, our Father, we praise you for your desire to reveal yourself to us through your Word. You have blessed us by preserving your gracious promise and pronouncement through the Scriptures, which you inspired by your own Holy Spirit. Now, through that same Spirit, you are teaching us about your Son, and your glorious plan to restore all things in him. How we bless your high and holy name for your living and abiding Word, and we ask that you would grant to us your wisdom as we learn together the power and greatness of your Word.
>
> Merciful God, heavenly Father, Thou hast said to us through the mouth of Thy dear Son, our Lord Jesus Christ, "Pray the Lord of the harvest," Upon this Thy divine command, we pray from our hearts, that Thou wilt give thy Holy Spirit richly to these Thy servants, together with us and all those who are called to serve Thy word. Amen.
>
> ~ Martin Luther. *Devotions and Prayers of Martin Luther.* Trans. Andrew Kosten. Grand Rapids: Baker Book House, 1965. p 77.

Scripture Memorization Review

No Scripture memorization this lesson.

Assignments Due

No assignments due this lesson.

CONTACT

A Question of Expertise

1. In general society today it is normal for most people who have professional or personal problems to either handle it on their own, or consult the "experts" – scientists, doctors, counselors, or others who are perceived as the ones who can enable them to overcome their difficulties or solve their problems. What place does the Word of God have today in solving people's problems? In what ways do you see or fail to see a respect for the teaching of the Word of God in society today?

Where Does the Authority Lie?

2. Imagine that a critical issue comes up in the youth group of your local church ministry about pre-marital sex. Many of the kids are being taught in their local high schools that sexual activity is normal and expected, and is fine as long as they take precautions against sexually transmitted diseases and the risk of getting pregnant. The arguments being made in high school are becoming somewhat attractive to some of the students in your youth group, who are wondering just how the standards of an ancient book like the Bible relate to them as young people today. What would you say to those kids who are teetering on the brink of rejecting the authority of Scripture for their lives, those who are becoming more and more persuaded that things are okay if we handle them responsibly and openly?

Jesus – Yes; the Bible – No!

3. There are many people who profess a deep allegiance to the person and teaching of Jesus, but have a problem with the truthfulness of the Bible. Jesus taught love, humility, and good will among people; the Bible, however, is filled with odd teachings about angels, demons, and miracles, things which many modern people find hard or impossible to believe. Do you think it is possible to embrace the person of Jesus Christ while, at the same time, calling certain things of the Bible into question? Can you say "Yes!" to Jesus, but a "No!" or "I'm not sure" to many things in the Scriptures? Must you believe everything that the Bible teaches in order to claim a true relationship and faith in Jesus? Why or why not?

The Word That Creates

Rev. Dr. Don L. Davis

Summary

The Word of God is the means by which the Holy Spirit creates new life in those who believe. Therefore, continuing in and receiving this implanted Word of God is the true sign of discipleship and authentic adoption into the family of God. As saints of God, we receive the Word of God together in his covenant community. Finally, because of the trustworthiness of the Word, it alone can declare to us the ultimate purpose of the created universe, which is the glorification of Almighty God.

Our objective for this lesson, *The Word That Creates,* is to enable you to see that:

- God's Word is infused with God's very life, and therefore, no spirituality or authentic religion is possible without the life-giving power of the Word of God. God creates new life in believers through his Word, enlightened by the Holy Spirit.

- The true sign of discipleship is to abide in and continue in the ongoing reception of the Word of God as spirit and truth. Spiritual maturity is directly connected to hearing and obeying God's Word in the Church.

- Because of its infallible authority, only the Word of God can provide us with the ultimate purpose for the created universe, which is to bring God honor and glory in all things.

Video Outline

I. **The Word of God Is Infused with God's Own Life, and Therefore Creates New Life in Those Who Believe.**

   A. The Word creates spiritual life in response to belief in the work of Jesus Christ.

      1. The Word of God is absolutely primary in creating new spiritual life in the believer.

         a. James 1.18

b. James 1.21

2. The Word of God is the instrument, the imperishable seed, that births new life in us through our faith in Jesus Christ, 1 Pet. 1.22-23.

3. The Gospel concerning Jesus and his Kingdom is not of human origin, but "is itself the very Word of God," 1 Thess. 2.13.

B. Spiritual life is created by the living Word of God: we live by every word which proceeds from the mouth of God.

1. We hold this view on the authority of Jesus Christ.

    a. The temptation of Jesus

    b. The quotation of Deuteronomy: the singular role of the Word of God, Deut. 8.3, cf. Matt. 4.4

2. The Word of God has remarkable spiritual vitality and creative power to spiritually enlighten the soul, Ps. 19.7-11.

3. No part of the Word of God is to be considered useless or superfluous; every jot and tittle will be fulfilled, and none of it shall pass away.

4. God absolutely refuses to break his covenant promise: the Scriptures are reliable because God is faithful.

    a. 2 Kings 13.23

b. 1 Chron. 16.14-17

C. God provides understanding for his Word through the sending of his Holy Spirit to believers, 1 Cor. 2.9-16.

1. The unbeliever (i.e., "natural man") does not have the Holy Spirit, and therefore cannot understand the Word's message or teaching.

2. The spiritual person, (i.e., the one who has and is led by the Holy Spirit), not only understands what the Word of God says, but escapes the judgment of those who fail to comprehend it.

3. The same Spirit who inspired the Word is the one who interprets it, 2 Pet. 1.21.

II. The True Sign of Discipleship Is to Continue In and Abide In the Word of God as Nourishment.

A. The sign of true discipleship is to continue in and abide in the Word of Christ.

1. John 8.31-32

2. "Abide" is to remain present, to make one's home in, to dwell in, Ps. 1.1-3.

3. The sense of abiding is similar to the OT notion of meditation.

a. Ps. 1.1-3

b. Josh. 1.8

B. Spiritual growth and maturity are dependent on feeding upon the truths in the creative and life-giving Word of God.

1. Believers are to desire the pure milk of the Word of God in order that we might be able to grow as we feed upon it, 1 Pet. 2.2.

2. Paul, in his challenge to the elders of Ephesus, commended them to God and the Word of his grace "which is able to build you up and to give you the inheritance among all those who are sanctified," Acts 20.32.

3. The Colossians are exhorted to let the Word of God dwell richly in them, Col. 3.16.

4. Paul gives Timothy authoritative charge to study to show himself a workman to God approved as he rightly divided (dissected) the Word of truth, 2 Tim. 2.15.

5. There are many ways to abide in the Word of God.

   a. We are to *read* it. Revelation 1.3 promises a blessing to those who read the Word of God.

   b. We are to *memorize* it. In Psalm 119.11 David says he hides God's Word in his heart that he might not sin against the Lord.

   c. We are to *meditate* upon it. Psalm 1.3 says that the godly man meditates, murmurs and chews on the Word of God day and night.

d. We are to *study* it. The Bereans are called "more noble" than the Thessalonians in Acts 17.11 because they not only heard the words of the Apostle Paul, but studied the Scriptures daily to validate Paul's Gospel.

e. We are to *hear it preached and taught* in the Church. We are not to despise prophesies, but hear the Word for, as Romans 10.17 suggests, "faith comes by hearing, and hearing by the Word of God."

f. We are to *include it in all our living and conversation*. The Word that creates must become the dominant force in our lives as spoken in the words of the Shema, Deut. 6.4-9.

C. This creative Word of God must be heard and obeyed in the context of Christian community.

1. Do not despise prophesying, nor quench the Holy Spirit, 1 Thess. 5.19-22.

2. The Word will come in the midst of the assembly, 1 Cor. 14.26.

3. God has given to the Church men and women specially endowed by the Holy Spirit to teach the Word of God, Eph. 4.11-13.

III. The Word Reveals God's Eternal Purpose for the Universe: That All Things Might Bring Glory and Honor to Him as Lord.

A. One underlying pulse of energy throbs from the heart of the Divine Story. All things were created to bring glory, honor, and praise to the Lord and his glorious Name.

1. All things were created for God's designed purpose, Prov. 16.4.

2. All things in heaven and in earth, whether visible or invisible, all angels, creatures, whether human or animal, and all that exist were created by God and for his glory.

    a. Col. 1.16

    b. Rev. 4.11

    c. Ps. 150.6

3. The nation of Israel, God's chosen people, were selected for his ultimate glory.

    a. Isa. 43.7

    b. Isa. 43.21

    c. Cf. Isa. 43.25; 60.1, 3, 21

4. God saves humankind in order to bring glory and honor to himself, Rom. 9.23; Eph. 2.7.

5. All the service and the works that God's people accomplish are to be done for God's ultimate glory, 1 Cor. 10.31; John 15.8; Matt. 5.16.

6. Believer's high purpose: personal witness to the glory of God in Christ, and sharing in that same glory at his appearing.

> *Taken as a whole, the Bible differs in its subject and purpose from any other book in the world. It stands supreme as reflecting the place of [humankind] and [its] opportunity of salvation, the supreme character and work of Jesus Christ as the only Savior, and gives in detail the infinite glories that belong to God himself. It is the one book that reveals the Creator to the creature and discloses the plan by which all [humankind] in all [its] imperfections can be reconciled in eternal fellowship with the eternal God.*
>
> ~ Lewis Sperry Chafer. *Major Bible Themes.* Grand Rapids: Zondervan, 1974. p. 29.

      a. John 17.22

      b. Col. 3.4

B. When we submit to God's creative Word, it provides us with strength and direction in order to accomplish this purpose of honoring and glorifying him.

  1. It discloses our inner motives and desires, Heb. 4.12.

  2. It aligns our wavering hearts with the majesty of God's eternal purpose.

      a. Scripture as the joy and rejoicing of our hearts, Jer. 15.16

      b. The Word of God causes great movement deep inside our hearts as we yield to its power, Jer. 20.9.

  3. It transforms us by the renewing of our minds to the perfect will of God, Rom. 12.1-2.

Conclusion

- The Word of God is infused with God's own life and is the means by which the Holy Spirit creates new life in those who believe.

- True disciples of Jesus Christ abide in this implanted Word.

- The Holy Spirit teaches us that the ultimate purpose of the created universe is to glorify Almighty God.

- The Scriptures, the Word that creates, enable us through the Spirit to glorify God as we live under God's rule.

LESSON 1 | CONVERSION AND CALLING: THE WORD THAT CREATES / 39

Student Questions and Response

The following questions were designed to help you review the material in the video which focused on the life-giving properties of the Word of God in our lives. Be clear and concise in your answers, and where possible, support with Scripture!

1. How does the Bible describe the role that the Scriptures play in providing new life to the one who believes in Christ? What role does faith play together with the Word to create the new birth?

2. In what way does Jesus' temptation teach us of the power of the Word of God for our lives? What truth did Jesus cite when confronted with the devil and his deceptions in the wilderness?

3. What role does the Holy Spirit play in helping the spiritual person grasp the meaning of the Holy Scriptures? What about the natural person – can they understand them? Why or why not?

4. What is the true sign of discipleship in Jesus Christ? Describe the relationship between spiritual growth and feeding upon the Word of God?

5. What are some of the ways that Scripture suggests that one can abide in the Word of God? How does abiding in the Word connect to living in Christian community?

6. What particular people has God given to the Church to help it understand and apply the Word of God? What is their role in helping equip Christians to do ministry?

7. According to Scripture, what is God's eternal purpose for the created universe?

8. Ultimately, what is the high purpose that God has appointed for believers, and how are they to carry that purpose out in their lives?

9. In what way are the Scriptures unique and supremely above all other books in the world?

10. What can we expect to occur in our hearts and our lives when we submit to God's creative Word? Explain.

CONNECTION

Summary of Key Concepts

This lesson highlights certain critical aspects of the creative power of the Word of God, objectively in the creation of the universe, and subjectively, in the creation of new spiritual life in the heart of the believer. In every sense, the notion of the Word of God is significant for understanding God's work in the world, and throughout human history.

- The Holy Scriptures are the living and eternal Word of God. They are as identified directly with God's person and his work.

- The Word of God, being authored by the Holy Spirit and therefore infused with God's own life, is the critical instrument by which new life is created in those who believe in Jesus. The message of the Gospel is the spiritual seed that causes us to be born from above.

- The authentic sign of true discipleship in Christ is abiding in and continuing in the Word of Jesus, which liberates and sets believers free.

- God has granted to every believer the Holy Spirit in order that we might understand and grasp the meaning of the Scriptures that he inspired (1 Cor. 2.9-16 cf. 2 Pet. 1.21-22).

- The Holy Spirit teaches us that the ultimate purpose of the created universe is to glorify Almighty God (Isa. 43.7; Prov. 16.4; 1 Cor. 10.31).

- The Scriptures, the Word that creates, enable us through the Spirit to glorify God as we live under God's rule.

Student Application and Implications

Now is the time for you to discuss with your fellow students your questions about the power of the Word that creates. What particular questions do you have in light of the material you have just studied? Perhaps the questions below might spark your discussion together, and help you form your own, more specific and critical questions.

- When we say that the Scriptures are inspired by God, do we mean the "original autographs" (i.e., the documents that prophets and Apostles wrote), the translations, copies of the translations, or everything?

- What impact on discussions about evolution does our belief that God created the world through his Word have? Is evolutionary theory something we need to be concerned about or not?

- If the Word of God is living and active and creative, why doesn't it seem to work the same way in every person's heart that hears it? Why do so many people reject the message of the Word today?

- What exactly is the relationship between the Word of God in Jesus and the Word of God in Scripture? Which one is to take precedence over the other; are they meant to be taken and revered in the same way?

- How are we to relate to the Holy Spirit, practically speaking, so we can know that he will teach us as we study the Word of God?

- If I am to study the Word of God in the context of community, what is the role and importance of my personal study of the Word of God? What if I disagree with some of the things that are being taught in my church, or by my pastor – what am I to do then?

CASE STUDIES

A Serious Case of Disagreement

1. As a church has been going through a series of teachings on the Second Coming of Christ, a young Christian leader has encountered teachings in the pastor's sermons that she doesn't understand, and, on first glance, does not agree with. She has spent some time discussing with the pastor some of the points, and none of them are critical, in the sense that they deny anything taught in the Scriptures. The pastor has made it plain that these are merely his opinions about the Scriptures, but is a strong teacher and many are finding his ideas convincing. The pastor is a biblical leader, a fine Christian teacher, and a humble brother in Christ. What ought the sister to do in this situation?

A Denial of the Faith?

2. In a science class at school, one of the students in the youth group is having to write a term paper on the theory of evolution. This same student has been learning at church how God created the worlds through the Word of God, and even more specifically, through Jesus Christ. He believes the Scriptures, that the Bible's teaching on creation is correct, and yet the Bible does not appear to address all of the issues that he is encountering in class about science. He does not want to turn his science class into a religious discussion group, but he is struggling with finding a way to talk about the Bible's view of creation in his high school science class. If this young brother came to you for advice, what would you counsel him to do or not do?

God's Word according to King James of England

 Serious disagreement and conflict has arisen in one of the church's home Bible studies over which translations are okay to be used. One faction of older believers has asserted that the only Bible we should use in the group is the King James Bible, a tried and true translation that has long been revered and treasured in the church. A group of younger folk are insistent on using some of the "modern" translations, because they find them so much easier to study and memorize. To those of the older faction, when verses are read from the newer translation, it is as if the entire meaning of the verse has changed. Both sides know that the Bible was not written originally in English, but no one in either faction understands Hebrew or Greek. As pastor, how would you resolve this dilemma in the home group?

You Need the Holy Spirit

 After hearing a teaching on television that said no one can understand the Bible without the aid of the Holy Spirit, one of the deacons at church is deeply concerned about his own lack of understanding of the Bible. While he understands that the Holy Spirit has indwelt and sealed him once he believed (e.g., Rom. 8.1-18; Eph. 1.13; Gal. 5.16-23), he doesn't know what it means to be "taught" by the Holy Spirit. He is deeply skeptical of going through a lot of emotional exercises in order to say that he is being taught by the Spirit, and everyone recognizes this dear brother to be a mature, godly, and Christlike servant in the church. Still, he wants to understand what it means to be taught by the Spirit. How would you instruct this brother to understand the role of the Holy Spirit's teaching ministry in his ongoing understanding of the Bible?

Restatement of the Lesson's Thesis

The Holy Scriptures are the Word of God, a written record of the Lord's own living and eternal Word. Because they are inspired by the Holy Spirit (literally, God-breathed) they are absolutely trustworthy and reliable in all they assert and claim. The Word of God provides us with God's eternal purpose for creation, that is, that all things were made through God's creative and life-giving Word for his ultimate glory. The Lord God identifies himself completely with the Word of God in Jesus Christ. He is the One through whom God reveals himself, redeems the world, and will restore the universe under his righteous rule. This Word by the Spirit creates new life in those who believe. True discipleship is abiding in this Word in the Church, which produces in the believer spiritual maturity, depth, and growth in God's purpose and will.

Resources and Bibliographies

If you are interested in pursuing some of the ideas of *The Word That Creates*, you might want to give these books a try:

> Fee, Gordon D. and Douglas Stuart. *How to Read the Bible for All Its Worth*. Grand Rapids: Zondervan, 1982.
>
> Montgomery, John Warwick. *God's Inerrant Word*. Minneapolis: Bethany Fellowship, 1973.
>
> Sproul, R.C. *Knowing Scripture*. Downers Grove: InterVarsity, 1977.
>
> Tenney, Merrill. *The Bible: The Living Word of Revelation*. Grand Rapids: Zondervan, 1968.

Ministry Connections

Now is the time to try to nail down your study of the creative power of the Word of God to a very real practical ministry connection that you are facing or have faced; one which you will think about and pray for throughout this next week. How in particular does the creative power of the Word of God need to be demonstrated in your life and ministry this week? Have you gained some insights in this lesson that need to be emphasized in what you are doing in your ministry at church? What particular concept has the Holy Spirit suggested that you need to understand better, or something you ought to take up to study more thoroughly? Meditate in the presence of the Lord for a moment and ask him to reveal to you specifically how you can make more plain the reality that his Word is a Word that creates in your church, your family and your life.

Counseling and Prayer

Ask God the Holy Spirit to illumine your heart regarding the life-giving power and divine energy which animates and fills the Word of God. Ask God to give you greater insight into the meaning of the Word of God, and to give you more and better time to spend reading, studying, memorizing and meditating on the Word in your life during the week. Pray too that God would make the sermons and teachings from your church come alive for you as you listen and meditate on these truths. Above all, ask God to use you more and more as a Spirit-taught teacher of the Word of God to make the person and purpose of God more plain through your teaching. The better you understand the Word of God, the more it seeps into your own soul and mind and influences you, the greater the impact your ministry and witness will have, both in your church and through the various responsibilities God has given you to represent him.

ASSIGNMENTS

Scripture Memory — 2 Timothy 3.16-17

Reading Assignment — To prepare for class, please visit *www.tumi.org/books* to find next week's reading assignment, or ask your Mentor.

Other Assignments — Read the assigned reading and summarize each reading with no more than a paragraph or two for each. In this summary please give your best understanding of what you think was the main point in each of the readings. Do not be overly concerned about giving detail; simply write out what you consider to be the main point discussed in that section of the book. Please bring these summaries to class next week. (Please see the "Reading Completion Sheet" on page 16.)

Looking Forward to the Next Lesson — In our next lesson, *Bible Interpretation: The Three-Step Model*, we will introduce an effective method of biblical interpretation designed to help you approach your study of Scripture so as to bridge the gap between our ancient and contemporary worlds. We call it the *Three-Step Model*, which helps us to understand the original audience, discover general principles, and make applications to life. The Bible's own remarkable claim of its transforming power ought to be reason enough to challenge us to master the Word of God. "All Scripture is breathed out by God and profitable for teaching, for reproof, for correction, and for training in righteousness, that the man of God may be competent, equipped for every good work" (2 Tim. 3.16-17). The God-breathed Word of God in the words of humankind is sufficient to enrich us, delight us, and make us competent and equipped for every good work. Truly, the Word of God cannot be broken, will always accomplish its purpose, and will ensure the person of God enjoys good success in all they do to advance the Kingdom of God wherever they are (John 10.35; Isa. 55.8-11; Josh. 1.8).

FOR FURTHER STUDY

Please see the following resources in *Picturing Theology: An A-Z Collection of TUMI's Key Diagrams, Charts, Graphics, and Articles*:

- *From Before to Beyond Time*, page 141
- *The Story of God: Our Sacred Roots*, page 401
- *From Deep Ignorance to Credible Witness*, page 143
- *Summary Outline of the Scriptures*, page 416
- *Theories of Inspiration*, page 478

LESSON 2

Bible Interpretation
The Three-Step Model

Lesson Objectives

Welcome in the strong name of Jesus Christ! After your reading, study, discussion, and application of the materials in this lesson, you will be able to:

- Give evidence to show how the *Three-Step Model* is an effective method of biblical interpretation designed to help us understand the truth of Scripture and bridge the gap between our ancient and contemporary worlds.

- Provide a definition of the *Three-Step Model* of biblical interpretation, and recite it without aids: "to so understand the meaning of the original situation that we may discover general principles of truth which may be applied in our personal lives in the Spirit's freedom."

- Highlight the ways in which all study of the Word of God must unfold the meaning and message of God's final revelation to us in the person and work of Jesus Christ.

- Demonstrate your knowledge of how the *Three-Step Model* corresponds to the grammatical-historical method of Scripture interpretation, which affirms the plain sense of its meaning, God's progressive revelation in Christ, the unity of the Bible, and the integrity of the text.

- Reproduce the critical reasons for each step in the *Three-Step Model*, including why each is necessary, the difficulties associated with each, the key attitude required in each step, the activities associated with each one, as well as an example of each step in Scripture.

- Distinguish between the kinds of attitudes necessary for each phase of study in the *Three-Step Model*: humility, thoroughness, and liberty for each of the phases respectively.

- Show through personal use of the *Three-Step Model* how each of the key stages focuses on the text in such a way as to credibly discern its purpose of illumination of the text's meaning, and the transformation of our lives through the joy of discovering biblical principles for life.

- Discern the key elements, cautions, and procedures in investigating the original situation of the text, discovering biblical principles, and making correct applications of the Scripture's teaching to your life.

Devotion

A Heart Prepared to Study, Do, and Teach the Word of God

Ezra 7.10 – For Ezra had set his heart to study the Law of the LORD, and to do it and to teach his statutes and rules in Israel.

Is your heart prepared before God?

A glance at the major saints of the Scriptures reveals that our God uses men and women whose hearts have been prepared before him to study his Word, to practice it diligently within their lives, and then be used as his vessel to communicate his truth to others. Perhaps one of the clearest examples of this is recorded in the OT historical book of Ezra which details the return of the Israelites during the post-exilic era back to Judah from Babylon in order to spiritually revive the faithful and reestablish the worship of the Lord in the temple. The worship of the Lord in a way that is appropriate and right is a key theme in all the books of the OT written during the time after Israel and Judah were sent into captivity because of their sin against God. Included in these books are 1 and 2 Chronicles, Ezra, Nehemiah, Haggai, Zechariah, and Malachi (with perhaps the book of Esther being the only exception). Those who returned were ready and willing to acknowledge their guilt before the Lord, their confidence that he would reestablish them in the land he had given them, and that he and he alone was worthy to be worshiped and able to usher in his kingdom reign through the coming Messiah.

Actually, there were three returns to the land of Israel from Babylon, which occurred approximately in the years 538, 458, and 444 B.C.E. This corresponds to the fact that there had been three times that the population was deported to Babylon from Israel in the years 605, 597, and 586 B.C.E. respectively. The returns were led by godly servants of God, the first in 538 B.C.E. by Zerubbabel (Ezra 1-6; Haggai; Zechariah), whose efforts resulted in the rebuilding of the temple. The second return occurred in 458 B.C.E. under the leadership and supervision of Ezra (Ezra 7-10), which focused on the reform and instruction of the people, their *spiritual revival*, and the need for them to come back to the Lord through the fulfillment of the covenant. Finally, Nehemiah led the third return to the land in 444 B.C.E., whose major concerns dealt with rebuilding devastated Jerusalem's broken down walls, and with Ezra, to bring God's people back to the Lord with spiritual renewal and covenant obedience. Many scholars believe that

Malachi was probably written in Nehemiah's time, and that Esther was written during the events recorded in Ezra 6 and 7. This eventful time in Israel's history provides key insights in the need for prepared men and women for the task of God.

Our single text for the devotion records the kind of inner life and motive of the person that God uses to bring revival, renewal, and refreshment to his people. "For Ezra had set his heart to study the Law of the LORD, and to do it and to teach his statutes and rules in Israel." According to our text, Ezra had "set his heart," literally "fixed his soul" to do three things on behalf of the Lord.

First, Ezra had set his heart to study the Law of the Lord. There would be no half-hearted, sleepy-eyed scanning of God's Word, but a disciplined, passionate, focused *study* of God's law. The Bible simply can be mastered in no other way; without seeking the knowledge of the Lord as treasure hunters seek gold, the hidden depth and meaning of the text simply cannot be found nor understood (Prov. 2.1-9). The lazy, undisciplined heart will never come to know the riches of God's wisdom regarding his plan of salvation in Christ.

Second, he had set his heart to *do it*. Simply put, Ezra was not *living to study*, rather, he was *studying to live*. The intent of the Word of God is not merely to hear the will of God regarding faith, obedience, love, and service. The purpose is to do it, and the blessing of the text is associated not merely with those who reflect upon it but to those who respond to it with humility and diligence as it is the very Word of God (James 1.22-25). The wisdom of the Lord comes to those who actually carry out his will as they discover it in his holy Word (cf. Psalm 111.10 – The fear of the Lord is the beginning of wisdom; all those who practice it have a good understanding. His praise endures forever!).

Finally, Ezra has set his heart to "*teach his statutes and rules in Israel.*" Once the Word of God is mastered through study and fulfilled through obedience, then the servant of God is ready to fulfill his or her ministry through the teaching ministry. Ezra's priorities regarding his approach and ministry of the Word were in the proper order: he prepared himself to study God's perfect Law, to do it, and then to teach it. This kind of careful consideration and heart preparation is the veritable stuff of which saints, Christian workers, prophets, and apostles are made of. The focus is not upon the mission, or the work, or the blessing, or the gifts. The focus is upon the Word of God – on studying it, mastering it, putting it into practice, and then, once known and obeyed, sharing it with passion and clarity. This is precisely what occurred in the ministry of Ezra to the people; because of his heart priorities, God used him mightily to bring revival and renewal to God's people, and lay a foundation for a movement that would eventually prepare the nation for the coming of Messiah. And all this, because a single person in love with God prepared his heart for the Word.

Is your heart set before God to study, do, and teach his Word to his people, for his glory? Do you focus on *yourself* – *your* gifts, *your* blessing, *your* opportunities, or are you clear in your desire simply to master the Word of God so *you* can put it into practice in your life, and be released of the Holy Spirit then to teach his Word to the people of God? Let's learn from the example of this humble and brave preacher of the Word of God whose ministry began not with grand plans of influence, but the humility of a heart set to know and do God's will as he learned it from the Word of God. Truly, *this* is the pattern for all fruitful ministry in the name of the Lord.

Nicene Creed and Prayer

After reciting and/or singing the Nicene Creed (located in the Appendix), pray the following prayer:

> O God Almighty, Father of our Lord Jesus Christ: Grant us, we pray, to be grounded and settled in your truth by the coming down of the Holy Spirit into our hearts. That which we know not, reveal; that which is wanting in us, fill up; that which we know, confirm; and keep us blameless in your service; through the same Jesus Christ our Lord. Amen.
>
> ~ Presbyterian Church (U.S.A.) and Cumberland Presbyterian Church. *The Theology and Worship Ministry Unit. Book of Common Worship.* Louisville: Westminster/John Knox Press, 1993. p 26.

Scripture Memorization Review

Review with a partner, write out and/or recite the text for last class session's assigned memory verse: 2 Timothy 3.16-17.

Assignments Due

Turn in your summary of the reading assignment for last week, that is, your brief response and explanation of the main points that the authors were seeking to make in the assigned reading (Reading Completion Sheet).

CONTACT

Only Formal Training Will Do

1 ▸ Many churches and denominations today are convinced that those who desire to go into ministry must have some formal training in a Bible Institute, Christian liberal arts college, or graduate school/seminary. Those who hold such a view are simply convinced that the rigors, problems, and situations of ministry cannot be left to one's own personal preparation. Rather, the likelihood that one will be successful in urban ministry increases greatly, they argue, if a student is given the opportunity to receive formal training. Unfortunately, for those unable either to afford or to qualify for such training, they are de facto eliminated from the candidate pool of ministry. What is your opinion about the role of formal training in biblical, theological, and pastoral training and the prospect of urban ministry? Is it possible to have a fruitful urban ministry without having been trained formally? If it is, then what is the role and function of formal academic preparation for urban ministry?

Discerning the Mind of the Holy Spirit Is My Method

2 ▸ While many believe that having a clear, rational method for approaching Bible study is essential to discern the meaning of Scripture, a great many today remain skeptical of the role of *method* for spiritual discernment. Having seen the doubt and confusion produced by modern historical criticism of the Bible, many hold that any allegiance to a form of method is dangerous in study. Rather than using scientific methods of approach, these often argue for a more spiritual, intuitive approach to Bible study. They approach study as a *spiritual* discipline not an intellectual one, and want to be taught by the Holy Spirit. This is perceived not as the wooden following of some method, but a heart and soul preparation that allows the Holy Spirit himself to be their teacher. If, in fact, the Holy Spirit alone is the true teacher of the Word of God, what is the usefulness of seeking a method to read, study, and apply the Scriptures? In what ways might a commitment to method in biblical interpretation either help or hinder our understanding of the Word of God?

Attitude vs. Method:
Which One Is Most Critical in Biblical Interpretation?

3 ▸ While most acknowledge that some form of disciplined approach to the Scriptures is helpful to understand God's purpose and meaning in the Bible, it is often not clear how to weigh the importance between *attitude* and *method* in study. On the one hand, many believe that without the proper attitude, no understanding of Scripture is possible. Whatever method we employ to discern the meaning of the Bible, it requires the humble, broken, and contrite spirit that God says throughout Scripture is his true sacrifice and the requirement for his leading and teaching. On the other hand, we can point to many examples where humility and kindness, zeal and passion severed from knowledge produced horrible spiritual results. Attitude without knowledge did not produce spiritual discernment but resulted in tyranny, confusion, even heresy. What is the relationship between proper heart preparation and attitude, and following a disciplined method and approach to the Bible? How should we order and place them in our study of Scripture?

The Three-Step Model

Bridging the Gap between the Ancient and Contemporary Worlds

Rev. Dr. Don L. Davis

CONTENT

Summary

The *Three-Step Model* is an effective method of biblical interpretation designed to help us understand the truth of Scripture and bridge the gap between our ancient and contemporary worlds. It focuses upon our efforts to understand the original audience, discover general principles, and make applications to life.

Our objective for this lesson, *Bridging the Gap between the Ancient and Contemporary Worlds,* is to enable you to see that:

- The *Three-Step Model* is an effective method of biblical interpretation designed to help us understand the truth of Scripture and bridge the gap between our ancient and contemporary worlds.

- A clear and concise definition of the *Three-Step Model* is "to so understand the meaning of the original situation that we may discover general principles of truth which may be applied in our personal lives in the Spirit's freedom."

- While studying individual words, phrases, paragraphs, chapters, sections, and books of the Scriptures is both edifying and necessary, all of our insights into the Scriptures ought to be in sync with the message of the whole Bible, i.e., the meaning and message of God's final revelation to us in the person and work of Jesus Christ.

- The *Three-Step Model* resonates and corresponds to the grammatical-historical method of Scripture interpretation, which affirms the plain sense of the Bible's meaning, God's progressive revelation in Christ, the unity of the Bible, and the integrity of the text as it communicates to us in different genres and forms.

- Each step associated with the *Three-Step Model* has its own particular aim and logic, reasons and basis, and key attitudes, and are fulfilled with a particular sequence and list of activities. To master the model we must become familiar with and skilled at these steps and activities.

- The critical preparation for the use of any form of biblical study is the attitude of the student of the Scriptures, as the phases of study in the *Three-Step Model* demands humility, thoroughness, and liberty for each phase respectively.

- As slaves to righteousness under Christ's lordship, we are called to obey his Word in every facet of our lives and ministries, and therefore, all legitimate biblical interpretation seeks to discern God's Word for the purpose of *life transformation*, not *mind information*.

Everyone Has a System for Bible Interpretation

Believe it or not, everyone has a method of interpreting the Bible. But not all methods are equally profitable. Some use the magic finger approach. It consists of acting upon some supposed divine directive, locating a particular verse – usually with the eyes closed – and taking that portion of Scripture as an answer or truth provided by God. We may laugh at that, but often come quite close to that when we ignore contexts. Then there are those who read the Bible a lot, but never seem to get very far in putting it altogether. They can quote at great length, but have difficulty seeing what the passage means. Others follow an extreme devotional approach. They read only what "warms" them at the moment, as if the Bible were intended to make them feel good continually. All of these people have systems of interpreting the Bible, and it is not difficult to see why such methods do not lead to spiritual soundness. As a result of these approaches – which are really partly Bible study methods and partly interpreting methods – many are spiritually weak and discouraged about their prospects of getting anything solid from the Bible. Such practices never lead to a mature ability to handle the Bible with power and fruitfulness.

> Methods of interpretation can be haphazard or systematic, and even systematic interpretation can be either profitable, or unprofitable, so that it does violence to the meaning of the Bible. God's desire is that believers come to the place where they are able to read the Bible with understanding, balance, and facility in relating various portions of the Scriptures to each other.
>
> ~ Paul Karleen. *The Handbook to Bible Study*. (electronic ed.). New York: Oxford University Press, 1987.

Video Outline

I. **Definition, Purpose, Elements, Benefits of the Three-Step Model of Biblical Interpretation**

   A. Definition: "To so understand the meaning of the original situation that we may discover general principles of truth which may be applied in our personal lives in the Spirit's freedom"

   1. *To so understand the meaning of the original situation*: the first step focuses on understanding what the text meant in its original setting.

   2. *That we may discover general principles of truth*: the second step focuses on drawing out of the text biblical principles which are binding and applicable to believers today.

   3. *That may be applied in our personal lives in the Spirit's freedom*: the third step is applying the principle of truth in our personal lives in the power of the Spirit.

   B. Purpose

   1. To learn what the author meant in the context of its original writing

2. To discover biblical principles which summarize the teaching of Scripture and offer God's wisdom and insight which are binding upon all and can be applied to all

3. To change our belief and practices and conform our lives to the truths contained in the Word of God

C. Elements

1. It corresponds to the *grammatical-historical method*: determine the meaning of the text in its *original setting* before applying its meaning to another time and place.

2. This model looks for the *plain sense* of the text.

3. This model affirms *progressive revelation*.

   a. The Bible shows that God unfolds the meaning and method of his purpose, culminating (i.e., "summing up") in Jesus Christ, Heb. 1.1-3.

   b. Jesus *surpasses* and *fulfills* the meaning of all that God communicated before (i.e., John 1.14-18; Matt. 5.17-18; John 5.39-40; Luke 24.27, 44-48).

4. It affirms *the unity of the Scriptures*.

   a. The Bible is a single canon (collection, library) of texts, written by a single author, 2 Tim. 3.16-17; 2 Pet. 1.20-21.

b. The explicit subject of the Scriptures is *Jesus Christ and his Kingdom*, Acts 28.23,31; Col. 1.25-27; Eph. 3.3-11; Rom. 16.25-27.

5. This model assumes the *integrity of the text*: the authors, carried along by the Holy Spirit, communicated the perspective and truth God intended for the original hearers, which we can discover and appropriate, 1 Cor. 10.1-6.

D. Benefits

1. An *exegetical* approach to the Scriptures

2. A method emphasizing understanding *before* application

3. Searching for the *timeless principle* arising from the *temporal particulars*

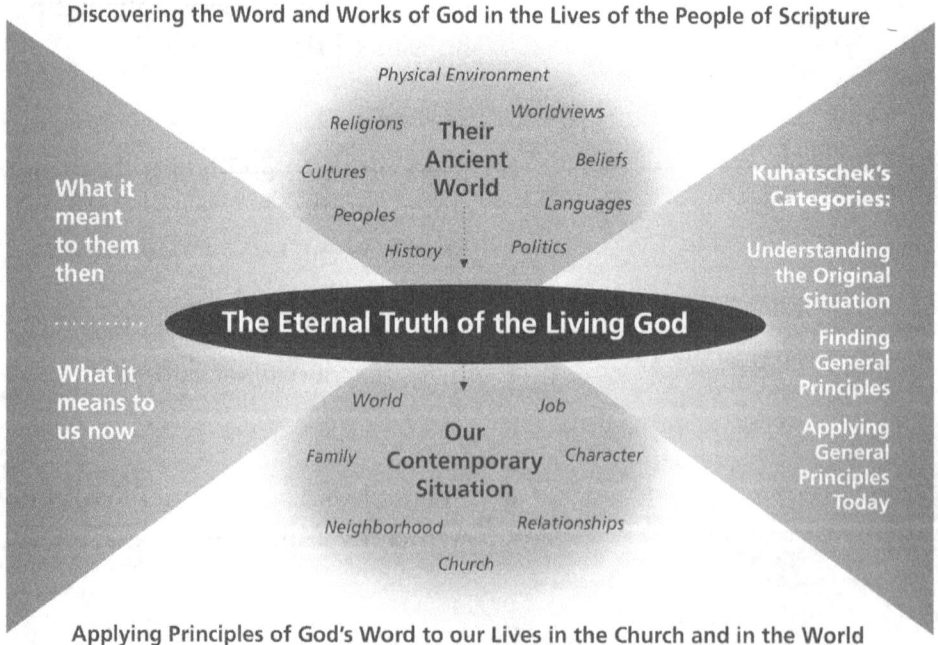

II. Step One: Understanding the Original Situation (*Engaging the Text on Its Own Terms*)

A. Critical reasons exist for seeking to understand a text *first* in its original situation.

1. *Major cultural barriers* exist between the original culture and our time.

2. The *languages* are different from our own (Hebrew, Aramaic, and koine Greek).

3. We are *ethnocentric* (completely immersed in our own culture, and believe naturally that ours is *preferable*).

4. We read the Bible *anachronistically* (i.e., we tend to read our own situation in the present day *back into* the biblical time).

5. We are prone to make *geographical, historical, and social blunders*.

B. Why is it so difficult to understand the original situation?

1. We weren't there!: *no one alive today was present* during the events when the reports of the Scriptures were given.

2. We do not know *the usages or nuances of the biblical languages* (Greek, Aramaic, and Hebrew).

3. Our *personal opinion filters* constantly interfere with our understanding of the original situation.

4. We are conditioned to *read it the way we've always read it* (i.e., we allow past readings to bias our present readings).

5. We *jump to conclusions* without considering what it meant to the people.

C. Key attitude needed: ***humility***, James 1.5

1. Acceptance of the distance between ourselves and the actual situation of the text

2. Willingness to admit the differences and the barriers that exist between our own time and that of the authors and audiences of the text

3. Openness to suspend judgment until we learn more of the situation *before we pass judgment on what the text meant*

4. Cultivating a deep respect for the original meanings and situations

D. Steps in understanding the original situation

1. Take the time to do your homework on the original situation, Prov. 2.1-6.

2. Respect the process of critical analysis, Ezra 7.10.

3. Recognize and take seriously the reality of distance: *Sitz im Leben* (situation in life).

4. Acquire and learn to use the proper Bible study tools that will help recreate for you the original situation.

E. Example: the Passover, 1 Corinthians 5.7, 8

III. Step Two: Discover and Draw Out General Principles

A. Why do we need to discover general principles?

1. "Facts are dumb things": biblical facts require *interpretation*, and interpretation leads to *understanding*.

2. Without principles we are left with pieces and no mosaics: we confront thousands of unconnected facts in the Bible.

3. General principles allow us to draw out wisdom from the experience of others: the power of biblical case studies, Prov. 24.30-34.

   a. *Careful personal observation* of a particular situation

   b. Reflection and *consideration of the meaning* of those facts

   c. The *formation of a principle (proverb)* that can be applied to a number of different but related situations

4. General principles allow us to predict with accuracy *what will occur if certain conditions are met*, drawing clear conclusions from universal truth.

5. Principles provide us with *the big picture underlying particular events*, giving us insight into the whole of human experience and God's spirituality.

B. Why is it hard to draw out general principles from Scripture?

1. *Too many facts, stories, and details* to process

2. Irony: there are not enough facts to process!

3. *Personal reading and devotional habits* interfere with our ability to generalize rightly.

4. *Most principles*: many principles are not explicitly written.

5. *Requires labor and time* to check our findings against the Word of God for their validity

   a. Prov. 8.17

   b. Matt. 7.7-8

   c. Prov. 9.9

   d. Eccles. 7.25

C. Key attitude: *thoroughness*, Acts 17.11

1. Develop a willingness to search out the Word to find universal truths.

2. Refuse to jump to conclusions without checking them against the Scriptures.

3. Orient yourself to patiently pray and discuss, in your search, for principles in the Word of God.

D. Steps to discover principles

1. Expect to find God's practical wisdom in your study of the Word of God, 2 Tim. 3.16.

2. When analyzing individual texts, always be on the lookout for larger patterns, structures, principles, and connections in the text to other Scripture.

3. Do not be hasty in declaring one of your proverbs a universal principle: test your findings against Scripture.

   a. 1 Thess. 5.21

   b. Prov. 23.23

   c. Phil. 4.8

   d. 2 Thess. 2.15

4. *Acid test of principle formation*: if your proverb is true, you ought to be able to find cases in life where the truth of your proverb is easily observed to be true.

E. Examples: "The Love Commandment" and "Sowing and Reaping"

1. Loving God and loving neighbor is the summation of all God's moral demands in the OT.

   a. The entire ethical demand of God hinges on loving him with all the heart, and one's neighbor as oneself, Matt. 22.36-40.

   b. Love is the fulfilling of the law of God, Rom. 13.8-10.

2. You will certainly reap what you sow, Gal. 6.7-8.

IV. Step Three: Apply the Principle to Life in the Power of the Spirit

A. What are the reasons for applying God's Word to our lives?

1. We are to be doers of the Word and not merely hearers (i.e., students) of the Word, James 1.22-25.

2. Disciplined practice of the Word produces godliness, 1 Tim. 4.7-9.

3. By consistent application of the Word we mature and become able to teach others, Heb. 5.11-6.2.

4. Faith without works is useless, James 2.14-17.

5. Applying the Word establishes our lives on a firm foundation, Matt. 7.24-27.

B. Why is it so difficult to apply the Word?

1. Our sin nature: we are naturally inclined to disbelieve and disobey, Gal. 5.16-21.

2. We avoid the challenge and stimulation of other believers.

    a. 2 Cor. 9.2

    b. Heb. 10.24-25

    c. Heb. 3.13-14

3. We seek to apply the truth of the text in fleshly power and effort, Phil. 3.2-3.

4. We are easily distracted by things that do not matter.

    a. 2 Tim. 4.10

    b. Luke 9.62

    c. Luke 14.33

    d. Luke 16.13

e. Luke 17.32

f. Phil. 2.21

g. 1 Tim. 6.10

h. 1 John 2.15-16

5. We embrace a common fallacy: "knowing about something is the same as doing."

C. Key attitude: *liberty in Christ*

Gal. 5.1 – For freedom Christ has set us free; stand firm therefore, and do not submit again to a yoke of slavery.

Rom. 7.6 – But now we are released from the law, having died to that which held us captive, so that we serve not under the old written code but in the new life of the Spirit.

2 Cor. 3.17 – Now the Lord is the Spirit, and where the Spirit of the Lord is, there is freedom.

1. Freedom is the dominant theme of Jesus' liberation.

a. John 8.34-36

b. Rom. 6.18

c. Rom. 8.2

d. 2 Cor. 3.17

e. Gal. 4.26

f. Gal. 4.31

g. Gal. 5.13

h. 1 Pet. 2.16

2. As slaves of righteousness under Christ's lordship, we are free to express obedience to the Word in every facet of our lives.

3. We must cultivate a willingness to experiment in our obedience under the Spirit's direction, 2 Cor. 3.17-18.

4. Openness to the *voice of the Lord* as he calls us to do certain things day by day, Heb. 3.7-8

D. Steps to applying the Word of God

1. Be prayerful and open to *the Holy Spirit*.

2. *Listen to your heart* and let God speak, Heb. 3.15.

3. Set practical, feasible goals, Ps. 119.164.

4. Ask your mentors and body members to hold you accountable.

E. Example: Zacchaeus, Luke 19.1-10

Conclusion

- The *Three-Step Model* of biblical interpretation takes seriously the need to understand the meaning of the Bible in its own context, to draw out biblical principles, and to apply them in our lives today through the Spirit's direction and leading.

- This method is a sure and certain way to approach the Word with reverence and clarity as we seek to become disciplined students of the Word of God.

Student Questions and Response

Please take as much time as you have available to answer these and other questions that the video brought out. In this session we saw how the *Three-Step Model* is an effective method of biblical interpretation designed to help us understand the truth of Scripture and bridge the gap between our ancient and contemporary worlds. As students of Scripture, we need a method that respects the nature of the Scriptures as ancient literature, as well as the living Holy Spirit in the Church who is our teacher and guide as we seek the mind and will of God (1 Cor. 2.9-16). Review the materials of the video through the following questions, and use the Scriptures themselves to support your claims.

Not Just Knowing What It Is, But Also How to Handle It

When Paul tells Timothy to strive to be someone who "correctly handles the word of truth" (2 Tim. 2.15), the assumption is that it is dangerously possible to be someone who does not correctly handle the word of truth. And that raises important questions about how to interpret the Bible. To approach the Bible wisely it is necessary not only to know what it is, but how to handle it.

~ Donald A. Carson. *New Bible Commentary: 21st Century Edition.* (electronic ed. of the 4th ed.). Downers Grove, IL: InterVarsity Press, 1997.

1. What is the definition of the *Three-Step Model* of biblical interpretation? How is this method particularly designed to help us bridge the gap between our ancient and contemporary worlds? Why is this activity of overcoming the distance between us and the world of the Bible so important for an *accurate interpretation* of the Bible?

2. Where in the Bible does it mention that an attention to method is important for understanding its meaning (cf. Acts 17.11; Isaiah 8.20; Ezra 7.10; etc.)?

3. What are the benefits and cautions associated with using *any method* in biblical interpretation? What safeguards do we have against becoming overly dependent on methods and our own understanding as we seek to discover the truths of God in Scripture and apply them to our lives?

4. Why is it always important to keep the "big picture" and "whole message" of the Bible in mind when engaging in studies of particular "parts" of the Scriptures? In what way should any study of the Word of God somehow directly connect with and explain the meaning and message of God's final revelation to us in the person and wok of Jesus Christ? Give examples of your answer.

5. What is the "grammatical-historical" method of Bible study, and how does the *Three-Step Model* relate to it? In the same way, how does the *Three-Step Model* help us understand the plain sense meaning of the text, and the overall unity of the Bible?

6. Why is it key to respect the *integrity of the text* as it has come to us in its various forms (e.g., poetry, songs, epistles, history, etc.), and how does the *Three-Step Model* do so?

7. Outline briefly the critical reasons involved in each step of the *Three-Step Model*. How does each of the three steps help us overcome some of the difficulties associated with understanding what the Bible teaches as an *ancient text* written in *languages which are no longer spoken or used as they were at the time of the Bible's writing*? Explain your answer thoroughly.

8. How do humility, thoroughness, and a love of liberty in Christ affect our ability to know and apply God's Word? What is the relationship between attitude and method in seeking to discern the Bible's meaning? Which is most important? Give an example that illustrates your opinion.

9. Explain and defend the statement: "all legitimate biblical interpretation seeks to discern God's Word for the purpose of *life transformation*, not *mind information*." How does the *Three-Step Model* help keep our focus on life transformation and not just analysis of texts and words?

CONNECTION

Summary of Key Concepts

To master the Word of God is the central and definitive skill for the man or woman of God, for it is the God-breathed Scripture that is able to make us competent workers and faithful servants of the Church, to enable us to equip others for ministry, and minister to the real needs of those both within and outside the Church (2 Tim. 3.16-17). There is no way that we can overemphasize the importance of your ability to handle the Word accurately (2 Tim. 2.15), to meditate upon it day and night in order to ensure success in the endeavors of God (Josh. 1.8), and guarantee the kind of fruitfulness and power you desire in every phase of your work for the Lord (Ps. 1.1-3). Listed below are the central concepts covered in this lesson on the *Three-Step Model*, so please review them diligently and carefully. Understanding this model can enable you to gain the knowledge and skills to become a workman of the Scriptures, approved of God and without shame as you handle his Word accurately and rightly.

The Importance of the First Reader: The Key to the Three-Step Model

When interpreters and translators ask themselves how the first readers would have understood a passage, they are not asking a merely hypothetical question impossible to answer (since we have no access to their minds). Rather, this is simply a way of getting at a host of subsidiary questions: How would these words have been understood at the time? What issues and themes were of resounding importance? What kind of conceptual framework would the biblical text confront? To raise such questions is not to affirm that we can always find perfect answers. Sometimes we can infer responsible answers by "mirror-reading" the text itself.

~ Donald A. Carson. *New Bible Commentary: 21st Century Edition.* (electronic ed. of the 4th ed.). Downers Grove, IL: InterVarsity Press, 1997.

- The *Three-Step Model* is an effective method of biblical interpretation designed to help us understand the truth of Scripture and bridge the gap between our ancient and contemporary worlds. The *Three-Step Model* defined is "to so understand the meaning of the original situation that we may discover general principles of truth which may be applied in our personal lives in the Spirit's freedom."

- While studying individual words, phrases, paragraphs, chapters, sections, and books of the Scriptures is both edifying and necessary, all of our insights into the Scriptures ought to be in sync with the message of the whole Bible, i.e., the meaning and message of God's final revelation to us in the person and work of Jesus Christ.

- The *Three-Step Model*, as a logical and methodical way of understanding Scripture, resonates and corresponds to the grammatical-historical method of Scripture interpretation, which affirms the plain sense of the Bible's meaning. It also takes into account God's progressive revelation in Christ, the unity of the Bible, and the integrity of the text as it communicates to us in different genres and forms.

- The critical preparation for the use of any form of biblical study is the attitude of the student of the Scriptures, and the phases of study in the *Three-Step Model* demand humility, thoroughness, and liberty for each phase respectively.

- As slaves to righteousness under Christ's lordship, we are called to obey his Word in every facet of our lives and ministries, and therefore, all legitimate biblical interpretation seeks to discern God's Word for the purpose of *life transformation*, not *mind information*.

- The *Three-Step Model* may be fruitfully employed with a number of units of Bible materials (words, paragraphs, chapters, books, sections).

- All study of the Word of God begins with our submission to the Holy Spirit, who alone is the author of the Scriptures and the only one sufficient to instruct us in its meaning and significance for our lives today. Our dependence on the Holy Spirit *enhances our diligent study of the Word* and is not meant to be a substitute for it.

- The first step in employing the *Three-Step Model* is observing the details of the text, establishing the background of the book, its author and audience, its purpose for being written, as well as its rendering in different translations.

- Finding general principles of the text or passage is the second step of the *Three-Step Model*, and involves finding the central messages, truths, commands, or teachings contained in the text. This step involves going from what the text *meant in its original setting*, to what the text now *means to us in our lives today*. These principles must be stated clearly, compared with teachings throughout the Scriptures, and made plain for further study and application.

- After we have observed the details and drawn out principles, we go to the third step of the *Three-Step Model* which is our goal to apply the spiritual principles in the power of the Holy Spirit. An application is an *expression of the heart to the truth of God as the Spirit leads*. It demands discernment and a readiness to obey God's will for our lives.

- All biblical interpretation is given in order to strengthen our discipleship in Christ, and is essentially a *variation on the common themes* emphasized throughout the Scriptures. Love for God and neighbor, using our freedom to build up others and glorify God constitute the heart of the Bible's ethic in both the Old and New Testaments.

Student Application and Implications

Now is the time for you to discuss with your fellow students your questions about your understanding of the *Three-Step Model*, and methodical Bible study in particular. The kinds of relationships between our own attitude, our chosen method of study, the Spirit, resource tools, other Christians, and our leaders demand clarity and wisdom. Scholars, church workers, pastors and preachers, and lay-persons alike have struggled with the questions of biblical interpretation for centuries, and now is your chance to join the conversation! Use the questions below to start you on your journey of exploration about the nature of your own biblical study.

- With all the confusion and doubt caused by modern biblical criticism, should we be skeptical at using any method, including the *Three-Step Model* as our way of studying Scripture? How do we know that even the *Three-Step Model* won't be twisted and lead to a denial of the orthodox doctrines of the Christian faith?

- How can we say that employing a method like the *Three-Step Model* is not merely an enlightened form of "don't lean on your own understanding" (Prov. 3.5-6)?

- With the abundance of studies being done on every imaginable subject under the sun, how do we ensure that all of our insights line up with the message of the whole Bible? How do we avoid "majoring on the minors" in our study of the Bible? Give practical examples.

- What role do our leaders (i.e., bishops, pastors, mentors, well-known Christian leaders, etc.) play in taking our own personal interpretations as *authoritative*? Should we hold to an interpretation of Scripture that we have found in our study if it is contradicted by what Christianity has taught in the creeds and throughout Church history? Explain.

- Why should we be open to having others criticize our findings and ideas *before* we begin to suggest that we have discovered general principles that are binding on all members of the Church? What kind of attitudes should we demonstrate when we speak about new things we have learned from the Lord in our studies?

- How should we take a person, however scholarly or well-studied, who is unwilling to have their own ideas weighed and checked against the teaching of the Scriptures themselves? How does the Berean example and reaction to the teaching of Paul inform our own need to be open to checking the findings of others against the Scriptures themselves (cf. Acts 17.11)?

- Since we are not all Bible teachers and scholars, what ought to be our goal as we engage in our own work of biblical interpretation? Should it concern us that some members of the body will discover more in their study than we did? How do spiritual gifts figure into this equation?

- Why is it important not merely to depend on others for the insights and wisdom that the Bible provides for us? What kind of errors may occur when we become overly dependent on others for our instruction and growth in Christ?

- Why is it impossible to suggest that our dependence on the Holy Spirit in our personal study is a substitute for the hard work of biblical interpretation? How can you know if you are not depending on the Holy Spirit for insight in your personal study? Likewise, how can you tell when you are being lazy in the way you are handling the Word of truth?

- Why is it always important to study the Bible in the light of the *great themes* emphasized by our Lord, along with the apostles and prophets? How do their teachings on love for God and neighbor help us understand that both the Old and New Testaments have a *common subject and purpose*? Explain.

CASE STUDIES

Only What the Pastor Says Counts

1. In many traditions, whatever the method of personal study employed to understand the meaning of the Bible, the heart of what the Scriptures teaches is dependent upon the church tradition and/or official leaders of the church. This is plainly seen, for example, in the Catholic approach to biblical interpretation. While individual study is encouraged and applauded as good and edifying, the discoveries of the individual can never take precedence over the teaching of the Church as we have understood it down through the centuries, and as it is represented presently in the teaching of the bishops and the Pope. Protestants do not hold to this view, but in many Protestant churches, individual interpretation is not considered credible unless it corresponds to what the pastor or spiritual leaders believe and teach. What is the place of pastoral and spiritual leadership authority in our personal interpretation of the Bible? Should all that we discover be confirmed by our leaders, or are they, like us, subject to the same responsibility to align their views with the Scriptures in order for them to be considered credible and acceptable?

How Then Do We Prove Anything from Scripture?

2. (Based on a true story). While in a graduate school situation, a budding pastor encountered an idea that challenged and somewhat confused him. During a class on the methods of the *scientific study* of religion, he was told by the professor that simply using the Bible to prove the points of the Bible is "tautological," or arguing in a circle, proving nothing. The professor went on: "If you want to prove that something in the Bible is true, you cannot use the Bible to prove it. In the scientific method you prove things on the basis of *independent verification*, not on the basis of those who have something to gain from the outcome of the study." The professor went on to suggest that because the prophets and the apostles were believers in Christ, they had too much at stake to say anything about Jesus except *what they wanted other people to believe*. As a result, he held, we cannot take their word as true regarding Jesus of Nazareth and his claims. Confused and bewildered, the pastor in the class felt handicapped. How can he prove the teaching of the Scriptures *without using the Scriptures themselves as proof*? What do you think about the professor's comments, and what would you advise the pastor to do in order to complete his study in that course?

Your Native-Tongue Bible Isn't Enough

(Based on a true story). While turning in an exegetical project for credit during a class on Romans, a student was advised by his professor (who had skimmed his first attempt at the study) that he had broke fundamental rules in using tools of language. The professor explained: "You simply cannot go to a theological dictionary or lexicon and assume that all the usages written down of a word are the *meanings in this particular place*. You wouldn't use an English or Spanish dictionary that way; you would look up the word, find the definition that fit, and then apply *that single meaning* to the text. You applied all the meanings of the term to your study, and therefore made a fundamental error in your study." The professor went on to say that only when you know how an individual author used a word (e.g., Peter's, Paul's, or John's use of a word in all of his writings) could you then be sure that you were using your language sources right. Since the Bible was written in Hebrew, Aramaic, and Greek, and since many of us do not know these languages, how then are we to know that we are reading the text right? How are we to use language tools if we don't know an author's *entire use of a word or phrase*?

Confusing the Twigs for the Trees and the Forest

One of the immediate problems with those who discover the *Three-Step Model* is that they begin to use their new-found methods to analyze the specific details of numerous passages as a single part. With no guidance as to how to *connect and integrate* their insights into the overall meaning of the Scriptures, they multiply themes, topics, and studies without ever bringing them all together under a single, understandable banner. In your opinion, do the Scriptures have a single, coherent theme that would allow all of our study to be placed underneath it, allowing us to interpret our insights in light of it? How do we as students of the Bible avoid becoming focused on the details of single passages so much so that we miss the "big picture," the larger message and meaning of the Bible itself? How do we avoid the distinctive problem of the Pharisees, who mastered the details of the Scriptures but had great difficulty in seeing and applying the weightier matters of Scripture to their lives (i.e., they saw trees fine, but missed the forest). How can we see the Bible as a *whole* and still find nourishment as we study its *parts*?

Restatement of the Lesson's Thesis

The *Three-Step Model* is an effective method of biblical interpretation designed to help us understand the truth of Scripture and bridge the gap between our ancient and contemporary worlds. The *Three-Step Model* defined is "to so understand the meaning of the original situation that we may discover general principles of truth which may be applied in our personal lives in the Spirit's freedom." This method corresponds to the grammatical-historical method of Scripture interpretation, affirms the plain sense of the Bible's meaning, and respects the integrity of the text as it communicates to us in different genres and forms. The Bible's central message of salvation in Jesus Christ must take precedence over all study of individual words, phrases, paragraphs, chapters, sections, and books of the Scriptures. All study demands a spirit of humility, diligent thoroughness, and a love for Christ's liberty as we seek to be transformed by the life-giving message of Scripture.

All study of the Word of God begins with our submission to the Holy Spirit, who alone is the author of the Scriptures and the only one sufficient to instruct us in its meaning and significance for our lives today. Our dependence on the Holy Spirit *enhances our diligent study of the Word* and is not meant to be a *substitute for it*. The steps of the *Three-Step Model* are simple and clear. First, we observe the details of the text, establishing the background of the book, its author and audience, its purpose for being written, as well as its rendering in different translations. Next, we discover general principles which summarize our findings about what the text *meant in its original setting*, and what the text now *means to us in our lives today*. Finally, we apply the spiritual principles in the power of the Holy Spirit. As we express our heart obedience to God, we ought to remain mindful of *the common themes* emphasized throughout the Scriptures which underlie his will for all believers in both Old and New Testaments – loving God and loving neighbor through faith in Christ, all for the glory of God.

Resources and Bibliographies

If you are interested in pursuing some of the ideas of *Bible Interpretation: The Three-Step Model*, you might want to give these books a try:

Fee, Gordon D. *New Testament Exegesis: A Handbook for Students and Pastors*. 3rd ed. Louisville, KY: Westminster John Knox Press, 2002.

Grenz, Stanley J., and Roger E. Olson. *Who Needs Theology?: An Invitation to the Study of God*. Downers Grove, IL: InterVarsity, 1996.

Grenz, Stanley J., and John R. Franke. *Beyond Foundationalism: Shaping Theology in a Postmodern Context*. Louisville, KY: Westminster John Knox Press, 2000.

Stuart, Douglas K. *Old Testament Exegesis: A Handbook for Students and Pastors*. 3rd ed. Louisville, KY: Westminster John Knox Press, 2001.

Traina, Robert A. *Methodical Bible Study*. Grand Rapids: Zondervan Publishing Company, 1985.

Ministry Connections

The use of the God-breathed Scripture in many ways is the very center of valid kingdom ministry. Like Ezra in our devotion, your ability to study the Law of the Lord and to do it is the key to your teaching the truth of God in the midst of his people, the Church, and to those who do not believe. Every facet and strand of ministry relates directly to your mastery of the Word of God, and your willingness to allow that Word to master you! Reflect some time on the dimensions of your current ministry at home, on the job, in the church and the community, and ask the Holy Spirit to show you how your interpretation and application of the Word might enhance some dimension of your life and witness. Ask the Lord to reveal to you some area where the power of his Word must become more real and vital, and be open to changing your attitude or behavior in any particular situation that the Spirit brings to your mind.

Counseling and Prayer

We Apply the Word of God in Community with Each Other

Newbigin has suggested there is only one way the people of God can make the gospel credible: "*the only answer, the only hermeneutic of the gospel*, is a congregation of men and women who believe it and live it . . . they have power to accomplish their purpose only as they are rooted in and lead back to a believing community." These ecclesia [church, assembly] of real people, in real places, dealing with real issues, and in touch with human reality, as Calvin said, are the "real" expressions of Christ on earth as the community of God is in heaven.

~ Gareth Weldon Icenogle. *Biblical Foundations for Small Group Ministry*. (electronic ed.). Downers Grove, IL: InterVarsity Press, 1994.

God has given us sure and certain promises regarding the power of prayer to transform us, empower us, and supply us with the provision and direction of the Lord. As discussed throughout this lesson, it is simply not possible to understand and apply the Word of God without prevailing prayer, the kind that with deep fervency and contrition asks God to supply us with the necessary wisdom to know and do his Word. Take time with your fellow students to share your requests to the Lord, without anxiety and with thanksgiving, making your requests (and not your demands!) known to God. He has promised that his provision and peace will keep your hearts and minds in Christ Jesus (Phil. 4.6-7). Remember one another during the week, and take note of your requests and those of others, and see how God answers your petitions for wisdom, power, and blessing.

ASSIGNMENTS

Scripture Memory

Psalm 1.1-3

Reading Assignment

To prepare for class, please visit *www.tumi.org/books* to find next week's reading assignment, or ask your Mentor.

Other Assignments

Again, make certain that you read the assignments above, and as last week, write a brief summary for them and bring these summaries to class next week. (Please see the "Reading Completion Sheet" on page 16.) Also, now is the time to begin to think about the character of your ministry project, as well as decide what passage of Scripture you will select for your exegetical project. Do not delay in determining either your ministry or exegetical project. The sooner you select, the more time you will have to prepare!

Looking Forward to the Next Lesson

In our next lesson, *The Old Testament Witness to Christ and His Kingdom: The Promise Given*, we will examine the relationship of the Old Testament to the New Testament through the idea of progressive revelation. We will look at the complimentary connections which exist in the OT and NT as they relate to the person of Christ and his Kingdom, and consider the unique motif of *promise and fulfillment*, and how this integrates and makes one the teaching of Scripture on the person of Jesus Christ. This unity of truth is seen in God's marvelous promise to send a redeemer to humanity through whom God's enemy would be destroyed, and humankind would be redeemed. In the *protoevangelium* (i.e., the first telling of the Gospel in Genesis 3.15), through the covenant promise of Abraham and its extensions we see how the Messianic hope is the unifying principle of the Old Testament and the joyous fulfillment of the New, all finding their climax in the person of Jesus Christ. He is both the seed of the woman and the seed of Abraham. May the Hebrew Scriptures unveil his glory to us, and transform us as we become diligent students of God's holy Word!

FOR FURTHER STUDY

Please see the following resources in *Picturing Theology: An A-Z Collection of TUMI's Key Diagrams, Charts, Graphics, and Articles*:

- *Bible Study Tools Worksheet*, page 16
- *Chart of Biblical Studies*, page 35
- *How to Interpret a Narrative (Story)*, page 180
- *Keys to Bible Interpretation*, page 208
- *Use of Reference Tools for Interpreting the Bible*, page 519

The Old Testament Witness to Christ and His Kingdom
The Promise Given

Lesson Objectives

Welcome in the strong name of Jesus Christ! After your reading, study, discussion, and application of the materials in this lesson, you will be able to:

- Define the relationship of the Old Testament to the New Testament through the idea of *progressive revelation*, which affirms that God has revealed himself progressively and definitively throughout the history of his people, and finally through Jesus Christ.

- Lay out the various aspects of progressive revelation, including God's continuous revelation of himself to us through creation, through specific manifestations and occasions, and in these last days through his Son.

- Show how the OT explains and reveals the NT through the person of Christ, and how both testaments focus upon God's final and full revelation of himself in Jesus Christ and his kingdom reign.

- Reproduce Augustine's epigram (saying) on the relationship between the two testaments: "In the OT the NT lies hidden; in the NT the OT stands revealed."

- Highlight the complimentary concepts which connect and explain the relationship of the Old and New Testaments, including the OT providing the introduction to the NT's conclusion about Christ, the OT as anticipation of Christ and the NT as its climax, the OT as the shadow (prefiguring) of the person and work of Christ and the NT as the embodiment of those figures, the OT as the ineffective former revelation of God's salvation and the NT revelation in Christ as the consummated latter, and the OT as the particularized form of God's salvation universalized to all nations in the NT.

- Lay out the definition and elements of the *promise and fulfillment* motif in OT revelation, which affirms the promise of God for his own chosen one to redeem humankind and to destroy the devil's work, a promise fulfilled in the person of Jesus of Nazareth.

- Identify the central texts in Scripture which affirm how the OT's work is to provide a compelling and definitive witness to the person of Messiah fulfilled in the person of Jesus Christ (cf. Luke 22.25-27, 44-48; Matt. 5.17-18; John 1.45; 5.39-40; Heb. 10.5-10 with Ps. 40.6-8).

- Describe the implications of the *promise-fulfillment* motif for OT study, especially the way in which it suggests that a clear picture of Messiah can be seen in the history of the patriarchs, the nation of Israel, the Messianic prophecies, and the moral standards of the Law.

- List the ways in which the *promise and fulfillment* motif affirms the unity of the Old and New Testaments, in terms of God's intention to reveal himself, to redeem his people, and to do this through the promise made to Abraham and his descendants fulfilled in the person of Jesus of Nazareth.

Devotion

The Original Promise Keeper

Gen. 3.15 – I will put enmity between you and the woman, and between your offspring and her offspring; he shall bruise your head, and you shall bruise his heel.

Do you keep your promises, or do you renege on what you say you will do? A popular men's group has given itself the name of "Promise Keepers," laying out seven areas in which the members pledge to the Lord and to each other their fidelity to him and the Kingdom. The idea of promise is a significant concept in our society, from our common romance notions of engagement, "I'm promised to Sherri," to the promissory notes associated with business and law. Truly, the idea of the promise is a significant and important notion in all of our modern day relationships: promises are made between nations, world leaders, militaries, business partners, family members, and contractors. Without the notion of making and keeping promises, our entire societal machinery would grind to a halt.

One of the simplest and most direct ways of comprehending the biblical story is the motif of promise and fulfillment. In one sense the entirety of the Bible can be seen as a movement of the sovereign God, the God of Israel, Yahweh, the God and Father of our Lord Jesus Christ who makes a promise to the rebellious first human pair and the serpent who deceived Eve. In this text God makes a promise, a promise that will affect the serpent and the seed of the woman. In theological circles this promise is called the "*protoevangelium*," the very first mention or telling of the Gospel message of salvation of humankind that occurs in Bible.

Here God lays out the entire plan of salvation in a short passage that summarizes one of the most important ideas in Scripture.

The setting of this episode related to the text is that tragic moment when the first human pair, Adam and Eve, are caught in their shameful admission of eating the fruit of the knowledge of the Tree of Good and Evil against the direct commandment of the Lord. The serpent, who deceived Eve into her disobedient act, Eve, and Adam are all before the Lord who is calling down his judgment upon them. In speaking to the serpent, God makes a declaration about the future that literally makes this text the beginning of the end of the entire written revelation of Scripture.

God here unequivocally states that his sovereign purpose for the serpent will be perpetual and unending hostility between the serpent and the seed of the woman, between its offspring and that of the woman. This "seed" would have his heel bruised by the serpent, but the serpent would have his entire head crushed in by the seed of the woman. This graphic image of the serpent and seed lies at the heart of the salvific vision of the Bible. God says that as a result of the voluntary human rebellion, he has established relationships in the universe which will perpetually be in place, unbroken hostility and enmity between the serpent and the seed of the woman, between its offspring and that of the woman.

From the earliest readings of this text, Jewish scholars saw it as the first mention of the divine promise of the Messiah, this seed, this person who would come of the woman and yet would bring a brutal and final end to the serpent and its accursed lying, deception, and ill-will toward the human race. We know that this promise is renewed with Abraham whose seed would be blessed and would be a blessing to all the nations (Gen. 12-13). This promise of a seed, an heir, a blessed warrior who would make an end of the works of the devil, was renewed with Abraham's sons, Isaac and Jacob, and then passed on to Jacob's son Judah (Gen. 49). The promise weaves through the OT, through the house of Judah, until it is made explicit that the seed would be an heir of the house of David (cf. 2 Sam. 7), and the prophets add even more color, knowledge, and revelation about the character and work of this seed (e.g., Isa. 9.6-7; 53.1-12).

Finally, the seed is revealed in the NT to be the person of Jesus of Nazareth, who himself is the fulfillment of the ancient promise of the Lord to bring to the earth one who would redeem his people, restore creation, and reign forever as the Lord and King of God's universe. The apostles make it explicit that Jesus of Nazareth is in fact the long sought for seed of Abraham (e.g., Paul in Galatians 4.4, "But when the fullness of time had come, God sent forth his Son, born of woman, born under the law"). Likewise, John makes it plain what the purpose of Jesus of Nazareth was in coming in to the world: 1 John 3.8 "Whoever makes a practice of sinning is of the devil, for the devil has been sinning from the beginning. The reason the Son of God appeared was to destroy the works of the devil."

Truly, Jesus of Nazareth is the fulfillment of the ancient promise of Yahweh to send through the line of humankind, the seed of the woman, a person who would both redeem humankind from its guilt, as well as finally destroy the works of the devil. This image of the serpent whose head is crushed by the victorious warrior of the Lord is dominant in the imagery and rhetoric of the apostles. Notice these themes in the following representative texts of the NT:

> Rom. 16.20 – The God of peace will soon crush Satan under your feet. The grace of our Lord Jesus Christ be with you.

> Eph. 4.8 – Therefore it says, "When he ascended on high he led a host of captives, and he gave gifts to men."

> Col. 2.15 – He disarmed the rulers and authorities and put them to open shame, by triumphing over them in him.

> Heb. 2.14-15 – Since therefore the children share in flesh and blood, he himself likewise partook of the same things, that through death he might destroy the one who has the power of death, that is, the devil, [15] and deliver all those who through fear of death were subject to lifelong slavery.

> 1 John 3.8 – Whoever makes a practice of sinning is of the devil, for the devil has been sinning from the beginning. The reason the Son of God appeared was to destroy the works of the devil.

> 1 John 5.5 – Who is it that overcomes the world except the one who believes that Jesus is the Son of God?

These and other texts lay out for us the power of the promise of the Lord to "crush the head of the serpent" in his own self-chosen, anointed "seed of the woman." God has determined to connect the entirety of human history to the fulfillment of a single promise that he made in regard to the restoration and redemption of his creation through Jesus of Nazareth.

We now know that this promise has in part already been fulfilled in the coming and work of Jesus of Nazareth, and soon he will consummate his work that he began on the cross at his Second Coming. Is it not amazing that all of the history of the entire world and universe can be boiled down to a single promise and our sovereign and faithful God's absolute determination to fulfill his Word? This is the ground of our faith, the heart of our worship, and the basis of our reading of the Scriptures. This divine promise coursed through the sacred history of the people of Israel until it was fulfilled in the person of Jesus of Nazareth. He is the center and end of all salvific work that God conducts in this world.

Isn't it amazing that our God, this great God, is a God of promise who fulfilled it in the person of Jesus Christ? Isn't it wonderful to know that the one who promised us will never change his mind, but will fulfill his sacred promise, to the glory of his name, and the salvation of his own? Let us declare our faith in the simple affirmation of the promise of the apostle, and live as if we believe it with all of our hearts and minds:

> 1 Thess. 5.23-24 – Now may the God of peace himself sanctify you completely, and may your whole spirit and soul and body be kept blameless at the coming of our Lord Jesus Christ. [24] He who calls you is faithful; he will surely do it.

The God who laid out his sovereign purpose for the world in the Garden, the God and Father of our Lord Jesus Christ, indeed, he is the *original Promise Keeper*!

Nicene Creed and Prayer

After reciting and/or singing the Nicene Creed (located in the Appendix), pray the following prayer:

> O everlasting God and Father of our Lord Jesus Christ, grant us thy grace that we may study the Holy Scriptures diligently, and, with our whole heart, seek and find Christ therein, and through him obtain everlasting life; through the same Jesus Christ our Lord. Amen.
>
> ~ John W. Doberstein, ed. *A Lutheran Prayer Book*. Philadelphia: Fortress Press, 1960. p. 102.

Scripture Memorization Review

Review with a partner, write out and/or recite the text for last class session's assigned memory verse: Psalm 1.1-3.

Assignments Due

Turn in your summary of the reading assignment for last week, that is, your brief response and explanation of the main points that the authors were seeking to make in the assigned reading (Reading Completion Sheet).

CONTACT

Are We Using the Right Book in the Wrong Way?

1. One of the ongoing issues and problems associated with the mastery of the OT is its misuse by so many interpreters, both conservative and liberal. The OT is such a diverse library of literature that many OT scholars no longer seek to provide us with a coherent, unified OT theology. In place of a single unity, it is seen as a heavily edited (redacted) text that covers many centuries, dozens of authors, and one which provides no consistent or unified message for the interpreter. Even for many evangelical Christians, the Bible remains a closed book. Used primarily for devotional readings in the Psalms and Proverbs, large portions of the OT remain unpreached and unread by many evangelicals. What is the reason that these dear saints who love the Bible give for their systematic neglect of the OT? It is simply too hard to understand and use. For them it is seldom referred to because it is unintelligible, filled with difficult passages, and too heavily concentrated in portions of ceremonial law and/or symbolism and imagery. Frankly, for the new or growing Christian it is easier to focus on the NT and read the Epistles, and, if one is so bold, go to the Gospels and read the words of the Lord. But, in terms of understanding and desirability, many Christians testify that the OT is not an integral part of their spiritual journeys. What do you make of this situation, and how does the neglect of the OT play itself out in your experience?

Is the God of the OT the Same God as the God of the New?

2. In a day of tolerance, political correctness, and overall squeamish feelings about anything that smacks of judgment or punishment, the OT is a much maligned book. Admittedly, it is filled with many stories which cover all the dark shadows of human existence, and include graphic portrayals of murder, rape, violence, war, and tragedy. Examples of tough judgment are given in many of the stories, and those of certain beliefs and lifestyles are not only morally condemned, but in graphic detail we see them judged by the community and the Lord. The statements of God against a number of modern lifestyle choices makes the OT especially the lightning rod for much debate and discussion. Some liberal Christians have gone so far as to denounce the OT as the product of a primitive culture whose theological and moral ideas were more a reflection of their era and environment than what we as "reasoned and tolerant Christians" would find acceptable. What should we make of these modern attempts to drive a wedge between the God of the OT and the God of the NT, as revealed in the person of Jesus of Nazareth? What is the continuity between the two? Should we admit, even a little, that there might be a difference between the God of the OT and the God of the NT? Explain.

Jesus and Meaning of the OT

When Jesus of Nazareth referred to the Bible or Scripture, his referent was our OT. Today, it is referred to in non-Christian circles as the "Hebrew Bible," and the discussions are heated about the *meaning* of the OT. For most Christians, the highest and best authority on the meaning of the OT is the person of Jesus, who unequivocally in at least five different passages in the NT said that he himself was the theme of the Hebrew Bible (cf. Luke 24.25-27; 44-48; Matt. 5.17-18; John 5.39-40; 1.41ff.; Heb. 10.5-10 with Ps. 40.6-8). These texts give the sense that Jesus believed that the OT, the Hebrew Bible, was essentially a text that pointed to his person in terms of figure and prophecy, and that a correct reading of the OT had to, in some fundamental sense, find its meaning in his own person. This claim, by the way, lies at the heart of the constant controversy between Jesus and the teachers of the Bible of his own day; such a claim, that the entirety of the Scriptures found their theological and spiritual end in relationship to him as the Messiah of God was unacceptable to them, even blasphemous. This Christo-centric use of the Bible is equally controversial today, especially in the world of biblical criticism, which sees such a laser-guided approach to such a diverse set of literature problematic. What is your thought? Based on what you know today, how would you understand the nature of the OT in its relationship to Jesus Christ? How far can you take this kind of hermeneutic before you skew or misread the basic message of the OT?

The Promise Given

Promise and Fulfillment in the Old and New Testaments

Rev. Dr. Don L. Davis

CONTENT

Summary

The relationship of the Old Testament to the New Testament can be effectively understood through the idea of *progressive revelation*, which affirms that God has revealed himself progressively and definitively throughout the history of his people, and finally through Jesus Christ. God in diverse manners and at different times made himself known to the nation of Israel in limited ways, but in these last days he has spoken to us through his Son. Jesus of Nazareth is God's final and full revelation of himself, now testified of in Scripture. As Augustine suggests: "In the OT the NT lies hidden; in the NT the OT stands revealed." The testaments have a complimentary relationship, the OT providing the introduction to the NT's conclusion about Christ, the OT as anticipation to the NT's climax about God's salvation story in Christ. Furthermore, the OT prefigures Christ's person and work fully embodied in the NT.

While the OT is the ineffective former revelation of God's salvation, the NT can be seen as the consummated latter, and the universalized call of which the OT is particularized to the nation of Israel. The connection of the testaments can be seen in the *promise and fulfillment* motif, especially in the way the NT affirms how the OT's work is to provide a compelling and definitive witness to the person of Messiah fulfilled in the person of Jesus Christ in the history of the patriarchs, the nation of Israel, the Messianic prophecies, and the moral standards of the Law.

Our objective for this lesson, *Promise and Fulfillment in the Old and New Testaments,* is to enable you to see that:

- The relationship of the Old Testament to the New Testament can be effectively understood through the idea of *progressive revelation*, which affirms that God has revealed himself progressively and definitively throughout the history of his people, and finally through Jesus Christ.

- The concept of *progressive revelation* includes God's continuous revelation of himself to us through creation, through specific manifestations and occasions, and in these last days through his Son. The OT explains and reveals the NT through the person of Christ, and both testaments focus upon God's final and full revelation of himself in Jesus Christ and his kingdom reign.

- Augustine's epigram (saying) nicely summarizes the relationship between the two testaments: "In the OT the NT lies hidden; in the NT the OT stands revealed." This complimentary relationship is seen in how the OT provides an introduction to the NT's conclusion about Christ, the OT's anticipation of the person and work of Messiah, and the NT's identification of Jesus of Nazareth as the climax of that anticipation. Also, the OT serves as the shadow (prefiguring) of the person and work of Christ and the NT as its embodiment, and the OT is seen as the ineffective former revelation of God's salvation consummated later in the NT revelation of Jesus. Finally, what was particularized to Israel in the OT was universalized to all nations in the NT.

- The motif of *promise and fulfillment* in OT revelation affirms the promise of God for his own chosen one to redeem humankind and to destroy the devil's work, a promise fulfilled in the person of Jesus of Nazareth.

- The NT provides several central texts which affirm how the OT's work is to provide a compelling and definitive witness to the person of Messiah fulfilled in the person of Jesus Christ (cf. Luke 22.25-27, 44-48; Matt. 5.17-18; John 1.45; 5.39-40; Heb. 10.5-10

LESSON 3 | THE OT WITNESS TO CHRIST AND HIS KINGDOM: THE PROMISE GIVEN / 85

with Ps. 40.6-8). This witness can be seen in the history of the patriarchs, the nation of Israel, the Messianic prophecies, and the moral standards of the Law.

Video Outline

I. Progressive Revelation: Affirming the Connection Between the Old and New Testaments

Augustine's epigram (little saying) about the relationship between the two testaments:

"In the Old Testament the New Testament lies hidden; in the New Testament the Old Testament stands revealed."

A. Definition of progressive revelation: God has revealed himself progressively through history and finally through Jesus Christ.

Heb. 1.1-2 – Long ago, at many times and in many ways, God spoke to our fathers by the prophets, [2] but in these last days he has spoken to us by his Son, whom he appointed the heir of all things, through whom also he created the world.

B. Aspects of progressive revelation

1. Through human history, God has provided a continuity (connected reality) of revelation to humankind.

2. God communicated on numerous occasions in the past using many different ways to speak to diverse individuals and groups.

3. God's earlier words, although entirely true, were partial and required completion.

   a. God's latter revelations explain the meaning of the earlier.

   b. God's earlier revelations give shape and meaning to the latter.

4. In these last days, God has spoken to us through his Son.

a. Matt. 3.17

b. Matt. 17.5

c. John 1.14

d. John 1.17-18

e. Jesus as the center of biblical revelation bridges the testaments, himself being the Shadow of the Old Testament and the Substance of the New.

f. He fulfills the sayings of the OT, including the prophecies of the Law and the Prophets, Luke 24.25-27.

g. He reveals the very person of God in his own person (i.e., he is the express image of his glory, the "Word made flesh," cf. John 1.14-18).

5. The Old Testament explains and reveals the meaning of the New Testament.

C. Implication of progressive revelation for Christ-centered approach to Scripture interpretation

1. The testaments are intimately connected to each other.

2. The testaments both focus on God's revelation regarding Jesus Christ and his kingdom reign.

II. Complimentary Concepts that Connect the Old and New Testaments

Augustine's epigram (little saying) about the relationship between the two testaments:

"In the Old Testament the New Testament lies hidden; in the New Testament the Old Testament stands revealed."

A. *Introduction and conclusion*: the Old Testament provides us an introduction to the truths about Christ and his Kingdom, and the New Testament brings these to a conclusion (e.g., the teachings of Isaiah of the Servant in chapters 42-55 introduces a figure who in fact is shown to be Jesus Christ at his first advent [cf. 1 Pet. 1.22-25]).

B. *Anticipation and climax*: what is anticipated regarding Christ and his Kingdom in the Old Testament is brought to its final climax in the New Testament (the salvation of the remnant of Israel in Zech. 12.10-13.1 anticipates the climax of Jesus' return in Revelation 19).

C. *Shadow and substance*: what is embodied and prefigured in the Old Testament regarding Christ and his Kingdom is revealed and given substance in the New (the physical tabernacle of Hebrews 8.5 is the shadow of the true tabernacle mentioned regarding Jesus as priest in heaven).

D. *Ineffective former and consummated latter*: what is demonstrated and found to be ineffective in the Old Testament is finalized and consummated in the New (e.g., the entire book of Hebrews speaks of the insufficiency of the old sacrificial system to actually take sins away; Jesus' death is the effective reality behind the OT example, e.g., Heb. 10.1-10).

E. *Particular and universal*: what is particularized in the experience of the people of Israel in the Old Testament is extended and expanded to all who believe in the New.

III. Promise and Fulfillment: the Christo-centric Nature of the Old Testament Revelation

Christ Is the Theme of Each of the Eight Sections of the Bible

(Cf. Geisler, *A Popular Survey of the Old Testament*, pp. 21-24)

1. The Law (Genesis - Deuteronomy): Laying the Foundation for Messiah
2. History (Joshua - Esther): The Preparation for Messiah
3. Poetry (Job - Song of Solomon): The Aspiration for Messiah
4. Prophecy (Isaiah - Malachi): The Expectation of Messiah
5. Gospels (Matthew - John): The Manifestation of Messiah
6. History (Acts): The Propagation of Messiah
7. Epistles (Romans - Jude): The Interpretation and Application of Messiah
8. Prophecy (Revelation): The Consummation of All Things in Messiah

A. *Definition of the promise-fulfillment motif:* the promise of God for someone to redeem humankind from its sin and destroy the devil's work is fulfilled in the person of Jesus Christ.

B. Jesus gives convincing testimony within Scripture that the Old Testament's purpose is to give witness concerning his person and work.

1. The road to Emmaus

    a. Luke 24.25-27, 32

    b. Here is a picture of Christ interpreting all the Scriptures (i.e., OT) as to how they explain and point toward his own identity.

2. The post-resurrection appearance to his own

    a. Luke 24.44-48

    b. Christ opened their minds to understand the Scriptures (i.e., the OT) concerning himself.

3. The Sermon on the Mount

    a. Matt. 5.17-18

    b. Christ's explicit teaching that he had come not to abolish the Scriptures but to fulfill them completely.

4. Dialogue with the Pharisees

    a. John 5.39-40

    b. Jesus explaining to the experts in Scripture that reading them without having his identity in mind is poor, ineffectual exegesis.

5. Prophetic quotation in Heb. 10.5-10 cf. Ps. 40.6-8

    a. Ps. 40.6-8

    b. Heb. 10.5-10

    c. A prophetic psalm is attributed to Jesus Christ as he relates a text to his own offering of his body as a sacrifice for sin.

C. Implications of the promise-fulfillment motif

Luke 24.44-48 – Then he said to them, "These are my words that I spoke to you while I was still with you, that everything written about me in the Law of Moses and the Prophets and the Psalms must be fulfilled." [45] Then he opened their minds to understand the Scriptures, [46] and said to them, "Thus it is written, that the Christ should suffer and on the third day rise from the dead, [47] and that repentance and forgiveness of sins should be proclaimed in his name to all nations, beginning from Jerusalem. [48] You are witnesses of these things."

1. In the history of the Patriarchs, the nation of Israel, and its historical and spiritual development, the Old Testament provides us with a clear picture of Christ.

2. The central promise of God in the OT (i.e., that God would send a Seed/Servant who would remedy the downfall of his creation and all humankind) is fulfilled in the manifestation of Jesus Christ recorded in the NT.

3. The actual subject matter of the Scriptures is singular and dynamic: the revelation of Jesus Christ.

4. The OT can be profitably studied as the outline of God's promise for salvation and kingdom restoration of which the New Testament is its fulfillment.

Conclusion

- The notion of *progressive revelation* unites our understanding of the Old and New Testaments in the person of Jesus Christ and his kingdom reign.

- Both the Old and New Testaments compliment each other, and through the biblical motif of *promise and fulfillment* we can comprehend the meaning and application of the Old Testament.

Student Questions and Response

Please take as much time as you have available to answer these and other questions that the video brought out. In this lesson we explored the relationship of the Old Testament to the New Testament in the ideas of *progressive revelation*, as well as the *promise-fulfillment* motif. The idea of progressive revelation affirms that God has revealed himself progressively and definitively throughout the history of his people, and finally through Jesus Christ. Likewise, the motif of promise-fulfillment suggests that the promise God made to redeem and restore his creation and people, made in the OT, is fulfilled in the person of Jesus of Nazareth in the NT. Explore these and the other ideas covered in this lesson by reviewing the material through the questions below. Include Scripture in your answers, where appropriate.

1. What is the meaning of *progressive revelation*, and what does this idea affirm regarding God and his determination to make himself known in the world? Be specific.

2. How does the concept of *progressive revelation* help us understand how God has revealed himself to humankind before Christ? Now that Christ has come, what further revelation can we expect from God about himself and his purposes for his universe?

3. What saying of Augustine nicely summarizes the relationship between the two testaments? Explain its meaning.

4. What are some of the ways in which the OT and the NT are complimentary to each other, that is, explain and reveal one another? Be specific, and highlight what each concept means.

5. What does it mean to say that the OT serves as *the shadow* (prefiguring) of the person and work of Christ *embodied* in the NT? Give examples.

6. How can it be said that the OT is the *ineffective former revelation* of God's salvation, of which the NT is the *consummated latter* of that same salvation in Jesus?

7. In what sense does the NT make available for all people what was particularized to Israel in the OT? Explain.

8. How does the motif of *promise and fulfillment* affirm how the entire Bible can be understood as God making his promise for salvation which is fulfilled in the person of Jesus of Nazareth? Explain.

9. What are the central texts which affirm how the OT's theme and subject is the person of Messiah fulfilled in the person of Jesus Christ? How is this theme developed and laid out in the OT?

CONNECTION

Summary of Key Concepts

This lesson focuses upon the various motifs and approaches that will allow us to see the Old and New Testaments as fundamentally and intimately connected – through *progressive revelation*, the *promise-fulfillment motif*, and the complimentary relationships that the testaments have as they both come to fulfillment in the person and work of Jesus of Nazareth. Carefully review the concepts below as a mastery of these themes is essential if you are to adopt exegetical strategies that will enable you to see the unity as well as the diversity of the Old and New Testament literature.

- The relationship of the Old Testament to the New Testament can be effectively understood through the idea of *progressive revelation*, which affirms that God has revealed himself progressively and definitively throughout the history of his people, and finally through Jesus Christ.

- The concept of *progressive revelation* includes God's continuous revelation of himself to us through creation, through specific manifestations and occasions, and in these last days through his Son. The OT explains and reveals the NT through the person of Christ, and both testaments focus upon God's final and full revelation of himself in Jesus Christ and his kingdom reign.

- Augustine's epigram (saying) nicely summarizes the relationship between the two testaments: "In the OT the NT lies hidden; in the NT the OT stands revealed." This complementary relationship is seen in how the OT provides an introduction to the NT's conclusion about Christ, the OT's anticipation of the person and work of Messiah, and the NT's identification of Jesus of Nazareth as the climax of that anticipation. Also, the OT serves as the shadow (prefiguring) of the person and work of Christ and the NT as its embodiment, and the OT is seen as the ineffective former revelation of God's salvation consummated later in the NT revelation of Jesus. Finally, what was particularized to Israel in the OT was universalized to all nations in the NT.

- The motif of *promise and fulfillment* in OT revelation affirms the promise of God for his own chosen One to redeem humankind and to destroy the devil's work, a promise fulfilled in the person of Jesus of Nazareth.

- The NT provides several central texts which affirm how the OT's work is to provide compelling and definitive witness to the person of Messiah fulfilled in the person of Jesus Christ (cf. Luke

22.25-27, 44-48; Matt. 5.17-18; John 1.45; 5.39-40; Heb. 10.5-10 with Ps. 40.6-8). This witness can be seen in the history of the patriarchs, the nation of Israel, the Messianic prophecies, and the moral standards of the Law.

- The major motif that links all biblical revelation in Scripture is the *promise and fulfillment* motif. This theme affirms the unity of the Old and New Testaments, in terms of God's intention to reveal himself, to redeem his people, and to do this through the promise made to Abraham and his descendants fulfilled in the person of Jesus of Nazareth.

I Find My Lord in the Bible

I find my Lord in the Bible, wherever I chance to look,
He is the Theme of the Bible, the center and heart of the Book;
He is the Rose of Sharon, he is the Lily fair,
Where ever I open my Bible, the Lord of the Book is there.

He, at the Book's beginning, gave to the earth its form,
He is the Ark of shelter, bearing the brunt of the storm
The Burning Bush of the desert, the Budding of Aaron's Rod,
Where ever I look in the Bible, I see the Son of God.

The Ram upon Mount Moriah, the Ladder from earth to sky,
The Scarlet Cord in the window, and the Serpent lifted high,
The Smitten Rock in the desert, the Shepherd with staff and crook,
The face of the Lord I discover, where ever I open the Book.

He is the Seed of the woman, the Savior virgin-born
He is the Son of David, whom men rejected with scorn,
His garments of grace and of beauty the stately Aaron deck,
Yet he is a Priest forever, for he is Melchizedek.

Lord of eternal glory Whom John, the Apostle, saw;
Light of the golden city, Lamb without spot or flaw,
Bridegroom coming at midnight, for whom the virgins look.
Where ever I open my Bible, I find my Lord in the Book.

~ Author Unknown

Student Application and Implications

Now is the time for you to discuss with your fellow students your questions about your own grasp and application of the concepts of progressive revelation and the promise-fulfillment motif. What you must do is ask pointed, direct, and open questions about your own understanding and mastery of these principles, and seek the ways in which you might need to apply this material directly to your own spiritual journey today. The questions below seek to anticipate some of the particular questions you may have in light of the material you have just studied.

- What is my relationship to the Old Testament material – do I know all the books of the OT, have I read through the OT at least once, and do I have a steady habit of reading and applying the OT in my life and ministry today?

- Did I have any grasp of the principle of progressive revelation before this unit of study, and if so, how did my knowledge of this actually influence the way in which I read and applied both the Old and the New Testaments?

- Do I tend to emphasize the connection and continuity between the Old and New Testament, or the differences between them? Explain.

- Do I tend to read all of the Bible with an eye toward the ways in which this text or these Scriptures might connect either *backward* to the life and revelation contained in the Old Testament, or *forward* to the life and work of Jesus of Nazareth, who is the fulfillment of the Old and full revelation of the New? How so?

- Could I have written what Augustine said: "In the OT the NT lies hidden; in the NT the OT stands revealed." Does the way I handle the Scriptures *really show* how much I believe in the unity of the OT to the New?

- In the church I attend, does the preaching and teaching reflect the connections between the Old and New Testament brought out in our discussion of the complimentary relationships between them (i.e., that the OT provides introduction to the NT's conclusion about Christ, the OT's anticipates the person and work of Messiah with the NT identifying Jesus of Nazareth as the climax of that anticipation, etc.)?

- How much do I worship and serve God with this kind of historical understanding that the motif of *promise and fulfillment* brings out? Do I focus most of my time on the past, the present, or the future in my Bible reading, meditation, and prayer?

- Do I tend to see Jesus both as the seed of the woman who will destroy the devil's work, as well as the seed of Abraham through whom all the families of the earth will be blessed? What is the primary way in which I view Jesus in light of these revelations about him?

- Do I (more often than not) affirm Jesus' teaching that he himself is the key theme and subject of all biblical revelation (cf. Luke 22.25-27, 44-48; Matt. 5.17-18; John 1.45; 5.39-40; Heb. 10.5-10 with Ps. 40.6-8)? How do I *most often* use the Bible in my life – as an affirmation of the person of Jesus or more related to my own troubles, needs, and issues? How ought we use the OT in light of Jesus' teaching about it?

CASE STUDIES

It Was Our Hebrew Bible before it Was Your Old Testament

1. Gang violence has been on the climb in your community for some time. In a show of unity and support, various religious groups have sent their religious representatives to an ecumenical panel discussion on violence, tolerance, and respect for others. As one of the panel members began to share his views about the "Old Testament" the local rabbi very warmly but firmly suggested the following: "As I know that many followers of Christ, Christian believers, are in attendance, and that it is their habit to refer to the first portion of their Bibles as the Old Testament, I would suggest that during our time together that we would refer to the Christian Old Testament as the Hebrew Bible. You see, for us, believers in Judaism, it has never been an old book; it is our Scripture and we refer to it as our Hebrew Scriptures. Would it be too much for us to refer to it in this way, as we dialogue together about respect, unity, and support for one another?" How would you answer the rabbi in this setting? Is this much ado about nothing, or is there something important about refusing to see the OT as merely the old portion of the Bible? How does viewing the "Hebrew Bible" as the "Old Testament" limit our ability to see its relevance for Christians today?

The OT and Equipping the Saints

2. It is quite clear that the Scriptures that Paul referred to in 2 Timothy 3, which could make God's woman or man outfitted for the work of the ministry, was the OT. The Bible of Jesus and the apostles was, in fact, our OT, and from even a cursory reading of the epistles we see that they quoted and referred to it often in their writings to new believers and emerging congregations. Unlike them, however, it is difficult to find follow-up material and discipleship curriculum where the teaching, stories, figures, and prophecies of the OT are made the heart and soul of the material. In some ways, the OT is in some sort of exile in many evangelical church settings. It is rarely read, and often even more rarely preached. A story here, a proverb there, but rarely do you find even expositors spending weeks or months in OT literature in the instruction of Christians. Obviously, this neglect has produced a kind of illiteracy of the OT in many Christians, those who have never had ongoing, systematic teaching of the OT. What should we make of this neglect of the OT in our churches – is it a product of the times, something more fundamental, or something else altogether?

A Gentilized Faith?

 If you were not aware of it, the casual observer would take Christianity as essentially a Euro-centric faith, one that essentially began as a result of the Protestant revolt against Catholic extremes during the period of the Reformation in 16th Century Europe. And no wonder that they would suppose this, especially in evangelical settings, which tend to rarely if ever refer to the Jewish roots of the Christian faith, giving it little or no time in a Christian experience that is informed by middle class American values and trends. Unfortunately, many minority groups are growing in hostility to Christianized forms of "religion," seeing essentially the term "Christian" to be synonymous with holding deep affinity with white, middle-class, conservative perspectives and moral values. A growing movement of thinkers and scholars are referring to the need to de-Gentilize our faith, arguing that we have swung too far to interpreting Christian experience as merely an American value system with a religious twist. Obviously, many who do not find this attractive are rejecting Christian faith before even being exposed to the biblical claims about the person of Jesus of Nazareth as outlined in the Old and New Testament. How might a rediscovery of the OT (admittedly, a distinctively Hebrew book) help us mature beyond the Gentilization of much of the Christian faith and practice today?

Too Hard and Not on Point

 A well-studied and beloved youth group leader in a growing church was recently struck by how few of the members of his youth group understood any of even the most basic stories and figures of the OT. We are not speaking of some of the lesser characters, but the main figures: Moses, Elijah, Elisha, etc. were not known, either. In an attempt to remedy this difficulty, the youth group leader started a Bible teaching series entitled "Defining Moments" which would take selected key points of the OT and show how it related to Christ and his Kingdom spoken of in the NT. After a few weeks, the character of the youth group changed greatly. Some students, finding the stories and materials too hard and not real exciting, quit the group altogether, and another group has found the stories intriguing, but not relevant to where they see themselves at. A small group, however, have flourished under the teaching, and for the first time believe that they are coming to understand the OT. Pressure is growing in the church to go back to the good ol' days of teaching on contemporary issues that were easier to teach (and to hear!), but the leader has determined to finish the series, which has another three months to go. If the youth group leader asked your opinion, how would you advise him on making the OT come alive in his group without alienating and confusing some of the "weaker brethren" complaining about it?

Restatement of the Lesson's Thesis

The relationship of the Old Testament to the New Testament can be effectively understood through the idea of progressive revelation, which affirms that God has revealed himself progressively and definitively throughout the history of his people, and finally through Jesus Christ. God in diverse manners and at different times made himself known to the nation of Israel in limited ways, but in these last days he has spoken to us through his Son. Jesus of Nazareth is God's final and full revelation of himself, now testified of in Scripture. As Augustine suggests: "In the OT the NT lies hidden; in the NT the OT stands revealed." The Testaments have a complementary relationship, the OT providing the introduction to the NT's conclusion about Christ, the OT as anticipation to the NT's climax about God's salvation story in Christ. Furthermore, the OT prefigures Christ's person and work fully embodied in the NT. While the OT is the ineffective former revelation of God's salvation, the NT can be seen as the consummated latter and universalized call of which the OT is particularized to the nation of Israel. The connection of the testaments can be seen in the promise and fulfillment motif, especially in the way the NT affirms how the OT's work is to provide compelling and definitive witness to the person of Messiah fulfilled in the person of Jesus Christ in the history of the patriarchs, the nation of Israel, the Messianic prophecies, and the moral standards of the Law.

The major motif that links all biblical revelation in Scripture is the promise and fulfillment motif. This theme affirms the unity of the Scriptures; God intends to reveal himself and redeem his people through the seed, the one promised to Abraham and his descendants.

This seed is fulfilled in the person of Jesus of Nazareth. The seminal text in Scripture outlining the promise is the *protoevangelium*, the first telling of the Gospel in Genesis 3.15. Here God promises the certainty of hostility between the serpent and the woman and their respective "seeds," the bruising of the heel of the woman's seed, and the crushing of the serpent's head by the seed. In the NT, Jesus of Nazareth is revealed to be this divine seed commissioned to destroy the devil's work and to redeem humankind to God. Yahweh's covenant promise with Abraham serves as the progressive continuation of God's divine promise for a Savior. In his covenant with Abraham, God promised to supply him a "seed" who would bring redemption and restoration to Abraham's descendants and all the nations of the earth. In the NT, Jesus of Nazareth is declared to be the seed of Abraham, the restorer and redeemer of creation and the world.

Resources and Bibliographies

If you are interested in pursuing some of the ideas of *The Promise Given*, you might want to give these books a try:

Baron, David. *Rays of Messiah's Glory: Christ in the Old Testament.* Eugene, OR: Wipf and Stock Publishers, 2001.

Clowney, Edmund P. *The Unfolding Mystery: Discovering Christ in the Old Testament.* Phillipsburg, NJ: P & R Publishing, 1991.

Drew, Charles D. *The Ancient Love Song: Finding Christ in the Old Testament.* Phillipsburg, NJ: P & R Publishing, 2000.

Ministry Connections

As you go through this lesson, probing the nature of the OT's witness to Christ, you will want to examine the ways in which these insights and perspectives can affect your own understanding and practice of ministry. How do *you* study and investigate the OT, what are *your attitudes and responses* to the OT literature, and in what way does your own preaching and teaching need to be impacted by a fresh and more unified understanding of the relationship of the testaments? Ask the Holy Spirit to help you identify the key ways in which you might want to make a direct practical ministry connection with the perspectives and ideas that you covered in this lesson, and ones that you can think about and pray for throughout this next week. The key to dynamic growth and innovation in ministry is being dramatically open to the Holy Spirit's promptings about growth, change, and application. Ask him to point out particular situations where you can integrate these new insights into your own personal walk and ministry.

LESSON 3 | THE OT WITNESS TO CHRIST AND HIS KINGDOM: THE PROMISE GIVEN / 99

Counseling and Prayer

Spend time in prayer for yourself and your colleagues, asking that God would enable you to grow in your knowledge and application of the biblical concepts of *progressive revelation*, of the *promise-fulfillment* motif, and of your own mastery and appreciation of the unity underlying both the Old and New Testament. Ask God to grant you a new love and insight into the Bible's revelation about the majesty and centrality of Jesus Christ, and ask him for a fresh filling of the Holy Spirit so you can prove in experience Augustine's epigram: "In the OT the NT lies hidden; in the NT the OT stands revealed." Prayer is a powerful, effective, and God-ordained way to receive his wisdom (James 1.5), never underestimate the power of prayer in your study of the Word of God. Pray fervently for yourself and for your fellow students, and ask the Lord for his generous supply and help – he is more than willing to provide it.

ASSIGNMENTS

Scripture Memory

Luke 24.44-48

Reading Assignment

To prepare for class, please visit www.tumi.org/books to find next week's reading assignment, or ask your Mentor.

Other Assignments

As usual you ought to come with your reading assignment sheet containing your summary of the reading material for the week. Also, you must have selected the text for your exegetical project and turn in your proposal for your ministry project.

Looking Forward to the Next Lesson

In our next lesson, *The New Testament Witness to Christ and His Kingdom: The Messiah Opposed*, we will explore the Jewish concept of the Kingdom of God at the time of Jesus. We'll see how the nation of Israel, oppressed by political powers, believed that when Messiah came, the Kingdom of God would come in power, restoring the material universe and saving humankind from the control of Satan. Of course, Jesus proclaimed the Kingdom present, and demonstrated its reality in his healings and exorcisms, revealing the Kingdom's presence in his own person and ministry. Again, there can be little doubt that the depth of our ministry and leadership can proceed no further than the depth of our knowledge of Jesus Christ, the Messiah of God and Lord of all.

FOR FURTHER STUDY

Please see the following resources in *Picturing Theology: An A-Z Collection of TUMI's Key Diagrams, Charts, Graphics, and Articles*:

- *Analytic vs. Christocentric Approach to Old Testament Study*, page 3
- *Degrees of Authority Given to Fruit of Christocentric Use of the Old Testament*, page 67
- *Old Testament Names, Titles, and Epithets for the Messiah*, page 305
- *Old Testament Witness to Christ and His Kingdom*, page 307
- *Promise vs. Prediction*, page 334

The New Testament Witness to Christ and His Kingdom
The Messiah Opposed

Lesson Objectives

Welcome in the strong name of Jesus Christ! After your reading, study, discussion, and application of the materials in this lesson, you will be able to:

- Detail the Jewish concept of the Kingdom of God at the time of Jesus, influenced as it was by their oppression from political powers, including their belief that the Kingdom of God would come in power, restoring the material universe and saving humankind from the control of Satan.

- Defend the biblical evidence that supports the idea that Jesus proclaimed the Kingdom present, and demonstrated its reality in his person, and works of healings and exorcisms.

Devotion

The Servant and His Lord

Read John 15.18-26. Can a disciple of Jesus maneuver through this world without experiencing the kind of rejection, persecution, and tribulation known and experienced by our Lord? Was our Lord's experience *sui generis* (utterly unique) to him, or must all of his own also experience a level of the world's hatred and rejection, even as he did? One of Jesus' favorite sayings was the familiar word, "Truly, truly, I say to you, a servant is not greater than his master; nor is a messenger greater than the one who sent him" (John 13.16 [ESV]). A servant is not greater than his master, nor is the one who is sent greater than the one who sent him. Jesus, the truly great and sovereign Master of all, endured the persecution and hatred of the ungodly and hardhearted, and his obvious word in our devotional text is that if the world hated him, they will hate us as well. No genuine disciple of Jesus can go through this world without scars, with no opposition, operating gloriously scot-free; we all must experience the rejection and opposition of God's enemies. We have to fight, we will be opposed, even hated, for the sake of Christ. We need not marvel at this, however. Jesus himself, our Lord and Master, was rejected and hated and we, because of our union with him, will experience the same. God will grant to those who belong to Christ the same grace that he received, which enabled our Lord to endure such hateful treatment and abuse for the sake of the Father.

	Always remember, as you endure troubles and trials, tribulation, hatred, and hardship, that our Lord endured the same, and will help us to persevere till the end.
Nicene Creed and Prayer	After reciting and/or singing the Nicene Creed (located in the Appendix), pray the following prayer: Almighty God, whose blessed Son was led by the Spirit to be tempted by Satan: Come quickly to help us who are assaulted by many temptations; and, as you know the weaknesses of each of us, let each one find you mighty to save; through Jesus Christ your Son our Lord, who lives and reigns with you and the Holy Spirit, one God, now and for ever. Amen. ~ Episcopal Church. *The Book of Common Prayer and Administrations of the Sacraments and Other Rites and Ceremonies of the Church, Together with the Psalter or Psalms of David.* New York: The Church Hymnal Corporation, 1979. p. 218.
Scripture Memorization Review	Review with a partner, write out and/or recite the text for last class session's assigned memory verse: Luke 24.44-48.
Assignments Due	Turn in your summary of the reading assignment for last week, that is, your brief response and explanation of the main points that the authors were seeking to make in the assigned reading (Reading Completion Sheet).

Is the Health-Wealth Gospel Heretical?

Many now proclaim a gospel which promises ease, comfort, and blessing in the face of a world becoming increasingly violent, vicious, and unjust. The heart of this gospel is the belief that the death of Jesus won for the believer a triumphant victory which touches every area of life without stain or admixture of trouble or trial. If our faith is firm, if our confession is clear, and our affirmation of the Word of God steadfast, we will receive the health and wealth of the Lord, the blessings which come to those whose faith remains unwavering and strong. This lifestyle of blessing and victory is indicative of saving faith; those who cling to God are assured of a level of blessing and grace that will not diminish, as long as their faith remains resolute. What do you believe about this "gospel?" Is it biblical, extreme, or even heretical?

A Question for the City: Kinds of Misery

 It appears in the urban neighborhoods of today that many people suffer daily in misery. Some go without housing and food, without shelter and clothing, without the bare necessities of life and health. Many are victims of abuse and violence, and many live daily in loneliness and despair. What is the role of misery in the Christian life? Why do terrible things happen to some of the best people, and some of the most wicked and unjust people appear to live problem-free lives? Are there different kinds of misery; is there a kind of misery and opposition that actually leads to godliness and growth, or are all versions of misery expressions of sin and the enemy's hatred of God's people?

Blame the Right One

 Who is precisely to blame for the opposition and hatred that oftentimes occurs in the life of those who belong to Jesus? While it is entirely obvious to see that Jesus suffered opposition from various quarters due not to himself but to the evil intentions of his enemies, can the same be said of us? Do we as disciples of Jesus experience opposition because we are associated with him, or do we sometimes experience opposition due to our own sinfulness and ungodly reactions to others? If that is true, then how can we tell when we are receiving persecution because of *our allegiance to Jesus*, and when we are receiving persecution due *to our own sinful behavior in this world*?

The Messiah Opposed

Opposition from Spiritual Forces

Rev. Dr. Don L. Davis

CONTENT

Summary

Even though the contemporary Jewish concept of the Kingdom of God at the time of Jesus emphasized the glory of Israel and defeat of the Gentiles, Jesus came announcing the Kingdom of God as present and visible in his person and works. In the person of Jesus of Nazareth, the long-awaited Kingdom of God had arrived, but not in a way that the Jews had predicted. Still, in his person and through his good deed works of miracles, Jesus proclaimed the Kingdom present, and demonstrated its reality in his healings and exorcisms.

Our objective for this lesson, *The Messiah Opposed: Opposition from Spiritual Forces*, is to enable you to see that:

- The Jewish concept of the Kingdom of God at the time of Jesus was rooted in the power and glory of the nation of Israel, and the hope of Israel to defeat their oppressing Gentile powers.

- The Jewish concept further understood the Messiah as one who would come in mighty and awesome power, restoring the Kingdom of God in the material universe, and in a decisive moment of salvation would liberate humankind from the control of Satan.

- Jesus' view of the Kingdom conflicted with his contemporaries in that Jesus proclaimed the Kingdom to be present in his very person and works of power, demonstrated in his healings and exorcisms.

- As the true – albeit unexpected – Messiah, Jesus opposed those underlying spiritual powers which have held the world and humanity captive since the fall.

- Jesus of Nazareth fulfills the kingdom promise, and therefore as Messiah opposes the effects of the curse and the works of the kingdom of darkness.

Video Outline

I. Background of the Jewish Concept of the Kingdom of God

A. "Kingdom" in the ancient world

1. *"Kingdom"* at the time of Jesus in that milieu meant "lordship," "rule," "reign," or "sovereignty."

2. *Sovereignty of God or Rule of God* = Kingdom of God

3. In most Jewish sources, *"Kingdom of God"* and *"Kingdom of heaven"* both refer to God's reassertion of his rule over his creation (Dan 7.27).

B. Old Testament references to the Kingdom of God (a representative sample)

1. Exod. 15.18

2. 1 Sam. 2.12

3. 1 Chron. 29.11

4. Ps. 22.29

5. Pss. 93.1; 95.10; 97.1; 99.1

6. Ps. 145.11-13

7. Isa. 9.6-7

8. Dan. 4.34

9. Dan. 7.14

10. Dan. 7.27

11. Much of the Jewish literature of the time of Jesus had numerous references to the idea of God's kingdom authority (e.g., Tobit 13.1; Wisdom of Solomon 6.4; 1 Enoch 41.1, etc.).

C. The Jewish worldview of the Kingdom at the time of Jesus

This overview is a summary of a few of the basic assumptions held by Jewish believers who were contemporaries of Jesus at his first coming. These ideas are assumed to serve as the backdrop of the events and teachings of the Hebrew Scriptures (i.e., our Old Testament).

1. God is the King of all heaven and earth (as Creator of the universe, he alone possesses the absolute right to rule over all the good things he has made).

2. God's sovereign right to rule has been contested in the universe.

   a. It has been contested by "*Satan*" (= "adversary"), a spiritual being which rebelled against God's right to rule.

   b. Through the deception of Satan, *humankind* fell into rebellion, losing their freedom under God, and passed under the control of Satan's rule and domination.

   c. Because of their rebellion against God, human beings have passed from the *Kingdom of God* (God's rule and influence) to the *kingdom of Satan* (the devil's rule and influence).

3. The *kingdom of the devil* rules in the present world system.

   a. His influence and presence touches all phases of this present world order.

   b. The *kingdom of Satan* functions in both the material universe and the affairs of humankind.

4. The *kingdom of the devil* and the *Kingdom of God* are in mortal conflict and combat with each other.

   a. God is reasserting his right to rule over his creation, and the *kingdom of the devil* resists this effort with all its fury and energy.

   b. At issue in this battle is this: *who will possess the absolute right to rule and reign over creation and humankind.*

D. Israel's special vision of the Kingdom related to its identity.

The idea of the Kingdom affected the Jewish view of spiritual opposition in regard to the forces of the material world, human affairs, and Israel's place as a nation.

1. Israel as a nation is wrapped up in this struggle between God and Satan for the control of the world.

   a. They are God's special people because of the Covenant, Gen. 12-17.

   b. Though called as God's special people, they live in a *milieu* (situation) that is dominated by the *kingdom of Satan*.

      (1) Political, governmental, and other social forces which were hostile to Israel are in fact under Satan's control.

      (2) God used these systems for his purposes (even though they were not aware of it).

2. The *Kingdom of God* would come in power through the Messiah and would bring an end to Satan's control and influence over the world and humankind.

a. A dramatic invasion of God's power to once and for all end Satan's control over humankind

   (1) God's kingdom invasion would be immediate (it would happen suddenly).

   (2) God's kingdom invasion would be cataclysmic (it would involve all the world).

   (3) God's kingdom invasion would be decisive (it would bring an end to Satan's rule).

b. A reversal of fortune for God's people (i.e., when the Kingdom came, Israel would become the greatest of all peoples on the earth)

3. The Kingdom of God would come through the line of the Hebrew kings.

   a. The kings of the Hebrews were rulers under the authority of God.

   b. God's Kingdom would come through the line of the Davidic kings (2 Sam. 7; Ps. 89).

   c. *Messiah* is spoken of often in Old Testament Scripture as a "*son of David*" (cf. Isa. 9.6-7; Jer. 23.5-6; Ps. 2).

   d. Appearance of the *Messiah* would be the evidence that the *Day of the Lord* had come, and that the Kingdom had arrived.

4. The *Kingdom of God*, when it finally arrived, would bring about dramatic change.

a. It would produce *deliverance of the nation of Israel from political oppression and domination*.

b. It would result in *the refreshing and renewing of all nature back to its Eden-like glory and splendor*.

c. It would *establish peace and righteousness with justice* among all the nations, with Israel at its head.

d. It would produce *global spiritual transformation*, with all nations changed to serve and worship the true God, YHWH.

e. It would be *apocalyptic* in its power: it would come suddenly, in the future, affecting all the world, both the material world and human affairs.

II. **Jesus' Appearance Is the Presence of the Kingdom of God in the Here and Now: He Opposes and Overcomes the Effects of the Curse and the Kingdom of the Devil.**

A. Jesus Christ in his person represents the *Kingdom of God in the here and now*.

1. Jesus announced himself to be the *promised Messiah* through whom all of the effects of the curse, sin, demonic oppression, and social injustice would be overcome.

a. He announced with his coming the Kingdom as present, Mark 1.14-15.

b. He declared himself to be Yahweh's Servant who would end all oppression in his person, Luke 4.18-19.

c. He is *the Word made flesh*, the actual manifestation of God in human form come to earth, John 1.14-18.

2. Jesus is the *presence of the future*.

a. The fulfillment of the promise of Abraham, Gal. 3.13-14

b. The one appointed to rescind the effects of the curse, cf. Isa. 11

c. The Victor who would bring a final and full end to Satan's rule and authority, cf. Gen. 3.15 with 1 John 3.8

d. The Messiah anointed by God to inaugurate the age to come in this present age

B. General outline of Jesus' role as *Messiah* fulfills the kingdom promise of the one who would bring down the effects of the curse and the works of the devil

1. The *mission* of Messiah Jesus was to destroy the works of the devil, 1 John 3.8.

2. The *birth* of Messiah Jesus represents the invasion of God's reign into Satan's dominion, Luke 1.31-33.

3. The *message* of Messiah Jesus was that the Kingdom of God was at hand, present for all to see in his person, Mark 1.14-15.

4. The *teaching* of Messiah Jesus represents the ethics of the Kingdom, Matt. 5-7.

5. The *miracles* of Messiah Jesus reveal to all his kingly authority and power to overcome the effects of the curse on God's material creation, e.g., in Mark 2.8-12 where he demonstrates his authority to forgive and heal.

6. The *exorcisms* of Messiah Jesus represent the "binding of the strong man" as spoken in Luke 11.14-20.

7. The *matchless* character of Messiah reveals the Father's own divine splendor and glory, John 1.14-18.

8. The *death* of Messiah represents the payment for our sin debt and its penalty, along with the defeat of Satan, as Paul says in Colossians 2.15, Christ made an open show and display of his victory on the cross, where our sin's indebtedness and unrighteousness was paid in full.

C. The Kingdom is Already, but Not Yet: two manifestations of the Kingdom of God.

1. In Jesus' presence, the Kingdom was displayed, and the reign of God inaugurated. Through his death and resurrection, the rebellious prince, Satan, the great deceiver and blasphemer was wounded, crippled, bound, but his destruction comes later, cf. 1 John 3.8; Heb. 2.14-15; Col. 2.15.

2. At Christ's Second Coming (what scholars call the *Parousia* [Greek for "Second Arrival"]) Satan will be finally destroyed, his rule finally put down, and the full manifestation of God's kingly power will be revealed in the glorification of the saints, and in a restored heaven and earth, 1 Cor. 15.24-28.

III. Messiah Opposed by Spiritual Powers: Healings and Exorcisms in the Life of Jesus

A. The Kingdom has come in Jesus: healings and miracles

1. Jesus' healings were signs of his Messiahship and the Kingdom's presence in the world.

2. *Jesus opposed the effects of the curse*: he was endowed with authority over all the effects of the curse, including disease, corruption, even death.

   a. He opened blinded eyes, John 9.1-7.

   b. He fed over 5,000 with a few loaves and fish, Mark 6.30-44.

   c. He commanded the raging winds and storms, Matt. 8.23-27.

   d. He healed the lame, the paralyzed, and the crippled, Mark 2.1-12.

   e. He even raised the dead, John 11.

3. All of Jesus' miracles were signs of his kingly authority as Messiah to reassert God's kingdom rule on earth.

   a. Jesus' ministry is signs of his kingly right to demonstrate God's power in our world, Acts 10.36-38.

b. Everywhere Jesus went, he demonstrated through his miracles and healings God's kingdom rule come to earth, Matt. 4.23-25.

B. The Kingdom come in Jesus: exorcisms and demonic oppression

1. Jesus' overthrow of the demons in exorcism and command are signs of his Messiahship.

    a. He healed the demon-possessed boy, Mark 9.14-29.

    b. He cured the raving demoniac of the Gadarenes, Matt. 8.28-34.

    c. Demons wailed in terror at his presence, Mark 1.24-25.

2. *Jesus opposed the kingdom of the devil*: he was endowed with the authority to defeat and bind all the powers of the devil, and to destroy his works over God's creation and all humankind.

    a. Jesus' destruction and domination over the forces of the devil prove his kingly authority and the presence of the Kingdom in the earth, Luke 11.14-23.

    b. With Jesus' kingly presence, the Kingdom came in the midst of the people, Luke 17.20-21.

    c. Jesus' public ministry is a plundering of the house of the strong man, the devil, and the reassertion of God's right to rule over his own house, Matt. 12.24-29.

3. All of Jesus' encounters with the devil can be viewed as signs of his kingly authority as Messiah to reassert God's kingdom rule on earth.

   a. Heb. 2.14

   b. 1 John 3.8b

Conclusion

- Jesus is the fulfillment of the Messianic promise of the Old Testament in its hope for the Kingdom come.

- The coming of Messiah in Jesus differed from the contemporary Jewish view, and yet fulfilled the Messianic promises of the Kingdom.

- Jesus as Messiah received opposition from and overcame great spiritual forces during his public ministry on earth, including the effects of the curse and the renegade lordship of the devil.

Student Questions and Response

The following questions were designed to help you review the material in the video. In the person of Jesus of Nazareth the Kingdom of God has come, reasserting God's right to rule in the midst of a world plagued by the effects of the curse and the vicious oppression of the devil. Be clear and concise in your answers, and where possible, support with Scripture!

1. In a short paragraph or statement, explain the various elements which made up the Jewish concept of the Kingdom of God at the time of Jesus. Why did the Jews of Jesus' day find it difficult to believe that he, a humble carpenter's son from Nazareth, might actually be the Messiah?

2. In regards to the element of time, how did the Jewish concept of the Kingdom differ from Jesus' own view of the Kingdom's coming?

3. In what sense does Jesus declare the prophecies of God's coming Kingdom to be fulfilled in his person at the time of his ministry? Be specific.

4. How do Christ's healings and exorcisms demonstrate that the promise of the Kingdom of God have actually come to pass in Jesus' own day?

5. Jesus' confrontation with the powers of the enemy reveal his authority in this world. How does his conflict help us to understand the ministry of Messiah in the world today?

6. If the Kingdom has come in Jesus, then why haven't all evil forces and influences been utterly destroyed? Is there a future dimension to Jesus' consummation of the Kingdom, and if so, what is it?

7. Jesus of Nazareth fulfills the kingdom promise, and therefore as Messiah opposes the effects of the curse and the works of the kingdom of darkness. How do we apply this kingdom authority in our own ministries and lives, here in the inner city?

CONNECTION

Summary of Key Concepts

This lesson focuses upon the opposition our Lord received, not only from his contemporaries in the nation of Israel, but those larger spiritual forces of the curse, the devil, and moral evil at work in the world. Jesus of Nazareth fulfills the kingdom promise of God, reasserting the rule of God in the earth, and demonstrating tangibly in his person and work God's victory over sin, Satan, and death.

- The Jewish concept of the Kingdom of God at the time of Jesus, influenced as it was by their oppression from political powers, included their belief that the Kingdom of God would come in power, restoring the material universe and saving humankind from the control of Satan.

- Jesus' view of the Kingdom conflicted with his contemporaries in that Jesus proclaimed the Kingdom to be present in his very person and works of power, demonstrated in his healings and exorcisms.

- As the true albeit unexpected Messiah, Jesus opposed those underlying spiritual powers which have held the world and humanity captive since the fall.

- Jesus of Nazareth fulfills the kingdom promise, and therefore as Messiah opposes the effects of the curse and the works of the kingdom of darkness.

Student Application and Implications

Now is the time for you to discuss with your fellow students your questions about the practical meaning of Jesus' opposition in his life and ministry as Messiah in Israel. A brief overview of the biblical teaching of Jesus' opposition reveals that the core principle of Jesus' work was to experience unrelenting conflict with those who opposed him in his kingdom advancing work. As you consider this critical element of Messiah's work, what kinds of questions do you have concerning your own life and ministry? How does opposition and conflict influence the various dimensions of your own service for the Lord today? Maybe some of the questions below might help you form your own, more specific and critical questions.

- What does the level and frequency of opposition, conflict, and persecution in the life of Jesus tell us about the nature of all kingdom advancing ministry today?

- To what extent can the disciple of Jesus today expect the kind of rejection and opposition that accompanied Jesus' life? In what ways is Jesus' life a pattern for us, and in what ways is his life utterly unique to himself? Explain.

- Jesus of Nazareth fulfills the kingdom promise in his person, so, in a very real sense, the Kingdom of God has come. What does this kind of teaching mean for inner city ministry and life? Are there signs of the Kingdom come in your neighborhood? Where?

- How does the health-wealth version of the Gospel either agree with or conflict with Jesus' view of the Kingdom come in his own person?

- In a sense, the Kingdom of God is already here, but not yet consummated (i.e., the Already/Not Yet Kingdom). What aspects of the Kingdom of God still await the full consummation and disclosure at Jesus' Second Coming?

- In what ways do the ministries of the Church continue to display Jesus of Nazareth's fulfillment of the kingdom promise through his victory over the effects of the curse and the works of the kingdom of darkness?

CASE STUDIES

Demonic Oppression, Possession, or Both?

1. The fact that the Kingdom of God has come in the person of Jesus completely redefines the believer's and the Church's relationship to the devil. Because of Jesus' work on the cross, the believer is no longer subject to the domination and power of the devil; the victory of God is available to every believer who claims the work of Christ as his or her own (1 John 3.8; Heb. 2.13ff; James 4.7; 1 John 5.4; Eph. 6.10-18; 2 Cor. 10.3-5). What is the possibility of believers to be oppressed by demons, to be possessed by demons, or both, or neither? What must a believer do to experience continuously the victory won for him or her through the blood sacrifice of Jesus (Rev. 12.9ff.)?

Suffering: An Absolute Necessity?

2. According to Paul, it has been granted to believers not only to hold him in confidence, but also to suffer for the sake of the Lord Jesus (Phil. 1.29ff.). Some teach the Gospel as if the victory won by our Lord over sin and the devil means practically that we are no longer subject to suffering and persecution. This teaching would suggest that when a believer finds himself or herself sick, depressed, struggling, doubtful, or hurting, that the problem must be *self-caused*, due to a *lack of faith*. How would you describe the necessity or lack thereof of suffering in the life of the godly disciple of Jesus? Must every blood-washed believer also expect a baptism of fire of persecution from the enemy and God's enemies, or can they be avoided altogether by the proper walk with God?

A Shame to Christ?

3. A common teaching in many evangelical circles is that our Lord died expressly to eliminate the possibility for certain negative realities to be encountered and endured. By his stripes we are healed, they declare, and this means that we are to confess continuous, unbroken health and prosperity *on the very basis of Jesus' suffering on the cross*. The fact that Christ suffered for these things means that the believer ought not to attempt to shame Christ by either ignoring his victory or undercutting it by a weak or unbiblical faith. To what extent does the work of Jesus on the cross guarantee that certain effects of sin and the curse are to *no longer be experienced by believers in Jesus*?

We Killed Our Son

4. This is the title of a book by a dear Christian couple who, confessing the healing of their diabetic son, saw him die due to a lack of insulin, and likewise saw themselves accused and found guilty of negligence in the death of their own son. How would you instruct new believers to pray the prayer of faith for healing, transformation, and blessing, while, at the same time, allowing God the right to withhold anything from his child for the sake of discipline, training, and growth?

Restatement of the Lesson's Thesis

The historical context which surrounded Jesus at the time of his appearing in his public ministry (i.e., Rome's domination of the world) influenced greatly the reaction of Jesus' contemporaries to his offer of the Kingdom. The critical groups included the Sadducees, Pharisees, Essenes, Zealots, and the Herodians. The Jewish concept of the Kingdom of God at the time of Jesus, influenced as it was by their oppression from political powers, included the belief that the Kingdom of God would come in power, restoring the material universe and saving humankind from the control of Satan. Jesus, on the other hand, proclaimed the Kingdom present in himself, and demonstrated its reality in his person and works of healings and exorcisms.

Resources and Bibliographies

If you are interested in pursuing some of the ideas of *The Messiah Opposed*, you might want to give these books a try:

Ladd, George Eldon. *Crucial Questions About the Kingdom of God.* Grand Rapids: Eerdman's, 1952.

Willis, Wendell, ed. *The Kingdom of God in 20th-Century Interpretation.* Peabody, MA: Hendrickson Publishers, 1987.

Ministry Connections

To understand the nature of the opposition that Messiah experienced is to begin to prepare for kingdom ministry today. After you have reflected much on the biblical evidence of Messiah's enduring of constant opposition to his person and work, you must apply this teaching to your own Christian life and service. If you are serving Jesus, you know already much of the truth of these simple texts. Now, in your life and ministry today, how would the Holy Spirit want you to be encouraged in your own struggle against sin, the devil, your flesh, and the world? What internal struggles are you fighting with lust and passion, what external influences call for your distraction and disobedience in the world's temptation, and what infernal conflicts do you wage with the enemy's lies and doubts? Try to pinpoint those areas that the Lord would have you consider in your life and practical ministry, and prayerfully consider what steps he would have you take to re-engage in the fight as Christ's soldier and child.

Counseling and Prayer

If anything is clear from the teaching of the Scriptures, many of the fights of the believer are done in a group; the enemy does not merely fight me, rather, he fights us. For your support, answerability, and growth, you need the prayers and counsel of others engaged in the same battle and struggle you face, even as they face the same (1 Pet. 5.8-10). Do not hesitate to ask believers whom you trust to pray specifically for you in the areas you need God's strengthening and aid. God will hear and answer the prayers of his believing children (James 5.16). Seek the face of the Lord together for his strength and power, and do not be discouraged; he knows we have need of him and his supply (Phil. 4.13).

ASSIGNMENTS

Scripture Memory

John 15.18-20

Reading Assignment

To prepare for class, please visit *www.tumi.org/books* to find next week's reading assignment, or ask your Mentor.

Other Assignments

Your ministry project and your exegetical project should now be outlined, determined, and accepted by your instructor. Make sure that you plan ahead, so you will not be late in turning in your assignments.

Looking Forward to the Next Lesson

In our next lesson, *The Kingdom of God: God's Reign Inaugurated*, we will explore God's intent to eradicate all disobedience and rebellion as a result of the Fall – God becomes a Warrior in this fallen realm. Jesus of Nazareth is the Kingdom's presence realized, with God's reign demonstrated in his incarnation, death, resurrection, and ascension. The Story of the Kingdom is the story of Jesus, and God's intent is to bring the world back under his rule in him. We praise God for his kingdom story, and your interest as a student of his Holy Word!

Please see the following resources in *Picturing Theology: An A-Z Collection of TUMI's Key Diagrams, Charts, Graphics, and Articles*:

- *General Facts Concerning the New Testament*, page 144
- *The Life of Christ according to Seasons and Years*, page 259
- *Miracles of Jesus*, page 290
- *Portrayals of Jesus*, page 329
- *Messiah Yeshua in Every Book of the Bible*, page 269

Theology and Ethics

The Kingdom of God:
God's Reign Inaugurated

God the Father:
The Triune God – The Greatness of God

God the Son:
Jesus, the Messiah and Lord of All – He Died

God the Holy Spirit:
The Person of the Holy Spirit

Introduction to Theology and Ethics Unit

Greetings, in the strong name of Jesus Christ!

Welcome to the second unit of the Cornerstone Curriculum, *Theology and Ethics*.

Of all the subjects preached and taught by Jesus of Nazareth, none are as significant and controversial as the subject of the Kingdom of God. Both conservative and liberal scholars agree that Jesus' favorite subject, the one he preached and taught upon most often, is the Kingdom of God. It was his salvation message, master plan, and heart theology. Sadly, the modern Church seems to pay little attention to what Jesus considered to be most important in his prophetic and Messianic ministry. Our hope is that your heart will be gripped by the kingdom story – the King and his Kingdom – and see its importance in the life of personal discipleship and ministry.

In our first lesson, *The Kingdom of God: God's Reign Inaugurated*, we will explore God's intent to eradicate all disobedience and rebellion as a result of the Fall – God becomes a Warrior in this fallen realm. Jesus of Nazareth is the Kingdom's presence realized, with God's reign demonstrated in his incarnation, death, resurrection, and ascension. The Story of the Kingdom is the story of Jesus, and God's intent is to bring the world back under his rule in him. We praise God for his kingdom story, and your interest as a student of his Holy Word!

The study of the person of our God, the Father Almighty, is one of the richest of all studies in the Word of God. It affects every part of our discipleship, worship, and ministry; truly, as our Lord Jesus said, "And this is eternal life, that they know you the only true God, and Jesus Christ whom you have sent," (John 17.3).

In our second lesson, *God the Father: The Triune God – The Greatness of God,* we will look at the biblical evidence for the Trinity, God's triune personhood. The Scriptures teach that there is only one God, and yet this same God reveals himself as God the Father, Son, and Holy Spirit. The members of the Trinity are one, diverse and equal, the one true God, Father, Son, and Holy Spirit. Truly, our God the Father Almighty is the one, true, and glorious God of heaven. Knowing him better will equip us to represent him with honor as his servants. May God bless you as you explore the untold riches of Scripture regarding our great and mighty God!

The identity of the person and work of Jesus of Nazareth is a critical subject in all Christian reflection and ministry. Indeed, it is impossible to minister in the name of the Lord Jesus Christ if that ministry is based upon false and ignoble views of who he was (and is), what his life signified, and what we are to make of him today. Everything is at stake in our right conception of his life, death, resurrection, ascension, and return.

In our third lesson, *God the Son: Jesus, the Messiah and Lord of All – He Died*, we will explore the theological implications of Jesus' humiliation and death, his descent in his divine person on our behalf. We will consider Jesus' humiliation in the Incarnation, his life and ministry, as well as his death. In considering his sacrifice on Calvary, we will explore some of the historical models for understanding his work on the cross. These include the perspective of his death as a ransom for us, as a propitiation (divine satisfaction) for our sins, as a substitutionary sacrifice in our place, as a victory over the devil and death itself, and as a reconciliation between God and humankind. We will also explore some of the historical alternative views of Jesus' death. These include his death as 1) a moral example, 2) a demonstration of God's love, 3) a demonstration of God's justice, 4) a victory over the forces of evil and sin, and 5) a satisfaction of God's honor. Perhaps no study of doctrine can compare with the thrill of understanding from a biblical and creedal way the richness, wonder, and mystery of God's Son, Jesus of Nazareth. His humiliation and ascension is the heart of the Gospel, and the center of our devotion, worship, and service. May God use this study of his glorious person to enable you to better love and serve him who alone has been given the preeminence by the Father.

There are few theological truths in the history of the Church that have sparked as much controversy, disagreement, and schism as the doctrine of the Holy Spirit. From ancient disagreements about Trinity and "procession" to modern disagreements about the baptism and gifts of the Holy Spirit, there is much that might cause us to approach this lesson with caution; but, I sincerely hope that this is not the case. The doctrine of the Holy Spirit lies at the very heart of the way that we understand who God is and how we experience his living presence in our midst. The Spirit is sent to empower and lead the Church of God and to give new life to all those who respond in faith to its message about Jesus. Our hope is that the truths you learn about the Holy Spirit will not only be "formal theology" which helps you to understand God better, but will be also "practical theology" which allows you *to depend on the Holy Spirit* in ever increasing measure as you minister in God's Church and witness in the world.

The fourth lesson, *God the Holy Spirit: The Person of the Holy Spirit*, focuses upon God the Spirit as the third person of the one Trinitarian God. We will talk about the Spirit as the "Life-giver" and show how the names, titles, and symbols of the Spirit in the Scriptures portray him as the source and sustainer of physical and spiritual life and as the one who is at work to renew all things. The person of the Holy Spirit is as real and vital as God the Father and God the Son. The Spirit is sent by the Father and the Son into the world so that we can experience loving fellowship with them and so that we can be empowered to obey God's commands and accomplish his mission. Our prayer is that your dependence on the Spirit will grow as you study the Scriptures together.

Unit Assignments

Exegetical Project

As a part of your participation in the Cornerstone Curriculum, you will be required to do an exegesis (inductive study) on a passage in the Word of God:

a. Luke 11.15-23

b. Isaiah 40.22-26

c. Philippians 2.5-11

d. Romans 8.13-25

The purpose of this exegetical project is to give you an opportunity to do a detailed study of a major passage on the nature and function of the Word of God. As you study one of the above texts (or a text which you and your Mentor agree upon which may not be on the list), our hope is that you will be able to show how this passage illumines or makes plain the significance of the Word of God for our spirituality and for our lives together in the Church. We also desire that the Spirit will give you insight as to how you can relate its meaning directly to your own personal walk of discipleship, as well as to the leadership role God has given to you currently in your church and ministry.

Memory Verses

The memorized Word is a central priority for your life and ministry as a believer and leader in the Church of Jesus Christ. There are relatively few verses, but they are significant in their content. Each class session you will be expected to recite (orally or in writing) the assigned verses to your Mentor.

   a. Luke 11.20-23

   b. Matthew 3.16-17

   c. Hebrews 2.14-17

   d. Romans 8.15-17

Textbooks

Each Cornerstone Curriculum unit has assigned textbooks which are read and discussed throughout the course. We encourage you to read, reflect upon, and respond to these with your professors, mentors, and fellow learners. Because of the fluid availability of the texts (e.g., books going out of print), we maintain our *official* Cornerstone Curriculum Required Textbook list on our website. Please visit *www.tumi.org/books* to obtain the current listing of this unit's texts and reading assignments.

Ministry Project

Our sincere desire is that you will apply your learning practically, correlating your learning with real experiences and needs in your personal life, and in your ministry in and through your church. Therefore, a key part of completing the Cornerstone Curriculum will be for you to design a ministry project to help you share some of the insights you have learned from this course with others.

Unit Exam

At the end of each unit, your Mentor will give you a unit exam (closed book) to be completed at home. You will be asked a question that helps you reflect on what you have learned in the unit and how it affects the way you think about or practice ministry. Your Mentor will give you due dates and other information when the Unit Exam is handed out.

LESSON 1

The Kingdom of God
God's Reign Inaugurated

Lesson Objectives

Welcome in the strong name of Jesus Christ! After your reading, study, discussion, and application of the materials in this lesson, you will be able to:

- Show from Scripture that since the Fall, the reign of God has been inaugurated in this present world.

- Articulate how Jesus of Nazareth in the world represents the Kingdom's presence realized in his incarnation, death, resurrection, and ascension.

- Recite from memory a passage relating to the inauguration of God's reign.

Devotion

Have You Heard the Announcement?

Read Mark 1.14-15. We all like to hear things announced. We like to hear good news, especially when it involves getting a gift, receiving a blessing, obtaining something you have longed for. When Jesus spoke these words in Mark, he had just recently started to proclaim the Good News. Having been baptized by John the Baptist and having endured the temptation of the devil in the wilderness, Jesus comes to Galilee. Mark gives us a time frame to gauge the date by: it is the time after John was put in prison. So, it was early in the ministry of Jesus, late in the announcement that John the Baptist had made regarding Jesus as the coming Anointed One. Jesus, at this critical moment in salvation history comes announcing, literally inaugurating (commencing), his kingdom preaching and ministry. Jesus recognized the importance of that time, suggesting that "the time is fulfilled," that is, that time spoken of by the prophets that God's reign had arrived. Without fanfare, without trumpets, fireworks, or great gatherings and official dignitaries, the Messiah announces that the Kingdom has come, i.e. that it was "at hand." God's rule, which had been promised and longed for, had now arrived with the coming of Jesus of Nazareth into the world. As spectacular and great as this announcement, very few heard it for what it was – the inauguration of the reign of God, the end of the devil's rebellion, the end of the curse, and the promise of new life in God's Kingdom. Only a handful got the message that day. What about today? Do you hear the Son of God proclaim in our time today that "the Kingdom of God is at hand?" His advice is as life-giving and wonderful today as it was that most ordinary-looking day back in Galilee; if we hear him speak now, today, we can return to God, turn from sin, and embrace the truth of the Good News in Christ. We can come under God's reign only if we respond to the announcement, to the voice of the Savior today.

Nicene Creed and Prayer

After reciting and/or singing the Nicene Creed (located in the Appendix), pray the following prayer:

> Almighty God, through the death of Thy Son Thou hast destroyed sin and death, and by his resurrection hast brought innocence and eternal life, in order that we, being redeemed from the power of the devil, may abide in Thy Kingdom. Grant that we may believe this with a whole heart and, steadfast in faith, praise and thank Thee; through Thy Son Jesus Christ our Lord, Amen.
>
> ~ Martin Luther in Andrew Kosten. *Devotions and Prayers of Martin Luther.* Grand Rapids: Baker Book House, 1965. p. 49.

Scripture Memorization Review

Review with a partner, write out and/or recite the text for last class session's assigned memory verse: John 15.18-20.

Assignments Due

Turn in your summary of the reading assignment for last week, that is, your brief response and explanation of the main points that the authors were seeking to make in the assigned reading (Reading Completion Sheet).

How Would You Answer the Following Question?

"God began to inaugurate (i.e. start out, commence) his kingdom reign in my life when . . . ." Can you pinpoint the time that God began his kingdom work in your life? Did he begin it the day you repented and believed? The day that you became a member of your local church fellowship? On the day when you were physically born, or before that? If you had to suggest a date when God's kingdom work began in your life, what would you say?

True or False?

 "It is best to suggest that the Kingdom of God has never had any beginning or inauguration, since God has always been God, and as God, he has always been in charge." What is right about this statement? Is there anything here that could be misleading? Does the reign of God in a person's, a family's, or a nation's life have a beginning, or has God always been Lord of our lives, whether we acknowledge it or not?

Free Will

 Throughout the history of philosophy and theology, godly, sincere people have debated over the question of free will, that is, do we actually have any such thing as free will? Think about it for a moment. If you were asked, "Are we free?", what would you say? What are we as human beings, free to do? Are we slaves to sin, to God, or do we have a choice in everything that we consider, do, and encounter? If we do not have free will, how can God hold us accountable for what we say and do?

God's Reign Inaugurated

Rev. Dr. Don L. Davis

CONTENT

Summary

God has been working since the beginning to eradicate all disobedience and rebellion as a result of the Fall, through the unfolding of his covenant promise to Abraham to bring a Seed. This promise can be traced through God's covenant people, through Judah, David. In spite of God's people's moral failure and idolatry, through them emerged the Anointed One, Jesus of Nazareth, who represents the Kingdom's presence realized. With final power and authority, God's reign has been demonstrated in Jesus' incarnation, death, resurrection, and ascension.

Our objective for this lesson, *God's Reign Inaugurated*, is to enable you to see that:

- In the person and works of Jesus of Nazareth, God's kingdom Reign has been gloriously inaugurated (in a final sense), and realized in the world.

- Jesus gave witness and life to God's reign as the *Christus Victum* in his suffering, death, and burial.

- Jesus provided indisputable proof of the Kingdom's inauguration and realization as *Christus Victor* in his glorious resurrection and ascension.

Video Outline

I. The Kingdom Reign of God Has Been Inaugurated and Realized (in a Final Sense) in the Person and Works of Jesus Christ.

"The distinctiveness of the Kingdom of God, in the person and work of Jesus of Nazareth, is that the reign of God has come and is now present, in some degree on earth."

A. Jesus of Nazareth declared himself to be the fulfillment of Messianic promise.

1. Luke 4.18-19

2. Fulfillment of the Year of Jubilee prophecy of Isaiah 61

B. Jesus of Nazareth is the Word made flesh: Jesus is himself the Incarnation of the Kingdom.

1. John 1.14-18

2. Jesus' coming into the world represents the fulfillment of the promise of Abraham, the beginning of the end of Satan's rule and authority, and the inauguration of the age to come in this present age.

C. Signs of the Kingdom's presence realized in Jesus' coming

1. Luke 17.20-21

2. Luke 10.16-20

3. Luke 11.17-20

D. In Jesus' entrance of the world we experience the "presence of the future," G.E. Ladd, "the already/not yet" Kingdom.

1. In Jesus the Kingdom has already come, Luke 17.20.

    a. Kingdom power and beauty displayed

    b. The reign of God is inaugurated.

    c. The rebellious prince, Satan, the great deceiver and blasphemer was wounded, crippled, bound, through Jesus' death and resurrection.

2. The final consummation of the Kingdom is not yet.

    a. The final destruction of the devil comes later, Rev. 20.

    b. The Church engages in warfare with the enemy in this present time, Eph. 6.10-18.

    c. The Second Coming or *parousia* (Greek for "Second Arrival")

        (1) Satan will be destroyed, his rule finally put down.

        (2) The full manifestation of God's kingly power will be revealed in the glorification of the saints, and in a restored heaven and earth.

E. Display of the Kingdom as "already" (inaugurated and realized)

1. His *mission*, 1 John 3.8

2. His *birth* represents the invasion of God's reign into Satan's dominion, Luke 1.31-33.

3. His *message* was that the Kingdom of God was at hand, Mark 1.14-15.

4. His *teaching* represents the ethics of the Kingdom, Matt. 22.37-38.

5. His *miracles* reveal for all to see his kingly authority and power, Mark 2.8-12.

6. His *exorcisms* represent the "binding of the strong man," Luke 11.14-20.

7. His *life and deeds* reveal the glory of the Kingdom, John 1.14-18.

8. His *death* represents the defeat of Satan, and the penalty of sin, Col. 2.15.

II. **Second, God's Reign Is Inaugurated and Realized through Jesus as *Christus Victum*, the Warrior Whose Death Defeats the Powers of Evil, and Pays the Penalty of Sin.**

A. Jesus Christ as Paschal Lamb of the Covenant

1. As the spotless lamb was the sign of God's covenant mercy, so Jesus now has become the Paschal Lamb of the new covenant, 1 Cor. 5.7-8.

2. In Jesus of Nazareth, the Passover of God, the fulfillment of God's penalty on sin and forgiveness to his people is done.

B. As Ultimate Sacrifice and Great High Priest: the body and blood of Jesus

1. Jesus is the completion of the Levitical priesthood and sacrificial system of the old covenant.

2. Furthermore, Jesus stands as our one and final High Priest who sacrifices his own blood in the Tabernacle in the heavens before the Father.

3. Heb. 9.11-12

C. Twice strong: Jesus' suffering and death (penalty for sin, power over evil)

1. Jesus as God's Divine Warrior, through his suffering and death, defeats Satan, the curse, hell, and our punishment by bearing it in his own body.

2. Jesus bears further on the cross the penalty of our sin, and the power of evil to plague and destroy our lives.

3. The destruction of death and the message of freedom, Heb. 2.14-15

4. Jesus as Warrior of God in the cross

III. Finally, the Kingdom Is Inaugurated in Jesus as the *Christus Victor*, the One Who Overcomes through His Resurrection and Ascension.

A. The cardinal revelation of Christianity, according to the Apostle Paul, is the teaching of the resurrection of Christ. If Christ has not been raised, says Paul:

1. The preaching of the Apostles was worthless.

2. Our faith in their testimony is in vain.

3. The Apostles are charlatans, liars, since they are found to have misrepresented God.

4. Our faith is futile.

5. We are still in our sins.

6. Those Christians who have fallen asleep have completely perished, having hope only in this life.

7. Finally, we are the most pitiful people on the planet.

8. But thank God! 1 Cor. 15.20.

B. The resurrection of Jesus is the sign of God's propitiation, the proof of our justification, and the sign of Jesus' exaltation.

C. The certainty of the resurrection: testimony and appearances

1. Jesus predicted his death and resurrection, Matt. 16.21.

2. Appearances

    a. Mary Magdalene, John 20.11-17

    b. The women at the tomb, Matt. 28.9-10

    c. Peter, Luke 24.34

    d. The disciples on the road to Emmaus, Mark 16.12-13

    e. The ten with Thomas absent, John 20.19-24

    f. The eleven disciples a week after the resurrection, John 20.26-29

    g. Seven disciples by the Sea of Galilee, John 21.1-23

    h. The five hundred, 1 Cor. 15.6

    i. James, the Lord's brother, 1 Cor. 15.7

    j. The eleven disciples on the mountain of Galilee, Matt. 28.16-20

k. The disciples at his ascension, Luke 24.44-53

l. Stephen prior to his martyrdom, Acts 7.55-56

m. Paul on the road to Damascus, Acts 9.3-6

n. Paul in Arabia, Acts 20.24

o. Paul in the temple, Acts 22.17-21

p. Paul in prison at Caesarea, Acts 23.11

q. The Apostle John at the Apocalyptic vision of Revelation, Rev. 1.12-20

D. What his resurrection signifies

1. His resurrection is a sign of his divine Sonship, Rom. 1.4.

2. His resurrection is a fulfillment of the Davidic covenant as Peter suggests in his sermon at Pentecost, Acts 2.25-31.

3. His resurrection also reveals that Christ is now the source of new life for all who believe in him, 1 John 5.11-12.

4. His resurrection is to a place of headship and exaltation as Head of the Church, Eph. 1.20-23.

5. His resurrection proves that our justification before God has been accomplished through him alone, Rom. 4.25.

6. And Jesus, as Lord of life, was resurrected as the first fruits of the great company of believers who will share in his resurrection glory, 1 Cor. 15.20-23.

E. The ascension is a visible sign of Jesus' authority and headship, his exaltation as God's triumphant Warrior, and Commander of the armies of God.

In conjunction with the inauguration of the Kingdom of God through Jesus of Nazareth, Jesus has ascended into heaven. Why?

1. As a visible sign of his authority and headship, worshiped above by God's holy angels, Heb. 1.3-4

2. As Head of the armies of God and Lord of the harvest, Matt. 28.18-20

3. As Head of the Church, Eph. 1.20-23

4. As a sign of his absolute preeminence and lordship over all, Phil. 2.9-11

Conclusion

- Jesus of Nazareth is supreme, the Anointed One of God through whom the promises of Abraham have been fulfilled.

- In him, the Lord of all, the Kingdom's presence realized, demonstrated in his incarnation, death, resurrection, and ascension.

Student Questions and Response

The following questions were designed to help you review the material related to Jesus' inauguration and realization of the Kingdom of God. Answer the questions, concentrating on the "big ideas" and principles associated with the inauguration idea, as well as Jesus' role in bringing the Kingdom into reality. Be clear and concise in your answers, and where possible, support with Scripture!

1. In what ways can it be claimed that Jesus of Nazareth declared himself to be the fulfillment of the Old Testament witness to the Messiah?

2. What are some of the signs in Jesus' life that testify that in him the Kingdom has been inaugurated and realized to some degree?

3. Explain the relationship embodied in the phrase, "the already/not yet" Kingdom. In what ways can the Kingdom be said to be already present? In what ways can we also know that the Kingdom is still yet future?

4. What is the meaning of the word *parousia*, and how does it relate to the whole idea of the Kingdom yet to come?

5. How does Jesus compare with the Passover Lamb of the Old Testament celebration? In what ways could Jesus be said to be the Paschal Lamb of the new covenant?

6. In what two ways does the death of Christ reveal the power of the Kingdom of God present today?

7. According to Paul, why is the resurrection the cardinal teaching of Christianity? How do we know that the resurrection of Jesus is a certainty – what evidence is there for it?

8. What are some of the things that the resurrection signifies about the Kingdom?

9. As a sign of Jesus' authority and Headship, how does the ascension contribute to our understanding that in Jesus, the Kingdom has been inaugurated?

CONNECTION

Summary of Key Concepts

This lesson focuses upon the critical ways that the Old and New Testaments give witness that the Kingdom of God has been inaugurated, through God's covenant promise to Abraham and the Patriarchs, through the tribe of Judah and family of David, and finally in the person of Jesus

Christ, who as *Christus Victum* (i.e. through his death on the cross) and *Christus Victor* (i.e. through his resurrection and ascension) has ushered in this present age the Kingdom of God.

- God renewed his covenant promise from Abraham, to Isaac and Jacob, to the people of Israel, to the tribe of Judah, to the family of David, and finally through Jesus Christ, who has realized the Kingdom in a final sense through his person and work.

- In Jesus of Nazareth, the covenant promises of Abraham and the prophetic promises of the Old Testament witness to Messiah have been fulfilled. Jesus is the fulfillment of the Messianic promise.

- In Jesus's life and ministry, the authority and power of God's reign has been inaugurated and manifested. Although much of the Kingdom's fulfillment is future, the Kingdom already has been demonstrated in the incarnation of Jesus on earth.

- Jesus' death broke the power of the devil and his minions, as well as paid the penalty for our sins. As ultimate sacrifice and Great High Priest, Jesus has paid it all for humankind, as the *Christus Victum*.

- Jesus' resurrection occurred: a sign of his divine Sonship, a fulfillment of the Davidic covenant, a confirmation that God has forgiven us for our sins, and a token of the first fruits of all those who one day will rise again to eternal life through faith in him.

- The ascension of Jesus to the Father's right hand is a visible sign of Jesus' authority and headship, as Head of the Church and the armies of God, as Lord of the harvest work of mission, and as Conquering Lord of all, who soon will come and consummate the Kingdom.

Student Application and Implications

Now is the time for you to discuss with your fellow students your questions about the Kingdom of God inaugurated and realized today. The implications of Jesus having brought the Kingdom into view are numberless and important, and undoubtedly you will have questions regarding the significance of his work on your life and ministry. What particular questions do you have in light of the material you have just studied? Maybe some of the questions below might help you form your own, more specific and critical questions.

- If the Kingdom is already present in some degree today, why is the world still so incredibly unjust and oppressed? More specifically, why are the poor still mistreated, abused, and overlooked if the Year of Jubilee has come into focus already?

- Will the specific promises about a literal, physical Kingdom be fulfilled, or are they to be understood only in a spiritual way?

- Why does it appear as if the devil is still so powerful and strong if Jesus defeated him decisively on Calvary at the cross? How much can we as believers appropriate of this great power, and how do we do it?

- What role does the city play in terms of the Kingdom of God today? If the Kingdom is already present in some fashion, what does this mean for us in urban ministry?

- To what extent can we ask God to do the same works in and through us that he did in Jesus, if the kingdom authority is present in our midst today?

- Why are so few Christians and churches experiencing the explosive authority and power of God's rule if Jesus in some real sense ushered in God's reign?

- Christians disagree much regarding end time prophecy and doctrine. How does this teaching of the Kingdom help resolve or make even more difficult to understand the Bible's teaching on the end times?

CASE STUDIES

A Triumphant Discovery

1. A sincere Christian brother, after hearing the teaching that the Kingdom of God is already present, took it to mean that all of the kingdom power and blessing is available for us today. He immediately began to teach in his Sunday school class that Jesus has ushered in the Kingdom, and therefore we no longer need to experience any of the devil's interference or jabs. Specifically, he began to teach the teens that they no longer had to get sick, or be without money, or sin, or even be emotionally discouraged. As a result of his teaching, factions broke out among the teens and their parents. Some sided with the Christian brother, while others affirmed that "in the world we will have tribulation." Both sides

have gone to the Bible and have emphasized those Scriptures which support their respective points; that we have victory in Christ, or, that we struggle and fight in this world, with the flesh, the devil, and this wicked system of temptation. With both sides mildly bruised and a little confused, they ask you to come and clarify the meaning of the "already" in the "already/not yet" Kingdom. How would you help this struggling fellowship come to understand the true meaning of the "already" and the "not yet" in regards to the Kingdom of God?

Everything Is for Later

 In sharing the teaching of this lesson with some friends in church, a visiting graduate student of a well-known seminary begins to say how this view is heretical. Believing strongly in the view that all kingdom life and power has been postponed to a future age, the graduate student begins to share how Israel was given a kingdom offer but refused it, killing the Messiah who invited them. Having rejected Jesus' kingdom offer, he says we are now in the Church-age which comes in between the time of Jesus' kingdom offer, and the time of the Second Coming, when Israel will eventually accept God's kingdom offer, and the Davidic Kingdom will be set up in the future. Now, no manifestation of the Kingdom is present, everything dealing with the Kingdom is for later. What would you say to this student? Does his view sound credible? How would you answer such an interpretation in light of what you learned in today's sessions?

Restatement of the Lesson's Thesis

Since the Fall, God has sought to eradicate and overturn its effect by bringing his reign into this present world. He began to demonstrate his rule concretely by taking the predisposition as a Warrior over his enemies. Through his covenant promise to Abraham, God determined to bring a Seed into the world which would crush the serpent's head and bless the families of the earth. The promise was renewed in the patriarchs, in Israel, to the tribe of Judah and the family of David. Finally, in the person and works of Jesus of Nazareth, the kingdom rule of God has been inaugurated in a final sense in this world. As *Christus Victum*, he delivered us from the power of the devil, sin, and death, and as *Christus Victor*, he has risen from the grave and ascended into heaven as Lord of all. Although not fully realized, the Kingdom has come in the person of Jesus Christ.

Resources and Bibliographies

If you are interested in pursuing some of the ideas of *God as a Divine Warrior*, you might want to give these books a try:

Dawson, John. *Taking Our Cities for God*. 2nd. ed. Altamonte Springs: Charisma House, 2001.

Lind, Millard. *Yahweh is a Warrior: The Theology of Warfare in Ancient Israel*. Scottsdale: Herald Press, 1980.

Ministry Connections

The interconnections of Jesus' victory have great relevance for every part of our ministry. Now is the time to try to nail down this high theology to a real practical ministry connection, one which you will think about and pray for throughout this next week. What in particular is the Holy Spirit suggesting to you in regards to the reign of God, and its challenge today? What situation comes to mind when you think about how the truth of God's reign being inaugurated, and your own life and ministry today? Give yourself time to meditate in the presence of the Lord on these matters, and he will reveal to you what it is, and what you ought to do as a result of what he reveals.

Counseling and Prayer

The appropriate kind of prayer in light of the teaching of this lesson is worship, praise, and thanksgiving. To see the resolve of the triune God to come to our aid, to fight our foes, to overturn the effects of the Fall, to send his Son who took on the devil and death for us – this mighty love ought to produce in us a dramatic outpouring of thankful praise. God did not abandon us in our weakened state, but gave his best for us. We ought to find ways to show what it means to appropriate the victory of Jesus over our enemies and watch God work through our humble faith. Perhaps there are those in your family or church, at work or in the neighborhood whom we can lift up to God on behalf of Jesus.

ASSIGNMENTS

Scripture Memory

Luke 11.20-23

Reading Assignment

To prepare for class, please visit *www.tumi.org/books* to find next week's reading assignment, or ask your Mentor.

Other Assignments

Read the assigned reading and summarize each reading with no more than a paragraph or two for each. In this summary please give your best understanding of what you think was the main point in each of the readings. Do not be overly concerned about giving detail; simply write out what you consider to be the main point discussed in that section of the book. Please bring these summaries to class next week. (Please see the "Reading Completion Sheet" on page 16.)

Looking Forward to the Next Lesson

In our next lesson, *God the Father: The Triune God – The Greatness of God*, we will look at the biblical evidence for the Trinity, God's triune personhood. The Scriptures teach that there is only one God, and yet this same God reveals himself as God the Father, Son, and Holy Spirit. The members of the Trinity are one, diverse and equal, the one true God, Father, Son, and Holy Spirit. Truly, our God the Father Almighty is the one, true, and glorious God of heaven. Knowing him better will equip us to represent him with honor as his servants. May God bless you as you explore the untold riches of Scripture regarding our great and mighty God!

FOR FURTHER STUDY

Please see the following resources in *Picturing Theology: An A-Z Collection of TUMI's Key Diagrams, Charts, Graphics, and Articles*:

- *Kingdom of God Timeline*, page 217
- *Jesus of Nazareth: The Presence of the Future*, page 204
- *Living in the Already and the Not Yet Kingdom*, page 261
- *Models of the Kingdom*, page 293
- *Once Upon a Time*, page 308

God the Father
The Triune God – The Greatness of God

Lesson Objectives

Welcome in the strong name of Jesus Christ! After your reading, study, discussion, and application of the materials in this lesson, you will be able to:

- Show from Scripture a general outline of the Bible's teaching about the doctrine of the *Trinity*, God's triune personhood.

- Explain that the Bible teaches us both that there is only one God, and yet this same God reveals himself as God the Father, Son, and Holy Spirit.

- Demonstrate from the Scriptures how God is spoken of as one God yet also as *plural*, that is, more than one person, which speaks of the Father, the Son, and the Holy Spirit as being persons within the Godhead.

- Recite some of the major historical understandings of the Trinity.

- Recognize the meaning of God's trinitarian nature, affirming that the members of the Trinity are one, diverse, and equal, the one true God, Father, Son, and Holy Spirit.

Devotion

The Blessed Trinity

> 2 Cor. 13.14 – The grace of the Lord Jesus Christ and the love of God and the fellowship of the Holy Spirit be with you all.

It ought to never surprise us that God is beyond our comprehension, that mystery, wonder, and awe are associated with an infinite spirit being who spoke and twirled millions of galaxies on nothing and flung them into the blackness of space. Modern people cannot stand mystery; science and knowledge must (it is asserted) pull back the curtains of every false wizard pulling cords and speaking into megaphones like the false wizard in *The Wizard of Oz*. Everything can be explained by appeal to logic, evidence, and reliable processes of truth seeking. Our cultures today have no patience nor confidence in any faith that does not first make itself valid at the bar of the explainable and the testable.

The religion of the Jehovah's Witnesses is a perfect example. Everything in the Bible that cannot be immediately understood is changed to conform to their plumb line of reason and logic. For instance, since they cannot understand completely God as a tri-unity, they reject the scriptural teaching on the Trinity even though the Bible clearly asserts the divinity of the Father, the Son, and the Holy Spirit. In their theology, Jesus becomes the archangel Michael and the Holy Spirit becomes an "active force," like electricity. If you want to look full face at a religion stripped of all mystery and wonder you'll find it in the teachings of the Witnesses.

Regardless of what our intellects might scream at us, the simple word of the Apostles and prophets should be our ground and foundation. We are to baptize in the name (singular) of the Father, Son, and Holy Spirit, and at the baptism of Jesus, the Holy Spirit rests upon him as a dove, and the Father's voice declares that he is well pleased with our Lord (Matt. 3.17). This text in 2 Corinthians speaks of the grace of Jesus, the love of God and the communion of the Spirit (2 Cor. 13.14). All of the members are referred to as God, and all of them share the same attributes of greatness. Yet, the Bible states that there is only *one God*, not *three*. The Trinity is the result of biblical affirmation, not our own logic.

Should it surprise us that our God is beyond our thought, that God as he is in himself cannot be known or comprehended? Let us kneel before the Lord our Maker, asserting with joyful heart the very word of our Lord in Matthew 11:

> Matt. 11.27 – All things have been handed over to me by my Father, and no one knows the Son except the Father, and no one knows the Father except the Son and anyone to whom the Son chooses to reveal him.

Let's affirm the truth of Scripture and give praise and honor to the God of heaven, Father, Son, and Holy Spirit.

Nicene Creed and Prayer

After reciting and/or singing the Nicene Creed (located in the Appendix), pray the following prayers:

> O God, you are infinite, eternal and unchangeable, glorious in holiness, full of love and compassion, abundant in grace and truth. Your works everywhere praise you, and your glory is revealed in Jesus Christ our Savior. Therefore we praise you, blessed and holy Trinity, one God, forever and ever. Amen.
>
> ~ Presbyterian Church (U.S.A.) and Cumberland Presbyterian Church, The Theology and Worship Ministry Unit. *Book of Common Worship*. Louisville, KY.: Westminster/John Knox Press, 1993. p. 51.

> O Father, my hope; O Son, my refuge; O Holy Spirit, my protection. Holy Trinity, glory to Thee.
>
> ~ Compline, Eastern Orthodox, St. Joannikios
> Appleton, George, ed. *The Oxford Book of Prayer.*
> Oxford/New York: Oxford University Press, 1988. p. 183.

Scripture Memorization Review

Review with a partner, write out and/or recite the text for last class session's assigned memory verse: Luke 11.20-23.

Assignments Due

Turn in your summary of the reading assignment for last week, that is, your brief response and explanation of the main points that the authors were seeking to make in the assigned reading (Reading Completion Sheet).

A Faith that Doesn't Make Sense?

One of your church members, Mrs. Jackson, was visited by a Jehovah's Witness the other day, and the conversation has haunted her ever since. For over an hour Mrs. Jackson listened carefully to the clean, simple, and appealing logic of the Witnesses who visited her home. She felt completely overwhelmed as these visitors ran down their laundry list of errors they say that the organized Church believes. Rejecting a host of doctrines as simple falsehoods and historical blunders, the Witnesses argued passionately against the personality of the Holy Spirit, the doctrine of the Trinity, the deity of Christ, the existence of hell, salvation by grace, and on and on. Frustrated, the member asked the Witnesses, "You guys seem to have everything figured out; you don't seem to believe anything that does not line up with your reason." "That's right," shot back the head person of the Witness team, "for why do you want a faith that doesn't make sense to you?" That phrase has been with your member since it was spoken. How would you answer the question of the Witness: must everything in the Bible make "sense" to us before we believe its testimony? Are we or are we not obliged to believe whatever the Bible asserts, even if it goes beyond our knowledge and logic?

And Greatly to Be Praised?

 Arguing that God is worthy of our best and most excellent worship, the music minister at your church is making a pitch for a dramatic increase in the budget for sound, music, and the worship band. Having been deeply impacted by the pastor's preaching series on the attributes of God, he realized, he says, that he has been giving God wounded sacrifices, reserving the best resources and monies for his own personal needs and desires. With great passion and clarity, he articulated that if God is infinitely great, he is greatly to be praised! "The most important way," he suggests, "we can really show this great God that we love him is to give him our very best, and that means immediately!" If you were a member in the business meeting, what would you suggest about your music minister's understanding of the greatness of God, and his views that this should immediately influence the way in which we conduct business, spend money, and offer worship?

Much Ado about Nothing

 On his return from seminary, Bill is upset because none of the people in his church seem as concerned about the things he has been learning as he is. After many semesters of wrestling with the great doctrines of the faith, he is anxious to share his answers to all their doctrinal questions, but they appear to have none. As a matter of fact, they find the discussions of doctrine and such "quite boring; it's much ado about nothing" as one deacon said. What is the relationship between the need to know and defend what the Bible asserts about God and his Kingdom and the simple faith of most people in the pew who simply cling to the Bible as God's Word? What advice do you have for Bill?

The Triune God: The Greatness of God

God's Greatness (Natural Attributes)

Rev. Dr. Don L. Davis

CONTENT

Summary The Word of God plainly asserts that there is only one God (the *Shema*, Deut. 6.4), and yet also affirms the deity of God the Father, the Son, and Holy Spirit. The doctrine of the Trinity is the product of accepting the Bible's teaching on God's oneness, while at the same time, affirming what it says regarding the divine nature of the persons of the Father, the Son, and the Holy Spirit.

LESSON 2 | GOD THE FATHER: THE TRIUNE GOD – THE GREATNESS OF GOD

Our objective for this lesson, *God's Greatness*, is to enable you to see that:

- The doctrine of the Trinity refers to the Bible's teaching about God's triune personhood.

- The Scriptures assert that God is one, and that there is none other than the one God, and yet they also assert that the one God reveals himself as God the Father, Son, and Holy Spirit.

- Each member of the Trinity (Father, Son, and Holy Spirit) possesses the attributes and does the work of God, is called God, and exercises authority as God.

- The Bible affirms both God's oneness and God's plurality (that the Godhead is more than one person), with the persons Father, Son, and Holy Spirit addressed together as being persons within the Godhead.

- The Church has attempted to draft understandings of the Bible's teachings on the Trinity, with varying degrees of acceptance among believers.

- We must assert God's trinitarian nature, affirming that the members of the Trinity, though God in three persons, are in fact one, diverse, and equal, together comprising the one true God, Father, Son, and Holy Spirit.

Video Outline

I. The Lord God Is a Triune God.

    A. The logic and biblical necessity of the Trinity

        1. Trinitarian doctrine arises from an attempt to take the Bible seriously on its teaching about the nature of God.

        2. The essence of the trinitarian argument: the Scriptures mandate a triune understanding of God.

            a. First, the Bible asserts that there is only one God.

b. Yet, the Bible also speaks of three different persons within this Godhead who share the same authority, substance, and essence.

c. God, therefore, must be a triune God.

3. Basic implications

a. The Trinity, while the word is not in Scripture, is essentially a biblical teaching, or rather, an attempt to take the Bible seriously.

b. The Trinity is incomprehensible (beyond our ability to understand).

c. The Trinity should inspire awe, humility, and worship.

B. God is one God.

1. The Decalogue, Exod. 20.1-6

a. The Lord God is the one true God. No other gods are to receive his worship and due.

b. All other gods are idols. Only the Lord made the heavens and delivered his people.

c. God is jealous; he will not share his glory with other deities or idols.

2. The *Shema*, Deut. 6.4-5

    a. Asserts the divinity of Yahweh God as the only God

    b. Asserts the unity and singleness of Yahweh

3. Jesus' affirmation of the unity and oneness of God, Mark 12.29-30

C. God exists in three Persons.

1. The Father is spoken of and referred to as God.

    a. Eph. 1.17

    b. John 10.29

    c. John 20.17

    d. Rom. 15.6

    e. 2 Cor. 1.3

    f. 2 Cor. 11.31

    g. Phil. 2.11

2. The Son is spoken of and referred to as God.

    a. Phil. 2.5-11

    b. John 1.1-18

    c. Heb. 1.1-12

    d. John 8.58

3. The Holy Spirit is spoken of and referred to as God.

    a. Acts 5.3-4

    b. John 16.8-11

    c. 1 Cor. 12.4-11

    d. Matt. 28.19

    e. 2 Cor. 13.14

4. Yet, there are not three Gods, but one blessed God, Father, Son, and Holy Spirit.

D. Biblical evidence for viewing God as one God in three persons

1. All the different members of the Trinity share the same attributes.

    a. Eternal

        (1) Rom. 16.26

        (2) Rev. 22.12

        (3) Heb. 9.14

    b. Holy

        (1) Rev. 4.8

        (2) Rev. 15.4

        (3) Acts 3.14

    c. True

        (1) John 7.28

        (2) John 17.3

        (3) Rev. 3.7

    d. Omnipresent

        (1) Jer. 23.24

        (2) Eph. 1.23

        (3) Ps. 139.7

e. Omnipotent

   (1) Gen. 17.1 with Rev. 1.8

   (2) Rom. 15.19

   (3) Jer. 32.17

f. Omniscient

   (1) Acts 15.18

   (2) John 21.17

   (3) 1 Cor. 2.10-11

g. Creator

   (1) Gen. 1.1 with Col. 1.16

   (2) Job 33.4

   (3) Ps. 148.5 with John 1.3

   (4) Job 26.13

h. Source of eternal life

   (1) Rom. 6.23

   (2) John 10.28

   (3) Gal. 6.8

i. Raising Christ from the dead

   (1) 1 Cor. 6.14 with John 2.19

   (2) 1 Pet. 3.18

2. Old Testament witness as to God's oneness

    a. Deut. 6.4

    b. 2 Kings 19.15

    c. 2 Kings 19.19

    d. Ps. 86.10

    e. Isa. 43.10

    f. Isa. 44.6

3. Old Testament witness as to God's plurality

    a. The plural form of the noun for God: *Elohim* (cf. Gen. 1.26 with Isa. 6.8)

    b. The self-mention of God at the creation of the *imago Dei* in humankind, Gen. 1.27 with 2.24

4. Trinitarian formulae (plural names of the Lord as triune in the New Testament)

    a. The baptism of Jesus, Matt. 3.16-17

b. The Great Commission, Matt. 28.19

c. The Corinthian benediction, 2 Cor. 13.14

5. Jesus' claim of oneness with the Father

   a. John asserts that Jesus is the Word, being with God, who is God, and giving revelation of God, John 1.1-18.

   b. Jesus and the Father are one, John 10.30.

   c. The one who sees Jesus has seen the Father, John 14.9.

   d. The Father and Jesus shared a fundamental glory before his self-emptying for our salvation, cf. John 17.21 with Phil. 2.6-8.

II. Views of the Trinity from History

A. *The Economic View:* the three persons are involved in various dimensions through both creation and redemption.

   1. Hippolytus and Tertullian (early fathers of the Church)

   2. This view made no attempt to explore the relations among the three members of the Trinity.

   3. Focused on creation and redemption: Son and Spirit are not the Father, but are connected to God in his eternal being

B. *Dynamic Monarchianism:* God coming in power upon the person Jesus

1. Developed in the late 2nd and 3rd centuries, originated by Theodotus

2. God was present in the life of the man, Jesus of Nazareth.

    a. God was a working force upon, in, or through Jesus, but no real presence within Jesus.

    b. Before his baptism, Jesus was simply an ordinary man (although a remarkably virtuous one), cf. Matt. 3.16-17.

    c. At the baptism, the Spirit descended on Jesus, and God's power flowed through him from that point onward.

3. This view never became popular in the Church.

C. *Modalistic Monarchianism:* One God manifesting himself in three forms

1. There is one Godhead, which may be designated as Father, Son, or Spirit.

2. These terms do not stand for real distinctions of different members or personalities within the Godhead.

3. These terms refer to the one God working at different times in different modes.

4. Father, Son, and Spirit are the same person acting in three different modes (one person with three different names, activities, or roles).

5. This view cannot explain fully what the Bible actually teaches about the Father, Son, and Holy Spirit.

D. *The Orthodox Formulation* (The Council of Constantinople [381] and the view of Athanasius [293-373] and the "Cappadocian fathers" [Basil, Gregory of Nazianzus, and Gregory of Nyssa])

1. God has one essence or substance (ousia) which exists in *three persons (hypostases)*.

2. God has a common essence, but exists in *three separate persons*.

3. The Cappadocian focus

    a. Individual *hypostases* is the ousia of the one God.

    b. Each member has characteristics or properties *unique to him* (e.g., individual people within universal humanity).

4. The orthodox view is *monotheistic*, not *tri-theistic* (i.e., belief that the Trinity teaches three separate Gods).

III. We believe in God: The Threefold Affirmation of Nicea (325)

A. The Nicene Creed confesses each member of the one Godhead.

1. We believe in *God the Father Almighty* – the Father is God.

2. We believe in *Jesus Christ the Lord* – the Son is God.

3. We believe in *the Holy Spirit* – the Spirit is God.

B. The need to affirm the true nature of *the one* God, Father, Son, and Holy Spirit

1. Affirm the *unity* of God.

2. Affirm the *diversity* of the members within the Trinity.

3. Affirm the *equality* of the members (in glory, substance, and majesty).

Conclusion

- The Word of God teaches that there is only one God, and yet this same God reveals himself as God the Father, Son, and Holy Spirit.

- Furthermore, the Scriptures teach not only that God is one God, but also speaks of God in three persons, as the Father, the Son, and the Holy Spirit.

Student Questions and Response

Please take as much time as you have available to answer these and other questions that the video brought out. The biblical teaching on the Trinity is neither easy nor quick to comprehend and understand. What must be understood, however, is that the Trinity is an attempt to accept with full authority and honesty the *scriptural testimony* of God's unity as one God, and yet the divinity of the Father, the Son, and the Holy Spirit. Rehearse the key concepts on this important teaching, and make sure that you are able to defend any claims you make with the Scriptures themselves (Acts 17.11).

1. What is the meaning of the "doctrine of the *Trinity*?" To what of the Bible's teaching does this term refer?

2. Summarize how the Scriptures assert both God is one, while at the same time, affirming the divinity of the Father, Son, and Holy Spirit.

3. Give examples of some of the biblical evidence for asserting that each member of the Trinity (Father, Son, and Holy Spirit) are God, (i.e., show from the Bible how the various members possess the attributes of God, do the work of God, are called God, and exercise authority as God).

4. In what sense can we affirm both God's oneness, and God's plurality?

5. What is the meaning and relationship of God's persons and God's single essence? How has the Church attempted to understand the Bible's teachings on the Trinity (list an example).

6. Why is it absolutely necessary never to state the idea of Trinity as meaning three gods? Why has the Church been so careful to distinguish between the single Godhood of God while affirming the *three persons of God*?

7. How do the creeds help us to understand how something is not doctrinally true about the Trinity? Can you deny either of these ideas and still have an acceptable view of the Trinity: the unity of God, the *differences* between the Father, Son, and the Holy Spirit, and the *equality* of the members?

CONNECTION

Summary of Key Concepts

This lesson concentrates on both the triune nature of the Trinity as well as the attributes of greatness of God the Father Almighty. The doctrine of the Trinity affirms Scripture's claims that God is both one and yet exists as three distinct persons, all who are referred to as God, and share the glory of the divine nature. God the Father, the first person of the Trinity, possesses attributes which speak powerfully and definitively as to his greatness. As God the Father is spirit, he possesses life in himself, has authentic personality, is infinite in his divine nature and character, and possesses an essence that never changes.

- The doctrine of the *Trinity* refers to the Bible's teaching about God's triune personhood.

- The Scriptures assert that God is one, and that there is none other than the one God, and yet they also assert that the one God reveals himself as God the Father, Son, and Holy Spirit.

- Each member of the Trinity (Father, Son, and Holy Spirit) possesses the attributes and does the work of God, is called God, and exercises authority as God.

- The Bible affirms both God's oneness, and God's plurality (that the Godhead is *more than one person*), with the persons Father, Son, and Holy Spirit addressed together as being persons within the Godhead.

- The doctrine of the Trinity asserts that God exists in three persons, and that all the members share the same essence, are distinct in their personalities and work, and yet are co-equal in glory, together comprising the one true God, Father, Son, and Holy Spirit.

Student Application and Implications

Now is the time for you to discuss with your fellow students your own tough questions about the Trinity and the divine attributes of the Father's greatness. Undoubtedly you have some questions that have come to mind as you have listened, studied, prayed, and reflected on these great topics of the Word of God. Take a moment to gather up your own particular questions on these and related subjects, and share them with your fellow learners. Interact together on the issues and concerns that have now surfaced in your study of the materials. Perhaps questions below might point you in some different directions.

- Can a person be a Christian and deny the doctrine of the *Trinity*? Is it as important as the doctrine of salvation by grace through faith, or can a person have a different view of God than the Trinity and still be considered "orthodox?"

- Since the word "Trinity" is not itself in the Bible, how can theology make it out to be an "essential doctrine" of the faith?

- Can one believe something about God like what the Jehovah's Witnesses believe (God the Father alone is God; Jesus is the second greatest being made by God and the Spirit is God's power for service) and still be considered biblical? Why or why not?

- How can you so understand the greatness of God that it affects all that you do: your worship, your conduct and character, and your ministry? How do you translate this high truth into a radical lifestyle for God?

- So many look at God as one who wants to meet their needs, and not as the triune and sovereign God of the universe. How do you make the switch *from seeing God as one who lives for me to the God for which all things exist*?

- What are practical ways to help growing believers desire and learn the "deeper truths" of the Word of God regarding God's attributes, character, and name?

- The attributes of God's greatness (i.e., his spirituality, life, person, infinitude, and constancy) speak of a being far beyond our comprehension.

- How does our faith in Jesus Christ make the Father more accessible to us (cf. John 1.18; John 14.7-9)?

CASE STUDIES

"It Don't Seem Relevant"

1 During a series on the attributes of God in the Pastor's mid-week Bible study, a young, hungry new believer raises her hand and makes a comment about the study. "Pastor," she says nearly apologetically, "I know that this may be important in a seminary kind of setting, but honestly, I am struggling to see why we ought to be studying all of these funny words and things about God. Why do we have to understand what Christians believed long ago about the nature of God, or use any other words like *ousios* or *homousia* or any of the fifty dollar terms. I just want to know about Jesus, really I don't care much for doctrine anyway. Can you tell me why on earth I, as a new Christian, should be interested in all of this stuff – to me, it just don't seem to matter much, it just don't seem relevant to anything I do." As pastor, how would you respond to the genuine question being raised by this dear sister in Christ?

One God, in Three Modes

2 A popular televangelist/preacher has recently come out with a view of the Trinity that has many eyebrows raising in the Christian community. Rather than affirm the traditional Christian view of the Trinity as one God who manifests himself in three distinct persons (Father, Son, and Holy Spirit), this popular teacher believes that there is one God who actually displays himself in three modes depending on the situation. In other words, while he affirms that God is one, he denies that the persons of the Trinity are distinct persons. There is only one God who manifests himself in three different modes. Why is this view unacceptable according to the Word of God? Would you count this view to be heresy? Why or why not?

"A Little too Friendly"

 So many of the praise and worship songs today highlight the intimacy and personal relationship that the believer now has with God. Many of the songs speak of God as friend, confidant, even as lover, with a strong emphasis on the *personal dimension* of our relationship with God. Yet, it is clear that with the absence of solid doctrinal teaching in many of our churches, and with hymns being sung less and less in most fellowships, many believers have no orientation to the attributes of the *greatness* of God the Father Almighty. In a real sense, the God of many churches is only large enough to meet the needs of our hearts, not tackle the problems of the world, let alone redeem a universe out of control. As one has characterized this state: "the God of many churches is a good pal, but doesn't seem to be the great God and our Savior, the God and Father of our Lord Jesus Christ. We seem to be just a little too friendly with him who is a consuming fire."

Imagine that the Lord has called you to be a minister of music and worship in a church. List out eight different emphases or things you could do to help believers in your church gain a greater, richer, and more biblical appreciation for the greatness of God in your worship and life together.

Restatement of the Lesson's Thesis

The doctrine of the Trinity is a biblical doctrine which asserts that God's nature is a tri-unity of three persons who share the same essence as God. The Bible claims that God is one God (Deut. 6.4), and yet this one God exists in three distinct yet co-equal, co-eternal persons, each of whom is referred to as God in Scripture, and is said to share the glory of the divine nature. The Holy Trinity (i.e., God the Father, the Son, and the Holy Spirit) is the name given to affirm Scripture's own assertion of the unity, diversity, and equality of the members of the one Godhead. God the Father Almighty, the first person of the Trinity, possesses attributes which speak powerfully and definitively as to his greatness. As God, the Father is spirit, possesses life in himself, has authentic personality, is infinite in his divine nature and character, and his essence never changes.

Resources and Bibliographies

If you are interested in pursuing some of the ideas on the nature of the Trinity and the greatness of God the Father Almighty, you might want to give these books a try (be warned, these are not easy readings!):

Charnock, Stephen. *The Existence and Attributes of God.* Grand Rapids: Baker Book House, 1996.

O'Collins, Gerald, S. J. *The Tripersonal God: Understanding and Interpreting the Trinity.* Mahwah, NJ: Paulist Press, 1999.

White, James R. *The Forgotten Trinity: Recovering the Heart of Christian Belief.* Bloomington, MN: Bethany House Publishing, 1998.

Ministry Connections

The doctrine of the Trinity and the greatness of God the Father are not merely theological themes to be studied and filed away. On the contrary, these are the great truths of the faith, and those who meditate long upon them are changed forever as a result of the reflection. Relating these great truths to your life and ministry can transform them; the price is concentrated application of the Word of God to your own life. As you meditate on the teaching in this lesson, ask the Lord how he might want you to enrich, change, or alter your ministry approach because of the truths the Holy Spirit has pointed out to you here. As you meditate on these truths, and think about your own life and ministry connected to them, seek to discern what the Spirit might be calling you to do right now, if anything, about these truths. Spend time before the Lord meditating on the truth of God's nature and greatness, and ask him how and in what way you might creatively apply the teaching here. Also, as you consider writing your ministry project for this unit, you might want to connect your assignment to some theme here. Seek the Lord regarding his direction, and come back next week ready to share your insights with the other learners in your class.

Counseling and Prayer

In pondering these truths on the nature of God as triune Lord and on the greatness of God the Father Almighty, one begins to see the sufficiency of our God to meet every need, not only in one's personal life but in the lives of those whom we love and serve. Maybe in the course of this lesson, while meditating on the greatness of the Father, some pressing need has been made known to you. The Holy Spirit has caused you, perhaps, to focus on a particular issue, need, or concern, and you need to seek the Lord for his strength and aid in it. Now is the time to share your need and pray for one another. If time does not permit for you to intercede together now, enlist a prayer partner with whom you can share your burden and who will lift up your requests to the Lord. Of course, know that your instructor will be willing and open to pray with you, as well as your church leaders, especially your pastor. Listen to the Lord, and allow the Holy Spirit to lead you into sharing your needs with the Father Almighty, our great and sovereign Lord of all.

ASSIGNMENTS

Scripture Memory: Matthew 3.16-17

Reading Assignment: To prepare for class, please visit *www.tumi.org/books* to find next week's reading assignment, or ask your Mentor.

Other Assignments: Again, make certain that you read the assignments above, and as last week, write a brief summary for them and bring these summaries to class next week. (Please see the "Reading Completion Sheet" on page 16.) Also, now is the time to begin to think about the character of your ministry project, as well as decide what passage of Scripture you will select for your exegetical project. Do not delay in determining either your ministry or exegetical project. The sooner you select, the more time you will have to prepare!

Looking Forward to the Next Lesson: In our next lesson, *God the Son: Jesus, the Messiah and Lord of All – He Died*, we will explore the theological implications of Jesus' humiliation and death, his descent in his divine person on our behalf. We will consider Jesus' humiliation in the Incarnation, his life and ministry, as well as his death. In considering his sacrifice on Calvary, we will explore some of the historical models for understanding his work on the cross. These include the perspective of his death as a ransom for us, as a propitiation (divine satisfaction) for our sins, as a substitutionary sacrifice in our place, as a victory over the devil and death itself, and as a reconciliation between God and humankind. We will also explore some of the historical alternative views of Jesus' death. These include his death as 1) a moral example, 2) a demonstration of God's love, 3) a demonstration of God's justice, 4) a victory over the forces of evil and sin, and 5) a satisfaction of God's honor. Perhaps no study of doctrine can compare with the thrill of understanding from a biblical and creedal way the richness, wonder, and mystery of God's Son, Jesus of Nazareth. His humiliation and ascension is the heart of the Gospel, and the center of our devotion, worship, and service. May God use this study of his glorious person to enable you to better love and serve him who alone has been given the preeminence by the Father.

FOR FURTHER STUDY

Please see the following resources in *Picturing Theology: An A-Z Collection of TUMI's Key Diagrams, Charts, Graphics, and Articles*:

- *The Father, Son, and Holy Ghost Share the Same Divine Attributes and Works*, page 128
- *God's Three-In-Oneness: The Trinity*, page 162
- *Giving Glory to God*, page 147
- *Names of Almighty God*, page 295
- *The Story of God: Our Sacred Roots*, page 401

God the Son
Jesus, the Messiah and Lord of All – He Died

Lesson Objectives

Welcome in the strong name of Jesus Christ! After your reading, study, discussion, and application of the materials in this lesson, you will be able to:

- Articulate with Scripture and concrete examples the significance of the *humiliation* of Jesus Christ, that is, his descent in his divine person and glory to come to earth and die on our behalf.

- Illustrate and state the major points of Jesus' humiliation in his Incarnation and in his life and ministry.

- Elaborate with Scripture and clear reasons how this humiliation of Jesus is specifically revealed in his death.

- Expand upon some of the key historical perspectives on Jesus' death and the way in which these dimensions enable us to understand the blessing our Lord's death was for humankind.

- These include the view of his death as a ransom for us, as a propitiation for our sins, as a substitutionary sacrifice in our place, as a victory over the devil and death itself, and as a reconciliation between God and humankind.

- Elaborate on how the Nicene Creed unequivocally confesses that our Lord Jesus Christ died and was buried, and how this act was the culmination of our Lord's humiliation upon earth in his descent from his heavenly, preexistent glory.

Devotion

The Iniquity of Us All

Isa. 53.1-12 – Who has believed what they heard from us? And to whom has the arm of the Lord been revealed? [2] For he grew up before him like a young plant, and like a root out of dry ground; he had no form or majesty that we should look at him, and no beauty that we should desire him. [3] He was despised and rejected by men; a man of sorrows, and acquainted with grief; and as one from whom men hide their faces he was despised, and we esteemed him not. [4] Surely he has borne our griefs and carried our sorrows; yet we esteemed him stricken, smitten by God, and afflicted. [5] But he was wounded for our transgressions;

he was crushed for our iniquities; upon him was the chastisement that brought us peace, and with his stripes we are healed. [6] All we like sheep have gone astray; we have turned every one to his own way; and the Lord has laid on him the iniquity of us all. [7] He was oppressed, and he was afflicted, yet he opened not his mouth; like a lamb that is led to the slaughter, and like a sheep that before its shearers is silent, so he opened not his mouth. [8] By oppression and judgment he was taken away; and as for his generation, who considered that he was cut off out of the land of the living, stricken for the transgression of my people? [9] And they made his grave with the wicked and with a rich man in his death, although he had done no violence, and there was no deceit in his mouth. [10] Yet it was the will of the Lord to crush him; he has put him to grief; when his soul makes an offering for sin, he shall see his offspring; he shall prolong his days; the will of the Lord shall prosper in his hand. [11] Out of the anguish of his soul he shall see and be satisfied; by his knowledge shall the righteous one, my servant, make many to be accounted righteous, and he shall bear their iniquities. [12] Therefore I will divide him a portion with the many, and he shall divide the spoil with the strong, because he poured out his soul to death and was numbered with the transgressors; yet he bore the sin of many, and makes intercession for the transgressors.

One of the greatest mysteries of the Christian faith relates to the profound humility of the Godhead as revealed in the death and passion of Jesus Christ. His lowliness and submission causes us to wonder and marvel at the *nature* of the divine. His willingness to follow the Father's command with such fierce loyalty and obedience, no matter what the cost, reveals the heart of a Savior which is boundless in virtue and grace. In this significant chapter of Messianic prophecy, Isaiah scripts out the contours of the one who would come in great humility for the sake of redeeming those who in fact were guilty and unconcerned. The lack of empathy and understanding for those who would receive his gift of grace makes the lowliness even more astounding.

One of the high points of the text leads us gently into the depths of the truth regarding the humility of our Lord and his death on our behalf. Isaiah 53.3-6 highlights his humiliation: "He was despised and rejected by men; a man of sorrows, and acquainted with grief; and as one from whom men hide their faces he was despised, and we esteemed him not. Surely he has borne our griefs and carried our sorrows; yet we esteemed him stricken, smitten by God, and afflicted. But he was wounded for our transgressions; he was crushed for our iniquities; upon him was the chastisement that brought us peace, and with his stripes we are healed. All we like sheep have gone astray; we have turned every one to his own way; and the Lord has laid on him the iniquity of us all." On close look at the text we are amazed at the disposition of people toward him.

He was despised, rejected, a man of sorrows, acquainted with grief, unesteemed and unloved. Though ironically perceived as one who was stricken by the Lord, he was actually bearing our griefs, wounded for our transgressions, crushed for our iniquities, chastised for our peace, and beaten viciously for our healing. We like sheep have wandered and gone astray in directions that have nothing to do with the Lord, we've turned each one to our own way, *and the Lord has laid on him the iniquity of us all*.

This truth, that his humiliation was the result of our rebellion and sin, ought to produce in each of us a deep sense of sobriety and angst. Hymnody has captured these inclinations in surveying the wondrous cross, in seeing the sacred head wounded on account of our own foolishness and transgression. The Lord's love to reconcile, redeem, and restore led him to punish his own Servant in our place, laying on *him* the iniquity of us *all*.

No other truth, no other idea, can bring in us such a deep level of self-awareness of the real consequences our sin wrought upon our Lord. His blows, beatings, rejection, and despising was caused directly by our own disobedience, lies, lust, and greed. Our waste and hatreds, our irritations and jealousies and our foolishness and profanities are the reasons for our Lord's horrible treatment and death. When we come to understand just how responsible we are for his suffering, only then will we be able to truly empathize with our Lord, and bear daily the cross that we are to share with him.

We must admit our part in Calvary, that contribution that made his death necessary *for our redemption*. Yes, we have gone our own way; yes, we have gone astray like wandering sheep without a shepherd, and the Lord has laid on him the iniquity of us all.

Nicene Creed and Prayer

After reciting and/or singing the Nicene Creed (located in the Appendix), pray the following prayer:

> Holy and everliving God who revealed the glory of your Son when he was exalted on the cross: Accept our praise and thanksgiving for the power of his victory and grant us never to be afraid to suffer or to die with him; our crucified King who is alive, and reigns in all eternity with you and the Holy Spirit one God for ever and ever.

~ The Church of the Province of South Africa.
Minister's Book for Use With the Holy Eucharist and Morning and Evening Prayer.
Braamfontein: Publishing Department of the Church of the Province of South Africa. p. 47.

Scripture Memorization Review

Review with a partner, write out and/or recite the text for last class session's assigned memory verse: Matthew 3.16-17.

Assignments Due

Turn in your summary of the reading assignment for last week, that is, your brief response and explanation of the main points that the authors were seeking to make in the assigned reading (Reading Completion Sheet).

CONTACT

The Cross in Your Pocket

1. The Cross is arguably one of the most visible symbols of the Christian faith, and least understood. Today, the Cross is represented in every conceivable way, from trinkets and lockets, on bracelets and T-shirts, to church art and architecture. It is a staple in the West and despised in many places of the world. One company makes a cross of coin-size that fits in the pocket to remind you of the price paid for our sin. What is your view of the commercialization of the cross, and how might such activities dull us to the true meaning of the passion of Christ?

The Passion of the Christ

2. In response to the blockbuster film, *The Passion of the Christ*, many evangelical churches held evangelistic meetings designed to share the Good News in conjunction with the debut of the film. The graphic nature of the sufferings of the Messiah shown in the film have produced wide ranging responses, from deep feelings of remorse and love to shock and horror. The film is perhaps the most dramatically violent depiction ever of the sufferings of Jesus. Some have said such showings simply go too far in highlighting the violence of Calvary without really dramatically revealing the underlying reasons for it. What is your opinion about such dramatic interpretations of the passion of Jesus. Ought we to produce more of these, or have we had enough of them for now?

A Strange Silence

3. In many of our more "seeker sensitive" churches, we are witnessing a strange silence to the stigma and passion of Calvary. Many of the

sermons and homilies are on subjects of wide public interest, usually avoiding topics and themes which are overtly theological and doctrinal. When the cross is presented, it is usually done in a way that highlights the self-actualization of the hearer rather than as an explicit solution to the transgression of humankind. Teachings on the blood sacrifice of Messiah have been replaced by homilies on positive thinking and building family memories. Many of the old hymns which highlighted the wonder, power, and mystery of the cross have been replaced by a flood of choruses, all of which focus on the joy of the worshiper and not the underlying suffering that makes worship possible. While many churches continue to emphasize the cross as the central event in salvation history, our methods of evangelism and outreach tend to focus on more positive themes for the sake of attracting new visitors. What is your opinion as to the growing and strange silence of the cross in the preaching, teaching, and worship in our churches today?

Jesus, the Messiah and Lord of All – He Died

His Humiliation and Death

Rev. Dr. Don L. Davis

CONTENT

Summary

The humiliation of Jesus Christ, to use the theologian Oden's language, deals with his descent from the heavenly realms in his divine glory to come to earth and die on behalf of the world. This lowliness was reflected in every dimension of Jesus' Incarnation and earthly life, from his birth to his life and ministry. The culmination of this lowliness and humility is revealed in his passion and death on Calvary. His death may be understood through various dimensions which enable us to understand better the nature of our salvation in him: his death was a ransom for us, the propitiation for our sins, a substitutionary sacrifice in our place, a victory over the devil and death itself, and a reconciliation between God and humankind.

Our objective for this lesson, *His Humiliation and Death*, is to enable you to see that:

- The humiliation of Jesus Christ is represented by his descent from the heavenly realms in his glory to come to earth to suffer and die on behalf of the world.

- Jesus revealed his lowliness and humility in every dimension of his Incarnation, in his birth and throughout his life and ministry.

- The culmination of this lowliness and humility is revealed in the passion and death of Jesus Christ.

- The death of Jesus may be understood through various dimensions which enable us to understand the blessings his suffering provided to the world.

- These include the concept of Jesus' death as a ransom for us, as a propitiation for our sins, as a substitutionary sacrifice in our place, as a victory over the devil and death itself, and as a reconciliation between God and humankind.

- The Nicene Creed unequivocally confesses that our Lord Jesus Christ died and was buried for our sins. This was the culmination of our Lord's humiliation upon earth in his descent from his heavenly, preexistent glory.

Video Outline

By means of a tree, we were made debtors to God. Likewise, by means of a tree [the cross], we can obtain the remission of our debt.

~ Irenaeus (c. 180, E/W), 1.545. David W. Bercot, ed. *A Dictionary of Early Christian Beliefs*. Peabody, MA: Hendrickson Publishers, 1998. p. 184.

I. The Humiliation of Jesus Christ

Phil. 2.6-8 – . . . who, though he was in the form of God, did not count equality with God a thing to be grasped, [7] but made himself nothing, taking the form of a servant,[a] being born in the likeness of men. [8] And being found in human form, he humbled himself by becoming obedient to the point of death, even death on a cross.

Gal. 4.4-5 – But when the fullness of time had come, God sent forth his Son, born of woman, born under the law, [5] to redeem those who were under the law, so that we might receive adoption as sons.

A. Humiliation in the Incarnation: the self-emptying of Jesus Christ

    1. He gave up his equality with God.

        a. Giving up the presence of the Father and the Spirit

        b. Form of spirit and infinite glory

2. He made himself nothing and took the form of a servant (in human likeness).

   a. Born of a woman in dramatically humble surroundings

   b. Raised in anonymity (no one knew who he was for the majority of his life)

   c. Yielded his will without limit to the Father

      (1) John 4.34

      (2) John 6.38

      (3) Matt. 26.39

The cross was to express grace by the letter "T."
~ Barnabas (c. 70-130, E), 1.143. *Ibid.* p. 96.

3. As a human being, he humbled himself becoming obedient to the point of death on the cross.

   a. He was born under the law and lived subject to it.

      (1) He was circumcised.

         (a) Gen. 17.12

         (b) Lev. 12.3

         (c) Luke 2.21

      (2) He was brought to the Temple for his mother's time of purification, Luke 2.22-39.

      (3) He fulfilled both the letter and spirit of the Law in his own person, Matt. 5.17-18.

   b. He surrendered the independent use of his divine attributes.

      (1) He was wholly dependent on his Father, John 5.19-20.

(2) He strictly and wholeheartedly obeyed the Father's commandment in every particular.

   (a) John 5.30

   (b) John 8.28

   (c) John 12.49

   (d) John 14.10

B. Humiliation in his death: the significance of Jesus' death

> *Christ is called a Sheep and a Lamb who was to be slain.... Christ is also called a Stone. ...He Himself is both Judge and King.*
> ~ Cyprian (c. 250, W), 5.521-5.527. *Ibid.* p. 370.

1. It is critical as the *central doctrine in apostolic witness and spirituality*.

   a. 1 Cor. 15.3-8

   b. Gal. 6.14

   c. Rom. 1.16

   d. 1 Cor. 1.22-24

   e. 1 Cor. 2.2

   f. Gal. 2.20

   g. Gal. 5.24

   h. 2 Cor. 4.8-10

2. *It is critical for its dramatic preeminence in the Holy Scriptures.*

   a. Jesus claimed this was the heart of the OT scriptural theme.

      (1) Luke 24.27

      (2) Luke 24.44-45

   b. It ranked among the critical subjects researched by the OT prophets, 1 Pet. 1.10-12.

3. It is critical as the *clear reason for his Incarnation.*

   a. Heb. 2.14-15

   b. 1 John 3.5

   c. Matt. 20.28

4. It is critical for it appears to be the *compelling theme of heaven.*

   a. Luke 9.30-31

   b. Rev. 5.8-12

II. The Meaning of Jesus' Death

A. Jesus died as *a ransom for many.*

> *It is impossible to teach the Father except by His Son Jesus Christ.*
> ~ Cyprian (c. 250, W), 5.542. *Ibid.* p. 574.

1. The biblical evidence

    a. Matt. 20.28

    b. Gal. 3.13

    c. 1 Tim. 2.5-6

    d. 1 Pet. 1.18

2. Picture: lost souls as in a slave market, bound, subject to domination and abuse, held in bondage

    a. Ezek. 18.4

    b. Rom. 7.14

3. Through his death, Jesus liberates the captives from the tyranny of the devil and sin, purchases us by his own blood and becomes our new Owner and Master."

    a. 1 Cor. 7.23

    b. Heb. 9.12

    c. Rev. 5.9

By believing in Him you will live. But by disbelieving, you will be punished. For "he that is disobedient to the Son will not see life."

~ *Apostolic Constitutions* (compiled c. 390, E), 7.449. Ibid. p. 575.

B. Jesus died as *a propitiation for our sins*.

1. The biblical evidence

   a. Rom. 3.25-26

   b. Heb. 2.17

   c. Heb. 9.5

   d. 1 John 2.2

2. Picture: the Ark of the Covenant, which was called a propitiation ("mercy seat")

   a. Exod. 25.17-22 (cf. Heb. 9.5)

   b. Lev. 16.15

   c. The transgression of sin is covered, and pardoned because propitiation provides a way that a righteous God may justly forgive the transgressor.

   d. The propitiation affirmed God's righteous anger against sin, covered the sin of the transgressor, and allowed God to be merciful to the penitent sinner.

   e. The propitiation allows God to affirm his infinite holiness while, at the very same time, pardon the guilty sinner: his righteousness is not compromised in the display of mercy.

3. Through his death, Jesus becomes our propitiation, he himself in his own death becomes our all-sufficient sacrifice for propitiation.

    a. Rom. 5.9

    b. 1 John 2.2

    c. 1 John 4.10

C. Jesus died as *a substitutionary sacrifice (our Passover)*.

    1. The biblical evidence

        a. Isa. 53.5-6

        b. Rom. 8.3

        c. 2 Cor. 5.21

        d. Gal. 3.13

        e. Eph. 5.2

        f. Heb. 10.12-14

        g. 1 Pet. 2.24

        h. 1 Pet. 3.18

> *Because of the love He had for us, Jesus Christ our Lord gave His blood for us by the will of God. He gave His flesh for our flesh, and His soul for our souls.*
>
> ~ Clement of Rome (c. 96, W), 1.18. Ibid. p. 42.

2. Picture

   a. The Passover Lamb of the Exodus story (Exod. 12) where the life of an innocent sacrifice is substituted for the life (*in the place of, instead of*) of the other, cf. Exod. 12.11-13

   b. The sacrifice of Isaac, where in the place of Isaac, a ram was substituted *in place of, instead of* Isaac, Gen. 22.13

3. Through his death, Jesus becomes our Paschal Lamb, the one whose own body absorbs and takes the punishment for our lawlessness, iniquity, and transgression, (*Christus Victum*: Christ, the Victim for us).

   a. 1 Cor. 5.7

   b. 1 Pet. 1.19-20

   c. Rev. 5.12

D. Jesus died in order to *destroy the devil and his work*.

   1. The biblical evidence

      a. Ps. 68.18

      b. Matt. 12.29

      c. John 12.31-33

God had foretold that this seed would proceed from the woman, and that he would trample on the head of the devil.

~ Cyprian (c. 250, W), 5.553. Ibid. p. 594.

            d. Rom. 14.7-9

            e. Col. 2.15

            f. Heb. 2.14-15

            g. 1 John 3.8

        2. Picture: through his own death, Jesus destroyed the one who has the power of death (the devil).

            a. Isa. 25.8

            b. Hos. 13.14

            c. 1 Cor. 15.54-55

            d. 2 Tim. 1.10

        3. Through his death, Jesus destroys the devil, ending any legitimate right he has on humankind, being totally disarmed in his ability to lie, accuse, enslave, and destroy those who were legitimately blamed by him before the Father, Rev. 12.9-10.

    E. Jesus died as *a reconciliation between God and creation (including humankind)*.

        1. The biblical evidence

            a. Rom. 5.10

Our Lord Jesus Christ endured man's condition on our behalf, so that He could destroy all sin and furnish us with the provision necessary for our entrance into eternal life.

~ Phileas (c. 307, E), 6.162. *Ibid.* p. 47.

b. 2 Cor. 5.18-21

c. Eph. 2.16

d. Col. 1.20

e. Rom. 8.19-23

2. Picture: hostility and bitterness between two parties, having it removed by the settling of the accounts

   a. Isa. 52.7

   b. Isa. 57.19

3. Through his death, Jesus effects a reconciliation and peace between God and his creation; he brings to a final and lasting conclusion the alienation between God and humankind, 2 Cor. 5.18-20

Conclusion

- Jesus Christ in his descent from the heavenly realms humbled himself in his Incarnation and death.

- Through his work on the Cross, Jesus has laid the foundation for our faith, worship, and witness to the world.

- Jesus' death has been historically understood through the dimensions of a ransom sacrifice, a propitiation for our sins, a vicarious or substitutionary offering in our place, a triumph over Satan's hold on us through death, and a reconciliation between God and humankind.

Student Questions and Response

Please take as much time as you have available to answer these and other questions that the video brought out. In many ways, the humility and lowliness of our Lord constitutes the heart and soul of our personal ethic of the Kingdom of God. We are called to suffer with him, to bear our cross daily, and follow him. Only if we experience the fellowship of his sufferings can we fully be liberated as his vessels of worship and witness. The significance of the cross cannot be overestimated for Christian leadership or effective urban ministry. Answer the following questions with an eye to apply these truths as the Spirit leads. Be clear and concise in your reasoning and support your answers with biblical proofs.

1. What is the meaning of the phrase "self-emptying of Jesus Christ?" In other words, what specifically did Jesus "empty" himself of in his Incarnation and ministry on earth?

2. How did the life and ministry of Jesus demonstrate his servanthood, humility, and lowliness? What are the implications of this for our own lives of discipleship and ministry today?

3. What is the relationship between Jesus humbling himself and him surrendering the "independent use" of his divine attributes while on earth?

4. Why is the death of Jesus so important for an overall understanding of Incarnation?

5. How are we to understand the death of Jesus as a ransom sacrifice for the world? Explain your answer.

6. What does it mean that Jesus' death is a propitiation for our sins?

7. In what ways does Jesus' death parallel for us the meaning of the Passover and substitutionary sacrifice?

8. What are the characteristics of conflict and struggle shown between Jesus' death and the devil, in other words, in what way did the death of Jesus destroy the devil's work?

9. How does the death of Jesus reconcile God with his creation and with humankind, even as both have been so dramatically affected by sin and the curse?

LESSON 3 | GOD THE SON: JESUS, THE MESSIAH AND LORD OF ALL – HE DIED

CONNECTION

Summary of Key Concepts

This lesson focuses upon the humiliation of Jesus Christ in the Incarnation and ministry, and in the meaning of the death of Jesus Christ as it relates to our salvation and redemption. In some ways, the truths associated with these topics constitute both warp and woof of God's loom of the Kingdom of God. All threads of God's revelation of himself as Maker and Redeemer are connected to the person of Jesus of Nazareth, his perfect life and substitutionary death on the cross. Our obligation as Christian leaders on these matters is crystal clear: we must not only understand these truths from a biblical and historical perspective, we must also reflect and embody them in our lives and ministries. *We* are to die, even as he did, and we are to suffer, even as our Lord suffered for us. Carefully consider these implications as you review the key concepts below.

- The humiliation of Jesus Christ, to use the theologian Oden's language, deals with his descent from the heavenly realms in his divine glory to come to earth and die on behalf of the world.

- The lowliness of Jesus was reflected in every dimension of his Incarnation and earthly life, from his birth to his life and ministry. The culmination of this lowliness and humility is revealed in his passion and death at Calvary.

- Jesus' death may be understood through various dimensions which enable us to understand better the nature of our salvation in him: his death was a ransom for us, the propitiation for our sins, a substitutionary sacrifice in our place, a victory over the devil and death itself, and a reconciliation between God and humankind.

Student Application and Implications

Now is the time for you to discuss with your fellow students your questions about the humiliation of Jesus and the culmination of that humility and lowliness through his death on the cross. As mentioned above, it is arguably one of the most important topics that we as Christian leaders can pursue. Understanding the meaning of the death of Jesus is the heart of our Christian confession and the pulse of our Christian service. Undoubtedly, certain questions have come to mind as you have discussed and studied these ideas. What particular issues have come to the light as you have studied the death of Christ so far? The questions below are given to provoke your own, more contextualized questions about Jesus' death.

- How should the self-emptying of Jesus Christ affect our attitudes about our own lives and ministries as we go forth to answer God's call on our lives?

- To what extent is Jesus' lowliness and humility a model for us, and in what ways is his submission to the Father unique to him alone? Explain your answer.

- How do you currently apply the following instruction of Jesus to your own life and ministry? Luke 9.23-25 – And he said to all, "If anyone would come after me, let him deny himself and take up his cross daily and follow me. [24] For whoever would save his life will lose it, but whoever loses his life for my sake will save it. [25] For what does it profit a man if he gains the whole world and loses or forfeits himself?"

- In what way should we incorporate texts like Philippians 2.5-11 and 2 Corinthians 8.9 into our understanding of Christian discipleship and ministry?

- Of all of the pictures given of Jesus' death and its meaning for our lives, which do you personally find most powerful for your life and ministry?

- Finish the following statement: "The one thing that still troubles me about my own grasp of Jesus' death that I need to learn more about is _____."

- What are the ways in which you will seek to make the death of Jesus more real in your life and ministry? Why is the Lord's Supper such an important ongoing practice to help us appreciate the meaning of his passion and death on our behalf?

- How might we better teach the humility and death of Jesus in our discipling, preaching, and teaching? Brainstorm together ways you can reemphasize the passion of Christ in your church life.

CASE STUDIES

A Bloodless Faith?

 Many modern presentations of the Gospel tend to focus on the *ethics of Christian faith*, that is, on the character of relationships and virtues associated with the Christian faith and not on the passion of Christ, his humility, sufferings, and death on Calvary. Many mega-churches associated with church growth and more contemporary approaches to Christian worship and witness are explicit in their insistence that dealing constantly with the violent and tortuous themes of death and sacrifice is ineffective in winning others. Churches that are growing deal with "real" issues, address people's concrete personal anxieties and worries, and concentrate on the quality of life issues that most mainstream Westerners worry about day to day. Our entree into their lives will not begin, it is argued, with tough teachings on the shed blood of Christ but more ground-floor issues like work, family, and self-development. *At what point ought we to introduce to genuine seekers of God the teaching surrounding the cross of Christ? Is it the ground floor or the end game of Christian witness? Explain your answer.*

Politically Incorrect Theories

In a world that is fragmented by political strife, many evangelical preachers have determined not to use the military metaphors of the NT to communicate the faith. Although much of Jesus' and the apostles' language uses military symbolism to make sense of Jesus' life and mission, including his death on the cross, few teachers seek to follow their example today. Some have gone so far as to suggest that using these pictures to communicate the nature of Christian faith would be a mistake at a time like this, where religious bigotry, jihads, and intolerance and violence is taking place in the name of gods and religion. The image of war is a horrible reality, and one that we ought not use without genuine caution. Others would argue that these images are *divinely inspired*, given in order to enable us to understand the *core meaning of redemption in Christ*. In other words, the image of war was selected because it communicates better than any other way the *true nature of spirituality; Jesus came to destroy the works of the devil* (1 John 3.8). The universe is *at war*, and no amount of squeamishness will change this fact. *Is using the image of war as a theory of atonement valid for us today?*

The Resurrection, Not the Passion

It is clear that the NT focuses on the nature of the resurrection as the central teaching of the Christian faith. First Corinthians chapter fifteen is the Magna Carta of Christian doctrine: apart from the resurrection Christianity would be a futile and false affirmation that changes nothing practically or spiritually for those deluded enough to embrace it. Some have argued that our focus should be upon the triumph of the resurrection and the victory of our Lord's work, rather than on the death of Jesus and the humiliation and violence associated with it. *Easter*, not *Good Friday*, is the defining event of Christian witness, these would argue, and would further state that a kind of obsession with the death and violence of Calvary is neither spiritually helpful nor psychologically healthy. It is clear, however, that the apostles' challenged believers in the early Church to model their attitudes and conduct on the basis of the sufferings of Christ and his death (e.g., Phil. 2.5-11; 1 Pet. 2.21ff; Gal. 2.20). Still, many tend to focus on the abundance, prosperity, health, and riches of the Christian experience rather than the fellowship of his sufferings in order to be conformed to his death (Phil. 3.10). *What is the relationship between emphasizing the resurrection of our Lord and his sufferings as it relates to a true communication of the Christian faith?*

Restatement of the Lesson's Thesis

The humiliation of Jesus Christ, to use the theologian Oden's language, deals with his descent from the heavenly realms in his divine glory to come to earth and die on behalf of the world. This lowliness was reflected in every dimension of Jesus' Incarnation and earthly life, from his birth to his life and ministry. The culmination of this lowliness and humility is revealed in his passion and death on Calvary. His death may be understood through various dimensions which enable us to understand better the nature of our salvation in him: his death was a ransom for us, the propitiation for our sins, a substitutionary sacrifice in our place, a victory over the devil and death itself, and a reconciliation between God and humankind. The death of Jesus has been understood in various ways throughout Christian history. These theories of the atonement each focus on a particular dimension of salvation, and taken together they enable us to gain an even greater understanding and appreciation of the significance of Jesus' death for us. Jesus' death and its meaning has been viewed as 1) an example, 2) a demonstration of God's love, 3) a demonstration of God's justice, 4) a victory over the forces of evil and sin, and 5) a satisfaction of God's honor. While none of these theories in and of themselves fully explains Jesus' death, each contains truth which can enhance our understanding of its larger meaning and truth.

Resources and Bibliographies

If you are interested in pursuing some of the ideas of *Jesus, the Messiah and Lord of All: His Humiliation and Death*, you might want to give these books a try:

Brown, Raymond E. *The Death of the Messiah*. New York: Doubleday, 1994.

Kiehl, Erich H. *The Passion of Our Lord*. Grand Rapids: Baker Book House, 1990.

Lohse, Eduard. *History of the Suffering and Death of Jesus Christ.* Philadelphia: Fortress Press, 1967.

Stott, John. *The Cross of Christ.* Downers Grove, IL: InterVarsity, 1986.

Ministry Connections

The humility and death of Jesus Christ is so central to faith and practice that we as Christian leaders must relate its insights and truths to our lives and ministries constantly. How you flesh this truth out in your own life will determine your effectiveness in articulating its relevance in your own church and witness. How God might want you to change or alter your ministry approach based on these truths is largely dependent on your ability to hear what the Holy Spirit is saying to you about where you are, where your ministry and pastoral leadership is, where the members of your church are, and what specifically God is calling you to do right now, if anything, about these truths. Plan to spend good time this week meditating on the meaning of the death of Christ, and how your own life needs to become better informed and enriched by its truth. Furthermore, as you consider your ministry project for this unit, you can possibly use it to connect it to the truth of Jesus' lowliness and death in a practical and direct way for your audience, whomever you choose to share your insights with.

Above all, we must seek the Lord's own application for us related to Christ's humility and death. Seek the Lord's face this week for his insight, and come back next week ready to share your insights with the other learners in your class.

Counseling and Prayer

As the Lord speaks to you, know that he will give you opportunity to pray and to be prayed for in the areas of growth that are needful for you today. Perhaps there are some specific needs which the Holy Spirit has surfaced through your study and discussion of this material on the death of Jesus. Seek out a partner in prayer who can share your burdens and heart, and lift up your burdens together before the Lord. Of course, your instructor is extremely open to walking with you on this, and your church leaders, especially your pastor, may be specially equipped to help you answer any difficult questions arising from your reflection on this study. Be open to God and allow him to lead you as he determines. Concentrate on your need to let the mind of Christ dwell in you, and for the death of Jesus to become more and more real in every dimension of your Christian character and witness.

ASSIGNMENTS

Scripture Memory — Hebrews 2.14-17

Reading Assignment — To prepare for class, please visit *www.tumi.org/books* to find next week's reading assignment, or ask your Mentor.

Other Assignments — As usual you ought to come with your reading assignment sheet containing your summary of the reading material for the week. Also, you must have selected the text for your exegetical project and turn in your proposal for your ministry project.

Looking Forward to the Next Lesson — The next lesson, *God the Holy Spirit: The Person of the Holy Spirit*, focuses upon God the Spirit as the third person of the one Trinitarian God. We will talk about the Spirit as the "Life-giver" and show how the names, titles, and symbols of the Spirit in the Scriptures portray him as the source and sustainer of physical and spiritual life and as the one who is at work to renew all things. The person of the Holy Spirit is as real and vital as God the Father and God the Son. The Spirit is sent by the Father and the Son into the world so that we can experience loving fellowship with them and so that we can be empowered to obey God's commands and accomplish his mission. Our prayer is that your dependence on the Spirit will grow as you study the Scriptures together.

FOR FURTHER STUDY

Please see the following resources in *Picturing Theology: An A-Z Collection of TUMI's Key Diagrams, Charts, Graphics, and Articles*:

- *In Christ*, page 195
- *Messiah Jesus: Fulfillment of the Old Testament Types*, page 265
- *Ethics of the New Testament: Living in the Upside-Down Kingdom of God*, page 121
- *Messianic Prophecies Cited in the New Testament*, page 271
- *Preaching and Teaching Jesus of Nazareth as Messiah and Lord*, page 330

LESSON 4

God the Holy Spirit
The Person of the Holy Spirit

Lesson Objectives

Welcome in the strong name of Jesus Christ! After your reading, study, discussion, and application of the materials in this lesson, you will be able to:

- Summarize the Old Testament view of the Spirit of God.

- Use the Scriptures to describe the life-giving role of the Spirit in creating and sustaining the world.

- Identify the major symbols associated with the Holy Spirit in the Scriptures and show how they contribute to our understanding of him as the Life-giver.

- Explain how the names and titles of the Holy Spirit in the Scriptures contribute to our understanding of him as the Life-giver.

- Explain why the ministry of the Spirit is a source of hope.

Devotion

The Spirit Who Makes God Known

Read 1 Corinthians 2.10-11 and Romans 8.26. The Spirit of God is remarkable. On the one hand, he explores the deepest mysteries of the Father's mind and will. He possesses infinite knowledge and understanding. And yet, on the other hand, it is the Spirit's special ministry to be near to us, to help us understand who God is and what he desires. The Holy Spirit is, in the teaching of 1 Corinthians 2, the one who reveals God's hidden wisdom and mysteries to us. And, as the reading from Romans points out, the Spirit will pray the will of God in and through us when our human understanding has reached its limits and we do not know what or how we should pray. As we begin our study of the theology of the Holy Spirit, we are faced with the great irony that we cannot understand the Spirit of God without having the help of the Spirit of God. If we truly grasp this truth it should produce both humility and gratitude. We are humbled because we realize that we cannot know God through their own efforts (no matter how hard we study), but only through the work of the Spirit. We are grateful because we know that Spirit is given to us through the sure promises of God and that he is already at work on our behalf to lead us into all truth.

Nicene Creed and Prayer

After reciting and/or singing the Nicene Creed (located in the Appendix), pray the following prayer:

> O gracious and holy Father, give us wisdom to perceive you, intelligence to understand you, diligence to seek you, patience to wait for you, eyes to behold you, a heart to meditate on you, and a life to proclaim you through the power of the Spirit of Jesus Christ our Lord. Amen.
>
> ~ St. Benedict.
> From William Lane, S. J. *Praying with the Saints*. Dublin, Ireland: Veritas, 1989. p. 26.

Scripture Memorization Review

Review with a partner, write out and/or recite the text for last class session's assigned memory verse: Hebrews 2.14-17.

Assignments Due

Turn in your summary of the reading assignment for last week, that is, your brief response and explanation of the main points that the authors were seeking to make in the assigned reading (Reading Completion Sheet).

CONTACT

Picture Book Theology

 Draw a simple picture that represents the Holy Spirit. After you have finished, be prepared to explain your drawing to others.

Contending for the Faith

 The Church in every age has encountered "false teachers" who twist the Scriptures, using them to teach ideas completely contrary to that of Jesus and his Apostles. These false doctrines (heresies) seem to get "recycled," so that the same mistaken ideas find new advocates in each generation. One wrong idea about the Holy Spirit that shows up repeatedly is the belief that the Spirit is some sort of spiritual energy (or spiritual consciousness) but not a Divine Person who speaks and acts as the Living God. (In our day, groups like the *Jehovah's Witnesses* or *The Unity School of Christianity* would teach this false view.) Most popular Christian teaching today focuses on the work of the Holy Spirit; what he *does* in the lives of believers. Can you think of any reason why it might be equally important to teach about who the Holy Spirit *is*?

Three-In-One

 What do we mean when we say that God is a Trinity? What illustrations have you heard used to try and describe the Trinity? What are the strengths and weaknesses of each illustration?

The Person of the Holy Spirit

The Life-Giver

Rev. Terry G. Cornett

CONTENT

Summary

In this lesson we will look carefully at a central theme that unites the many activities of the Holy Spirit in the world. We will see that the Spirit gives life to the world through his work in creation and providence. We will examine some of the most common symbols, names, and titles used to describe the Holy Spirit in the Scriptures and explore how each of these contributes to our understanding of the Spirit as Life-giver. Finally, we will conclude with a discussion of how the life-giving ministry of the Spirit brings hope for the future.

Our objective for this lesson, *The Life-Giver*, is to enable you to see that:

- Understand why the theological study of the Holy Spirit is called *Pneumatology*.
- Summarize the Old Testament view of the Spirit of God.
- Use the Scriptures to describe the life-giving role of the Spirit in creating and sustaining the world.
- Identify the major symbols associated with the Holy Spirit in the Scriptures and show how they contribute to our understanding of him as the Life-giver.
- Explain how the names and titles of the Holy Spirit in the Scriptures contribute to our understanding of him as the Life-giver.
- Explain why the ministry of the Spirit is a source of hope.

Video Outline

I. The Life-Giver

We believe in the Holy Spirit, the Lord and Life-giver, who proceeds from the Father and the Son, who along with the Father and Son is worshiped and glorified, who spoke by the prophets.

II. The Powerful Breath of God

A. The study of the doctrine of the Holy Spirit is known as pneumatology.

1. *Pneuma* is the Greek word for "wind or breath or spirit."

2. The Hebrew word *ruach* (which is used in the Old Testament Scriptures) carries the same basic meaning of "wind or breath or spirit."

B. The best description of the Holy Spirit as portrayed in the Old Testament Scriptures would probably be "the powerful breath of God."

1. In the Hebrew Scriptures, God's breath is a powerful force which both destroys (Exod. 15.10; Isa. 11.4) and creates (Ps. 33.6).

The Hebrew word for 'spirit' is **ruach**. The root **r-w-ch**, from which the noun is derived, means primarily "to breathe out through the nose with violence.".... The word **ruach** stands for hard, strong, violent breathing, as against **neshamah**, which means ordinary, quiet breathing.... The word **ruach** is frequently used of the wind; some eighty-seven times in all. Of these thirty-seven speak of the wind as the agent of Jehovah, mostly destructive, and always strong and violent.... The **ruach-adonai** [Spirit of the Lord] is the manifestation in human experience of the life-giving, energy-creating power of God. . . . . The **ruach-adonai** cannot be hindered (is not 'straitened'), but is like His word, which shall not return unto Him void, but will accomplish that which He pleases.

~ N. H. Snaith. Chapter VII, "The Spirit of God."
The Distinctive Ideas of the Old Testament. pp. 143-158.

2. Old Testament Judaism understood the Holy Spirit to be "the power of God in action." That power might be demonstrated as:

   a. Strength in battle (as when the Wind of God parts the Red Sea or when the Judges are empowered in their fight against Israel's enemies)

   b. Various kinds of wisdom (as with the craftsmen at the Tabernacle or Joseph or Daniel having special gifts for the administration of Government).

   c. Prophetic utterances (such as those given by Jeremiah or Ezekiel).

III. The Power that Gives Life

A. The Spirit is intimately involved in the creation of the world.

Gen. 1.1-2 – In the beginning, God created the heavens and the earth. The earth was without form and void, and darkness was over the face of the deep. And the Spirit of God was hovering over the face of the waters.

1. The Spirit's "hovering"

In the OT the spirit (rûah) of Yahweh is God's power in action. . . . A term for both breath blown out and wind blowing . . . rûah has vivid and awesome association when used of God's energy let loose. It is so used in nearly 100 of its nearly 400 OT appearances.

~"Holy Spirit." *New Dictionary of Theology.* Downers Grove, IL/ Leicester, England: Inter-Varsity Press, 1988. p. 316.

See Ray Pritchard, *Names of the Holy Spirit.* Chicago: Moody Press, 1995. pp. 11, 13, 34.

a. The Hebrew word translated "hovering" (rachaph) suggests careful tending (cf. Deut. 32.11). The Spirit of God tended the new creation preparing it to move from formlessness to order, from darkness to light.

   Gen. 1.2 – "with a *divine wind*"

b. The Spirit's role in physical creation is similar to the Spirit's role in "new creation" (salvation) (see John 3).

   John 3.8 – The *wind* blows where it wishes, and you hear its sound, but you do not know where it comes from or where it goes. So it is with everyone who is born of the Spirit.

2. The Spirit is the Breath of God which brings humanity to life.

   a. The first human being, Gen. 2.7

   b. All human beings, Job 33.4, 6

B. The Spirit is intimately involved with sustaining life in the world.

   1. The Doctrine of Providence

      a. Definition: Providence comes from the word *provide*. Through his providence God sustains, governs, and protects the life that he gave the earth and guides it toward the end for which it was created.

> The root meaning of Providence is to foresee, or to provide. The question of providence concerns how God thinks ahead to care for all creatures.... God's providing looks ahead for needs as yet unrecognized by creatures. But more than simply foresight, providence has to do with the active, daily caring of God for the world in its hazards.
>
> ~ Thomas C. Oden. *The Living God*. p. 271.

Throughout the universe the immense forces that are at work in suns, stars, and galaxies are energized by the Spirit of God. All energy and power are there by virtue of the divine Spirit.

~ J. Rodman Williams

  b. The work of the Holy Spirit in providence: the Life-giver.

    (1) The Spirit is at work to create, renew, and provide for all the forms of life that exist within the created order.

    (2) OT: Ps. 104.29-30; Isa. 32.14-15

    (3) NT: John 6.63; Rom. 8.2, 6, 11

 2. The scriptural symbols of the Holy Spirit reveal him as Life-giver.

  a. Water – the source of life.

    (1) Isa. 44.2-4a

    (2) John 7.37-39

    (3) John 4.14

    (4) 1 Cor. 6.11 (cf. Titus 3.5)

    (5) Rev. 22.17

See Ray Pritchard, Names of the Holy Spirit. Chicago: Moody Press, 1995. pp. 57, 69, 77, 100, 187.

  b. Oil – the sustaining of life

  In biblical times, olive oil was used for both food and medicine as well as for fuel for lamps which lit the house. It was so vital to daily life that it became a symbol for prosperity. One could not think of oil without thinking of healing, security, and abundance. It sustained life.

Oil as an image of the Holy Spirit, took on an even more important symbolic role because of the biblical practice of anointing. Prophets (1 Kings 19.16), priests (Exod. 28.41), and kings (2 Sam. 2.4; 1 Kings 1.34) were anointed with oil to set them apart for ministry. This pouring on of oil was a symbol which showed visibly that the person was having the Holy Spirit poured out on them. The anointing with oil shows that God had chosen and equipped a person to minister life, health, security, and abundance to his people. In the Old Testament Scriptures this special anointing (empowerment) of the Holy Spirit was usually limited to those who served as prophets, priests, or kings. In the New Testament, every believer in Christ, receives an anointing of the Spirit to be a minster of life to others.

(1) 1 Sam. 16.13a (cf. Isa. 61.1)

(2) Luke 4.18

(3) 2 Cor. 1.21-22

Ibid. p. 19.

(4) 1 John 2.20, 27 (compare with John 14.26)

c. Fire – the protection (purification) of life.

The ancient world did not have microbe killing medicines. The primary agent for cleansing and purification was fire. Garbage was burned to keep it from becoming a breeding ground for disease (Lev. 8.17). When disease had broken out, burning the infected person's clothes was often the only way to stop the disease from spreading (Lev. 13.47-59). Fire also refined metals and made them pure and useful (Mal. 3.2-3).

Throughout the Scriptures God uses the symbol of fire to speak about the purification of his people. The prophet Isaiah, for example, speaks about a day "when the Lord shall have washed away the filth of the daughters of Zion and cleansed the bloodstains of Jerusalem from its midst by a spirit of judgment and by a spirit of burning" (Isa. 4.4).

(1) Matt. 3.11-12

(2) Acts 2.3-4

(3) 1 Thess. 5.19

Ibid. p. 40, 110.

(4) The Holy Spirit as the fire of God, constantly purifies the Church, protecting it from the infection that sin might bring.

d. The Dove – the symbol of new life

In Genesis chapter 8, when God has destroyed all life on the earth because of sin, only Noah, his kinfolk, and a group of animals remain alive on the ark. As they wait for the waters to subside, they send out a dove to see if it can find dry land. Initially, just like the Holy Spirit at creation, the dove "hovers over the waters" but cannot find a resting place and returns to the ark. It is sent out a second time and returns with an olive leaf indicating that the water level is lowering. The third time it is sent out it does not return and Noah knows that dry land has appeared and it is safe to come out of the Ark and start life on the earth again. In the Noah story, the dove becomes the symbol of new creation and new hope for the earth.

(1) When God sends Jesus to the earth he also enters the waters, not of the flood, but of the Jordan River in baptism, Luke 3.22.

Ibid. p. 79.

(2) This incident is so important that it is recorded in all four of the Gospel accounts. The appearance of the Holy Spirit as a dove reminds the Jewish audience who sees Jesus baptized that, like Noah, this man is beloved of God and the means of new hope and new creation.

3. The scriptural names and titles of the Holy Spirit reveal him as Life-giver.

a. He is called the Spirit of Truth (John 14.16-17; 15.26; 16.13). He is the one who teaches us the words of life.

b. His is called the Spirit of Holiness (Rom. 1.4). He is the one who enables us to overcome sin and death.

c. He is called the Spirit of Grace (Heb. 10.29). He is the one who freely brings new life to those who could not obtain it through their own efforts.

Ibid. pp. 105, 123, 127, 131, 191.

d. He is called "the Spirit of Life" (Rom. 8.2). He has the ministry of bringing life and is the source of resurrection.

C. "Where there is Life there is hope": the results of the Spirit's life-giving ministry

Rom. 15.13 – May the God of hope fill you with all joy and peace in believing, *so that by the power of the Holy Spirit you may abound in hope*.

1. The Spirit's ministry of hope flows from his critical role in the life-giving renewal of all things.

    a. Ezek. 36.6-37.28

    b. Matt. 19.28 (cf. Titus 3.5)

2. The Spirit as the in-breaking presence of the "Age to Come"

    a. The firstfruits of a renewed creation, Rom. 8.23-24

    b. The guarantee of resurrection and eternal life, 2 Cor. 5.1-5

    c. The down-payment on the rule of Christ in the Age to Come, Eph. 1.13-14, 19-21.

Conclusion

[The] Spirit is at work in history, first bringing humankind into existence and then moving it toward the goal of union [with God]. Spirit is the power released to bring the divine plans to completion. He is Spirit of creation and new creation, concerned with creating community and bringing about the kingdom. Spirit is the power by which this present age will be transformed into the kingdom and which ever works to bring about ultimate fulfillment... The scope is breathtaking. God's breath is on the whole creation – we live and move and have our being in an ocean of love.

~ Clark Pinnock. *Flame of Love*. p. 61.

Student Questions and Response

The following questions were designed to help you review the material in the video. They focus on the Spirit's identity as one who gives life. Be clear and concise in your answers, and where possible, support with Scripture!

1. How are the Old and New Testament ideas about the Spirit of God alike? How are they different?

2. What is the Spirit's role in creation? What does this suggest about his role in the salvation of believers (new creation)?

3. What is providence? What part does the Spirit play in God's care of the world?

4. What are the key symbols of the Holy Spirit in Scripture? How do these contribute to our understanding of the Spirit as the one who gives life?

5. What are biblical titles of the Holy Spirit that emphasize his life-giving ministry?

6. How does the ministry of the Spirit bring hope to all believers?

CONNECTION

Summary of Key Concepts

This lesson focuses upon the person of the Holy Spirit. In it we discussed the following ideas.

- God the Holy Spirit is portrayed in Scripture as the Life-giver who is both the Creator and Sustainer of all life.

- The images and symbols used for the Holy Spirit in the Bible reinforce the idea that the Holy Spirit both gives and sustains all life.

- The scriptural titles of the Holy Spirit demonstrate the scope of his life-giving ministry and even directly name him as "the Spirit of Life."

- The life-giving mission of the Holy Spirit means that he is the source of hope for individuals, for the Church, and for the world.

Student Application and Implications

Now is the time for you to discuss with your fellow students your questions about the material we have covered in this lesson "The Person of the Holy Spirit." Even the most abstract theology is not intended to be an "academic exercise." Theological truth is meant to affect our lives. The most important part of asking and answering questions about the Holy Spirit, is discovering how God wants to change us through what we have learned. What particular questions do you have in light of the material you have just studied? Maybe some of the questions below might help you form your own, more specific and critical questions.

- One of the most consistent shared characteristics of "cults" is that they teach the wrong thing about who God is. (If someone misrepresents God's true nature as revealed in Scripture, they cannot help but misrepresent God's work in the world.) What kind of errors might result from thinking wrongly about the person of the Holy Spirit?

- What are the implications of the fact that the Spirit is sent as the Paraclete; the one called alongside us be the living presence of Jesus in our midst?

- How does the description of the Holy Spirit as the "bond of love" between the Father and the Son affect our understanding of the Spirit's role in our own lives and church communities?

- What are some of the practical ways in which our churches can "worship and glorify the Spirit" along with the Father and the Son?

- Is there any significance to the fact that the Hebrew and Greek words for Spirit also mean "breath" or "wind"? What do these closely related concepts tell us about the Spirit's work?

- How has the Holy Spirit operated as the Life-giver in your own experience? What are the implications of his life-giving power for the way we view ministry?

- Which of the scriptural symbols of the Holy Spirit have been particularly important in your own life? How have they helped you understand the Holy Spirit? How have they affected your understanding of Christian leadership?

- As Christians who are indwelt by the Holy Spirit, we often think of the Spirit's work in very personal terms: the Spirit is the one who lives in me and helps me know and obey God. Is it common for you to also think of the Holy Spirit as the one who is caring for the whole creation and who is preparing the world for the coming reign of Christ? (Explain your answer).

CASE STUDIES

Ready to Give an Answer

 You are teaching a bible study at your church on the doctrine of the Holy Spirit and you remind your students that he is rightly called the Lord and Life-giver. Sue, a visitor who has come to the study only a few times, perks right up when she hears your comment. Sue says, "I usually attend the Unity Church down the street and they gave me a book that talks about that very thing." She pulls out the book and flips through it until she finds these quotes, "God is Spirit, or the creative energy which is the cause of all visible things. . . . God is not a being or person having life, intelligence, love, power. . . . God is that invisible, intangible, but very real, something we call life. . . . Each rock, tree, animal, everything visible, is a manifestation of the one Spirit – God – differing only in degree of manifestation; and each of the numberless modes of manifestation, or individualities, however insignificant, contains the whole" (*Lessons in Truth*, H. Emilie Cady, published by The Unity School of Christianity, pp. 18, 19-20). You realize immediately that she has been studying with a group that does not have a correct doctrine of God or the Trinity. What will you say to her, and to the Bible study group, as you respond to the quote she read?

Searching for Clarity

 Carlos is a new believer in Christ who is trying to understand what the Bible teaches about the Holy Spirit. He says, "It is easy for me to understand who Jesus is. I can read the stories about him in Scripture and know exactly what he said and did. When I put my trust in Christ for salvation, I felt just like Peter did when he told the Lord that he couldn't go anywhere else because Jesus had 'the words of eternal life.' But the Holy Spirit seems very mysterious. I can't seem to imagine what he is like and I am not sure how I am supposed to have a relationship with him. Can you help me figure it out?" How can you use Carlos' current understanding of Jesus to help him understand the Holy Spirit?

Leading Trinitarian Worship

 Many Christian churches follow the Church calendar, setting aside special days and seasons to emphasize important events in the Gospels and the Book of Acts. Suppose your church was celebrating Pentecost Sunday* for the very first time. In your tradition, are there songs, benedictions, actions, decorations, colors, symbols, readings, spiritual giftings, or other forms of worship that particularly focus on the person and work of the Holy Spirit? If you were put in charge of that Pentecost Sunday worship service, what things could you plan that would help your congregation joyfully worship and glorify God the Holy Spirit?

Pentecost Sunday is the 7th Sunday after Easter, and is traditionally a service which remembers and celebrates the coming of the Holy Spirit in fulfillment of the prophecy of Joel (Joel 2.28-32) and the promise of Jesus (John 14.16-17; 16.7; Acts 1.8).

Restatement of the Lesson's Thesis

The Holy Spirit is the Lord; the third person of the one Trinitarian God. He is a distinguishable person in the Godhead who thinks, acts, and loves as fully as the Father and the Son and who fully shares their Divine Nature. As Lord, he is given worship and glory along with the Father and the Son. The Holy Spirit is the Life-giver: the Creator and Sustainer of all life. He is given symbols and titles in Scripture which help us more fully understand his life-giving work. He is also the one who gives new life (regenerates); first through the new birth by which people are made new creations in Christ; and one day still future when he gives birth to a new heavens and a new earth, the home of righteousness.

Resources and Bibliographies

If you are interested in pursuing some of the ideas of *The Person of the Holy Spirit*, you might want to give these books a try:

Bickersteth, Edward Henry. *The Trinity*. Grand Rapids, MI: Kregel Publications, 1977.

Saint Basil. *On the Holy Spirit*. Crestwood, NY: St. Vladimir's Seminary Press, 1980. Also available as an on-line text at the following web sites:

- www.newadvent.org/fathers/3201000.html
- www.monachos.net/patristics/basil/on_holy_spirit_a.shtml

Ministry Connections

Now is the time to try to nail down this high theology by applying it in actual ministry. What truth from the lesson did God quicken to your own heart? What particular situation comes to mind when you think about training people to understand the doctrine of the Holy Spirit? What part of this lesson will you think and pray about through the upcoming week. Reflecting on the person of the Holy Spirit has been challenging and difficult work in the history of the Church. You are called to enter into this long stream of theological reflection and see the practical implications for those that you lead and teach. Fortunately, you can ask the Holy Spirit himself to come and help you understand these deep truths and give you direct guidance as to how they need to affect your life and ministry. Do not neglect to ask the Spirit to illuminate the Scriptures we have studied. He will make clear their meaning and usefulness. The prayer that is located in the next section is a good way to get started on this.

Counseling and Prayer

Holy Spirit of God, "open my eyes to see wonderful things in your word." My understanding is limited, Your understanding is infinite. I "see through a glass darkly," You search the thoughts of the one "who dwells in unapproachable light." Teach me the meaning of the Scriptures you inspired. Illumine my mind to know the truth and to see what you want me to do because of it. Empower me to fulfill my ministry calling. Give me the wisdom to lead others to a true knowledge of You. All this I pray through Jesus Christ, who lives and reigns with You and the Father Almighty, one God, forever blessed. Amen.

ASSIGNMENTS

Scripture Memory Romans 8.15-17

Reading Assignment To prepare for class, please visit *www.tumi.org/books* to find next week's reading assignment, or ask your Mentor.

Other Assignments Your ministry project and your exegetical project should now be outlined, determined, and accepted by your instructor. Make sure that you plan ahead, so you will not be late in turning in your assignments.

Looking Forward to the Next Lesson In our next lesson, *Theology of the Church: The Church at Worship*, we'll consider salvation as the foundation of the Church's worship. We'll see that salvation comes by God's grace alone and that human beings can in no way earn or deserve it. Worship, therefore, is the proper response to the grace of God.

Without question, the Church of Jesus Christ is God's agent for his Kingdom, and the people of his presence. May your study of this material and the Word of God produce in you a deep love and devotion to live for and build up the holy people of God, the Church!

FOR FURTHER STUDY

Please see the following resources in *Picturing Theology: An A-Z Collection of TUMI's Key Diagrams, Charts, Graphics, and Articles*:

- *Areas of Disagreement among Christians Concerning Spiritual Gifts*, page 8

- *Spiritual Gifts Specifically Mentioned in the New Testament*, page 391

- *St. Basil, the Nicene Creed, and the Doctrine of the Holy Spirit*, page 396

- *Some of the Ways in Which Christians Disagree about Sanctification*, page 385

- *The Role of the Holy Spirit in Spiritual Guidance*, page 359

Part Two

Christian Ministry & Urban Mission

Christian Ministry

Theology of the Church:
The Church at Worship

Foundations of Christian Leadership:
The Christian Leader as Pastor – *Poimenes*

Practicing Christian Leadership:
Effective Worship Leading

The Equipping Ministry:
The Ministry of Proclamation – *Kerygma*

Introduction to Christian Ministry Unit

Greetings, in the strong name of Jesus Christ!

Welcome to the third unit of the Cornerstone Curriculum, *Christian Ministry*.

The Church of God in Jesus Christ is one of the most refreshing and important themes of all the Scriptures. Jesus of Nazareth, through his death, burial, and resurrection, has been exalted as head over his new people, those called to represent him in the earth and bear witness of his already/not yet Kingdom. To understand the Church's role in God's kingdom program is critical to every facet of personal and corporate discipleship; there is no discipleship or salvation apart from God's saving action in the Church. Grasping what God is doing in and through his people empowers God's leader to represent him with wisdom and honor. We invite you with enthusiasm to study the Church in order to fully appreciate the nature of ministry in the world today.

In our first lesson, *Theology of the Church: The Church at Worship*, we'll consider salvation as the foundation of the Church's worship. We'll see that salvation comes by God's grace alone and that human beings can in no way earn or deserve it. Worship, therefore, is the proper response to the grace of God.

Without question, the Church of Jesus Christ is God's agent for his Kingdom, and the people of his presence. May your study of this material and the Word of God produce in you a deep love and devotion to live for and build up the holy people of God, the Church!

The leaders of the Church of God are his precious gift to his people throughout the ages. The evidence that Jesus loves his people dearly is that he has granted unto them apostles, prophets, evangelists, pastors and teachers to equip his people to represent the Kingdom of God in this fallen and soon-to-end world (Eph. 4.9-16).

In our second lesson, *Foundations of Christian Leadership: The Christian Leader as Pastor*, we will discuss pastoral authority, and look at three biblical models and analogies of pastoral care: that of a nurturer and care giver, a protector and guardian, and a leader of the flock of God. It is hard to imagine a more wonderful gift to an assembly or group of assemblies than godly, Christlike leadership, true shepherds who guard and protect the flock of God. May God use this study to inspire you to nurture and care for his people, to emulate the Good Shepherd who laid down his life for his sheep.

We demonstrate our devotion to our Savior by practicing a kind of leadership that both honors and glorifies our Lord and edifies and builds up his people.

Our third lesson, *Practicing Christian Leadership: Effective Worship Leading* considers the idea of representation of the Lord Jesus as fundamental in practicing every dimension of Christian leadership as his agents and servants. Closely connected to this important idea, we will also consider carefully the role of ministering the Word and Sacrament among the people of God. What an adventure it is to serve the living God by caring for his dear people!

The ministry of the Word of God lies at the heart of the equipping ministry. Paul tells the Ephesians that God has given the Church apostles, prophets, evangelists, and pastors and teachers in order that they might equip the saints for the work of ministry, for building up the body of Christ (Eph. 4.11-12). There is no precedent for seeing a church as having a single minister: as believers we hold to the universal priesthood of believers (1 Pet. 2.8-9), in the universal ministry of the gifts of the Spirit (1 Cor. 12.1-11), and the universal functioning of the members of the body of Christ (Rom. 12.3-8).

In our fourth lesson, *The Equipping Ministry: The Ministry of Proclamation*, we will outline the three steps of planning out, delivering, and following up on the preached Word. As communicators of the Word of God, we must first establish contact with hearers, communicate the content of the Word clearly and boldly, and make connections with the truth of the message and the lives of the audience, proclaiming all in dependence on the Holy Spirit. A revolution can occur in urban ministry when gifted and available men and women minister the Word of God in such a way as to raise up a new generation of laborers in the city – those who can care for the hurting, share the truth of God, and declare the Kingdom to their neighbors. Your role in this ministry is urgent and needed.

May God bless your efforts as you seek to enhance your ability to know, preach, and teach God's living Word of truth!

Unit Assignments

Exegetical Project

As a part of your participation in the Cornerstone Curriculum, you will be required to do an exegesis (inductive study) on a passage in the Word of God:

a. Ephesians 4.1-16

b. Acts 20.24-28

c. 1 Peter 5.1-4

d. 2 Corinthians 4.6-12

The purpose of this exegetical project is to give you an opportunity to do a detailed study of a major passage on the nature and function of the Word of God. As you study one of the above texts (or a text which you and your Mentor agree upon which may not be on the list), our hope is that you will be able to show how this passage illumines or makes plain the significance of the Word of God for our spirituality and for our lives together in the Church. We also desire that the Spirit will give you insight as to how you can relate its meaning directly to your own personal walk of discipleship, as well as to the leadership role God has given to you currently in your church and ministry.

Memory Verses

The memorized Word is a central priority for your life and ministry as a believer and leader in the Church of Jesus Christ. There are relatively few verses, but they are significant in their content. Each class session you will be expected to recite (orally or in writing) the assigned verses to your Mentor.

a. Hebrews 10.19-22

b. Acts 20.26-28

c. 1 Peter 2.9-10

d. 2 Timothy 2.1-2

Textbooks

Each Cornerstone Curriculum unit has assigned textbooks which are read and discussed throughout the course. We encourage you to read, reflect upon, and respond to these with your professors, mentors, and fellow learners. Because of the fluid availability of the texts (e.g., books going out of print), we maintain our *official* Cornerstone Curriculum Required Textbook list on our website. Please visit *www.tumi.org/books* to obtain the current listing of this unit's texts and reading assignments.

Ministry Project

Our sincere desire is that you will apply your learning practically, correlating your learning with real experiences and needs in your personal life, and in your ministry in and through your church. Therefore, a key part of completing the Cornerstone Curriculum will be for you to design a ministry project to help you share some of the insights you have learned from this course with others.

Unit Exam

At the end of each unit, your Mentor will give you a unit exam (closed book) to be completed at home. You will be asked a question that helps you reflect on what you have learned in the unit and how it affects the way you think about or practice ministry. Your Mentor will give you due dates and other information when the Unit Exam is handed out.

Theology of the Church
The Church at Worship

Lesson Objectives

Welcome in the strong name of Jesus Christ! After your reading, study, discussion, and application of the materials in this lesson, you will be able to:

- Defend the idea that salvation comes by God's grace alone and that human beings can in no way earn or deserve it.

- Recognize that worship is the proper response to the grace of God.

- Explain the difference between the terms "sacrament" and "ordinance" and describe the theological perspective that lies behind each term.

- Understand the meaning of baptism and the Lord's Supper and discuss the key differences in the way Christians think about their meaning.

Devotion

We Bring the Sacrifice of Praise

Read Romans 12.1-2, Hebrews 13.15, and Habakkuk 3.17-19. One of the most common ideas associated with the Old Testament form of worship was the idea of sacrifice. In general public worship, as was connected to the services in the temple, those who draw near to God were in every case to bring sacrifices, whether during ordinary times of worship, or especially at important events like the dedication of the temple. At this high moment, the blood of the animals flowed greatly as the worshipers expressed their thanksgiving to God for his great blessing in the establishment of his house (2 Chron. 7.5). What is so amazing is that no one was to come before the presence of God without offering to him something to be sacrificed on his behalf. God deserves our best, highest, and most important offerings, and above our gifts and things, he deserves our very selves. We are to offer to him our highest praise, not merely during those times when we are most refreshed and most able, but even during the times of deepest hardship and greatest trial. Our God is impervious to change; he is worthy to be worshiped however things are going in our lives and ministries. Exalted high above all creation, he is the Lord God, deserving of our best and most focused energies, out best songs, our liveliest dancing, our greatest service, our most aggressive response. The Church at worship always provides to God a sacrifice fitting to his holiness and worthy of his acknowledgment. He is truly worthy to be worshiped, to be offered our praise.

Habakkuk the prophet illumines the way for us in terms of offering to God the sacrifice of praise:

> Hab. 3.17-19 – Though the fig tree should not blossom, nor fruit be on the vines, the produce of the olive fail and the fields yield no food, the flock be cut off from the fold and there be no herd in the stalls, [18] yet I will rejoice in the Lord; I will take joy in the God of my salvation. [19] God, the Lord, is my strength; he makes my feet like the deer's; he makes me tread on my high places.

Let us, therefore, heed the words of the writer to the Hebrews:

> Heb. 13.15 – Through him then let us continually offer up a sacrifice of praise to God, that is, the fruit of lips that acknowledge his name.

Nicene Creed and Prayer

After reciting and/or singing the Nicene Creed (located in the Appendix), pray the following prayer:

> Eternal God, our Father, God and Father of our Lord Jesus Christ, You alone are worthy of all praise, and as such, You require that we give You honor and glory and praise. We approach You in the name of Your beloved Son and our Savior, Jesus Christ, asking that You grant us the power of the Spirit in order to glorify You with our whole hearts in joyful worship in all of our meetings, in all our relationships, in all our actions, and in all our ministries. Receive all that we say and do as an acceptable sacrifice offered to You as the Lord our God, worthy of praise and glory, in Jesus' name we pray, Amen.

Scripture Memorization Review

Review with a partner, write out and/or recite the text for last class session's assigned memory verse: Romans 8.15-17.

Assignments Due

Turn in your summary of the reading assignment for last week, that is, your brief response and explanation of the main points that the authors were seeking to make in the assigned reading (Reading Completion Sheet).

CONTACT

Grace

 I heard a story about a person who was doing an experiment in human behavior. This person stood by the pumps at a gas station in a big city and tried to give away twenty dollar bills to the people who pulled up to the station. To his amazement, no one would take the money. Those of us who live in cities are probably not so surprised at this response. Most people in big cities have learned the hard way that "you don't get something for nothing" and that anyone who appears to be giving away something valuable for free is probably not to be trusted. We urbanites recognize that if something seems too good to be true, then it almost always is. It is natural for us to be suspicious of things that are free. Today's lesson is about worship as a response to the grace of God. The Gospel is the good news that everything we need and could not have is being given to us by God as a free gift of grace. Like the people at the gas pumps, most of us probably did not recognize at first that the grace of God is a completely free gift. When did you first realize that the gift of salvation could never be earned and comes only as a gift to be received?

Going a Little Too Far

 If your church had to answer this question, how would it do so: "All forms of worship and praise are enjoined to give to God, but as far as we are concerned, engaging in (X) is taking worship a little too far." What might it mean in some of our church contexts to go beyond the acceptable boundaries of the way worship is understood in your congregation? Should there be boundaries to our expression of worship, and if so, what ought the standards be to hold such boundaries in conjunction with our freedom in Christ, and our desire to express our love to God in new and unique ways?

Liturgy Is So Boring – Does God Like Us to Be Depressed?

 At the dinner table, one of the children of a church family commented on their view of the church service. In her 13-year-old opinion, church services were too formal, too similar, with a lot of language and activity that didn't mean anything to her. She wondered why the songs were so old, and the music was kinda like going to a funeral home. The whole atmosphere seemed sad and depressing; she didn't know why they had to chant, and sing at certain times, stand up sometimes, and read at other times. It all seems so boring and old-fashioned. She asked her folks why can't church be more exciting, like game shows on TV, or the excitement at athletic events. "Does God like us to be depressed?" she asked. What would you say to the 13 year old about her worship experience at her church, and how God wants her to understand and perceive worshiping together?

The Church at Worship

Rev. Terry G. Cornett

Summary The grace of God comes before all human decision or effort – only his grace can enable people to respond to him. It is because of this grace that the Church can worship God and all of the Church's worship, especially the Lord's Supper and baptism, is meant to be a testimony to, and an experience of, the grace of God.

Our objective for this lesson, *The Church at Worship,* is to enable you to:

- Give a definition of grace.
- Distinguish between grace and mercy.
- Identify and answer the Pelagian heresy.
- Explain the difference between the term "sacrament" and the term "ordinance."
- Name and briefly explain the four major Christian views about the Lord's Supper.

Video Outline **I. *Sola Gratia* (Grace Alone)**

Rev. 22.21
The grace of the Lord Jesus be with all. Amen.

    A. Grace is an essential attribute of who God is.

        1. Exod. 34.6-7

        2. John 1.14

3. Eph. 1.6

4. Heb. 10.29

B. Grace is undeserved favor. When God is gracious he acts lovingly toward us even though we have no reason to claim or expect that kindness.

C. The difference between "grace" and "mercy"

1. Mercy is God withholding what we actually deserve.

2. Grace is God giving us what we don't deserve.

3. In the New Testament Scriptures, grace means that God acts toward us just as he does toward his Son Jesus. Therefore, grace is truly unmerited and undeserved favor.

D. What do we mean when we insist that everything we have is *Sola Gratia*, by grace alone?

1. First of all, we mean that every human being who has ever lived comes into the world locked up under sin and is in a completely hopeless position, Rom. 3.10-12.

    The Pelagian error or heresy, is the belief that a person is not born with a sinful nature and can seek and believe in God completely out of their own free will. The Church has rejected the Pelagian error and taught from the Scriptures that a person can come to God only because the grace of God is already working in them.

> If anyone says that the grace of God can be conferred as a result of human prayer, but that it is not grace itself which makes us pray to God, he contradicts the prophet Isaiah, or the Apostle John who says the same thing, "I have been found by those who did not seek me; I have shown myself to those who did not ask for me"... The sin of the first man has so impaired and weakened free will that no one thereafter can either love God as he ought or believe in God or do good for God's sake, unless the grace of divine mercy has preceded him.
>
> ~ The Council of Orange (529 A.D.)

2. Secondly, we mean that because salvation comes only through faith it cannot ever be earned by anyone. Salvation can only be received as a free gift, not deserved through acts of goodness. Salvation is completely a gift of God's grace.

    a. Eph. 2.8-9

    b. Acts 20.24

    c. Gal. 2.21

    d. Any good work or righteous act we do is a result of God's grace working in us. Good works are the result of salvation not the cause of it. No good work gains us any extra favor with God. No one can be good enough to earn a relationship with God or eternal life with him in his Kingdom. We have his grace poured out on us because of Christ and what his work has done for us. Our good works are a response to the grace that God has given. Again, as the Apostle John says, "we love him because he first loved us," 1 John 4.19.

II. Worship Is the Church's Response to the Grace of God.

Worship is always the single most important responsibility of the Church because it is the starting point for living by grace. In worship, we acknowledge that as James wrote in his Epistle, "Every good gift and every perfect gift is from above, coming down from the Father of lights," James 1.17a.

A. Two pivotal events in Christian worship (the meal and the bath)

In every Christian tradition, the Lord's Supper and baptism are important parts of the way in which we experience the grace of God at work among us. Christians differ, however, as to how these acts of worship demonstrate God's grace in the Church. Some churches call the Lord's Supper and baptism "sacraments" and understand them as a "means of grace" while others refer to them as "ordinances" and understand them as a testimony to the grace of God. Let me explain the difference.

B. The meaning of "sacrament"

1. A sacrament is usually defined as "an outward and visible sign of an inward and spiritual grace." Those who use the term sacrament would see baptism and the Lord's Supper as a means by which the grace of God comes to us.

2. Although Catholics and Eastern Orthodox Christians have many sacraments, Protestants have usually reserved the term sacrament only for baptism and the Lord's Supper. These two sacraments have a special place in the history of the Church as a particularly important "means of grace" because they were directly instituted by the command of Jesus. Those who define the Lord's Supper and baptism as sacraments would argue that when they are received in faith, God is graciously at work in us to fulfill his promises.

C. The meaning of "ordinance"

1. There are many church traditions which understand the Lord's Supper and baptism as ordinances, rather than sacraments. The word "ordinance" means an "authoritative command" and so the Lord's Supper and baptism are done in obedience to the command of Christ. Rather than being a means by which God's grace comes to us, these churches argue that in baptism and the Lord's Supper we remember and testify to the grace of God which we have already received.

2. Exod. 12.14 – This is a day you are to commemorate; for the generations to come you shall celebrate it as a festival to the LORD – a lasting ordinance.

3. The focus of most Old Testament ordinances was to help people remember to obey by means of a command or religious ceremony. In the New Testament, baptism and the Lord's Supper serve as public testimony to the grace that God gave to us through Jesus' life, death and resurrection and reminds us that the Church exists and lives through this grace.

III. Baptism: How Is Baptism Related to Salvation?

A. Those who see baptism as a sacrament see it as a means by which God's grace becomes effective for salvation. In sacramental theology, baptism is important for regeneration.

1. Scriptural support for baptism as a sacrament or means of grace:

    a. Acts 2.38

    b. Acts 22.16

c. Mark 16.15-16

d. 1 Pet. 3.20-22

"The Thirty-Nine Articles of Religion" which is the core creed of churches in the Methodist and Episcopal tradition describes the sacramental doctrine of Baptism like this. "They that receive Baptism rightly are grafted into the Church; the promises of the forgiveness of sin, and of our adoption to be the sons of God by the Holy Ghost, are visibly signed and sealed; Faith is confirmed, and Grace increased by virtue of prayer unto God."

~John H. Leith, ed. *Creeds of the Churches.* Louisville: John Knox Press, 1983. pp. 275-76

---

2. It is important to understand that those who see baptism as a sacrament are *not* teaching baptismal regeneration.

    Baptismal regeneration is the false belief that baptism by itself will save a person simply because the act of baptism has been performed. At times in the past, the Catholic Church seemed to teach something very close to this, but today both Catholic and Protestant teaching agree that the key element of baptism is faith. The Church father Gregory of Nyssa emphasized that if a person is baptized but does not combine it with genuine repentance then, "in these cases the water is but water, for the gift of the Holy Ghost in no way appears in him who is thus baptismally born."

B. Those who define baptism as an ordinance see it as a symbol by which a person declares their identification with Christ and his Church. Baptism is important for incorporation into the Church.

1. Scriptural support for baptism as an ordinance or symbol:

    a. Acts 10.47

b. 1 Cor. 1.14-17

2. The key motivation for baptism is obedience.

The Holman Bible Dictionary, which represents the Baptist tradition, says:

Baptism is not a requirement of salvation, but it is a requirement of obedience. Baptism is a first step of discipleship. Although all meanings of baptism are significant, the one that most often comes to mind is water baptism as a picture of having come to know Christ as Lord and Savior. Baptism is never the event but, rather, the picture of the event. So the pattern of obedience is to come to Christ in trust and then to picture that through the symbol of baptism.

~ Trent C. Butler, Gen. ed. *Holman Bible Dictionary* (electronic ed.). Nashville: Holman Bible Publishers, 1991.

C. Baptism is equally important in both sacramental and ordinance traditions.

Baptism is given and commanded by Christ himself. It is never optional or dispensable. Therefore, both for those who see it as a sacrament and those who see it as an ordinance, baptism is the defining mark that a person has committed themselves to the lordship of Jesus Christ.

IV. The Lord's Supper

A. Common terms:

1. The Lord's Supper is a common name for this act of worship.

2. You may also hear it called the *eucharist* (which means "thanksgiving meal"), Communion, or the Lord's Table.

   The Lord's Supper was given to the Church by Jesus himself on the night before he was arrested.

B. Established by Jesus Christ

   1. Matt. 26.26-29

   2. 1 Cor. 11.23-26

C. Observed regularly from the earliest days of the Church onward

There is in the Lord's Supper a constant renewal of the covenant between God and the Church. The word 'remembrance' (anamnesis) refers not simply to man's remembering of the Lord but also to God's remembrance of his Messiah and his covenant, and of his promise to restore the Kingdom. At the Supper all this is brought before God in true intercessory prayer.

~ R. S. Wallace. "Lord's Supper." *Evangelical Dictionary of Theology.* Walter A. Elwell, ed. Grand Rapids: Baker, 1984. p. 653.

All the early evidence . . . indicated that while the elements of the service [of the early Church] had no fixed sequence, the climactic event of the weekly service on the Lord's Day was the sacrament of the Lord's Supper.

~ R. G. Rayburn. "Worship in the Church." *Evangelical Dictionary of Theology.* Walter A. Elwell, ed. Grand Rapids: Baker, 1996. p. 1193.

The [Lord's Supper] might be celebrated in the most becoming manner, if it were dispensed to the Church very frequently, at least once a week. . . . We ought always to provide that no meeting of the Church is held without the word, prayer, dispensation of the Supper, and [collecting money for the poor].

~ John Calvin. *Institutes.* 4.17.43-44.

A second reason why every Christian should [take communion] as often as he can is, because the benefits of doing it are so great. . . . The grace of God given herein confirms to us the pardon of our sins, by enabling us to leave them. As our bodies are strengthened by bread and wine, so are our souls by these tokens of the body and blood of Christ. This is the food of our souls: This gives strength to perform our duty, and leads us on to perfection. If, therefore, we have any regard for the plain command of Christ, if we desire the pardon of our sins, if we wish for strength to believe, to love and obey God, then we should neglect no opportunity of receiving the Lord's Supper; then we must never turn our backs on the feast which our Lord has prepared for us. We must neglect no occasion which the good providence of God affords us for this purpose. This is the true rule: So often are we to receive as God gives us opportunity. Whoever, therefore, does not receive, but goes from the holy table, when all things are prepared, either does not understand this duty, or does not care for the dying command of his Savior, the forgiveness of his sins, the strengthening of his soul, and the refreshing it with the hope of glory.

~ John Wesley. "Sermon 101: The Duty of Constant Communion." *The Works of John Wesley*. Vol. 7-8. p. 148.

D. The Lord's Supper is to be eaten in repentance and faith.

1. One of the reasons that Protestant reformers first broke away from Catholic churches was because they felt that the sacraments were being viewed as a magic action rather than as the grace of God received by faith.

2. The Lord's Supper is not like a magic ritual which causes grace to be given just by participating in the action.

The early Protestant reformers objected to the Catholic doctrine which was known as *ex opere operato*. (This is a Latin phrase that means "by the very fact of the action's being performed.") This meant that if the sacrament was given it produced the desired effect whether or not the person offering it or the person receiving it were acting in faith. Reformers objected that this had caused people to view the sacraments as magic: that getting baptized or taking the Lord's Supper made you into a Christian. Their response was that a person becomes a Christian and grows as a Christian "by faith alone."

Catholics continue to teach *ex opere operato* but have nuanced their teaching to reemphasize that receiving the sacraments in faith is not just a Protestant idea but is necessary to the Catholic view as well by saying that "[the sacraments] presuppose faith" and that, "celebrated worthily in faith, the sacraments confer grace."

~ *Catechism of the Catholic Church.*
Liguori, MO: Liguori Publications, 1994. pp. 291-293.

E. There are four basic Christian views on the Lord's Supper (see *The Lord's Supper: Four Views* on page 264 in *Picturing Theology: An A-Z Collection of TUMI's Key Diagrams, Charts, Graphics, and Articles*).

1. *Transubstantiation* is the belief that the bread and wine become the literal body and blood of Jesus Christ. This is the view of the Lord's Supper held by Roman Catholic Christians.

    a. Matt. 26.26

    b. John 6.53-60

By the miracle of the loaves and the fishes and the walking upon the waters, on the previous day, Christ not only prepared his hearers for the sublime discourse [of John 6] containing the promise of the Eucharist, but also proved to them that he possessed, as Almighty God-man, a power superior to and independent of the laws of nature, and could therefore, provide such a supernatural food, no other, in fact than his own Flesh and Blood.

~ Joseph Pohle. "Eucharist." *Readings in Christian Theology.* Vol. 3. Millard Erickson, ed.
Grand Rapids: Baker, 1973.

2. *Consubstantiation* is the belief that the bread and wine become the literal body and blood of Jesus without ceasing to be bread and wine. This is the view of the Lord's Supper held by Lutheran churches. This view accepts the basic idea discussed above that the real body and blood of Jesus is present in the Lord's Supper but has a different explanation of how they are present together.

3. The third view is the *Reformed* view. Presbyterian and Reformed churches teach that the body and blood of Christ are given to us in the Supper, not physically, but spiritually through the power and presence of the Holy Spirit.

    This tradition would point out that in the John 6 passage that as Jesus teaches about eating his flesh, he goes on to emphasize this as a spiritual truth:

    John 6.60-63 – On hearing it, many of his disciples said, "This is a hard teaching. Who can accept it?" Aware that his disciples were grumbling about this, Jesus said to them, "Does this offend you? What if you see the Son of Man ascend to where he was before! The Spirit gives life; the flesh counts for nothing. The words I have spoken to you are spirit and they are life."

In this sacrament Christ is present not bodily but spiritually.... His people receive him not with the mouth, but by faith; they do not receive his flesh and blood as material particles, but his body as broken and his blood as shed. The union thus signified ... [is] a spiritual and mystical union due to the indwelling of the Holy Spirit. The [effectiveness] of this sacrament as a means of grace is not in the signs nor in the service, nor in the minister, nor in the word, but in the attending influence of the Holy Ghost.

~ Charles Hodge. *Systematic Theology*. Abridged edition. Grand Rapids: Baker, 1992. pp. 496-498.

---

   a. Col. 3.1

b. John 16.7

Although most Pentecostal traditions are Memorialist, the Pentecostal scholar Gordon Fee defends a similar view to Calvin's when he says: "Indeed, one would not be far wrong to see the Spirit's presence at the Table as Paul's way of understanding the real presence. The analogy of Israel's having had 'Spiritual food,' and 'Spiritual drink' in 1 Corinthians 10.3-4 at least allows as much."

~ Gordon Fee. *Paul, the Spirit and the People of God.* Peabody, MA: Hendrickson Publishers, 1996. p. 154.

---

4. The Memorialist view believes that the bread and wine only symbolize the body and the blood of Christ and help us to remember what he had done for us.

    a. Unlike the first three views which all see the Lord's table as a sacrament, the Memorialist view sees the Lord's table as an ordinance.

The Lord's Supper has no regenerative power, it possesses no sanctifying grace. There is nothing magical or mystical about its nature. It is a symbol of the relation of the believer to Christ, who alone does the sanctifying. The outward tokens devised by Christ himself are the symbols of the atoning power and forgiving love of his great sacrifice, which was once and for all efficacious.

~ Williams Stevens. "The Lord's Supper." *Readings in Christian Theology.* Millard Erickson, ed. Grand Rapids: Baker, 1973.

---

    b. Luke 22.19

    c. 1 Cor. 11.23-24

F. What all the differing views about the Lord's Supper share in common:

1. Every part of Christian theology believes that the Lord's Supper is:

   a. An essential part of Christian worship

   b. A direct command of Christ to his Church

   c. A time that draws us closer to God and to our fellow believers

   d. A time that allows us to grasp hold of God's grace and respond to him with gratitude and praise

   e. Meant to be received in faith and to help us place our complete faith in the work of Christ

   f. A time in which sins can be dealt with and placed under God's forgiving mercy

2. We may disagree on how the Lord's Supper causes these things to happen but those disagreements should not cause us to lose sight of the fundamental importance of the Supper in our life of worship. It is a gift of God's grace to his Church.

Conclusion

- Worship is the response of the Church to the grace of God.

- Salvation comes completely by the grace of God and there is no human being that can say that they have earned their salvation by what they have done.

- Baptism and the Lord's Supper are especially significant parts of Christian worship.

- The Church differs on how to understand the Lord's Supper and baptism. Some believe that they are sacraments, that is a means by which the grace of God comes to us while others believe that they are ordinances which symbolize and testify to the grace of God.

Student Questions and Response

Please take as much time as you have available to answer these and other questions that the video brought out. These questions were designed to help you review the material in this lesson related to God's grace as the basis of the Church's worship. As you answer these questions, try to form clear convictions about what the Scriptures teach in regard to the grace of God. Since Bible believing Christians differ about how the grace of God comes to us in the Lord's Supper and baptism, please listen closely and respectfully to those in the class who may disagree with you. Be clear and concise in your answers, and where possible, support with Scripture!

1. What does *sola gratia* mean and why is it important?

2. What is the Pelagian heresy?

3. What is the difference between Christian traditions that describe baptism and the Lord's Supper as *sacraments* and those that think of them as *ordinances*?

4. What are the main biblical arguments for and against seeing baptism as a "means of grace"?

5. What are the four major views about the Lord's Supper?

6. Why is baptismal regeneration (the belief that being baptized causes salvation) an unscriptural doctrine? How is this different from a sacramental view of baptism?

7. Why did the Protestant reformers disagree with the Catholic doctrine of *ex opere operato*?

8. What role does faith play in our experience of the sacraments/ordinances?

CONNECTION

Summary of Key Concepts

This lesson focuses upon the foundational approach we as members of the Church have with God, that is, on the grounds of grace alone through faith in Christ, and how the experience of this grace expresses itself in authentic praise, adoration, thanksgiving and worship to God through Jesus Christ. In one sense, understanding these foundational concepts are at the heart of what it means to serve the Church as one of its leaders, and helps us to discern when a congregation is healthy or sick, depending on its experience of God's unmerited favor and grace in Christ, and the active expression of its gratitude through its way of life in worship. Below are some of the foundational concepts associated with worship, the Church's true vocation.

- Salvation is completely a free gift of God to be received by faith and cannot be earned or deserved.

- Human beings are so enslaved by sin that they cannot desire the right things unless the grace of God works in them first.

- God always is the first to act in bringing someone to salvation. "We love him because he first loved us."

- Because the Church is a community of people who have experienced the grace of God, worship is both the duty and the joy of the Church.

- The "meal and the bath" (Lord's Supper and baptism) are part of the way in which we experience and remember the grace of God. They are key elements of Christian worship.

- A sacrament is a means by which the grace of God is given to us while an ordinance is an action that acknowledges grace through obedience and remembrance. Both types of theology emphasize that participation in the Lord's Supper and baptism is helpful only if it is combined with repentance and faith.

- Christian leaders must study the Scriptures and decide whether it is best to understand the Lord's Supper and baptism as sacraments or as ordinances.

Student Application and Implications

Now is the time for you to discuss with your fellow students your questions about the Church at worship. To comprehend the strategic role of grace in establishing a relationship between God and the worshiping community, as well as the freedom and responsibility the Church has to exalt God is foundational to being a leader for God today. It may arguably be said that until a person understands and can articulate these truths with one's words and deeds, one cannot exercise effective leadership in the Church. Go over these questions to see if you fully grasp both the facts and implications of the material, and how it relates to you and your relationships in ministry. What particular questions do you have in light of the material you have just studied about your own understanding of these truths? Maybe some of the questions below might help you form your own, more specific and critical questions.

- Although most people have never heard of the "Pelagian heresy," there are many people who commit it. How would a person who misunderstood salvation in this way talk about what it means to become a Christian?

- Does your church (or denomination) understand the Lord's Supper and baptism to be sacraments or ordinances? Why?

- How often should a church take the Lord's Supper together? Why?

- To what extent does your worship team at your church fully grasp the facts and implications associated with worship as the Church's vocation?

- How free is the expression of your church's worship in terms of the physical and psychological expressions exhorted in the Bible? How much are these injunctions to shout, clap, and dance "cultural expressions" versus biblical mandates for worship? Explain your answer.

- What is the nature of your church's "liturgy," in other words, how your church organize its services and celebrations in order to "retell the story" in its worship services? What prevents this from being more effective in your church?

- How does one shift the cultural climate of a congregation from stiff, familiar worship to dynamic and life-giving praise? What are the steps to such a situation?

CASE STUDIES

Showing Off Unnecessarily

1. In a local congregation which has more than its fair share of gifted musicians and singers, the church has begun to grow through its dynamic and remarkably excellent worship services. Some have begun to complain, however, because the music minister has made it more difficult for so-called "ordinary" worshipers to be on the worship team or the praise band. All singers must be auditioned for their vocal quality and ability to read music, and no musicians are allowed to participate on the praise band who cannot read sheet music and accompany the beautiful (but difficult) arrangements selected for the songs. The minister of music is strong in his opinion that God is excellent and therefore our worship should be as excellent as possible. What would your counsel be to the music minister if he asked you to comment on the direction the worship was taking in this congregation?

You Can't Make Me Worship

2. The new worship leader in church has been emphasizing the need for active, physical expression during the worship service. He is very strong in his opinion that we ought to employ all the different means Scripture speaks of in expressing our love to God – clapping, lifting and waving our hands, shouting, dancing, kneeling, being silent, lying prostrate, making joyful noise – we ought to show our love to God with our bodies. A small but determined group in the church is dead set against all of this motion and commotion, and wants to end this emphasis on all this bodily expression. After all, this isn't a pro football game, but the worship of Almighty God. Conflict is brewing among the members about what is most appropriate for this church. How would you help them resolve this issue?

Grace Alone

3. A pastor is witnessing to a young woman about Jesus and invites her to attend church. The woman replies, "I'm not really good enough right now to be doing that. I'm interested in religion and stuff but I want to get my life together first. Once I clean some things up, then I'll come to church." What should the pastor say to this young woman?

Getting Down for the Lord

 A new jazz-funk-rock praise band has emerged from the church who call themselves *Selah*. They are determined to bring praise and worship to a whole new level of intensity and power in the congregation, but are doing it with an "in your face" kind of volume and showmanship that has many members of the church, even some of the staff, concerned about them. Selah is experiencing real popularity in their Saturday evening concerts, and have been used of the Lord greatly in some of the evangelistic outreaches around town. Yet, when you hear them, they sound exactly like secular bands. As a matter of fact, many of their songs use the melody of popular pop music songs set to Christian lyrics. Some people have admitted they come to their concerts to dance! How would you advise Selah as it attempts to give full expression to their love for God in worship, while continuing to, as the drummer says, "get down for the Lord?"

Restatement of the Lesson's Thesis

There is nothing we can do to desire or obtain salvation that is not given to us as a free gift by the grace of God. This experience of God's grace causes the Church to become community whose duty and delight is to worship God. We glorify God in our worship because of his perfect character – his solitary holiness, his infinite beauty, his incomparable glory and his matchless works. Through the grace of God in Jesus Christ, we have been set free to worship the true God, the Triune God in the power of the Holy Spirit. In addition, the Church worships God through its praise and thanksgiving, through liturgy, which emphasizes the Word and the sacraments, and through its obedience and lifestyle as a covenant community.

Resources and Bibliographies

If you are interested in pursuing some of the ideas associated with the themes brought up in this lesson, *The Church at Worship*, you might want to give these books a try:

Boschman, Lamar. *The Rebirth of Music*. Shippensburg: Destiny Image, 2000.

Bridges, Jerry. *Transforming Grace: Living Confidently in God's Unfailing Love*. Colorado Springs, CO: NavPress, 1993.

Engle, Paul E. *Baker's Worship Handbook*. Grand Rapids: Baker Book House, 1998.

Hill, Andrew E. *Enter His Courts With Praise!* Grand Rapids: Baker Book House, 1993.

Oden, Thomas C. *The Transforming Power of Grace*. Nashville: Abingdon Press, 1993.

Webber, Robert. *Planning Blended Worship*. Nashville: Abingdon, 1998.

Ministry Connections

Now is the time in the lesson to discover what facets of this biblical theology is most applicable to your personal life. Where might the Holy Spirit be calling you to most readily apply in your current ministry situation these teachings on the grace of God, and the worship that a full understanding of that grace leads to in our personal and church lives? Making clear and dynamic ministry connections is a major skill of any qualified leader, and now is an opportunity for you to practice this skill, especially in connection to your own life. Meditate on these truths and see which one(s) you might need to think about and pray for throughout this next week. Be open to how the Holy Spirit might want you to emphasize these truths as you minister to those under your care this week, and ask him for wisdom as you apply these truths to your particular situation.

Counseling and Prayer

Pray to God for yourself and those whom you serve, that you might specifically come to understand and appreciate the power of the transforming grace of God in your life and the lives of those whom you disciple and teach. Ask the Holy Spirit to make Christ's love more real in your personal life, and seek his power as to how you might become more free in expressing your praise and thanksgiving to God for all he is and has done in your life. Especially ask the Lord for insight into those things, areas, habits, or practices in your life which might hinder you from giving more and better praise to God, consistent with our vocation to bring maximum pleasure and honor to God.

ASSIGNMENTS

Scripture Memory Hebrews 10.19-22

Reading Assignment To prepare for class, please visit *www.tumi.org/books* to find next week's reading assignment, or ask your Mentor.

Other Assignments

Read the assigned reading and summarize each reading with no more than a paragraph or two for each. In this summary please give your best understanding of what you think was the main point in each of the readings. Do not be overly concerned about giving detail; simply write out what you consider to be the main point discussed in that section of the book. Please bring these summaries to class next week. (Please see the "Reading Completion Sheet" on page 16.)

Looking Forward to the Next Lesson

In our next lesson, *Foundations of Christian Leadership: The Christian Leader as Pastor*, we will discuss pastoral authority, and look at three biblical models and analogies of pastoral care: that of a nurturer and care giver, a protector and guardian, and a leader of the flock of God. It is hard to imagine a more wonderful gift to an assembly or group of assemblies than godly, Christlike leadership, true shepherds who guard and protect the flock of God. May God use this study to inspire you to nurture and care for his people, to emulate the Good Shepherd who laid down his life for his sheep.

Please see the following resources in *Picturing Theology: An A-Z Collection of TUMI's Key Diagrams, Charts, Graphics, and Articles*:

- *Salvation as Joining the People of God*, page 371
- *There Is a River*, page 479
- *Theology of the Church*, page 458
- *The Lord's Supper: Four Views*, page 264
- *Christus Victor: An Integrated Vision for the Christian Life*, page 43

Foundations of Christian Leadership
The Christian Leader as Pastor – *Poimenes*

Lesson Objectives

Welcome in the strong name of Jesus Christ! After your reading, study, discussion, and application of the materials in this lesson, you will be able to:

- Elaborate the three biblical models and analogies of what a pastor does in relationship to the flock of God, i.e., the pastor as nurturer and care giver, as protector and guardian, and as leader of the flock of God.

- Give evidence of the particular perils and promise for fulfilling the pastoral role in the inner city, as well as the specific ways we may equip urban pastors for their important duty.

- Discuss some of the more important principles in the practice of pastoring the urban congregation, as well as the wonderful promises associated with the pastoring of the flock of God.

Devotion

An Unusual Occupation

John 10.10-18 – The thief comes only to steal and kill and destroy. I came that they may have life and have it abundantly. [11] I am the good shepherd. The good shepherd lays down his life for the sheep. [12] He who is a hired hand and not a shepherd, who does not own the sheep, sees the wolf coming and leaves the sheep and flees, and the wolf snatches them and scatters them. [13] He flees because he is a hired hand and cares nothing for the sheep. [14] I am the good shepherd. I know my own and my own know me, [15] just as the Father knows me and I know the Father; and I lay down my life for the sheep. [16] And I have other sheep that are not of this fold. I must bring them also, and they will listen to my voice. So there will be one flock, one shepherd. [17] For this reason the Father loves me, because I lay down my life that I may take it up again. [18] No one takes it from me, but I lay it down of my own accord. I have authority to lay it down, and I have authority to take it up again. This charge I have received from my Father.

Jesus used vivid metaphors and images to communicate his understanding of caring for his people, and one of his most cherished was the image of the shepherd. He addressed himself as the "Good

Shepherd," the one who would, in obedience to his Father's command, gladly give his life for the sheep, his redeemed company. Throughout every dimension of his life and ministry our Lord stands out as one who offered care to those who were in need, whatever their lot, situation, or position. Whether spending time with one of the rulers in Israel in dialogue (Nicodemus) or befriending a lonely, spurned Samaritan woman, our Lord provided clear evidence of his caring heart, of the nature of true pastoral care.

Our Lord was neither biased nor bigoted, and never seemed to berate or belittle the individuals that he encountered and cared for. He met each particular individual in the moment and at the point of their specific need. In all of the representative examples of his rich ministry provided in the NT, our Lord respected the dignity and worth of each one, whether, child, woman, or man. Our Lord did not believe that "one size fits all" in terms of caring for the people he encountered in his ministry. Rather, he was careful to honor the individuality and uniqueness of each person's situation, and tailored his own particular response to that person's need, lack, and burden. This kind of specific, particular, and contextualized care is the heart and soul of the pastoral ministry, and is also why the art of pastoring is so little practiced today.

At a time when many pastors envision the role of the senior pastor as a religious CEO who does not "dirty his hands" in the details of people's lives, we desperately need a new (or rather, a truly old) kind of pastoral leadership. A great need exists to rediscover the nature of biblical caring, a kind of ministry which is focused on meeting the needs of individual persons, particular families, and specific neighborhoods and communities. Look again at the remarkable care of our Lord to specific individuals – the widow of Nain, the blind Bartemeus, Zacchaeus the publican, and the demoniac of the Gadarenes. In each case it is the same Lord loving, caring, comforting, but also in each case his grace and care are given in a particular way. Our Lord did not love from afar nor even at arm's length. He got close enough to touch the ones he ministered to, and as a result of his specific and particular love for each and every sheep in their own life context, he transformed their lives.

What kind of motivations and incentives will enable us to find individuals willing to give this kind of taxing, exhausting, and costly care to those who so desperately need spiritual shepherding? Ephesians 4 suggests that it is *God alone* who provides pastors to his people, gifted, available persons who like our Lord are willing to lay down their lives for the sheep. God alone can provide the kind of Christian leadership that his people need, care givers that will follow our Lord's example and become the kind of sacrificing shepherds that he was, which culminated with his remarkable act of dying on our behalf. In light of the shortage of godly pastors for our cities, we need to fervently and continuously ask God to give to us what he promised his people of Israel so many centuries ago: "And I will give you shepherds after my own heart, who will feed you with knowledge and understanding" (Jer. 3.15). How we desperately need pastors who, like our dear Lord, will lay down their lives for the sheep.

R. Robert Cueni has given a funny, fine, and factual summary of the odyssey of care giving as a pastor: Being a pastor is . . .

- Spending three years studying systematic theology only to discover that the most scholarly comment that people respond to is "God loves you."

- Never having enough money to pay one's bills and enough time to count one's blessings.

- Receiving two anonymous letters in the same week – one correcting the grammar in last Sunday's sermon and the other containing money to be given to a family experiencing difficulty.

- Seldom living near relatives but always near friends.

- Trying not to laugh when asked to say a blessing at the dedication of the town's new sewage treatment plant.

- Always working overtime but seldom feeling the need to watch the clock.

- Uniting with God's children at all of the turning points of life.

- Sharing the joys of the wedding, the birth of the child, the baptism of the believer, and tears in the hospital and the funeral home.

- Pushing the button of hope for those who have hit bottom.

May God give all of us, whether he calls us to the pastorate or not, to be care givers like our Lord, and be willing to lay down our lives for our brothers and sisters, for the glory of God through Christ.

Nicene Creed and Prayer

After reciting and/or singing the Nicene Creed (located in the Appendix), pray the following prayer:

A prayer for pastors...

O God, Father of our Lord Jesus Christ, who sent Thy Son not to be ministered unto but to minister, and who made him the great Head of the Church, set apart and consecrate this thy servant for the work of the ministry. Give him thy wisdom, and in counsel may he deal wisely as one who has the mind of Christ. Grant him thy spirit of compassion for human needs and fill him with love that he may tenderly care for every soul whom thou dost so graciously love. Strengthen and nourish his faith in thee and in the values of thy Church, that he may increase the faith of his fellow Christians. Cause his study to be meaningful and his work in thy Church fruitful. And give grace unto us all that working together, seeking to know thy will, we may advance thy cause in this place and throughout the world; to the glory of him who preached good news to the captives, even Christ our Lord. Amen.

~ John E. Skoglund. *A Manual of Worship.* Valley Forge, PA: Judson Press, 1968. p. 256.

Scripture Memorization Review

Review with a partner, write out and/or recite the text for last class session's assigned memory verse: Hebrews 10.19-22.

Assignments Due

Turn in your summary of the reading assignment for last week, that is, your brief response and explanation of the main points that the authors were seeking to make in the assigned reading (Reading Completion Sheet).

CONTACT

A Non-pastoral Pastor

It has now become fashionable in the culture of the mega-church for many senior pastors to delegate the responsibility for pastoral care to "staff" who do the menial work of counseling the depressed and bereaved, visiting the sick, and nurturing the individuals and families which make up the membership of the church. The role of the senior pastor is to be the "up front" person, the "public face" of the church, the one who teaches in the prime time of the congregation's public ministry, whether on television, radio, or the Internet. This kind of

phenomena has created the reality of the "non-pastoral Pastor," a person who is called the "pastor" of the church, but in fact, does virtually no pastoral ministry with actual families or individuals. What do you think of these kinds of trends in the church? Is the nature of the pastoral call to ministry to *specific individuals and families* or can you in fact pastor a congregation of 3,000, 5,000, or even 10,000 members? It is legitimate to delegate virtually all pastoral responsibility to others, while retaining the title of "pastor"?

Brother X on Television Is My Pastor

In a corresponding way, many now associate their spiritual authority and pastoral oversight to presenters on various religious broadcasts on television or radio. It is not uncommon today to meet believers who claim that their primary spiritual input and authority comes from this, that, or the other television preacher. They purchase their materials, religiously "attend" their presentations on the radio and television, and identify with their emphases, perspectives, and initiatives. They give to their ministries, and associate with their fellow followers. Is it possible or desirable to claim that a person who teaches on radio, television, or on the web *is your spiritual authority, and to see that person as your pastor?*

A Lost Art

An entire generation of urban pastors who were mentored in the art of offering care for the poor and the oppressed is about to be lost. We are speaking here of those faithful shepherds who have given themselves selflessly on behalf of little, anonymous congregations who needed the faithful guidance of a spiritually mature servant who was willing to pour out their lives for the sake of Christ's little ones in the city. Many of these dear pastors never received any formal theological training, yet served small urban congregations for little or no remuneration, and usually were forced to work another job in order to pastor their flocks. Still, in spite of hardship and sacrifice, these servants poured out their lives for others. What is interesting to note is that most of these pastors who served in this ways were mentored in this role, that is, they learned this art from others who had given the same kind of service for the poor. It is becoming increasingly rare to find those willing to give themselves with this level of selflessness and sacrifice, especially on behalf of congregations who can offer little in terms of financial support. How do we recover this "lost art" of equipping pastors who will care selflessly for congregations which will never be able to afford their full salary, benefits, and perks known in larger churches?

The Christian Leader as Pastor (*Poimenes*)

Models, Training, and Practice

Rev. Dr. Don L. Davis

CONTENT

Summary

The Word of God provides three clear models and analogies of what a pastor does as care giver to the people of God as his flock. The pastor is a nurturer who ensures that God's people receive proper nourishment, feeding, tending, and care. Furthermore, the pastor is a protector and guardian who guards the people of God against any predators or situations which would seek to harm or destroy them. Finally, the pastor is a leader called to go before the people of God and lead them into the fullness of the will of God for their individual and corporate lives. More than ever before the urban church needs pastors who will nourish, protect, and lead urban disciples of Christ to mature in Christ and give witness to the Kingdom of God in the city. God makes unequivocal promises to those who faithfully fulfill their work of shepherding the flock of God – they will receive the unfading crown of glory when the Chief Shepherd appears at the Second Coming.

Our objective for this lesson, *The Christian Leader as Pastor: Models, Training, and Practice*, is to enable you to see that:

- The Word of God provides three clear models and analogies of what a pastor does as care giver to the people of God as his flock: the pastor as nurturer, as protector, and as leader.

- The pastor is a nurturer who ensures that God's people receive proper nourishment, feeding, tending, and care.

- In addition, the pastor is a protector and guardian who guards the people of God against any predators or situations which would seek to harm or destroy them.

- Finally, the pastor is a leader called to go before the people of God and lead them into the fullness of the will of God for their individual and corporate lives.

- Because of the unique problems and challenges of urban communities, more than ever before the urban church needs pastors who will nourish, protect, and lead urban disciples of Christ to mature in Christ and give witness to the Kingdom of God in the city.

- God makes unequivocal promises to those who faithfully fulfill their work of shepherding the flock of God – they will receive the unfading crown of glory when the Chief Shepherd appears at the Second Coming.

Video Outline

I. Models and Analogies of the Pastorate

A. The pastor is a nurturer.

The pastor is a nurturer, one who ensures that the flock of God receives its proper nourishment and feeding, tending and care.

1. As the Shepherd of Israel, God's distinct role was to provide his people with feeding and nourishment that would cause them to grow, to be strengthened, and experience the abundance of his leading.

    a. Isa. 40.11

    b. Jer. 23.4

    c. Ezek. 34.23

2. A pastor is a nurturing shepherd; you can't shepherd if you don't have a flock.

3. A pastor will not tend a flock if he does not have a heart for them, Jer. 3.15.

4. A pastor is a nurturer not one who dominates or intimidates, 1 Pet. 5.3.

The apostle bids that such persons should be teachers. Let him be a patient ruler. Let him know when he may relax the reins. Let him terrify at first, and then anoint with honey. And let him be the first to practice what he teaches.

~ Commodianus (c. 240, W), 4.214., David W. Bercot, ed. *A Dictionary of Early Christian Beliefs*. Peabody, MA: Hendrickson, 1998. p. 159.

5. A pastor nurtures in a number of ways.

   a. By supplying *a godly example* of what it means to live as a disciple of Christ.

      (1) Titus 2.7

      (2) 1 Tim. 4.12

      (3) 2 Thess. 3.9

   b. By *teaching sound doctrine* and preaching the Word of God.

      (1) 1 Thess. 5.12-13

      (2) 1 Tim. 4.6

      (3) 1 Tim. 5.17

      (4) Acts 20.32

   c. By providing tender, loving, care on the journey as God leads the flock, John 21.16.

B. The pastor is a *protector and guardian*.

   1. A hireling flees at the first sign of danger of an approaching predator on the flock, John 10.12-13.

   2. The abandonment of a flock will certainly result in some of the lambs being eaten, others scattered, John 10.12.

   3. A pastor is a guardian, who like Messiah Jesus guarded and protected his sheep by dying for us on the cross.

      a. Christ never forsook us, but laid his life down for the sheep, John 10.11.

b. Christ's pastoral sacrifice for us is the standard by which we measure all other forms of caring for the flock, Heb. 13.20.

4. As guardians of the flock, our responsibility is to pay careful attention to their needs and guard them against those things that would seek to harm or destroy them.

   a. Jesus warned that wolves would in fact come within his flock.
      (1) Matt. 7.15
      (2) Matt. 10.16

   b. Fierce wolves will arise among the flock, Acts 20.28-31.

   c. Destructive heresies are certain to abound, 2 Pet. 2.1-3.

5. The nature of our guardianship as pastors

   a. *Extreme*: not willing to lose a single lamb, Luke 15.4

   b. *Critical*: no flock will survive if the shepherd is destroyed or abandons his flock, Mark 14.27.

   c. *Radical*: we may have to give up our very lives for the survival and abundance of our flocks, John 10.11.

   d. Rallying cry: a shepherd guards by leading the sheep in the right direction, away from those things which may cause them to stray or be destroyed, 1 Pet. 2.25.

C. The pastor is a *leader*.

1. Jesus, as the Chief and Good Shepherd, leads us into the way and the pastures that are beneficial to us.

    a. Ps. 23.1-2

    b. John 10.4

    c. John 10.16

    d. John 10.26-27

    e. John 10.3-5

2. The godly pastor leads the flock into the will of God through the Word of God: he will not lead the flock astray, Jer. 50.6.

3. As the godly pastor follows Christ as a disciple, he challenges members of the flock to follow his lead.

    a. 1 Cor. 11.1

    b. 1 Cor. 4.16

    c. 1 Cor. 10.33

    d. Phil. 3.17

e. 1 Thess. 1.6

f. 2 Thess. 3.9

4. The pastor *is the message*, as well as the one who gives messages, Titus 2.7.

5. The youth of the pastor is not an issue; *godly modeling is*, 1 Tim. 4.12.

II. Equipping Pastors for Urban Congregations: Critical Issues

A. The domination of management models among evangelical pastors

1. The *do-everything myself* pastor: the pastor as Jack of all trades (the super charismatic Christian)

2. The *managerial pastor*: the pastor as CEO of the Christian corporation

3. The *aloof pastor*: the pastor who brackets the various tasks he does, virtually isolating himself from the flock

B. The need for solid urban pastors

1. A *vulnerable, unsafe environment*: the primacy of the shepherding role of pastoral care

2. *Vicious predators*: those who would prey upon urban Christians

> *Deacons should remember that the Lord chose apostles – that is, bishops and overseers. In contrast, the apostles appointed deacons for themselves.*
>
> ~ Cyprian
> (c. 250, W), 5.366.
> *Ibid.* p. 156.

3. *Proneness to wander:* the inclination of sheep toward distraction and departure from the flock

4. *Dry, parched ground for grazing:* the increased amount of spiritual materials and doctrines in urban areas

5. *Hirelings abound:* many who feast upon the flock rather than protect it

C. Where do we find and how do we equip solid pastors for urban churches?

1. Pray for them: God said that he would provide them for us! Cf. Eph. 4.11-12.

2. Change our ways of producing them: many of our modern ways of training pastors are simply inadequate.

    a. They take too long.

    b. They focus on academic systems and structures.

    c. They are too expensive.

    d. They don't equip urban pastors to care for disciples in urban contexts.

    e. They don't give the training in the urban church setting.

3. Concentrate again on *biblical criteria* for leadership in the local church.

   a. Watch over the flock of God, (we're looking for people who never sleep when it comes to the well-being of the flock).

      (1) Acts 20.28

      (2) Heb. 13.7

   b. Counter false teaching and their heresies by nourishing the saints on the Word of God, Acts 20.29-32.

   c. Equip the saints for the work of ministry (training pastors who are skilled in the art of making disciples and disciple makers, 2 Tim. 2.2).

4. Simplify the process of recruiting, training, and commissioning pastors.

   2 Tim. 3.16-17 – All Scripture is breathed out by God and profitable for teaching, for reproof, for correction, and for training in righteousness, [17] that the man of God may be competent, equipped for every good work.

   a. The Gospel of Jesus Christ

   b. The Kingdom of God

   c. The Nicene Creed

   d. The Sacraments

   e. Teaching and preaching the Word of God

5. Let's rediscover the elegant simplicity of the early Church to equip undershepherds for the urban flocks around us.

   a. Authentic courage from *compassionate servants*

   b. Defenders of the apostolic tradition: *the Nicene Creed*

   c. Concentration on the essentials: *laying one's life down for the sheep*, John 10.11

6. Place calling and gifting before credential and education.

   a. God has raised up pastors for the body, Eph. 4.11-12.

   b. A single true call of God is worth 10,000 lesser endorsements, Rom. 11.29.

III. Principles and Practice of the Pastoral Ministry

A. Recognize the importance of the pastoral office.

1. No pastor, the sheep will be scattered and feasted upon, John 10.10-13.

2. No pastor, fierce predators will devour the sheep, 1 Pet. 5.8-9.

3. No pastor, no flock at all!

Do not receive any stranger – whether bishop, presbyter, or deacon – without commendatory letters. And when such are offered, let them be examined.
~ Apostolic Constitutions (compiled 390, E), 7.502. *Ibid.* p. 156.

B. Recruit workers to the pastoral ministry.

1. Appeal to their love for Jesus Christ, John 21.16.

2. Appeal to their desire for a growing healthy church, Col. 1.25-28.

3. Appeal to their passion to equip others for ministry, Eph. 4.11-12.

C. Emphasize biblical standards and criteria (i.e., the Word of God is sufficient to equip the man or woman of God for every good work), 2 Tim. 3.15-17.

1. It never fails, Isa. 55.8-11.

2. It nurtures the soul and spirit, 1 Pet. 2.2.

3. It brings to maturity, Heb. 5.11-14.

D. Redefine the pastorate in terms of care-giving, nurturing, and tending the lambs, not administrating the corporation.

E. Embrace styles and methods of training conducive to urban disciples.

1. Become all things to all people in order to save and edify them, 1 Cor. 9.19-23.

2. Emphasize your freedom in Christ for the sake of loving others.

   a. Gal. 5.1

   b. Gal. 5.13

3. Ground believers in Christ, not in the plaque of Christian tradition, Col. 2.6-10.

F. Place the focus on helping to multiply ministry by equipping the saints, Eph. 4.11-16.

IV. The Blessing, Benefit, and Reward of the Christian Leader as Pastor

The same promise to elders is the very same reward promised to the godly shepherd who serves the Lord by willingly, eagerly, and carefully tending the flock of God on behalf of the Chief Shepherd.

1 Pet. 5.1-4 – So I exhort the elders among you, as a fellow elder and a witness of the sufferings of Christ, as well as a partaker in the glory that is going to be revealed: [2] shepherd the flock of God that is among you, exercising oversight, not under compulsion, but willingly, as God would have you; not for shameful gain, but eagerly; [3] not domineering over those in your charge, but being examples to the flock. [4] And when the Chief Shepherd appears, you will receive the unfading crown of glory.

A. The charge: *shepherd the flock of God that is among you.*

B. The reward: *when the Chief Shepherd appears, you will receive the unfading crown of glory.*

Therefore, appoint for yourselves bishops and deacons worthy of the Lord.
~ Didache
(c. 80-140, E), 7.381.
Ibid. p. 158.

Conclusion

- The Word of God articulates three key images of the pastorate.

- A pastor is a nurturer and care giver, a protector and guardian, and a leader of the flock of God.

- The Word of God is able to equip the worker of God with all they need in order to fulfill their calling in leading God's flock.

- We must joyously flesh out the freedom that Christ has won for us in order to discover new, innovative ways to meet the deep needs of the lambs God has given to us to equip.

Student Questions and Response

The following questions were designed to help you review the material in the video. This lesson discussed Scripture's vision of the kinds of roles that a pastor offers the people of God in his function as shepherd of the body. The pastor is a nurturer who ensures that God's people receive proper nourishment, feeding, tending, and care, a protector who guards the people of God against any harm or damage, and a leader called to go before the people of God and lead them into the fullness of the will of God for their individual and corporate lives. As those called to exercise leadership for the church in the city, it is critical that we understand these dimensions and roles with care and exactness. As you review the questions below, please concentrate on how these roles will need to be fleshed out in the urban community, and look to apply the Scriptures with an eye toward the urban scene and needs.

1. In looking at the examples of shepherding in the Word of God, what are three clear models and analogies given to us of what kind of *persona* (i.e., identity) a pastor ought to adopt as he cares for the people of God?

2. Explain the role of the pastor as a nurturer of the people of God. What does this role involve, and how does one prepare for this kind of ministry in the church? How can you tell if one is fulfilling this role in a local congregation to the maturity and well-being of the members of the body?

3. Lay out the various dimensions of the pastor as protector or guardian of the people of God. What are some of the things that a pastor may have to protect God's people from? What kind of training or input do you need in order to be able to fulfill this ministry in the church? How can you tell if someone is doing a

good job at protecting a local congregation from predators and other things that may want to harm them?

4. What are the different kinds of things involved in providing overall leadership and direction for a local congregation? In what way should a pastor lead a congregation, and what kinds of things are emphasized in that leadership? What is the best way to help pastors learn how to lead others in the church? How can you tell if a pastor is not fulfilling this crucial role in the body?

5. Name three unique challenges of the urban community that makes nurturing, protecting, and leading an important ministry for Christian leaders in the city? How can urban churches identify, train, and release pastors who will nourish, protect, and lead urban disciples of Christ to mature in Christ and give witness to the Kingdom of God in the city?

6. How have modern views and models of management deeply impacted the way in which many churches have come to understand the pastoral ministry? Have these changes been healthy for the Church? Why or why not?

7. According to 1 Peter 5.1-4, what are the specific duties God requires for elders who are called to shepherd God's flock? How may these instructions be applied today specifically to shepherding small, poor congregations in the city?

8. What are the specific promises given to those who fulfill the high calling of shepherding the flock of God with integrity and excellence?

CONNECTION

Summary of Key Concepts

This lesson focuses upon the nature and meaning of the pastorate, that duty to shepherd the flock of God. The need for godly, dedicated, and well-equipped pastors is as great today as any time in the past, and perhaps even more necessary in urban communities which, for whatever reason, do not attract many who are willing to come and nurture, protect, and lead the people of God there. Review these foundational truths, making certain that you have a good grasp of the content of the statements, as well as their biblical support.

- The Word of God provides three clear models and analogies of what a pastor does as care giver to the people of God as his flock: the pastor as nurturer, as protector, and as leader.

- The pastor is a nurturer who ensures that God's people receive proper nourishment, feeding, tending, and care.

- In addition, the pastor is a protector and guardian who guards the people of God against any predators or situations which would seek to harm or destroy them.

- Finally, the pastor is a leader called to go before the people of God and lead them into the fullness of the will of God for their individual and corporate lives.

- Because of the unique problems and challenges of urban communities, more than ever before the urban church needs pastors who will nourish, protect, and lead urban disciples of Christ to mature in Christ and give witness to the Kingdom of God in the city.

- God makes unequivocal promises to those who faithfully fulfill their work of shepherding the flock of God – they will receive the unfading crown of glory when the Chief Shepherd appears at the Second Coming.

Student Application and Implications

Now is the time for you to discuss with your fellow students your questions about the calling, criteria, and character of the pastoral ministry. Whether or not God has called you to be the *pastor* of a church or congregation, it is clear that, in some sense, God is calling all Christian leaders to be *pastoral* in their need to be nurturing, protecting, and guiding figures for those whom they mentor and lead. Now, list out your own particular questions about the nature of the pastorate that this lesson has unearthed for you, and address specifically any unresolved issues that remain for you on the nature of the pastoral ministry. The questions below are meant to spur your own questions about this important ministry.

- Is it possible to be called to the pastorate even when in fact you don't want to be a pastor? Explain your answer.

- How specifically would you know that God wanted you to join the pastorate? Must this come from one's own sense of calling, from your leader's sense of your own gifting and ministry, or a combination of both?

- Are women allowed to be in the pastorate? What are we to make of the many denominations which recognize pastoral authority for godly, mature women today?

- Should there be only *one senior pastor* or should we always seek a plurality of pastors in charge of the church?

- How much of a church's operations (i.e., administration, finances, facilities, etc.) should be under the control and oversight of the pastor? Should a pastor's responsibility be limited to the *spiritual responsibilities* associated with leading the people of God, and the more mundane items be turned over to others? Why or why not?

- How long should the term of pastor, elder, or deacon be? Ought we to place any limits in regards to term limits for any Christian leaders in the church?

- How confidential must a pastor be in the various kinds of dealings that they have with the different members of the church? Do any circumstances exist where a pastor might have to break confidence, both for the good of the individuals and of the congregation. Site examples.

- Can a pastor function properly if they do not also have an *authority structure* that they must report and answer to? What are the implications of this for the kind of church government that churches ought to establish for their own and their pastor's benefit?

- What are the qualifications that we ought to use for identifying and selecting pastoral candidates for the ministry? How important ought things like salary, housing, insurance, and similar items be in selecting a congregation to lead? Explain your answer.

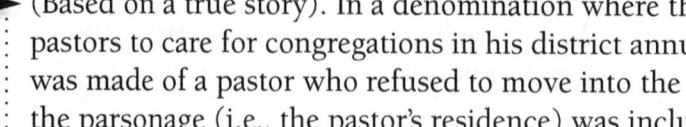

Not Until You Fix It Up

(Based on a true story). In a denomination where the bishop appoints pastors to care for congregations in his district annually, an appointment was made of a pastor who refused to move into the parsonage. Although the parsonage (i.e., the pastor's residence) was included in the financial package provided to the pastor, upon his arrival to the city and his first inspection of the parsonage, he decided that it was in too rundown of a condition for him to move his family into it. He refused to move into the parsonage until the leaders of the church funded its renovation. Staying at a local motel, the pastor of this poor urban church argued that asking your pastor, any pastor, to move into substandard housing was neither spiritually advisable nor fiscally desirable. The church had very few financial resources but, in obedience to their new pastor, renovated the inside of the parsonage, and after some weeks the pastor and his family moved into the newly decorated home. The actual tenure of the pastor at the church was both fruitful and cordial. What do you think of this pastor's insistence that the congregation provide for its leaders in an acceptable manner – did he go too far in his leadership here?

I Can't Submit to a Woman

A rift is beginning to occur among the members and leaders of a socially progressive evangelical church in a needy urban neighborhood. This congregation has become known around the city for its staunch stance against racism and sexism in any form. At its annual business meeting, the head elder announced the retirement of the church's current pastor, and in his place, the elders are recommending a godly, mature woman to pastor the church. Seminary trained, a gifted teacher, and deeply spiritual individual, this sister is liked by the entire congregation, whom she has served in various capacities over the last ten years. Some of the male members, however, struggle with this candidacy, not because she is not qualified spiritually, but because she is a woman. This has sparked a strong debate among the members, some of which feel so deeply that they have promised to leave the church if she is voted in. How ought the church approach and handle this issue of women and the pastorate?

No Wiggle Room to Maneuver

Many churches do not allow their pastor to be involved in the everyday decisions of administration, finance, personnel, or facilities. Arguing from the position of Acts 6, those who refuse this kind of participation for their pastors suggest that the role of the pastor is spiritual not administrative or technical. Issues of finance and administration are the province of others; the pastor ought to concentrate on issues surrounding the Word of God, prayer, and equipping the saints for ministry. Because of these restrictions, however, many pastors have little or no input into many things that affect the church's future, including their own salaries and benefits. What is the proper role for pastoral leadership in the ongoing operations of a church? Should they concentrate solely on spiritual matters, or should they be included in all decisions affecting the church. Make your case with Scripture, if possible.

Restatement of the Lesson's Thesis

In both the OT and NT, the image of shepherding is given for the leader of God's people, *roeh* in Hebrew and *poimen* in koine Greek, with both meaning "shepherd," "to shepherd," and to "provide pastoral care." The Lord God, rulers and kings, and the coming Messiah are all perceived as shepherds of God's people. The concept of pastor developed throughout the Church, from the care that all Christians provided to eventually a formal role for those individuals who would care for God's flock. Jesus himself is the prototype for the pastoral ministry, and God calls and gifts particular individuals to provide this care for the Church. Depending on the government structure of the church, the pastor exercises his care giving responsibility in different ways, but all through the functions of a *shepherd*, i.e., one who teaches and preaches the Word, administers the sacraments, comforts the bereaved, performs marriages, and equips the body for the work of the ministry.

The Word of God provides three clear models and analogies of what a pastor does as care giver to the people of God as his flock. The pastor is a nurturer who ensures that God's people receive proper nourishment, feeding, tending, and care. Furthermore, the pastor is a protector and guardian who guards the people of God against any predators or situations which would seek to harm or destroy them. Finally, the pastor is a leader called to go before the people of God and lead them into the fullness of the will of God for their individual and corporate lives. More than ever before the urban church needs pastors who will nourish, protect, and lead urban disciples of Christ to mature in Christ and give witness to the Kingdom of God in the city. God makes unequivocal promises to those who faithfully fulfill their work of shepherding the flock of God – they will receive the unfading crown of glory when the Chief Shepherd appears at the Second Coming.

Resources and Bibliographies

If you are interested in pursuing some of the ideas of *The Christian Leader as Pastor (Poimenes)*, you might want to give these books a try:

Dawn, Marva, and Eugene H. Peterson, Peter Santucci, eds. *The Unnecessary Pastor: Rediscovering the Call*. Grand Rapids: Eerdmans, 2000.

Hansen, David. *The Art of Pastoring: Ministering without All the Answers*. Downers Grove: InterVarsity Press, 1994.

Oden, Thomas C. *Pastoral Theology: Essentials of Ministry*. New York: HarperCollins Publishers, 1983.

Willimon, William H. Pastor: *The Theology and Practice of Ordained Ministry*. Nashville: Abingdon Press, 2002.

Ministry Connections — Whether or not God has called you to the pastorate, your understanding of this vital role of Christian leadership will affect every area of your own life and ministry through your church. You are called to be pastoral in terms of offering care and love to those to whom you minister, and through your own application of these truths, God may desire to change and/or alter your ministry approach. How has the Holy Spirit been influencing your own judgments about the pastorate as you studied this material? Have you sensed any calling from the Lord regarding your own appointment to this high ministry? What do you believe the Lord is specifically calling you to do right now, if anything, about these truths? Set aside good time this week to review these truths, and rethink your own understanding of the pastoral ministry. Also, as you consider your ministry project for this unit, you can possibly use it to connect to these truths in a practical way. Seek the face of God for insight, and come back next week ready to share your insights with the other learners in your class.

Counseling and Prayer — If for any reason you need spiritual direction for unanswered questions and/or unresolved issues in this lesson, seek the Lord's guidance about getting with your own pastor, spiritual supervisor, or leader to get further clarification. Also, be open to ask your fellow students to lift up your particular requests to God. Of course, know that your instructor is extremely open to discussing related questions to Christian leadership, the pastorate, or related questions with you, whatever they are related to the materials in this lesson. The more open you are to the Lord's counsel through his people the better you will be led to discover his particular insights and will for you. Be open to God and allow him to lead you as he determines.

ASSIGNMENTS

Scripture Memory — Acts 20.26-28

Reading Assignment — To prepare for class, please visit *www.tumi.org/books* to find next week's reading assignment, or ask your Mentor.

Other Assignments — Again, make certain that you read the assignments above, and as last week, write a brief summary for them and bring these summaries to class next week. (Please see the "Reading Completion Sheet" on page 16.)

Also, now is the time to begin to think about the character of your ministry project, as well as decide what passage of Scripture you will select for your exegetical project. Do not delay in determining either your ministry or exegetical project. The sooner you select, the more time you will have to prepare!

Looking Forward to the Next Lesson

Our next lesson, *Practicing Christian Leadership: Effective Worship Leading* considers the idea of representation of the Lord Jesus as fundamental in practicing every dimension of Christian leadership as his agents and servants. Closely connected to this important idea, we will also consider carefully the role of ministering the Word and Sacrament among the people of God. What an adventure it is to serve the living God by caring for his dear people!

FOR FURTHER STUDY

Please see the following resources in *Picturing Theology: An A-Z Collection of TUMI's Key Diagrams, Charts, Graphics, and Articles*:

- *Following the Life of Christ throughout Each Year*, page 139
- *The Role of Women in Ministry*, page 366
- *Nurturing Authentic Christian Leadership*, page 302
- *Six Kinds of New Testament Ministry for Community*, page 382
- *Suffering: The Cost of Discipleship and Servant-Leadership*, page 410

Practicing Christian Leadership
Effective Worship Leading

Lesson Objectives

Welcome in the strong name of Jesus Christ! After your reading, study, discussion, and application of the materials in this lesson, you will be able to:

- Recite the different ways in which leadership is a form of representation, i.e., representing the Lord, his person, his people, and his purposes in the community.

- Give reasons why in leadership we do not represent our own purposes or interests in our lives and ministries, but the Lord's purposes and interests in all we say and do.

- Outline the importance of the role of worship in bringing glory and honor to God in the midst of his people.

- Detail the importance of liturgy by worshiping God in the spirit, in truth, in order, and in faith.

Devotion

Learn How to Represent

Read Luke 10.1-16. In order to lead in a Christian way, you must never interpret your leadership in an overly personalized way. To lead is to represent another. This seems odd, but, after first glance, it becomes perfectly clear how this works. If you desire to lead others as a sergeant, you must be willing to follow the orders of the captain. If you reject the captain, you cannot order around privates, if you are a sergeant. The foreman on the factory floor must obey the department head, or he loses the right to lead those under him. The key to leadership is always submission. If you find a person who struggles with or is unwilling to submit to others, they forfeit the right to lead others.

Christian leadership is representation. As our Lord Jesus Christ represented the Father in all that he said and did while on the earth, so we, following his example, represent him in all that we do. Christian leadership is about the authority of Jesus, and the one who is unwilling to follow Jesus loses all right to serve and care for the members of his body in their own leadership. What is interesting about this, is that it works also for those who respond to the leader. In other words, if you are truly representing the Lord Jesus, then the one who rejects your word is rejecting him, and according to Christ's own testimony, also rejecting the Father who sent our Lord. The entire vision of Christian leadership is anchored therefore on a simple but profound idea: leadership is representation. No Christian leader can function on the basis of their own authority, power, and position. It is not gifting or resources or education or brilliance that makes a Christian leader legitimate. It is the call of God. If God has called a man or woman to represent him, then they must act as God's ambassador, God's representative, God's diplomat. We speak his words, represent his interests, share his burdens, carry out his commands. The emerging Christian leader who learns this lesson will not only carry out their ministry with dignity and excellence, but they will also open themselves up to be used by the Lord to transform others. In order to be God's leader, learn how to represent.

Nicene Creed and Prayer

After reciting and/or singing the Nicene Creed (located in the Appendix), pray the following prayer:

> You sent your Son Jesus Christ, who came not to be served but to serve, and to give his life a ransom for many. We praise you that he calls his faithful servants to lead your holy people in love; to proclaim your Word and to celebrate the sacraments of the new covenant.
>
> ~ Presbyterian Church (USA) and Cumberland Presbyterian Church. *Book of Common Worship.* Louisville: Westminister/John Knox Press, 1993. p. 137.

Scripture Memorization Review

Review with a partner, write out and/or recite the text for last class session's assigned memory verse: Acts 20.26-28.

Assignments Due

Turn in your summary of the reading assignment for last week, that is, your brief response and explanation of the main points that the authors were seeking to make in the assigned reading (Reading Completion Sheet).

CONTACT

"I Don't Need Your Permission."

During a rather heated discussion among the leaders of a local inner city church, the pastor claimed that he did not need the permission of his deacon board to go forward with his plan to expand the sanctuary. After all, they had called him to be the pastor, the by-laws said that he had the authority to establish and expand ministry in the church, and there were enough resources in the treasury to actually go forward with the building. While some of the deacons wanted further discussion of the wisdom of such a move, the pastor closed down debate. He announced that he believed the Lord wanted the church to proceed forward, and finished with the statement, "I really don't need your permission on this. I am the pastor, and God has called me to lead." What do you think about the style of the pastor's leadership?

"It Just Don't Seem Right."

In an effort to become more "contemporary" in their worship style with the youth service, the youth pastor has begun his new "Hip Hop Hallelujah" service. It is a worship service, but done completely in sync with the hip-hop culture which dominates the minds and hearts of the kids in the neighborhood. Although the service continues to expand and grow, attracting more of the lost kids around the community, some of the leaders are concerned with the flavor of the service. To them, it looks no different than an MTV program; the kids dress the same, they use all kinds of electronic instruments and turn-tables, and essentially is nothing more than worldliness with a little Jesus thrown in. As one of the deacons said about it, "Looking at what our youth pastor is doing, I just feel uneasy. It just don't seem right." What would you say to the deacon if he asked you about the hip-hop hallelujah service – is it right, is it wrong, does it matter what they're doing? How so?

Only the Believing

(This is based on a true story.) Recently, in a growing church, the pastor noticed that when he only made the Lord's Supper available to those who believed, that many unbelievers felt judged and isolated during their communion service. After consulting with his other leaders, the pastor decided to open up communion to whoever was present for the service. Remarkably, this opened up the service greatly and, brought much added enthusiasm to the service. The pastor actually testified that there have been some unbelievers who have actually come to faith in Jesus Christ as a result of participating in the Lord's Supper event! Some are troubled at his trend, believing that Communion should be reserved only for those who have repented and put their trust in Jesus for the salvation of their souls. While all believe that communion is an important service, they genuinely disagree about the pastor's "new direction." How would you counsel the pastor and the church to understand the Lord's Supper in the midst of the people of God?

Effective Worship Leading: Worship, Word, and Sacrament

Representing the People of God in Giving God His Due

Rev. Dr. Don L. Davis

Summary

In order to effectively lead the people of God in worship, we must be certain that we represent the Lord in our leadership, i.e., we have been appointed to act on his behalf as his agent before his people for his purposes.

Our objective for this lesson, *Representing the People of God in Giving God His Due*, is to enable you to see that:

- The biblical understanding of representation is the fundamental concept in practical Christian leadership.

- The Christian leader is called to represent the Lord and his purposes to his people and within the community.

- As those who belong to the Lord, our leadership can never be about ourselves, but rather we must speak and act for God as we strive to represent his purposes and interests in all we say and do.

- The critical role where this representation shows itself is how we lead the people of God into the presence of God, for his glory through Jesus Christ.

- Practical Christian leadership begins with the worship of God in Christ, leading the people of God in liturgy by worshiping God in the spirit, in truth, in order, and in faith.

Lesson 3 | Practicing Christian Leadership: Effective Worship Leading

Video Outline

I. The Christian Leader as God's Called Representative (i.e., His Ambassador)

2 Cor. 5.18-20

All this is from God, who through Christ reconciled us to himself and gave us the ministry of reconciliation; [19] that is, in Christ God was reconciling the world to himself, not counting their trespasses against them, and entrusting to us the message of reconciliation. [20] Therefore, we are ambassadors for Christ, God making his appeal through us. We implore you on behalf of Christ, be reconciled to God.

A. Definition: *a practicing Christian leader is one called by God to represent his purposes and interests in the midst of the people of God.*

1. Called by God: *the Christian leader is a person who has sensed from the Lord a particular call from God.*

    a. The leader has been placed in their position by *God's own choice*, John 15.16.

    b. A leader may be called *directly or through appointment*, but they still represent God in their leadership.

        (1) Direct call from God

            (a) John 20.21

            (b) 2 Tim. 1.11

            (c) Acts 26.17-18

        (2) Appointment through God's representatives

            (a) 1 Tim. 5.22

            (b) Titus 1.5

            (c) 2 Tim. 2.2

            (d) 1 Tim. 1.18

c. This calling is *irrevocable*. (God will not cancel a calling; his calling may be fulfilled or ignored, but he never takes it back.)

   (1) Rom. 11.29

   (2) 1 Tim. 1.11-12

   (3) Rom. 1.5

d. This calling is accompanied by *God's giftings and enablements.*

   (1) 2 Cor. 3.6

   (2) Eph. 3.7

   (3) Col. 1.25

2. To represent his purposes and interests: *this calling is focused on God's intentions and purposes, and not those of the leader.*

   a. The leader is an ambassador. He speaks and acts on behalf of another.

      (1) Eph. 6.20

      (2) 1 Cor. 9.16-17

   b. The leader has *no authority to go beyond his or her mandate* from the Lord to build up his people.

      (1) 2 Cor. 13.10

      (2) 2 Cor. 10.8

   c. Promotion and demotion comes from the Lord alone: *God sets up one and puts down another.*

      (1) Ps. 75.6-7

      (2) John 15.16

3. In the midst of the people of God: *the leader exercises authority and provides service to those who belong to God in the midst of Christian community.*

   a. There is no such thing as a leader who exists for themselves, Rom. 15.15-16.

   b. Jesus Christ is the prime example of a leader for others, Phil. 2.5-11.

   c. All of the efforts of the practicing Christian leader are to edify the people of God, to enable them to be what God intends for them to be, and to do what God intends for them to do.

B. Three dimensions of representing God as one called to lead his people

   1. The Leader *is first and foremost a Representative of Jesus Christ.*

      a. Jesus Christ is Lord and Head over all things to the Church, Eph. 1.20-23.

      b. He has selected men and women to represent his interests and will in the Church, John 15.16.

   2. The Leader is also *a Representative of the Christian Community.*

      a. They serve as undershepherds under God's authority.

         (1) 1 Cor. 12.28

         (2) 1 Cor. 12.7

         (3) 1 Pet. 5.1-4

b. They possess no authority to destroy or tear down, only to edify the saints, 2 Cor. 13.10.

c. We as leaders are to see God's people fulfill God's desire that they might represent him with honor in the world as his people and his witnesses, Eph. 2.10.

3. The Leader is finally *a Representative of the Christian faith.*

a. They are to contend for the faith, Jude 1.3.

b. They are to equip others to share their faith, Eph. 4.11-12.

II. Giving God His Due: Leading God's People into Worship

A. Definition: the practicing Christian Leader is one who ushers the people of God into the presence of God by giving God his due in acceptable worship.

1. Ushers the people of God into the presence of God: *the leader, as a worshiper of God, is charged with ushering God's people into his very presence.*

a. Rom. 15.15-19

b. Paul's aim is to so minister among the Gentiles that they might bring glory to God through his ministry, Rom. 1.5.

---

*Bob Webber in his book **Worship is a Verb** highlights eight indispensable principles of participating in worship. They are:*

1) Worship celebrates Christ

2) Worship tells and acts out the Christ-event

3) In worship, God speaks and acts

4) Worship is an act of communication

5) In worship we respond to God and each other

6) Return worship to the people

7) All creation joins in worship

8) Worship is a way of life

2. By giving God his due: *the goal of all worship, whatever the form, is to offer God the praise and glory due his name.*

   a. We are called to preach the unsearchable riches of Christ to those who do not know him, Eph. 3.7-8.

   b. This worship is linked directly to obedience, not merely our outward acts of religious devotion, Acts 26.20.

3. Through worship that is acceptable to him: *we are not to simply encourage outward religious show, but to lead in such a way that those who respond to our ministries may give to God the kind of service and obedience that bring pleasure and honor to him.* To bring about the obedience of faith was Paul's ministry aim, Rom. 16.26.

B. Implications of this high calling

1. No one can lead others unless they are out in front of them.

2. Only God can empower us to fulfill this high calling.

3. We are free to experiment and find as many ways as possible to bring more and more honor to the name of God through Jesus Christ.

III. Four Dimensions of Effective Worship Leading

A. Worship in the Spirit: being led by the Holy Spirit, John 4.22-24

1. We have access to God through faith in Christ by the Spirit.

   a. We are saved by the purpose of the Father, 2 Tim. 1.8-9.

   b. We are made whole through the blood of Christ, Heb. 10.12-14.

   c. These salvation blessings are made real in our lives by the Holy Spirit, John 16.13-14.

2. Worship is not proper form, but must be accompanied by a faith and lifestyle that makes the forms meaningful to him.

   a. Mere outward signs of devotion are not acceptable to God, Isa. 1.13-14.

   b. Worship must be accompanied by justice and righteousness to be acceptable to God, Isa. 1.16-17.

3. Being saved by grace through faith alone, we are now free in Christ to offer worship to God that corresponds to our own cultural identity, Gal. 5.1.

   a. In our own styles of music, hymns, worship, and celebration

   b. In our own styles of learning and presentation

   c. In our own ways of preaching, teaching, and sharing together

B. Worship in Truth: grounded in the true revelation of God, Phil. 3.3

1. Christ is the end of the law for righteousness: we do not worship God on the basis of liturgy and tradition alone, but by the filling and leading of the Holy Spirit, Rom. 10.3-4.

2. All acceptable worship, whatever the form or liturgy, is done in the name and person of Christ Jesus alone; he is our only access to God, John 14.6.

3. We put no confidence "in the flesh," that is, our own ability to please or draw near to God except through Jesus Christ, 1 Pet. 1.23-25.

C. Worship in Order: approaching God in liturgical order

1. God is a God of order and of peace: the Holy Spirit has given gifts to all members of the church to use, but these must be used wisely for the benefit of all.

    a. 1 Cor. 14.12

    b. 1 Cor. 14.26

    c. 1 Cor. 14.33

2. As God used times of remembrance and celebration in the yearly schedule of Israel to remind them of their history, so we can use the Church calendar and liturgical order to rehearse the great stories of our redemption in Christ.

    a. Paul referred to Christ as our Passover, 1 Cor. 5.7.

b. Paul referred to the great stories of deliverance in the history of Israel as signs for us, 1 Cor. 10.1ff.

c. The early Church developed liturgy (the Church calendar and the service order) to help members of the Church recall the important moments in our history of redemption.

3. As leaders of God's people, we employ order in worship not to encourage dead tradition, but to train others to lead in worship.

a. We are to be careful not to be faithful to our tradition and ignore the plain statements of the Word of God, Matt. 15.3.

b. Mark 7.13

c. Col. 2.8

4. We employ liturgy because it can help the family of God recall our salvation history (going through the key events and stories year by year for encouragement and instruction).

D. Worship in faith: avoid empty tradition to celebrate God and his provision.

1. Without faith, it is impossible to please God; regardless of the way in which we lead the people of God in worship, we must always beware of the power of tradition to become stale and meaningless.

a. Heb. 11.6

b. Col. 2.23

> *Worship in the Bible is the due response of rational creatures to the self-revelation of their Creator. It is honoring and glorifying of God by gratefully offering back to him all the good gifts, and all the knowledge of his greatness and graciousness, that he has given. It involves praising him for what he is, thanking him for what he has done, desiring him to get himself more glory by further acts of mercy, judgment, and power, and trusting him with our concern for our own and others' future well-being.*
>
> ~ J. I. Packer. *Concise Theology: A Guide to Historic Christian Beliefs.* (electronic version). Wheaton, IL: Tyndale House, 1995.

2. No one can approach God except through the person and work of our Lord Jesus Christ.

   a. Acts 4.12

   b. 1 John 2.23

3. Use and employ worship methods but do not substitute them for our need to approach and relate to God only through his Son.

   a. 2 John 1.9

   b. 1 Pet. 3.18

   c. Titus 2.14

Conclusion

- The fundamental concept of Christian leadership is representation. As representatives of Jesus, his Church, and the Christian faith, we are called by God to lead God's people to bring glory and honor to God.

- Perhaps the most critical way in which we represent God is to lead his people in worship.

- Worship is not mere form, tradition, and going through the motions of weekly service; true worship involves our obedience to the Spirit, according to the truth of God's Word, in proper liturgical order, grounded in a living faith that celebrates God and his work in the world.

- We lead the people into the presence of God in dependence on the Lord Jesus Christ alone to bring us before the Father.

Student Questions and Response

Please take as much time as you have available to answer these and other questions that the video brought out. This lesson outlined one of the critical concepts of practical Christian leadership, which is the representing of God in Christ before his people for his purpose and the advance of his Kingdom, to his glory. Be clear and concise in your answers, and where possible, support with Scripture!

1. What does it mean to say that "a practicing Christian leader is one called by God to represent his purposes and interests in the midst of his people?"

2. As ambassadors of God, how do we as practicing Christian leaders "stay in touch" with headquarters to speak and act on his behalf most accurately?

3. In what ways may a Christian leader be called to represent God's interests in the body?

4. What similarities are there between the role of an ambassador to his appointed nation and the Christian leader in relationship to Christ?

5. What are the three dimensions in which a Christian leader is called to represent God? Is there any authority from the Lord to tear others down or destroy? Explain.

6. Why do you think it might be important for the Christian leader to understand his or her role first as one who ushers the people of God into God's presence?

7. What role does the Holy Spirit play in leading others into the presence of God?

8. Why is it significant that all worship of God in Christ be grounded upon the truth of Scripture? What role does Christ himself play in giving God worship that is acceptable to him?

9. Why is order important in leading others into worship? Can form alone guarantee acceptable worship before the Lord? Why or why not?

10. In what ways can we avoid empty tradition as we lead others into the celebration and worship of God? What role does faith play in leading others to relate to God?

CONNECTION

Summary of Key Concepts

This lesson focuses upon the role of the practicing Christian leader as a representative of the Lord, one who is called to speak and act on behalf of the purposes and interests of the Lord. We demonstrate this representation first and foremost in our ushering people into the presence of God through our leading them in worship, through the nourishment of the Word of God in the lives of believers in the body, and through our ongoing celebration of the sacraments in our services of worship in the Church.

* The biblical understanding of representation is the fundamental concept in practical Christian leadership: the leader does not represent himself or herself but the authority and purpose of the Lord.

* The Christian leader has sensed his or her particular call from the Lord to represent his purposes to his people within the community.

* As those who belong to the Lord, our leadership can never be about ourselves, but rather we must speak and act for God as we strive to represent his purposes and interests in all we say and do.

* The critical role where this representation shows itself is how we lead the people of God into the presence of God, for his glory through Jesus Christ.

* The four dimensions of effective worship leading for the practicing Christian leader is to lead God's people to worship him in the Spirit, to worship him in truth, to worship him with order and peace, and to worship him in faith through Jesus Christ.

Student Application and Implications

Now is the time for you to discuss with your fellow students your questions about the insights you have gleaned in this lesson regarding our representation of the Lord, and our leading the body into the presence and purpose of God through worship, Word, and sacrament. What particular questions do you have in light of the material you have just studied? Maybe some of the questions below might help you form your own, more specific and critical questions.

* How do we know in fact that we have sensed a call from God to represent him? What role do other Christian leaders and the congregation play in confirming the authenticity of my call to ministry, to represent God in the church?

- Can you lead others into God's presence if you are not dwelling there yourself? Explain your answer.

- Why is it impossible to be a leader for the Lord and be isolated from the life, worship, and ministry of the local body?

- What kinds of attitudes and habits must be cultivated in order to be an effective worship leader in the way described in this lesson? Which of these do you express best, least?

- Why is commitment to the faithful Word of God so critical in all phases of representing God in the midst of the Church?

- What about those traditions which recognize other significant events and practices as sacraments, more than simply Baptism and the Lord's Supper?

- What role does tradition play in acknowledging these other practices as sacramental?

- Of all the aspects of effective worship leading, which ones do you believe are critical for the emerging Christian leader to master first?

- How do we ensure that members of the body continue to grow in the Word and sacrament even as they are faithful in attendance to our services of worship? How can we instill a sense of celebration and refreshment in our teaching and worship leading that continues to encourage them in their faith?

CASE STUDIES

"The Lord Told Me to Come."

1. A young person with real personality and apparent spiritual gifts begins to attend your church for a few weeks, but, as time has gone on, you have become concerned about his understanding of God's leading. He has more and more asserted himself as the Lord's prophet in the church, and will state authoritatively to others on some point of conduct or doctrine, "This is what I believe God is saying to you about this." You as pastor have heard more and more concern from members about some of the things this young fellow is saying, but you believe the Lord is upon him. The young fellow's constant word about himself in the church is "The Lord told me to come." How would you lead this young person to maturity in the body, i.e., to help him understand the principle of leadership as representation.

"You're Doing it all Wrong."

2. With the entrance of new ways of worship; singing, Scripture and responsive reading, and prayer into your services, some of your older members are concerned about the break with their traditional ways of worship. A growing divide is occurring between those who prefer more contemporary styles of worship and those who embrace more traditional forms and liturgies of service. One dear mother in the church, frustrated with the kinds of things going on in service, shared with the pastor recently, "This new kind of worship is not right. You're doing it all wrong. We need to return to how we always did it." How would you counsel the pastor in his leading the church in these new/old style dialogues about services of worship?

"I'm Not Being Fed."

3. While using the lectionary (i.e., those ordered yearly lists of texts shared by many denominations and assemblies guiding worship), you notice that many in the body are expressing dissatisfaction both in the subject matter and the presentation of the sermons. While many have commented that they are growing much through your teaching, a small but vocal group is expressing deep concern over your teaching. One dear member bluntly said the other week, "I am spiritually hungry. Your sermons and teaching aren't helping me grow. I'm not being fed!" If confronted with these concerns, how would you respond?

"I Don't Believe I Need to Do That."

4. While teaching the importance of our shared devotional life and ongoing practice of the sacraments together, one member disagreed openly. She believes that only her personal faith in Jesus Christ is necessary for her to mature in Christ. Salvation is through him, and growth is in him. She flatly disagrees with the idea that she must attend weekly services or participate in sacramental observances to grow. She has her faith, her Bible, and her love for Christ, and she is convinced that she needs nothing else. How would you go about seeking to persuade her that she cannot grow without her shared worship in the body, her nourishment of the Word in community, and her participation in the sacraments of the Church? What would you do if she remained firm and unconvinced?

Restatement of the Lesson's Thesis

The biblical understanding of representation is the fundamental concept in practical Christian leadership: the leader does not represent him or herself but the authority and purpose of the Lord. As those who belong to the Lord, our leadership can never be about ourselves, but rather we must speak and act for God as we strive to represent his purposes and interests in all we say and do. The four dimensions of effective worship leading for the practicing Christian leader is to lead God's people to worship him in the Spirit, to worship him in truth, to worship him with order and peace, and to worship him in faith through Jesus Christ. As we lead God's people into his presence, we must work tirelessly to ensure that each member of the family is properly fed and nourished with a full and steady diet of the Word of God.

Resources and Bibliographies

If you are interested in pursuing some of the ideas of *Effective Worship Leading: Worship, Word, and Sacrament*, you might want to give these books a try:

Boschman, LaMar. *Future Worship*. Ventura, CA: Gospel Light Publications, 1999.

Webber, Robert E. *Worship Is a Verb*. Peabody, MA: Hendrickson Publishers, 1992.

———. *Blended Worship*. Peabody, MA: Hendrickson Publishers, 1998.

Wiersbe, Warren W. *Real Worship*. Grand Rapids: Baker Books, 2000.

Ministry Connections

Now is the time to try to nail down this high theology to a real practical ministry connection, one which you will think about and pray for throughout this next week. In all that has been covered in this lesson on the nature of practical Christian leadership, what application or idea specifically connects with your experience in your life and ministry today? What in particular is the Holy Spirit suggesting to you regarding your own worship, your own nourishment in the Word of God, and your own celebration of the sacraments in the midst of the body? Are you growing in your sense of God's call on your life, and do you flesh out that call in the context of the local church, under the leadership of godly pastoral authority? What particular situation comes to mind when you think about how you might need to change or adapt something in your life so you could better represent the Lord in your worship, your ministry of the Word, and your practice and celebration of the sacraments?

LESSON 3 | PRACTICING CHRISTIAN LEADERSHIP: EFFECTIVE WORSHIP LEADING

Counseling and Prayer

Receiving prayer for the areas that the Spirit brings to mind is one of the key means of receiving the needed grace we must have to glorify God in our role as Christian leaders. Do not hesitate to share with your mentor and fellow students your need for prayer, and be careful to offer faithful intercession for them as you lift them up before the Lord. Prayer is not merely a little pause at the beginning and end of a session, it is the life blood of receiving Christ's ongoing aid in times of need. Remember the good advice of Hebrews:

> Heb. 4.14-16 – Since then we have a great high priest who has passed through the heavens, Jesus, the Son of God, let us hold fast our confession. [15] For we do not have a high priest who is unable to sympathize with our weaknesses, but one who in every respect has been tempted as we are, yet without sin. [16] Let us then with confidence draw near to the throne of grace, that we may receive mercy and find grace to help in time of need.

ASSIGNMENTS

Scripture Memory

1 Peter 2.9-10

Reading Assignment

To prepare for class, please visit www.tumi.org/books to find next week's reading assignment, or ask your Mentor.

Other Assignments

As usual you ought to come with your reading assignment sheet containing your summary of the reading material for the week. Also, you must have selected the text for your exegetical project and turn in your proposal for your ministry project.

Looking Forward to the Next Lesson

In our next lesson, *The Equipping Ministry: The Ministry of Proclamation*, we will outline the three steps of planning out, delivering, and following up on the preached Word. As communicators of the Word of God, we must first establish contact with hearers, communicate the content of the Word clearly and boldly, and make connections with the truth of the message and the lives of the audience, proclaiming all in dependence on the Holy Spirit. A revolution can occur in urban ministry when gifted and available men and women minister the Word of God in such a way as to raise up a new generation of laborers in the city – those who can care for the hurting, share the truth of God, and declare the Kingdom to their neighbors. Your role in this ministry is urgent and needed.

FOR FURTHER STUDY

Please see the following resources in *Picturing Theology: An A-Z Collection of TUMI's Key Diagrams, Charts, Graphics, and Articles*:

- *Faithfully Re-Presenting Jesus of Nazareth*, page 127
- *Fit to Represent*, page 137
- *Discerning the Call: The Profile of a Cross-Cultural Urban Church Planter*, page 78
- *Lording Over vs. Serving Among*, page 263
- *Representin': Jesus as God's Chosen Representative*, page 357

LESSON 4

The Equipping Ministry
The Ministry of Proclamation – *Kerygma*

Lesson Objectives

Welcome in the strong name of Jesus Christ! After your reading, study, discussion, and application of the materials in this lesson, you will be able to:

- Recite the three central steps in planning out, delivering the content, and making connection with the audience through the preached Word.

- Lay out the ways in which we establish contact with our hearers as we spotlight issues, concerns, ideas, or experiences that resonate in the lives of the audience, which can also be used as a springboard into our preaching content.

- List key principles as to how we can paint a picture through our words in the spiritual eyes of our hearers so as to show them our themes (not merely tell them about it), preaching messages which focus on Christ and his Kingdom, using the Bible's methods of images, symbols, and stories, being organized in a plain and simple manner.

- Explain how use of the liturgy and the Church calendar allow us to provide our audiences with a continuous retelling of the Story of God in the life and work of Jesus, and thus highlight the whole counsel of God annually through his story.

- Gain skill in making connections in our preaching with the audience by inviting them to specific and particular responses, helping them to understand their spiritual condition before God by making clear appeals and bold invitations for repentance and change, and when responses are made, gaining insight as to how these should be followed up on quickly and thoroughly.

Devotion

An Enemy of a Different Sort

2 Cor. 4.1-7 – Therefore, having this ministry by the mercy of God, we do not lose heart. [2] But we have renounced disgraceful, underhanded ways. We refuse to practice cunning or to tamper with God's word, but by the open statement of the truth we would commend ourselves to

everyone's conscience in the sight of God. [3] And even if our gospel is veiled, it is veiled only to those who are perishing. [4] In their case the god of this world has blinded the minds of the unbelievers, to keep them from seeing the light of the gospel of the glory of Christ, who is the image of God. [5] For what we proclaim is not ourselves, but Jesus Christ as Lord, with ourselves as your servants for Jesus' sake. [6] For God, who said, "Let light shine out of darkness," has shone in our hearts to give the light of the knowledge of the glory of God in the face of Jesus Christ. [7] But we have this treasure in jars of clay, to show that the surpassing power belongs to God and not to us.

How effective can our own preparation, investigation, practice, and work be in terms of communicating the Word of God with power? In many ways, our heartfelt desire as Christian leaders is to communicate the Word of God regarding Jesus of Nazareth in a convincing and compelling way. We spend untold hours of preparation, prayer, study, and instruction for this end. Yet, sometimes, in spite of all the hard work that we do to prepare ourselves for urban ministry, the results are the opposite of our desires. Why do our best laid plans, prayerfully conceived and diligently carried out, often result in fruitless, even hostile reactions? What exactly are we doing wrong to get such unwelcome, even mean-spirited responses to the Word of God?

Of course, it could be due to our own fault – in the way we communicated, our lack of humility and openness to others, the communication of a harsh, judgmental spirit or the lack of genuine love demonstrated in our sharing of the Gospel. More likely than these, however, is the presence of a very real enemy, one who masterfully interferes with the presentation of the Word of God to those who do not believe, and whose aim is to undermine all ministry done in the name of the Lord. Of whom do we speak?

Paul speaks about the hiddenness of the Gospel. This is unusual language for an apostle, even while shackled himself in the Roman prison, to say confidently that the Word of God cannot itself be imprisoned (cf. 2 Tim. 2.9 for which I am suffering, bound with chains as a criminal. But the word of God is not bound!). This same apostle says that the Gospel is hidden due to the demoniacal work of the "god of this age," the devil, who veils the Gospel to those who are perishing. He has blinded their minds to keep them from seeing the light of the Gospel of the glory of Christ. He impedes the work of those who proclaim the Word of God, interfering, lying, deceiving, and inhibiting them to fully comprehend the wonder and depth of God's salvation offer in Jesus Christ.

We need not, however, be either deterred or intimidated. We do not preach about ourselves; we are not the subject matter of our own ministries, but rather we preach Jesus Christ as Lord, and we, like Paul, are servants on behalf of those who hear and respond to our message of Christ and his Kingdom. We are confident of our message, because Jesus of Nazareth is the God-bearer; the very glory of God himself shines forth in the face of our Lord Jesus Christ. This remarkable treasure, this astounding Gospel exists in us, mere jars of clay, in order that the surpassing power of the entire preaching event may belong to God and him alone, and never to us. Only God can reveal, only God can redeem, and therefore only God deserves the glory and praise for the work of the ministry.

It may take us most of our ministry lives to grasp this basic yet essential point. Although we ought to in every way prepare ourselves to be the kind of vessels the Lord can use in ministry, we need never to forget that without the direct intervention of the illumination and convicting power of the Holy Spirit, we cannot in any way bring a person to saving faith in Jesus Christ. Apart from the drawing of God the Father of souls to the Lord Jesus (John 6.44), apart from the overcoming of the influence of the "strong man" in order that the Lord Jesus may despoil his goods (Matt. 12.29-30), and without the convicting power of the Holy Spirit of sin, righteousness, and judgment (John 16.7-11), no fruit will be borne. All the essential interior transforming grace must come from God, and not from us. This, of course, does not mean that we do not continue to prepare ourselves and others for the work of the ministry. What it does suggest, however, is that we recognize what must occur before fruit can be borne for God. See Paul's good wisdom in 1 Corinthians:

> 1 Cor. 3.5-9 – What then is Apollos? What is Paul? Servants through whom you believed, as the Lord assigned to each. [6] I planted, Apollos watered, but God gave the growth. [7] So neither he who plants nor he who waters is anything, but only God who gives the growth. [8] He who plants and he who waters are one, and each will receive his wages according to his labor. [9] For we are God's fellow workers. You are God's field, God's building.

In preparing for ministry we face many barriers, difficulties, and challenges, but the god of this age is *an enemy of a different sort*, one which only our triune God can face and overcome. Let us depend evermore on him to do what he alone can do – unveil the minds of unbelievers so they, like us, can see the glory of God in the face of Jesus Christ.

Nicene Creed and Prayer

After reciting and/or singing the Nicene Creed (located in the Appendix), pray the following prayer:

> Eternal, faithful God, we pray for our pastor. Grant him grace to speak boldly that he may proclaim thy Word unafraid, in season and out of season, and be a faithful steward of thy mysteries. Hold him fast to the one thing needful and give him strength for his ministry. And open thou our hearts, that we may gladly hear thy Word and never weary in the doing of thy holy will; through Jesus Christ our Lord. Amen.
>
> ~ John W. Doberstein, ed. *A Lutheran Prayer Book.* Philadelphia: Fortress Press, 1960. p 100.

Scripture Memorization Review

Review with a partner, write out and/or recite the text for last class session's assigned memory verse: 1 Peter 2.9-10.

Assignments Due

Turn in your summary of the reading assignment for last week, that is, your brief response and explanation of the main points that the authors were seeking to make in the assigned reading (Reading Completion Sheet).

CONTACT

Who You Are Is Shouting at Me

 In the last decade, the evangelical Church has suffered much in the moral breakdown of a number of its leaders who were exposed to public ridicule and shame due to their own sexual misconduct. Important and influential Christian leaders whose preaching and teaching ministries went around the world fell from dizzying heights to the hard earth of reality because their lives did not coincide with their messages. In some way these notable examples illustrate a fundamental spiritual truth: our lives communicate and shout to others as much as our language ever does. The little quip "Your life is talking so loud I can't hear what you are saying" seems to be more than just a little homespun wit. In your opinion, what is the relationship between the character of the preacher and the perceived validity of his message? How connected is our testimony and reputation to the integrity of the Word of God and to the credibility of our message?

The Convicting Power of the Holy Spirit and the Ministry of Preaching

 In John 16.7-11, the Lord Jesus provides us with astounding revelation about the nature of the Holy Spirit which has ramifications for the work of the preaching ministry.

> John 16.7-11 – Nevertheless, I tell you the truth: it is to your advantage that I go away, for if I do not go away, the Helper will not come to you. But if I go, I will send him to you. [8] And when he comes, he will convict the world concerning sin and righteousness and judgment: [9] concerning sin, because they do not believe in me; [10] concerning righteousness, because I go to the Father, and you will see me no longer; [11] concerning judgment, because the ruler of this world is judged.

Here, Jesus makes it plain that the Holy Spirit (not the evangelical preacher) is the one who convicts the world concerning sin, righteousness, and judgment. It is the Spirit who draws the world to the Lord, that enables them to see themselves as they really are – lost, desperate, without hope and without the Lord. If this is so, and only the Holy Spirit can truly convict the lost person of their need for God, what is the role of the "foolishness of preaching" (cf. 1. Cor. 1.18, 21)? If the Spirit is the only one who can truly transform, why do we need *preachers* at all? What does Paul mean when he suggests that people cannot hear *without someone preaching* (cf. Rom. 10.14-15: But how are they to call on him in whom they have not believed? And how are they to believe in him of whom they have never heard? And how are they to hear without someone preaching? [15] And how are they to preach unless they are sent? As it is written, "How beautiful are the feet of those who preach the good news!")?

Dependent on the Holy Spirit, or Just Plain Lazy?

Discipline and rigorous preparation in sermon preparation and study is absent from the lifestyle of many evangelical leaders today. Resting on the truth that without the Holy Spirit no spiritual fruit can be borne, many are substituting what they call the "faith walk" for diligent study of the Word of God. Overmuch concentration on preparation is viewed by these leaders as carnality, pride, and a denial of the fundament work of the Spirit. They rather "go with the flow," "look for the leading of the Lord at the moment," and "wait for the leading of the Spirit when the time is right." Others, equally committed to the Holy Spirit, believe that, like discipline and exercise, preparation does not hinder spontaneity but rather makes it possible. They argue that Michael Jordan could do all the remarkable things he attempted on the court because of untold hours of preparation during practice. Which "school of thought" do you think gets closer to the biblical injunctions both to "walk in the Spirit" as well as "study to show yourself a workman that needs not to be ashamed?"

The Ministry of Proclamation: *Kerygma*

Contact, Content, and Connection in the Preaching Ministry

Rev. Dr. Don L. Davis

Summary

Three essential steps are involved in preaching effective sermons: establishing contact with the mind and world of the audience, delivering the content of the Word of God with clarity and boldness, and making specific and dynamic connection with the audience on the meaning of the preached Word to their spiritual condition and lives. In the first step we *establish contact* with our hearers as we spotlight issues, concerns, ideas, or experiences that resonate in the lives of the audience, which can also be used as a springboard into our preaching content. In the second phase, we *communicate the content* of Scripture, painting a picture through our words to focus on the person of Christ and his Kingdom. The Church calendar or *liturgical year*, along with the resources, texts, and tools associated with it can provide our audiences with a continuous retelling of the Story of God in the life and work of Jesus. The final step in effective biblical preaching involves *making connections* with the truth, coming to feel and understand their spiritual condition before God, and responding so as to be transformed by the truth in a way appropriate to their life situation and place.

Our objective for this lesson, *Contact, Content, and Connection in the Preaching Ministry*, is to enable you to see that:

- Three essential steps are involved in preaching effective sermons: *establishing contact* with the mind and world of the audience, *communicating the content* of the Word of God with clarity and boldness, and *making specific and dynamic connection* with the audience on the meaning of the preached Word to their spiritual condition and lives.

- In the first step of effective biblical preaching, we establish contact with our hearers as we spotlight issues, concerns, ideas, or experiences that resonate in the lives of the audience, which can also be used as a springboard into our preaching content.

- The second phase of effective biblical preaching deals with delivering the content of Scripture. Our goal is to paint a picture through our words in the spiritual eyes of our hearers so as to show them our themes, not merely tell them about it. The content of our preaching ought to focus on the person of Christ and his Kingdom, and be presented in a manner that resonates with the biblical methods of images, symbols, and stories, being organized in a plain and simple manner.

- The Church calendar or *liturgical year*, along with the resources, texts, and tools associated with it can provide our audiences with a continuous retelling of the Story of God in the life and work of Jesus. Through its effective use, our preaching can thus highlight the whole counsel of God annually through a retelling of Jesus' story.

- The final step in effective biblical preaching involves making connections with the truths of our preaching and the specific and particular responses of the audience. Our aim must be to help our audiences come to feel and understand their spiritual condition before God through our clear appeals and bold invitations for repentance and change.

- Since the goal of biblical preaching is life transformation and formation, we ought to be open to the Spirit to follow up all responses made to our preaching, directing the hearer to the response appropriate to their life situation and place.

Video Outline

I. **Establishing Contact with Your Hearers: Turn Your SPOTLIGHT upon an Issue, Concern, Idea, or Experience that You Can Use as a Springboard into Your Theme**

   Prepare and preach sermons that get their attention by speaking directly to the context of your audience with language, in particular ways, and through forms they naturally perceive and easily understand.

   A. Speak directly to the context of your audience, 1 Cor. 9.19-23.

      1. Know the situation of your audience, 1 Chron. 12.32.

2. Use plain, non technical language, 1 Cor. 2.1-2.

3. Avoid an overly heady presentation.

   a. 1 Cor. 1.22-25

   b. 1 Cor. 4.10

   c. 2 Cor. 4.7-12

4. Key in on the things they are living and feeling, see Paul's quotation of Greek poetry in Acts 17.27-28.

B. Be visual, concrete, and simple: start with a picture or incident that the audience understands and knows, and go from there to *what they do not know.*

C. Develop a checklist to spur ideas.

   1. What is currently the "talk of the town" where you live?

   2. What are the big issues that people are concerned about?

   3. What are the opportunities that everyone is looking forward to?

   4. What are the fears of the people; their critical concerns?

Preaching Addresses the Non-Christian World

In the NT, preaching is 'the public proclamation of Christianity to the non-Christian world' (C. H. Dodd, The Apostolic Preaching and its Development, 1944, p. 7). It is not religious discourse to a closed group of initiates, but open and public proclamation of God's redemptive activity in and through Jesus Christ.

~ D. R. W. Wood. *New Bible Dictionary.* 3rd ed. Downers Grove, IL: InterVarsity Press, 2000, p. 950.

II. Communicate the Word of God Effectively: Paint the Picture in the Eyes of Your Listeners to Show Them Your Theme, Not Merely Tell Them About It.

Prepare and preach sermons that are biblical, outlining the Kingdom of God, and dealing with the whole counsel of God.

A. Preach the Word: focus on Christ.

2 Tim. 4.2 – **Preach the word**; be ready in season and out of season; reprove, rebuke, and exhort, with complete patience and teaching.

Col. 1.27-29 – To them God chose to make known how great among the Gentiles are the riches of the glory of this mystery, which is Christ in you, the hope of glory. [28] **Him we proclaim**, warning everyone and teaching everyone with all wisdom, that we may present everyone mature in Christ. [29] For this I toil, struggling with all his energy that he powerfully works within me.

1. Preach on numerous themes, end with a single subject.

2. Concentrate on Jesus and his Kingdom, Gal. 3.1.

3. Refuse to ignore the big picture; never teach anything without reference to Jesus Christ and him crucified.

    a. John 5.39-40

    b. Acts 4.2

    c. Acts 5.42

    d. Acts 8.35

Preach Christ and His Kingdom

One central motif in the Scriptures is the kingdom of God. It was the main thrust of Jesus' teaching and preaching. Jesus came as the fulfillment of John the Baptist's message, which was clear, precise, and simple: "Repent, for the kingdom of God is at hand."

~ R. C. Sproul. *Following Christ.* (electronic ed.). Wheaton, IL: Tyndale House Publishers, 1996.

e. Acts 17.3

f. Acts 18.28

g. Acts 28.23

B. Preach the Word in the way it speaks itself: with images, symbols, and stories.

1. Jesus is the living substance of all of the OT types and figures.

    a. Matt. 5.17-18

    b. Luke 24.27, 44-48

    c. John 5.39-40

2. Jesus spoke in parables, filled with imagery, stories, drama and irony.

    a. The Good Samaritan, Luke 10.29-37

    b. The Prodigal Son, Luke 15.11-32

    c. The Vine and the Branches, John 15.1-16

    d. The Lilies of the Field, Matt. 6.28-29

C. Organize your ideas in a plain, simple manner, 2 Cor. 11.2-3.

1. Keep your use of materials, outlines, and technology simple.

2. Anything that takes away from the message is not helpful.

3. Tricks, gimmicks, or goofy things will obscure the message.

D. Preaching is drama and theater: use your words and gestures to *paint the picture* in the mind of your audience, Gal. 3.1.

1. Recognize the literary craftsmanship of the story of Messiah and his Kingdom – it is quite literally the greatest story ever told!

2. Be *dramatic*: the stories and images beg for animation and action.

3. Be *transparent*: use personal examples and experience to stitch truths into your listeners' tapestries.

4. Be *visual*: concentrate on using metaphor, images, and symbols to communicate.

E. Teach the whole counsel of God.

1. Use the *Church calendar* to give an annual retelling of the Story of Jesus to your congregation.

2. Use the *lectionary* (the three year rotating preaching schedule) to teach through the entire Bible every year or three years.

3. Use your commitment to the whole counsel of God to help your people view the story of Christ and his Kingdom in every section and book of the Scriptures, Luke 24.44-48.

   a. He fulfills the Messianic prophecies.

   b. He embodies the OT figures.

   c. He is the climax of the Temple and its sacrifices.

   d. He keeps with perfect obedience the ethical standards of the Law.

F. Preaching that counts outlines the message of the Kingdom of God and the reign of God inaugurated in Jesus Christ, Acts 28.23, 31.

III. Make Connections with Their Response: Affirm the Word as a MIRROR to Reveal to the Listener Their Exact Spiritual Position and Condition before God.

Prepare and preach sermons that point to concrete ways that your hearers may respond in faith and obedience to God's Word.

A. Hold the mirror steady, James 1.22-25.

1. Speak directly to the point that your message and the Scriptures seek to make.

> **Preaching as Divine Compulsion**
>
> *Perhaps the most prominent feature in NT preaching is the sense of divine compulsion. In Mark 1.38 it is reported that Jesus did not return to those who sought his healing power but pressed on to other towns in order that he might preach there also – 'for that is why I came out'. Peter and John reply to the restrictions of the Sanhedrin with the declaration, 'We cannot but speak the things which we have seen and heard' (Acts 4.20). 'Woe to me if I do not preach the gospel', cries the apostle Paul (1 Cor. 9.16). This sense of compulsion is the sine qua non of true preaching. Preaching is not the relaxed recital of morally neutral truths: it is God himself breaking in and confronting man with a demand for decision. This sort of preaching meets with opposition. In 2 Cor. 11.23-28 Paul lists his sufferings for the sake of the gospel.*
>
> ~ R. H. Mounce. "Preaching." *The New Bible Dictionary*. D. R. W. Wood, ed. 3rd ed. Downers Grove, IL: InterVarsity Press, 1996. p. 951.

2. Be blunt and clear on what your point is.

3. Talk about the various responses possible in regard to this truth, and the results of making them.

   a. Warn the people of the consequences of ignoring the Word of God.

   b. Encourage the people with the blessing that comes from responding to the message of the Lord.

4. Ask for dramatic expressions of faith, and radical evidence of obedience.

B. Make a clear appeal.

1. Appeal to the heart: ask your listeners to consider where they stand in regard to your message.

2. Appeal to the mind: ask your listeners to believe the message of the Word of God.

3. Appeal to the will: ask your listeners to respond to the message in a concrete way.

C. Give a bold invitation: everyone is building something to live their lives upon, Luke 6.47-49.

1. To come to Christ as Savior and Lord

   a. Acts 16.31-34

b. Acts 20.21

c. Acts 22.16

2. To return to Christ from a backslidden condition

3. To increase and abound in discipleship

D. Follow up the response, Acts 2.37-41.

1. Those who respond should be interacted with: "What precisely do you want to do?"

2. Whatever their response, we should respond as compassionately and openly as possible.

3. Lay out the next steps for the responder.

4. Celebrate all true responses as gifts of the Spirit.

a. For those who come to Jesus for the first time in faith

b. For those who return to Jesus after turning their backs

c. For those who desire to give Jesus even more than they have before

Declare the Kingdom Come in Jesus Christ

In the Gospels Jesus is characteristically portrayed as One who came 'heralding the kingdom of God'. In Luke 4.16-21 Jesus interprets his ministry as the fulfilment of Isaiah's prophecy of a coming Servant-Messiah through whom the kingdom of God would at last be realized. This kingdom is best understood as God's 'kingly rule' or 'sovereign action'. Only secondarily does it refer to a realm or people within that realm. That God's eternal sovereignty was now invading the realm of evil powers and winning the decisive victory was the basic content of Jesus' kerygma.

~ R. H. Mounce. "Preaching." In *The New Bible Dictionary*. D. R. W. Wood, ed. 3rd ed. Downers Grove, IL: InterVarsity Press, 1996, p. 951.

Conclusion

- Three critical dimensions lie at the heart of planning and applying an effective preaching ministry.

- We must first *establish contact* with hearers, *communicate the content* of the Word clearly and boldly, and finally strive to *make connections* with the truth of the message and the lives of the audience.

- In all of these efforts, we must never forget that it is only the Holy Spirit who makes the delivered Word effective in our preaching.

Student Questions and Response

The following questions were designed to help you review the material in the video. In this lesson we saw how the preaching ministry involves three critical dimensions: *establishing contact* with hearers, *communicating the content* of the Word clearly and boldly, *making connections* with the truth of the message and the lives of the audience. As we prepare ourselves diligently in Scripture and depend on the Holy Spirit, we can learn how to represent the Lord with clarity and integrity through the preached Word. Review these three dimensions carefully through the questions below.

1. Give an overview of the three essential steps involved in effective biblical preaching. How do these dimensions recognize and build upon the essential ministry of the Holy Spirit in all effective presentations of the Word?

2. How do we establish contact with the audience? To what extent must we understand and incorporate issues of culture and custom into our work if we are to gain the ear of our audience? What limits exist in shaping our message with attention to culture, in other words, how do we keep from *changing the message itself* to accommodate the culture of those whom we address?

3. Why is it important to use contact *only as a springboard* into the larger context of the Word of God? What is liable to happen if we do not progress beyond the immediate concerns and issues of the hearers and move on to the word of God regarding Christ and his Kingdom?

4. What are some central principles we ought to keep in mind as we seek to communicate the Word of God with clarity and boldness to our hearers in a way they can appreciate culturally? What limits ought we to place on *the way in which we communicate* the Gospel? How does Paul's instruction in 1 Corinthians 9 help us to see the role of freedom in preaching the Word to others (cf. 1 Cor. 9.19-21)?

5. What did Jesus and the apostles preach as their actual content during their ministries, and how should their themes and focus affect what we choose to preach about today?

6. Why is it important to preach the content of the Bible in a manner that resonates with the Bible's own methods of presentation: the use of images, metaphors, symbols, and stories presented in a plain and simple manner?

7. How may our use of the *liturgical year* (along with the resources, texts, and tools associated with it) provide us with a way to expose our audiences with a continuous retelling of the Story of God, and in some way allow us to preach "the whole counsel of God" (cf. Acts 20.27)?

8. What are some practical ways in which our preaching can help our audiences *make connections* with the truths of our preaching? What is the difference between making connections and manipulating responses from an audience? What is the role of making invitations and appeals to our audience as we proclaim the Word to them?

9. Why should we place a large emphasis upon following up all responses made to our preaching, and how can we use these specific follow-ups to reinforce our messages to particular individuals and families?

LESSON 4 | THE EQUIPPING MINISTRY: THE MINISTRY OF PROCLAMATION / 299

CONNECTION

Summary of Key Concepts

This lesson focuses upon the ministry of proclamation, through the *kerygma*, the preaching of the Word of God in dependence upon the Holy Spirit. Through his influence alone, we can learn the art of obeying God as we proclaim his Word, responding obediently to the call of God to preach, convinced of the power of the Word of God for salvation and change, and gaining skill as we learn to establish contact, communicate the content the Word of God clearly, and make specific connection with the lives of our listeners. The following concepts underlie the principles of this lesson on the *kerygma*.

- Three essential steps are involved in preaching effective sermons: *establishing contact* with the mind and world of the audience, *communicating the content* of the Word of God with clarity and boldness, and *making specific and dynamic connection* with the audience on the meaning of the preached Word to their spiritual condition and lives.

- In the first step of effective biblical preaching, we establish contact with our hearers as we spotlight issues, concerns, ideas, or experiences that resonate in the lives of the audience, which can also be used as a springboard into our preaching content.

- The second phase of effective biblical preaching deals with delivering the content of Scripture. Our goal is to paint a picture through our words in the spiritual eyes of our hearers so as to show them our themes, not merely tell them about it. The content of our preaching ought to focus on the person of Christ and his Kingdom, and be presented in a manner that resonates with the biblical methods of images, symbols, and stories, being organized in a plain and simple manner.

- The Church calendar or *liturgical year*, along with the resources, texts, and tools associated with it can provide our audiences with a continuous retelling of the Story of God in the life and work of Jesus. Through its effective use, our preaching can thus highlight the whole counsel of God annually through a retelling of Jesus' story.

- The final step in effective biblical preaching involves *making connections* with the truths of our preaching and the specific and particular responses of the audience. Our aim must be to help our audiences come to feel and understand their spiritual condition before God through our clear appeals and bold invitations for repentance and change.

- Since the goal of biblical preaching is life transformation and formation, we ought to be open to the Spirit to follow up all responses made to our preaching, directing the hearer to the response appropriate to their life situation and place.

Student Application and Implications

Now is the time for you to discuss with your fellow students your questions about the Holy Spirit's role and the essential steps involved in preaching effective sermons. What particular questions do you have in light of the material you have just studied? Maybe some of the questions below might help you form your own, more specific and critical questions.

- How would you describe your own knowledge and relationship to the Holy Spirit? What kind of emphasis has the Holy Spirit had in your life from the beginning of your walk with God?

- In your preparation and teaching of the Bible, how have you sensed the leading and direction of the Holy Spirit? Can you describe a situation where you experienced the power of the Holy Spirit in a unique way as you were either preaching or sharing the Word with others?

- How would you say that the Holy Spirit has prepared your life as you have begun to read yourself for a richer, more fruitful ministry in Christ?

- Finish the following statement: "Of all the ways I have tended to hinder the work of the Spirit in my walk, my greatest challenge is in the area of . . ."

- In surveying the traits of the kind of person the Spirit uses, which areas are you most clear in, and which are your most needy areas? How has God been leading you recently to get you ready for the next level of growth and usefulness in ministry? Explain.

- How well do you understand and can you articulate a compelling "theology of the Holy Spirit?" Summarize your own belief about the Holy Spirit and his working in the preaching ministry in *three simple sentences only*.

- What kind of approach do you currently use when you share the Word of God with others? How can the "Contact, Content, Connection" help you in becoming more clear in your presentation of the Word to others?

- Are you the kind of person who can be flexible in the midst of your presentation – why or why not? How do you know that God wants you to change what you are going to say as you are sharing the Word with others?

- How well do you understand and can you defend the "content of Scripture," that is, the Scriptures' focus on the person and work of Christ and his Kingdom?

- Have you had any exposure to the Church calendar or liturgical year, or the lectionary? If not, spend some time outside of class researching some on the nature of these resources and how they can help us year by year to continuously retell of the Story of God in the life and work of Jesus.

- Finally, what kind of connections have you been making with the preached Word that you have heard over the last months? How have you personally responded to the appeals and invitations God has given you through the preached Word for both repentance and change?

CASE STUDIES

Interesting Plate, But No Solid Food

1. The new trends in the Church movement is the wholehearted acceptance of digital technologies and props in the presentation and preaching of the Word. Pastors use multi-media presentations, film clips, theater props, and even live animals in their presentations. Sermons are strictly forbidden to deal with "doctrinaire" issues and themes, and heavy theological jargon (even that of the NT itself!) is strictly avoided. Defined as "seeker sensitivity" the focus is on compatibility with culture and custom; to eliminate the distance between what the modern person is accustomed to in terms of quality of sound, picture, presentation, and experience in our fellowships. Choir members audition, the pastor is a production manager, and technical know-how is a standard. In a digital world, many have embraced this as the key to growth, and in fact, some mega-churches follow the same kind of protocol. What is noticeable in such venues, though, is that with short messages, softer subjects, and a lack of doctrine, the seeker friendly experience is not as effective in producing literate, ready disciples of Jesus. How do we (or should we) take seriously the digital world and seeker sensitive experience while, at the same time, preach the whole counsel of God from the pulpits of the city? Can we do the one without avoiding the other?

Nothing Succeeds Like Success – Or Does It?

 With the popularity of a handful of preachers and their congregations, many churches are moving wholesale to follow their example of success. The standard of success is plain and clear: large professional facilities, great and growing staff, solid financial base, growing numbers in attendance, and greater leverage in the larger secular world are added as indicators along with love for God and others, solid missions work, and steady growth. Moved by the outward signs of success, many preachers are more than willing to "learn from the best," and a host of preachers are now adapting their methods and directions from the more successful mega-churches. What is important in this experience is the new trend to be attentive to culture, and respond to it in our preaching and presentation. While we ought to be thankful for the outward signs of success with such attention to numbers, size, and influence, we ought to be open to critically examining the meaning of success in a preaching ministry. How do we measure success in the proclamation of the Word? Will a faithful declaration of the Word always lead to a large following, financial independence, and growth in terms of facilities? How do we know that we have been successful as a preacher of the Word of God?

Preaching as Performance – Taking the Drama of God too Seriously?

 A growing number of homiletical scholars are seeking to explore the relationship between preaching the Word of God and performing as an actor. While they are not emphasizing pretending to be something you are not, they are interested in exploring the connection between preaching as a kind of theater where the listener and the preacher encounter each other not in terms of the dry presentation of boring outlines, but in a living relationship where the spoken Word of the preacher becomes an event where God actually makes contact with the audience through the peaker. Surely, with the Bible's own unity built on the dramatic story of God that culminates in Jesus Christ, there may be room for us to understand how the Bible, more story world than philosophical outline, can be seen as the drama of God, and the preacher and congregation, as members in God's play. How important or distracting do you believe this emphasis on preaching as performance of the drama of God is for urban churches today? Can one truly ignore the dramatic, the world of imagery, metaphor, and symbol, and still be effective in communicating the heart and soul of the Bible, the story that we preach to the world and the Church?

Never Without an Invitation

 The nature of the content of the Gospel is that it demands response and action: repentance, surrender, obedience, faith, transformation. To preach the Word without this understanding has led many in both the pulpit and the pew to see preaching as largely a sharing of information rather than a challenge to transformation and formation in Christ. Baptistic and congregational traditions have for many years connected the preaching of the Word to an "Invitation to Discipleship," where the hearer, whether lost or saved, is enjoined to respond to the spoken Word right then and there while under the convicting power of the Holy Spirit. Although this practice has largely been abandoned in many evangelical settings today, this idea of invitation is literally built right into the liturgy of many Baptist congregations. The reasoning behind this is solid. They view the preaching of the Word as so important that it cannot be presented without call to response; and in some of these congregations they take the next hour to discuss the sermon and its implications. The heart of this understanding is the belief that every time the Word is proclaimed the Holy Spirit is present, and he may elect to so move on the heart of a person that without our invitation for action and acknowledgment, they may ignore his voice altogether. What do you believe about the role of this kind of invitation to the preached Word wherever it is given, whether to those who do not believe or to those in the Church? Should we always have an invitation to discipleship moment whenever the Word of God is preached? Why or why not?

Restatement of the Lesson's Thesis

The Holy Spirit of God, who both inspires and illumines the written Word of God, is central in every dimension of an effective preaching ministry. Apart from the Holy Spirit, the preached Word will produce no spiritual fruit, remaining ineffectual and unheeded in those who hear it. The Spirit works through individuals prepared for his leading, i.e., one who has obeyed the call of God to preach, embraced the power of the Word of God for salvation and change, and who seeks a mastery of the Word of God through disciplined study and liberated application, in his or her own life as well among those they seek to save and influence.

Throughout the preaching ministry process, the Spirit thwarts the devil as he seeks to veil and blind the minds of unbelievers, and empowers the preacher through his supply and gifting. He alone can convict the audience of the truth and confirm the spoken word with signs and wonders of its veracity. When the Holy Spirit is allowed to work, he converts and incorporates the new believer into the body of Christ.

Three essential steps are involved in preaching effective sermons: establishing contact with the mind and world of the audience, delivering the content of the Word of God with clarity and boldness, and making specific and dynamic connection with the audience on the meaning of the preached Word to their spiritual condition and lives. In the first step we *establish contact* with our hearers as we spotlight issues, concerns, ideas, or experiences that resonate in the lives of the audience, which can also be used as a springboard into our preaching content. In the second phase, we *communicate the content* of Scripture, painting a picture through our words to focus on the person of Christ and his Kingdom. The Church calendar or *liturgical year*, along with the resources, texts, and tools associated with it can provide our audiences with a continuous retelling of the Story of God in the life and work of Jesus. The final step in effective biblical preaching involves *making connections* with the truth, coming to feel and understand their spiritual condition before God, and response so as to be transformed by the truth in a way appropriate to their life situation and place.

Resources and Bibliographies

If you are interested in pursuing some of the ideas of *The Ministry of Proclamation: Kerygma*, you might want to give these books a try:

Allen, Ronald J. *Preaching the Topical Sermon*. Louisville: Westminster/John Knox Press, 1992.

Buechner, Frederick. *Telling the Truth: The Gospel as Tragedy, Comedy, and Fairy Tale*. New York: Harper & Row, 1977.

Craddock, Fred B. *As One Without Authority*. Nashville: Abingdon, 1971.

Fisher, Wallace E. *Who Dares to Preach? The Challenge of Biblical Preaching*. Minneapolis, MN: Augsburg Publishing House, 1979.

Gonzalez, Justo L. and Catherine G. Gonzalez. *Liberation Preaching: The Pulpit and the Oppressed*. Abingdon Preacher's Library. Nashville: Abingdon, 1980.

Koller, Charles W. *Expository Preaching Without Notes plus Sermons Preached Without Notes*. Grand Rapids, MI: Baker Book House, 1962.

Long, Thomas G. *Preaching and the Literary Forms of the Bible*. Philadelphia: Fortress Press, 1989.

Mitchell, Henry. *Black Preaching*. Nashville: Abingdon, 1990.

Ministry Connections

As an emerging leader interested in touching the lives of others with the Gospel of Christ, you should canvass the various principles covered in this lesson and seek to make your own ministry connection with an area in your life and ministry. What has been clear throughout this lesson is that it is not possible to ignore one's own life and expect to see God work in a direct and powerful way. God desires to work through us, and in order for this to occur, he must work within us. We must wrestle with the meaning of these truths for our own lives, and be willing for the Holy Spirit to work specifically afresh in our lives as the precursor for working through our lives. Spend time meditating on the truths in this lesson, and ask the Lord to reveal to you the area or concerns he would have you bring before him for his cleansing, sharpening, and development.

Counseling and Prayer

Take the time to pray with and for your fellow colleagues regarding the application of these truths on the Holy Spirit, and the preaching of the Word of God. Surely, any preaching that in fact claims to be both biblical and evangelical will always be nurtured by prayer. What you must seek from the Lord is not merely snatches and bits of hurried prayer, but a life orientation to the Spirit that will make every phase of your study and ministry an expression of prayer.

The relationship of prayer and obedience is clearly seen throughout the word of God. E. M. Bounds eloquently argues for our lives to be deeply prayerful if we are to make the insights of the Word of God come alive in our hearts and minds. Notice how he emphasizes how prayer opens the way for obedience, and obedience makes prayer effectual in our lives:

> Our Lord Jesus Christ, "holy, harmless, undefiled, separate from sinners," had full liberty of approach and ready access to God in prayer. And He had this free and full access because of His unquestioning obedience to His Father. Right through His earthly life His supreme care and desire was to do the will of His Father. And this fact, coupled with another – the consciousness of having so ordered His life – gave Him confidence and assurance, which enabled Him to draw near to the throne of grace with unbounded confidence, born of obedience, and promising acceptance, audience, and answer. Loving obedience puts us where we can "ask anything in His name," with the assurance, that "He will do it." Loving obedience brings us into the prayer realm, and makes us beneficiaries of the wealth of Christ, and of the riches of His grace, through the coming of the Holy Spirit who will abide with us, and be in us. Cheerful obedience to God, qualifies us to pray effectually.
>
> ~ E. M. Bounds. *The Necessity of Prayer.* (electronic ed.) Oak Harbor, WA: Logos Research Systems, Inc., 1999.

Truly, if the assertions we made in this lesson concerning the Holy Spirit are correct, our ministry of preaching, our very life is inseparable from our spirituality, that is, our relationship to the Holy Spirit. God longs to be longed for, and we must oblige him by admitting our need for his grace and aid. Share specific requests with your fellow students, and trust God together to provide you with the grace to have his will accomplished in your life. It has been attributed to John Calvin to have referred to prayer as "the soul of faith," and truly our faith is lifeless and empty without prayer. Seek to make contact with God on the issues covered in this lesson, and trust him for provision and direction.

ASSIGNMENTS

Scripture Memory

2 Timothy 2.1-2

Reading Assignment

To prepare for class, please visit *www.tumi.org/books* to find next week's reading assignment, or ask your Mentor.

Other Assignments

Your ministry project and your exegetical project should now be outlined, determined, and accepted by your instructor. Make sure that you plan ahead, so you will not be late in turning in your assignments.

Looking Forward to the Next Lesson

In our next lesson, *Foundations of Christian Mission: The Vision and Biblical Foundation for Christian Mission*, we will look at mission as the warfare of the ages. We will see the proclamation of God's kingdom rule in the person of Jesus of Nazareth. Beginning with the clear affirmation of God's sovereignty, we see God has determined to reestablish his rule over his creation, which fell from his grace through the rebellion of the devil and humankind at the Fall. Since this time, God has taken the position of warrior to bring the universe back under his rulership. In the person of Jesus of Nazareth, God is reasserting his right to rule over the universe, and mission is the proclamation of that Kingdom come in Christ.

FOR FURTHER STUDY

Please see the following resources in *Picturing Theology: An A-Z Collection of TUMI's Key Diagrams, Charts, Graphics, and Articles*:

- *Story: The Crux of Revelation*, page 402
- *Discipling the Faithful: Establishing Leaders for the Urban Church*, page 80
- *Spiritual Service Checklist*, page 395
- *Translating the Story of God*, page 505
- *The Hump*, page 193

UNIT 4

Urban Mission

Foundations for Christian Mission:
The Vision and Biblical Foundation for Christian Mission

Evangelism and Spiritual Warfare:
Spiritual Warfare – The Binding of the Strong Man

Focus on Reproduction:
Church Growth – Reproducing in Number and Quality

Doing Justice and Loving Mercy:
Let Justice Roll Down – The Vision and Theology of the Kingdom

Introduction to Urban Mission Unit

Greetings, in the strong name of Jesus Christ!

Welcome to the fourth unit of the Cornerstone Curriculum, *Urban Mission*.

The theme of mission has not received the kind of focus and attention in our urban churches that it should. Having been seen largely as a work across the ocean in far flung corners of the world, we have failed to give it the kind of critical analysis that it deserves. From one vantage point, the entirety of the Christian faith could be seen as a response of mission, the call to go to the nations and proclaim Jesus of Nazareth as Lord and King of the reign of God. The NT is a collection of missionary documents given to churches that were founded by the apostles, the original missionaries of the Christian faith. God himself is the original missionary, coming to the world in Christ and reconciling it to himself (2 Cor. 5.18-21). Indeed, Christianity is mission.

In our first lesson, *Foundations for Christian Mission: The Vision and Biblical Foundation for Christian Mission*, we will look at mission as the warfare of the ages. We will see the proclamation of God's kingdom rule in the person of Jesus of Nazareth. Beginning with the clear affirmation of God's sovereignty, we see God has determined to reestablish his rule over his creation, which fell from his grace through the rebellion of the devil and humankind at the Fall. Since this time, God has taken the position of warrior to bring the universe back under his rulership. In the person of Jesus of Nazareth, God is reasserting his right to rule over the universe, and mission is the proclamation of that Kingdom come in Christ.

Evangelism is proclaiming and demonstrating to the world that God has visited the world in the person of Jesus of Nazareth, and that this visitation is now accompanied by liberation from the devil and from the effects of sin! To evangelize is to prophesy deliverance in Messiah Jesus.

Our second lesson, *Evangelism and Spiritual Warfare: The Binding of the Strong Man*, shows that through the life, death, and resurrection of Jesus Christ, believers are delivered from Satan's dominion, as well as from the effects of the Curse through the power of the Spirit. Evangelism is proclaiming God's deliverance through Jesus Christ to the entire world in the power of the Holy Spirit. Our Lord Jesus desires that we bear much fruit to the glory and praise of God (John 15.8-16). May the Lord bless your study of his Word so you can join the harvest workers in gathering the fruit of the Lord's own salvation, to the Father's glory!

As 21st century disciples of Jesus in the cities of America, we desire to be fruitful in the work of God – ministering to the lost, and advancing the Kingdom of Christ (John 15.8, 16).

In our third lesson, *Focus on Reproduction: Church Growth – Reproducing in Number and Quality*, we survey Jesus' call to make disciples of all nations, to Evangelize, as well as to affirm that radical discipleship is proven in Christian community. Jesus has called us to evangelize the lost, equip new disciples to live the Christian life, and to empower his Church to reproduce itself, all for the glory of God. May his Spirit grant you the power and desire to make disciples where you live, and so multiply his Church, to the glory of his great name!

As disciples of the Lord Jesus Christ, we are responsible to display in our words and deeds the life of the Kingdom to Come in the midst of our churches, and through our lifestyles and ministries of compassion to others. As leaders of the church in the city, it is critical that we understand the richness of the biblical insights around this subject, as well as explore the possible ways in which we as believers and Christian ministers can demonstrate the love and justice of the Kingdom where we live.

Our fourth and final lesson, *Doing Justice and Loving Mercy: Let Justice Roll Down – The Vision and Theology of the Kingdom*, focuses on the *imago Dei* (i.e., the image of God) in Scripture. We will see the uniqueness of humankind, and explore its implications for viewing all individuals, families, peoples, and nations as precious and irreplaceable. In a world torn by violence, cruelty, and injustice, we desperately need representatives of the Kingdom who can demonstrate both the justice and mercy of our Lord Jesus Christ. Only the Church can reveal the righteousness, unity, and grace of the Kingdom of God in the midst of a world torn by malice, vengeance, and disunity. Only in Christ can we pursue a peace that is authentic and that will last. Until our Lord returns, we are called to display his righteousness in the earth. May God richly bless you in every way as you refresh your memory of our call to demonstrate justice and love mercy, in the Church and in the world, to the glory of God.

Unit Assignments

Exegetical Project

As a part of your participation in the Cornerstone Curriculum, you will be required to do an exegesis (inductive study) on a passage in the Word of God:

a. Matthew 28.16-20

b. 1 Corinthians 15.1-8

c. Acts 1.1-8

d. Isaiah 58.1-10

The purpose of this exegetical project is to give you an opportunity to do a detailed study of a major passage on the nature and function of the Word of God. As you study one of the above texts (or a text which you and your Mentor agree upon which may not be on the list), our hope is that you will be able to show how this passage illumines or makes plain the significance of the Word of God for our spirituality and for our lives together in the Church. We also desire that the Spirit will give you insight as to how you can relate its meaning directly to your own personal walk of discipleship, as well as to the leadership role God has given to you currently in your church and ministry.

Memory Verses

The memorized Word is a central priority for your life and ministry as a believer and leader in the Church of Jesus Christ. There are relatively few verses, but they are significant in their content. Each class session you will be expected to recite (orally or in writing) the assigned verses to your Mentor.

a. Matthew 28.18-20

b. Ephesians 2.8-10

c. Ephesians 6.10-13

d. Amos 5.20-24

Textbooks

Each Cornerstone Curriculum unit has assigned textbooks which are read and discussed throughout the course. We encourage you to read, reflect upon, and respond to these with your professors, mentors, and fellow learners. Because of the fluid availability of the texts (e.g., books going out of print), we maintain our *official* Cornerstone Curriculum Required Textbook list on our website. Please visit *www.tumi.org/books* to obtain the current listing of this unit's texts and reading assignments.

Ministry Project Our sincere desire is that you will apply your learning practically, correlating your learning with real experiences and needs in your personal life, and in your ministry in and through your church. Therefore, a key part of completing the Cornerstone Curriculum will be for you to design a ministry project to help you share some of the insights you have learned from this course with others.

Unit Exam At the end of each unit, your Mentor will give you a unit exam (closed book) to be completed at home. You will be asked a question that helps you reflect on what you have learned in the unit and how it affects the way you think about or practice ministry. Your Mentor will give you due dates and other information when the Unit Exam is handed out.

Foundations for Christian Mission
The Vision and Biblical Foundation for Christian Mission

Lesson Objectives

Welcome in the strong name of Jesus Christ! After your reading, study, discussion, and application of the materials in this lesson, you will be able to:

- Outline the motif of *Mission as the War of the Spheres*, which is perhaps the most dynamic image of mission in Scripture, the proclamation of God's kingdom rule in the person of Jesus of Nazareth.

- Give an overview of the reign of God in Scripture, beginning with the Lord as creator and sustainer of all, and the mystery of iniquity (the satanic rebellion in the heavenlies), which resulted in the temptation and fall of humankind, and the curse, yet ended with God's promise to crush the head of the serpent through the Seed of the woman. As a result of the Fall, the universe is at war and God is a warrior.

- Lay out the major points of God as the divine warrior in the OT, including God as warrior defeating evil in its symbolism as a river and sea, defeating Pharaoh and his armies, who led his people into victory as the great Lord of armies, and who fought against his own people because of their disobedience and rebellion. Also, Israel's prophets pictured God as a divine warrior who through his Messiah would finally destroy all evil once and for all time.

- Show how the promise of the Messiah in David's heir represented God's intent to provide a king who would restore the reign to his people, rule the nations with justice and righteousness, and bring a knowledge of God to the entire earth as Lord and King.

- Argue from Scripture how God's promised rule has been inaugurated through the person and work of Jesus Christ, who is the one from the Davidic line who will restore the reign of God. In him and the various aspects of his birth, teaching, miracles, exorcisms, deeds, death, and resurrection, the Kingdom of God is now here, already present in the life of the Church.

- Explain the "already/not yet dimension" of the Kingdom of God; although the Kingdom of God has come in the fulfillment of the

Messianic promise in the person of Jesus, the Kingdom will only be consummated at his Second Coming, when the full and final manifestation will occur. The Church is both sign and foretaste of the Kingdom present today, who is authorized to proclaim and demonstrate the victory of Christ over Satan and the curse as his agent and deputy.

- Draw out the main implications of the *Mission as the War of the Spheres* motif, including the reassertion of God's rule today over his universe in Jesus Christ, God as the warrior who through his anointed One has defeated the power of the devil and the effects of the curse, and how mission through this lens becomes the display and proclamation of the rule of God here and now. Making disciples among all nations is advancing the reign of God by testifying to its coming in the person of Jesus of Nazareth.

Devotion

The Divine Romance

Eph. 5.25-32 – Husbands, love your wives, as Christ loved the Church and gave himself up for her, [26] that he might sanctify her, having cleansed her by the washing of water with the word, [27] so that he might present the church to himself in splendor, without spot or wrinkle or any such thing, that she might be holy and without blemish. [28] In the same way husbands should love their wives as their own bodies. He who loves his wife loves himself. [29] For no one ever hated his own flesh, but nourishes and cherishes it, just as Christ does the church, [30] because we are members of his body. [31] "Therefore a man shall leave his father and mother and hold fast to his wife, and the two shall become one flesh." [32] This mystery is profound, and I am saying that it refers to Christ and the church.

One of the great wonders of Scripture is its deep and profound mysteries which are embedded in the lives and experiences of its great characters. In a real sense this quality of Scripture speaks to its inspiration; great lessons can be gleaned about the nature of God and his relationship with his people from the lessons learned in sync with its chief characters. The example of Adam and Eve, and their union together as man and wife is a symbolic representation of the great unity between Christ and his people, who, amazingly according to this text, is his bride.

What an amazing lesson for us today, one which reveals God's heart for humankind as it has been fulfilled in the Church. Almighty God has determined from the beginning of time to gather from among all peoples a peculiar possession for Jesus of Nazareth. Here this text reveals a profound mystery: at the heart of the universe lies a marvelous cosmic drama, a divine romance, a marvelous and epic true myth and legend of an undying love relationship between an Almighty God, and a people. We are living witnesses of it, and as those who believe in the truth of the Gospel regarding Jesus of Nazareth, we too have actually become a part of that people, called and chosen to live out that drama of the divine romance.

What is the nature of this divine romance? You see it in the Old Testament between God and his people Israel:

> Isa. 62.5 – For as a young man marries a young woman, so shall your sons marry you, and as the bridegroom rejoices over the bride, so shall your God rejoice over you.

Again, we read of the Lord's determination to delight in his people like a bridegroom:

> Isa. 62.4 – You shall no more be termed Forsaken, and your land shall no more be termed Desolate, but you shall be called My Delight Is in Her, and your land Married; for the Lord delights in you, and your land shall be married.

The righteous of the Lord will be adorned as a bride at a wedding – his wedding. (Cf. Isaiah 61.10: "I will greatly rejoice in the Lord; my soul shall exult in my God, for he has clothed me with the garments of salvation; he has covered me with the robe of righteousness, as a bridegroom decks himself like a priest with a beautiful headdress, and as a bride adorns herself with her jewels.") The God of heaven sees his people as a bride, and himself as her bridegroom and lover.

This same dramatic image is seen most clearly in the drama of Christ and his Church, with our Lord as the bridegroom and the Church as his bride. The following texts give a sampling of the reference of Jesus as the bridegroom of his people:

> Matt. 9.15 – And Jesus said to them, "Can the wedding guests mourn as long as the bridegroom is with them? The days will come when the bridegroom is taken away from them, and then they will fast."

> John 3.29 – The one who has the bride is the bridegroom. The friend of the bridegroom, who stands and hears him, rejoices greatly at the bridegroom's voice. Therefore this joy of mine is now complete.

> Rev. 21.2 – And I saw the holy city, new Jerusalem, coming down out of heaven from God, prepared as a bride adorned for her husband.

The clearest and most direct association occurs in our devotional text itself:

> Eph. 5.25-27 – Husbands, love your wives, as Christ loved the church and gave himself up for her, [26] that he might sanctify her, having cleansed her by the washing of water with the word, [27] so that he might present the church to himself in splendor, without spot or wrinkle or any such thing, that she might be holy and without blemish.

According to this text, the love that a man has for his wife should be patterned upon the love that Jesus has for his people. Furthermore, the heart and goal of all apostolic ministry should be the preparation of the people of God for the ceremony and union ahead: "I feel a divine jealousy for you, for I betrothed you to one husband, to present you as a pure virgin to Christ" (2 Cor. 11.2). Christ is building his Church, his sacred company of disciples from all eras, places, and times, those whom he personally purchased for himself, and those who will serve him, with not even the gates of Hades being able to overcome their onslaught (Matt. 16.15-19).

Any of us who have gone to a wedding know the difference between the bride as she ordinarily appears over against how she is adorned for the wedding day! In the same way, God is preparing for his Son a bride, a people, a divine assembly who will forever be at his side and who will reign with him in the coming Kingdom.

This makes it simple and easy to understand the role of mission: the task of mission is to gather the remaining souls unto Christ, to fill up that number that has been given to him by his Father (John 6.44). Simply stated, there can be no salvation apart from the people of God in the body of Christ. If there is no Church, there can be no Christianity, no salvation, no hope for this world. An urbanized version of a saying by the great Latin father, Cyprian, makes this even more plain: *"If the Church ain't yo' mama, then God ain't yo' daddy!"* Yes, and amen!

As believers we have been apportioned to the great mystery, the prospect of sharing eternity and the Kingdom with our bridegroom, who also is our Savior and Lord, the Lord Jesus Christ. The means by which we come to acknowledge our connection to him is not apart from the Church, but rather, as a part of her, as a member of the Church of God in Jesus. Unfortunately, some people never come to church except for their baptism, their marriage, and their funeral, or, as some might say, when they're hatched, matched, and dispatched! In my mind, no informed and biblical Christian can claim intimacy with God and deny and ignore the Church; such a one is confused at best, and perhaps not a Christian, at worst.

To be a Christian is to be a member of the bride of Christ, and be a part of the divine romance. In a real sense, the "two becoming one" will occur at the consummation of all things at the Second Coming, but the

Church knows this unity and intimacy now, today. Truly, the Church is utterly connected and integrated into and with the person of Jesus of Nazareth: we enjoy total identification and association with Christ. We are "made one in Christ" (1 Cor. 6.15-17), were baptized into him (1 Cor. 12.13), and died with him in his death on the cross (Rom. 6.3-4). Furthermore, we were buried with him by baptism into death (Rom. 6.3-4), and were raised with him in the resurrection (Eph. 2.4-7). We ascended with him (Eph. 2.6), we are seated with him in heavenly places (Eph. 2.6), and we suffer with him in this life as we serve him (Rom. 8.17-18). Soon, we will be glorified with him (Rom. 8.17), will be resurrected in him (1 Cor. 15.48-49), and will be made like him when we see him at his appearing (1 John 3.2). Then, we will inherit all things with him as joint-heirs with him (Rom. 8.17), and will reign forever with him as his co-regents in the new order (Rev. 3.21). What an extraordinary mystery, indeed, for the "two to become one flesh."

Take your place as a believer in Christ in the company of honored human beings who make up the one, holy, apostolic, Church, the bride of Christ, that sacred company that will rule with Christ in the Kingdom. What a blessing to be a part of the divine romance. The banquet is almost ready.

> Rev. 19.6-8 – Then I heard what seemed to be the voice of a great multitude, like the roar of many waters and like the sound of mighty peals of thunder, crying out, "Hallelujah! For the Lord our God the Almighty reigns. [7] Let us rejoice and exult and give him the glory, for the marriage of the Lamb has come, and his Bride has made herself ready; [8] it was granted her to clothe herself with fine linen, bright and pure" – for the fine linen is the righteous deeds of the saints.

Have you made yourself ready? Will you be there?

Nicene Creed and Prayer

After reciting and/or singing the Nicene Creed (located in the Appendix), pray the following prayer:

> God, Almighty Father who chose your servant Abraham and made him faithful to obey your call and to rejoice in your promise that all families on earth would be blessed in him: Grant us so firm a faith that your promises may be fulfilled in us; through Jesus Christ our Lord.
>
> ~ The Church of the Province of South Africa.
> *Minister's Book for Use With the Holy Eucharist and Morning and Evening Prayer.*
> Braamfontein: Publishing Department of the Church of the Province of South Africa. p. 15.

| Scripture Memorization Review | Review with a partner, write out and/or recite the text for last class session's assigned memory verse: 2 Timothy 2.1-2. |

| Assignments Due | Turn in your summary of the reading assignment for last week, that is, your brief response and explanation of the main points that the authors were seeking to make in the assigned reading (Reading Completion Sheet). |

The Mystery of Iniquity

Because of the heightened sense of the principalities and powers in some Christian circles, questions abound about the way in which we ought to speak and think about the dark powers mentioned in Scripture. The apostles were careful not to go into great detail regarding the inner workings of the demonic, or exorcisms, or providing instructions on these regions of the shadows; some ministries today, however, seem to specialize in this focus. Seeking to understand some of these highly developed demonologies and strategies to overcome the dark powers, many Christians become overwhelmed in their personal walks with a near preoccupation with the demonic, and its influence in their lives. Others, being afraid of this kind of over-emphasis, ignore altogether the frequent mention and reporting of the encounters of Christ and the apostles with the demonic. In light of our warfare with the rulers and principalities, what ought to be our perspective on the dark powers which Paul says we wrestle with in our Christian walk (cf. Eph. 6.11ff.)? How should we approach the description and appropriate Christian response to Satan, the demonic, and evil in general?

The Heart of Apostolic Ministry

The heart of apostolic ministry according to Paul is to prepare the people of God for the upcoming marriage to Christ (2 Cor. 11.2). The people of God are in fact the bride of Christ, being prepared by him to be a faultless and beautiful bride, a people without spot or wrinkle (Eph. 5), in every way outfitted for the great day of union and consummation when the people of God meet him and never leave his side (1 Thess. 4.13-17). In a real sense, all mission and ministry has a peculiar eschatological flavor: all evangelism adds to the number of the Lamb's bride who will inhabit the New Jerusalem, and all disciple making is preparing and readying the people of God for the great union and marriage of the Lamb (Rev. 19). How does or should it affect and influence our understanding of ministry to see it through the lens of feeling a divine jealousy for those whom we serve, of betrothing the people of God to one husband, to present them as a pure virgin to Christ (2 Cor. 11.2)? How might it impact our perspective and practice if we saw mission and ministry as the attempt to prepare God's people for the upcoming union with Christ? Is it too abstract, too symbolic, or is it dramatically empowering and clarifying?

The Vision and Biblical Foundation for Christian Mission

Mission as the War of the Spheres

Rev. Dr. Don L. Davis

CONTENT

Summary

The motif of Mission as the War of the Spheres is perhaps the most dynamic image of mission in Scripture, and begins with the sovereign rule of Yahweh God as creator and sustainer of all. God's reign was resisted in the rebellion of the mystery of iniquity (i.e., the satanic rebellion in the heavenlies), which resulted in the temptation and fall of humankind, and the curse of creation. God placed hostility between the Seed of the woman and the serpent, and sovereignly and graciously promised to end the rebellion through the Seed of the woman. As a result of the Fall, the universe is at war and God has declared himself at war with the serpent and those who side with him. God displayed himself as divine warrior in his conflict with evil symbolized as a river and the sea, his defeat of Pharaoh and his armies, and the nations of Canaan. Unfortunately, God also had to fight against his own people because of their disobedience and rebellion. In addition, Israel's prophets pictured God as a divine warrior who through his Messiah would finally destroy all evil once and for all time. This Messianic rule has been inaugurated in the person of Jesus, who in his birth, teaching, miracles, exorcisms, deeds, death, and resurrection has brought the Kingdom of God into being. The Kingdom is both "already" and "not yet;" it has already come in Jesus' fulfillment of the Messianic promise but will be consummated at his Second Coming. Today in this world and in our age, the Church of Jesus Christ is both the sign and foretaste of the Kingdom present, indwelt by the Holy Spirit, the pledge of the full inheritance. The Church is now authorized to proclaim and demonstrate the victory of Christ over Satan and the curse as his agent and deputy. Mission proclaims that God is presently reasserting his rule today over his universe in Jesus Christ, and through his agent, the Church.

Our objective for this lesson, *Mission as the War of the Spheres*, is to enable you to see that:

- The motif of *Mission as the War of the Spheres* is perhaps the most dynamic image of mission in Scripture, and deals directly with the establishment and proclamation of God's kingdom rule in the person of Jesus of Nazareth.

- A brief overview of the warfare motif in Scripture begins with Yahweh as creator and sustainer of all. At some time in the ancient and distant past, the mystery of iniquity occurred (i.e., the satanic rebellion in the heavenlies), which resulted in the temptation and fall of humankind, and the curse. Still, God placed hostility between the Seed of the woman and the serpent, and sovereignly and graciously promised to crush the head of the serpent through the Seed of the woman. As a result of the Fall, the universe is at war and God has declared himself at war with the serpent and those who side with him.

- Some of the major points of God as divine warrior include the image of God defeating evil symbolized as a river and the sea, as well as God as man-of-war defeating Pharaoh and his armies, and leading his people into victory over the nations of land as the great Lord of armies. Unfortunately, the Lord also had to fight against his own people because of their disobedience and rebellion. Also, Israel's prophets pictured God as a divine warrior who through his Messiah would finally destroy all evil once and for all time.

- Through his promise of the Messiah as the son of David, God revealed his intent to provide a king who would restore the reign to his people, rule the nations with justice and righteousness, and bring a knowledge of God to the entire earth as Lord and King. This Messianic rule has been inaugurated in the person of Jesus, the heir from the Davidic line who is restoring God's reign.

- In the various aspects of Jesus' birth, teaching, miracles, exorcisms, deeds, death, and resurrection, the Kingdom of God is now here, already present in the life of the Church. The Kingdom has already come, and yet is not yet consummated; although the Kingdom has come in the fulfillment of the Messianic promise in the person of Jesus, it will only be consummated at his Second Coming, when the full and final manifestation will occur.

- Today in this world and age, the Church of Jesus Christ is both the sign and foretaste of the Kingdom present, indwelt by the Holy Spirit, the pledge of the full inheritance. The Church is now authorized to proclaim and demonstrate the victory of Christ over Satan and the curse as his agent and deputy.

- The main implications of the *Mission as the War of the Spheres* motif is that God is presently reasserting his rule today over his universe in Jesus Christ, and through his agent, the Church. . God is the warrior who through his anointed One has defeated the power of the devil and the effects of the curse. Mission is the display and proclamation of the rule of God here and now, and making disciples among the nations advances the reign of God by testifying to its coming in the person of Jesus of Nazareth.

Video Outline

I. Mission as the *War of the Spheres*: God as the Warrior Reestablishing His Kingdom Rule over the Universe

Mission Announces God's War with Idolatry

The fundamental question of theology, 'What do we mean by "God,"' can be answered from a variety of angles by exploring God's various relations to the world and to ourselves. Ironically, the study of idolatry also gives us some insight into the nature of the true God. What constitutes a god? Martin Luther's answer, as he reflected on the first commandment in his larger catechism, was 'whatever your heart clings to and relies upon, that is your God; trust and faith of the heart alone make both God and idol'. We wish to confirm his view, but also to emphasize love and service: a god is that which one loves, trusts and serves above all else. This definition suggests both the possibility and the urgency of making clear the relevance of idolatry to the modern world. In one sense idolatry is the diagnosis of the human condition to which the gospel is the cure. The root problem with humans is not a horizontal 'social' problem (like sexual immorality or greed), but rebellion against and replacement of the true and living God with gods that fail (which lead to these destructive sins). If the story of the human race is a sorry tale of different forms of idolatry, the height of human folly, the Good News is that God reconciles his image-bearers back to himself in Christ. It is no coincidence that the prophets envisage a time when idols will finally be eradicated and replaced by true worship.

~ Brian S. Rosner. "Idolatry." *The New Dictionary of Biblical Theology.* T. D. Alexander, ed.(electronic ed.). Downers Grove, IL: InterVarsity Press, 2001.

A. The Triune God as Sovereign Lord over the heavens and the earth

1. The Lord is the creator and sustainer of all things, and rules all things according to his wisdom, Isa. 40.21-31, cf. Isa. 40.28.

    a. Ps. 33.6

    b. Ps. 104.5-6

    c. Ps. 136.6

    d. Jer. 10.16

2. As Sovereign Lord over all, God's will was supreme in all things among all beings in all places, Ps. 135.6.

    a. Ps. 33.11

    b. Ps. 115.3

    c. Dan. 4.35

B. The mystery of iniquity: war in the heavenlies through satanic rebellion, Isa. 14.12-17

1. At some point in time, after the creation of all things, there was rebellion in heaven fueled by God's creature, Lucifer, the son of the Dawn.

2. The source of his rebellion was envy toward God as a result of pride, Isa. 14.12-15.

3. His extraordinary beauty and glory caused him to rebel against the authority of God, Ezek. 28.12-18.

4. This spiritual rebellion is the root and cause of all other forms of rebellion among human beings today, 1 John 5.19.

C. The Fall as humankind's participation in the rebellion of the spheres: pride, lust, and greed, Gen. 3.1-7

1. Temptation and disobedience: Eve and the serpent, 2 Cor. 11.2

2. The loss of freedom: the entrance of sin and satanic bondage

3. The absence of wholeness: the inauguration of sickness and reality of death

4. The end of justice: the brokenness and fragmentation of human relationships

D. The *protoevangelium*: the first telling of the Gospel, Gen. 3.15

1. God will place hostility between the serpent's seed and the Seed of the woman.

2. The Seed of the woman will crush the head of the serpent.

3. The serpent will bruise the heel of the Seed of the woman.

4. This is the first telling of the Gospel and the outline of the story: the universe is at war, and God is the warrior.

E. Senses of God's role as divine warrior in the OT

1. In the times before the monarchy, God is viewed as a warrior who defeats the sea or river (Exod. 15.4-10; Judg. 5.19-21; Ps. 68.22-23; Hab. 3.8-15).

   a. The sea is a symbol of disorder and chaos, viewed with a kind of unstable, chaotic, even frightening sense.

   b. When God overcomes this enemy, nature returns to life and produces abundant crops, Deut. 23.28; Ps. 68.10-11.

2. God is a warrior, defeating Pharaoh and his armies as they sought to destroy his covenant people, Israel, Exod. 15.3-4.

3. The Psalms reveal the God of Israel to be a God who honors his rule, and will uphold his Davidic king with power and protection (e.g., Pss. 2; 18; 24; 46; 48; 76; 89; 97; 132; 144).

4. The prophets spoke of Yahweh God as a great Lord whose armies he led into battle on behalf of his people and his honor (Isa. 6; Mic. 1.2-4; Zeph. 1.14-18; Joel 2.1-11).

5. As a result of Israel's disobedience and rebellion against God, the Lord through his judgment and the captivity of Israel and Judah became a warrior who fought against his own people.

a. Jer. 12.7

b. Jer. 15.14

c. Lam. 2.3-5

6. As Israel's prophets continued to receive revelation about the coming of Messiah, they pictured God as a divine warrior who would engage the powers to come as in Israel's earliest divine warrior poetry (e.g., Isa. 26.16-27.6; 59.15b-20; 63.1-6; Zech. 9.1-17; 14.1-21).

F. The promise of David's son: a King to reign in righteousness

1. God gave a solemn promise through the prophets that he would restore his reign among his people and in the earth, Isa. 9.6-7.

2. The nations would respond to his lordship of justice and peace, Ps. 72.8-11.

3. This King of Israel, who would restore God's righteous rule, would be of David's house, 2 Sam. 7.8ff.

4. The nations of the earth would bow to this exalted ruler whom God enthroned in his authority, Ps. 2; Ps. 110.

5. As an apocalyptic figure, this ruler would rule over the nations as Lord and King, Dan. 2.35-44; Dan. 7.14, 27.

II. God's Rule has been Inaugurated through God's Covenant Promise Culminating in the Person and Work of Jesus Christ.

A. The coming of Jesus of Nazareth is viewed as the Davidic King who would restore the reign of God for Israel.

1. He would rule over the house of Jacob forever, Luke 1.31-33.

2. Jesus came proclaiming the Kingdom of God fulfilled with his appearing, Mark 1.14-15.

3. *Jesus is the Messiah, the prophesied Lord of the Davidic lineage who would restore God's reign in the earth.*

    a. Ps. 132.11

    b. Isa. 16.5

    c. Amos 9.11-12

4. Jesus announced himself as the fulfillment of the Messianic texts heralding the Day of Lord, cf. Luke 4.18-19 with Isa. 61.1-3.

5. In his overcoming of the signs of the curse and the dominion of the devil over people's lives, Jesus demonstrated that in his person the Kingdom had come!, Matt. 12.25-30.

    a. Mark 1.15

b. Mark 11.10

c. Luke 10.11

d. Luke 11.20

e. Luke 16.16

f. Luke 17.20-21

B. The Kingdom (rule of God) becomes present in Jesus of Nazareth: the Presence of the Future

1 John 3.8 – Whoever makes a practice of sinning is of the devil, for the devil has been sinning from the beginning. The reason the Son of God appeared was to destroy the works of the devil.

In every dimension, the life and ministry of Jesus of Nazareth represents the authentic presence of the prophesied Age to Come in the here-and-now, today!

1. His *mission*: to destroy the works of the devil, 1 John 3.8

2. His *birth*: the invasion of God into Satan's dominion, Luke 1.31-33

3. His *message*: the Kingdom's proclamation and inauguration, Mark 1.14-15

4. His *teaching*: kingdom ethics, Matt. 5-7

5. His *miracles*: his kingly authority and power, Mark 2.8-12

6. His *exorcisms*: his defeat of the devil and his angels, Luke 11.14-20

7. His *life and deeds*: the majesty of the Kingdom, John 1.14-18

8. His *resurrection*: the victory and vindication of the King, Rom. 1.1-4

9. His *commission*: the call to proclaim his Kingdom worldwide, Matt. 28.18-20

10. His *ascension*: his coronation, Heb. 1.2-4

11. His *Spirit*: the *arrabon* (surety, pledge) of the Kingdom, 2 Cor. 1.20-22

12. His *Church*: the foretaste and agent of the Kingdom, 2 Cor. 5.18-21

13. His *present session in heaven*: the generalship of God's forces, 1 Cor. 15.24-28

14. His *Parousia* (coming): the final consummation of the Kingdom, Rev. 19.11-19

C. Mission is the proclamation of the Kingdom come in the Lord Jesus.

In Jesus Christ, the Kingdom is both already present, but not yet fulfilled.

1. The apostles preached in their mission message that Jesus of Nazareth, who was crucified, was the Messiah, Acts 2.32-36.

2. Jesus understood himself as the fulfillment of the Messianic prophecies regarding the suffering Servant of God, Luke 24.26-27, 44-48.

3. The Jesus rejected by the leaders and the nation of Israel has been exalted to the position of the Cornerstone, Acts 4.11-12.

4. Jesus has been granted all authority by God, and is proclaimed as the exalted Lord of all, Matt. 28.18.

    a. Acts 5.30-31

    b. Acts 10.36 – As for the word that he sent to Israel, preaching good news of peace through Jesus Christ (he is Lord of all)

5. The heart of the apostles' message as they traveled and preached the Good News was the *Messianic fulfillment of Jesus Christ and the presence of his kingdom reign*, Acts 28.23, 31.

6. Jesus' rule acknowledged in Church history

    a. *Christus Victum*: Jesus as ultimate sacrifice for sin

    b. *Christus Victor*: Jesus as conquering Lord over God's enemies

    c. *Christus Vicar*: Jesus as exalted Head of his Church

God's Kingdom means the divine conquest over His enemies, a conquest which is to be accomplished in three stages; and the first victory has already occurred. The power of the Kingdom of God has invaded the realm of Satan – the present evil Age. The activity of this power to deliver men from satanic rule was evidenced in the exorcism of demons. Thereby, Satan was bound; he was cast down from his position of power; his power was "destroyed." The blessings of the Messianic Age are now available to those who embrace the Kingdom of God. We may already enjoy the blessings resulting from this initial defeat of Satan. This does not mean that we enjoy the fullness of God's blessings, or that all that is meant by the Kingdom of God has come to us. . . . The Second Coming of Christ is absolutely essential for the fulfillment and consummation of God's redemptive work. Yet God has already accomplished the first great stage in His work of redemption. Satan is the god of This Age, yet the power of Satan has been broken that men may know the rule of God in their lives.

~ George Ladd. *The Gospel of the Kingdom*.
Grand Rapids: Wm. B. Eerdmans Publishing Company, 1999. p. 50.

III. God's Rule Is Invading this Present Evil Age through the Church Militant

A. The empowering presence of the Holy Spirit of God

Eph. 5.18 – And do not get drunk with wine, for that is debauchery, but be filled with the Spirit.

1. The Spirit is the sign of the Kingdom's presence and certainty, 2 Cor. 1.21-22.

2. All believers in Christ have been sealed with the Spirit as a pledge of the future inheritance (i.e., a down payment of the full display of the Kingdom to come, Eph. 1.13; 4.30).

B. The Church as *Sign and Foretaste* of the Kingdom, Eph. 5.25-32

   1. Commissioned as his witnesses to the ends of the earth, Acts 1.8

   2. Ambassadors of Christ and his Kingdom, 2 Cor. 5.18-21

   3. Showcase of God's eschatological glory, 1 Pet. 2.9-10

   4. Deputies of Christ's authority, Matt. 28.18-20; 16.18-19

C. God's intent in this present age: to empower and authorize his Church to do battle against his foes, bearing witness to God's rule today

   1. Jesus' authority now in heaven and earth is absolute: he has been raised to the position of Lord of all by the Father, cf. Matt. 28.18 with Phil. 2.9-11.

   2. The strong man must be bound: Jesus' authority over Satan must be enforced (even though he is defeated), 1 Pet. 5.8 with James 4.7.

   3. The Church is the deputy and agent of the Kingdom of God: she has been granted the right and authority to represent Christ's authority in the earth, to do violence against all powers and entities which defy God's knowledge and authority, 2 Cor. 10.3-5.

D. Mission is engagement in the *War of the Spheres*.

1. Mission is nothing less than the announcement of the coming of God's rule to earth in the midst of the devil's own territory, 1 John 4.4.

2. Mission proclaims Messiah Jesus as the fulfillment of Messianic prophecy in our day and time, who must reign until all his enemies are under his feet, 1 Cor. 15.24-28.

3. The Church has been granted authority to use the weapons of God's warfare in their proclamation of the Good News of the Kingdom throughout the world.

E. The weapons of our warfare

2 Cor. 10.3-5 – For though we walk in the flesh, we are not waging war according to the flesh. [4] For the weapons of our warfare are not of the flesh but have divine power to destroy strongholds. We destroy arguments [5] and every lofty opinion raised against the knowledge of God, and take every thought captive to obey Christ.

1. The whole armor of God, Eph. 6.11

2. Authority (by identification and organic unity with Christ), Eph. 1.13

3. The Word of God, Eph. 6.17

4. The shield of faith, Eph. 6.16

5. The blood of Christ and the word of their testimony, Rev. 12.10-11

   Mission is nothing less than the insertion of God's shock troops into the enemy territory of the devil. Satanic opposition to Christ's victory and authority will be strong and vicious; only those commissioned with his sovereign Word and kingdom authority can stand in the evil day, Eph. 6.10-18.

F. Soon, God's rule will consummate in the Age to Come at the Second Coming of Jesus Christ, Rom. 16.20.

IV. Implications of Mission as the *War of the Spheres*

A. God's rule over his universe is now being reasserted in the person of Jesus Christ.

   1. Jesus of Nazareth is the prophesied Messiah, who has been charged with the responsibility to restore God's rule in the universe, John 1.41-45; Matt. 28.18.

   2. As a result of his obedience and death, he has been exalted to the Father's right hand, as Lord over all, Phil. 2.9-11; Eph. 1.20-23; Phil. 3.20-21.

   3. As Lord of all, he is the Lord of the harvest (of mission), and is leading his people to victory all over the world as they declare his glory to the nations, Acts 1.8; Matt. 9.35-38; Matt. 28.18-20.

B. God is the warrior whose authority in Messiah Jesus has defeated the powers of the devil and the effects of the curse.

   1. He has openly disarmed and shamed them through the cross, Col. 2.15.

2. He has granted to his people authority over the evil one by transferring them from the kingdom of darkness to the Kingdom of Christ, Col. 1.13.

C. Mission is the *display and proclamation of the rule of God in operation in the here and now.*

1. Mission is prophesying deliverance to the captives, Rom. 10.9-10.

2. We are set free from the bondage of the enemy in Christ, Heb. 2.14-15; 1 John 3.8; 1 John 4.4.

3. Satan's infernal rebellion has been put down, but he still has power to deceive and persecute, 1 Pet. 5.8; James 4.7.

4. His doom is sure; nothing can prevent the full restoration of the will of God over all things, Rev. 11.15-18, cf. 15.

D. Making disciples among all nations is *advancing the reign of God by testifying to its coming in the person of Jesus of Nazareth!*

Conclusion

- One of the most intriguing and powerful images of mission in Scripture is the proclamation of God's kingdom rule in the person of Jesus of Nazareth.

- Through the death, burial, and resurrection of Jesus, God has defeated the powers of the devil and rescinded the effects of the curse. Now, in the very life of the Church, the rule of God is present and alive on planet earth.

- The Kingdom is not yet fully consummated, however, and will not be until Christ comes again.

Student Questions and Response

The following questions were designed to help you review the material in the video. In our last section we briefly reviewed what may arguably be considered one of the most integrating and dynamic motifs of mission in the entire Bible: the *Mission as the War of the Spheres* motif which is anchored in the reassertion of the rule of God in the person of Jesus of Nazareth. This motif traces the notion of divine warrior through the Bible, a theme which finds its zenith in the person of Jesus, the Messiah of God. Through the death, burial, and resurrection of Jesus, God has defeated the powers of the devil and rescinded the effects of the curse. Now, in the very life of the Church, the rule of God is present and alive on planet earth. This motif carries special significance for urban communities, which especially are attuned to this kind of ongoing spiritual warfare. Be thorough and complete in your answers to the questions below, and make certain you understand the basic concepts related to this important motif.

1. Why can it be said that the motif of *Mission as the War of the Spheres* may be the most integrating and dynamic image of mission as well as spirituality in the entire Scriptures? How does this motif relate to the idea of the establishment and proclamation of God's kingdom rule in the person of Jesus of Nazareth? Explain.

2. Provide a concise overview of God as the divine warrior motif in Scripture. What does this motif assert about the "mystery of iniquity?" What occurred as a result of the resistance to God's reign in the heavenlies, and what was its result for creation?

3. Why is the *protoevangelium* so important for understanding God's role and identity as a warrior (cf. Genesis 3.15)? How did the mystery of iniquity, the Fall, and the curse change fundamentally God's relationship with his creation, especially with humankind?

4. How was God's conflict with evil symbolized in the OT? How did God's conflict with Pharaoh and the nations of Canaan help us understand God as divine warrior? Why did God also take up the position of warrior against his own people?

5. How did the prophets of Israel picture the coming of Messiah as an extension of God as a divine warrior, and how would this Messiah finally destroy all evil once and for all time?

6. Briefly lay out the ways in which the promise of the Messiah has been inaugurated in the person of Jesus, the heir from the Davidic line who is restoring God's reign. How do the various aspects of his birth, teaching, miracles, exorcisms, deeds, death, and resurrection show that the promised Kingdom of God is now here, already present in the life of the Church?

7. Explain the way in which the Kingdom of God can be said to be "already present" but "not yet consummated." Why is this distinction important to keep in mind when discussing the work of Jesus Christ in this present age?

8. In what sense can we say that the Church of Jesus Christ today in this age is both the sign and foretaste of the Kingdom present? In what sense is the Holy Spirit, who indwells the Church, providing evidence that the Kingdom of God has in fact arrived in Jesus? What is the Church now authorized to do on behalf of Christ for the sake of the Kingdom?

9. What are the main implications of the *Mission as the War of the Spheres* motif for mission? In light of God reasserting his rule today over his universe in Jesus Christ, what ought missionaries do and how ought they to represent their work and ministries among the lost?

10. Read the Ryken quote on the next page. Why is it important to see these various motifs of God as interrelated and connected, rather than isolated and separate? How does Ryken help us to connect these images as we use them to understand who God is and his actions in the world (which, in fact are the foundations for doing mission today)?

The God of the Promise Is also a God of War

When God appears as the divine warrior in the OT, he most often comes to save his people from their enemies. This happens from the time of the crossing of the Red Sea until late in the history of Israel. The divine warrior theme is closely connected to the idea of covenant in the OT. God reveals himself as king through covenant-treaty and then promises to protect his subject people from danger threatened by their enemies. We can see this in the blessings that flow if the law of the covenant is obeyed. In Deuteronomy 28.7 God the king promises that if Israel obeys him, "The Lord will grant that the enemies who rise up against you will be defeated before you. They will come at you from one direction but flee from you in seven" (NIV). He does this many times in the history of Israel, appearing in a variety of forms and using different means to win the battle. God often uses forces of nature, his own creation, as his weapons. At the crossing of the Red Sea when Israel is saved and Egypt judged, God uses the winds to push back the waters of the Sea to allow Israel safe access to the other side and then collapses the waters to kill the Egyptians (Exod. 14 and 15). Later when Joshua fights against a coalition of southern Canaanite kings, God uses large hailstones to kill the enemy and causes the sun to stop in the sky so there would be more daylight in which to finish the battle (Josh 10.1-15). On other occasions God uses his heavenly army to fight Israel's enemies.

~ Leland Ryken. *The Dictionary of Biblical Imagery*. (electronic ed.) Downers Grove, IL: InterVarsity Press, 2000. p. 211.

CONNECTION

Summary of Key Concepts

This lesson deals with one of the single most important motifs in all of Scripture, and not merely in relationship to the issue of mission. The motif of *Mission as the War of the Spheres* touches upon a truly significant theme that holds great significance for our understanding of the work of Messiah and of the Church. It could easily be argued that this theme is a central notion for grasping the meaning of not only mission, but the very identity and work of the Church. Therefore, review these concepts carefully, and ensure that you can support them with an appeal to Scripture.

- The motif of *Mission as the War of the Spheres* is perhaps the most dynamic image of mission in Scripture, and deals directly with the establishment and proclamation of God's kingdom rule in the person of Jesus of Nazareth.

- A brief overview of the warfare motif in Scripture begins with Yahweh as creator and sustainer of all. At some time in the ancient and distant past, the mystery of iniquity occurred (i.e., the satanic rebellion in the heavenlies), which resulted in the temptation and fall of humankind, and the curse. Still, God placed hostility between the Seed of the woman and the serpent, and sovereignly and graciously promised to crush the head of the serpent through the Seed of the woman. As a result of the Fall, the universe is at war and God has declared himself at war with the serpent and those who side with him.

- Some of the major points of God as divine warrior include the image of God defeating evil symbolized as a river and the sea, as well as God as man-of-war defeating Pharaoh and his armies, and leading his people into victory over the nations of land as the great Lord of armies. Unfortunately, the Lord also had to fight against his own people because of their disobedience and rebellion. Also, Israel's prophets pictured God as a divine warrior who through his Messiah would finally destroy all evil once and for all time.

- Through his promise of the Messiah as the son of David, God revealed his intent to provide a king who would restore the reign to his people, rule the nations with justice and righteousness, and bring a knowledge of God to the entire earth as Lord and King. This Messianic rule has been inaugurated in the person of Jesus, the heir from the Davidic line who is restoring God's reign.

- In the various aspects of Jesus' birth, teaching, miracles, exorcisms, deeds, death, and resurrection, the Kingdom of God is now here, already present in the life of the Church. The Kingdom has already come, and yet is not yet consummated; although the Kingdom has come in the fulfillment of the Messianic promise in the person of Jesus, it will only be consummated at his Second Coming, when the full and final manifestation will occur.

- Today in this world and age, the Church of Jesus Christ is both the sign and foretaste of the Kingdom present, indwelt by the Holy Spirit, the pledge of the full inheritance. The Church is now authorized to proclaim and demonstrate the victory of Christ over Satan and the curse as his agent and deputy.

- The main implications of the *Mission as the War of the Spheres* motif is that God is presently reasserting his rule over his universe in Jesus Christ, and through his agent, the Church. God is the warrior who through his anointed One has defeated the power of the devil and the effects of the curse.

- Mission is the display and proclamation of the rule of God here and now, and making disciples among the nations advances the reign of God by testifying to its coming in the person of Jesus of Nazareth.

Student Application and Implications

Now is the time for you to discuss with your fellow students your questions about these important motifs of mission in Scripture. The following questions are designed to help you grapple with the personal implications of this material, so strive to be as transparent as possible as you explore these and other questions related to the material.

- Have you ever studied thoroughly and clearly the motif of the *war of spheres* in Scripture, and if so, what were you major conclusions about them? Do either of these provide you with a clear grasp of "what the Bible is getting at," especially in terms of the unity between the Old and New Testaments?

- How important do you think this motif is for the *urban experience*? Why would a breakdown of the family and fidelity in man/woman relationships actually impact whether or not people would find the *divine romance* motif more or less compelling?

- Ought we concentrate only on motifs that people resonate with or like, or should we teach all the major motifs of the Bible, no matter what? Explain thoroughly your answer.

- How does the relationship of Israel with the Lord parallel your own relationship with the Lord? Are you more *like* the Israelites than *unlike* them? Explain how so.

- In what way are we to teach the history of Israel as *our history* for the sake of instruction, learning, and edification? (Cf. 1 Cor. 10.6-11: "Now these things took place as examples for us, that we might not desire evil as they did. [7] Do not be idolaters as some of them were; as it is written, "The people sat down to eat and drink and rose up to play." [8] We must not indulge in sexual immorality as some of them did, and twenty-three thousand fell in a single day. [9] We must not put Christ to the test, as some of them did and were destroyed by serpents, [10] nor grumble, as some of them did and were destroyed by the Destroyer. [11] Now these things happened to them as an example, but they were written down for our instruction, on whom the end of the ages has come.")

- Does the language of the Bible about warfare, conflict, and struggle line up with your own experience as a believer? How ought we to apply this language and symbolism to our own life as disciples of Jesus?

- Are there people in particular that you have not wanted to respond to the Lord? What does it mean to you that God may draw whomever he will at any time an from any place to be a part of his body and bride (cf. John 6.44)?

- Do you think of yourself as a soldier of Jesus Christ, and if not, why not? If you feel comfortable with this imagery, why don't you think it is more prominent and acceptable in our circles today?

- Is it prudent to be using images, metaphors, and symbols of war today, with all of the conflict taking place in the world and the global concern about terrorism? Ought we to de-emphasize these symbols so as not to be misunderstood by others today?

- Do you live as if you believe that the Kingdom of God has been reasserted in the presence of Jesus in the Church? Do you see your own local church as a "sign and foretaste of the Kingdom of God" on earth today? Why or why not?

- Complete the following sentence: "If there was just one thing I could do to make these motifs come alive in my life right now, where I am, it would be . . ."

CASE STUDIES

War Images Not Edifying for Faith

Although the Bible is abundant with the metaphors, images, symbolism, and mythic outline of cosmic war, of Yahweh as a warrior, and Christ as the great Victor over Satan, death, the curse, and the powers, many modern Christians feel squeamish about them. In a world torn by terrorism, conflict, and war, many sincere Christians do not believe that such imagery and focus is helpful. Rather than pointing to the heart of the Gospel, the love of God expressed in the death of Jesus Christ for the world, such warfare imagery confuses people, imports ideas that are hard to understand in the world today, and even blur the overall vision of God's compassion for the poor and the oppressed. Others (equally sincere and biblical) feel that to ignore or overlook the biblical emphasis on spiritual warfare is to miss perhaps the most commanding and important motif for understanding the spiritual world given in Scripture. These who see the value of warfare images would affirm that we do not fight against human beings, but for them against those powers which would seek to destroy them: "For we do not wrestle against flesh and blood, but against the rulers, against the authorities, against the cosmic powers over this present darkness, against the spiritual forces of evil in the heavenly places" (Eph. 6.12). These images provide us with substantial insight into the world of Christian struggle for good against evil, and we ought to learn from them. Which of these groups are correct in communicating the nature of the Christian faith in today's world: ought we seek for other motifs to understand and communicate the faith in a world torn by war and conflict, or ought we to use them so others can better understand what the nature of the fight really is, and how much is at stake in them understanding and applying these images to their lives?

Suburban vs. Urban Styles of Spirituality

In regard to the warfare motif of Christian discipleship and mission, one can notice a stark difference between urban and suburban styles of spirituality and battle. Speaking generally, for many suburbans who have attained a measure of affluence and convenience, a major emphasis in their spiritual journey is safety, protection, and security. Often the society is perceived as a evil counter force warring against the positive morals and decency of the nuclear family, and the goal is to conserve these values and belief systems to ensure that the family and neighborhood is kept secure from those forces which would seek to undermine that security. Urban styles of spirituality, on the other hand, tend to highlight the conflict and struggle with the world and its agents. Warfare is embraced as a necessary response to the ever-present evil all around that seeks to destroy and annihilate them. The predisposition of a mature Christian will be constant vigilance and engagement with powers, of struggling to overcome these powers on a daily basis. The assumptions are not rooted in conserving values, but liberating people from oppressive and dangerous structures that hold them in their grasp. With nothing to protect and no affluence to keep, they tend to embrace spiritual motifs which emphasize fighting, engagement, and struggle. What do you make of these different styles – are they simply the result of spiritual journeys based on different contexts, or is there something more fundamental in the different assumptions and their outworking in spiritual life?

Is Christianity a Western Religion?

Unfortunately, many wrongly have associated the entire Christian enterprise with a kind of controlling Euro-centrism that would see Christianity as Western, white, and middle class. Although the strongest and most intense Christian movements are currently third-world and involve people of color, the centers of power and finance for much of the Christian world are still white and western. Most of the seminaries, publishing houses, and church and parachurch organizations are run by those who are European or North American in background, usually white, and with connections of power and means. For many from the outside, then, Christianity does not appear to be a new people of God built on inclusion, equality, diversity, and unity – multi-national and multi-cultural, enjoying one bond in the Spirit. Rather, the body and bride of Christ appears to be Gentile in orientation, and western in domination. These perceptions are undermining our ability to enter into certain societies, which see Christianity as essentially a western, cultural religion; many nations are no longer open to receive Christian missionaries, seeing them as agents of western values and norms, not the representatives of the citizenry of heaven. With the ever increasing animosity towards Christianity and the West, how ought we as mission leaders think about the next generation of communicating Christ across cultures, especially those which are highly suspicious and skeptical of anything western and white?

Restatement of the Lesson's Thesis

The motif of *Mission as the War of the Spheres* is perhaps the most dynamic image of mission in Scripture, and begins with the sovereign rule of Yahweh God as creator and sustainer of all. God's reign was resisted in the rebellion of the mystery of iniquity (i.e., the satanic rebellion in the heavenlies), which resulted in the temptation and fall of humankind, and the curse of creation. God placed hostility between the Seed of the woman and the serpent, and sovereignly and graciously promised to end the rebellion through the Seed of the woman. As a result of the Fall, the universe is at war and God has declared himself at war with the serpent and those who side with him. God displayed himself as divine warrior in his conflict with evil symbolized as a river and the sea, and in his defeat of Pharaoh and his armies and the nations of Canaan. Unfortunately, God also had to fight against his own people because of their disobedience and rebellion. In addition, Israel's prophets pictured God as a divine warrior who through his Messiah would finally destroy all evil once and for all time.

This Messianic rule has been inaugurated in the person of Jesus, who in his birth, teaching, miracles, exorcisms, deeds, death, and resurrection has brought the Kingdom of God into being. The Kingdom is both "already" and "not yet;" its has already come in Jesus' fulfillment of the Messianic promise but will be only be consummated at his Second Coming. Today in this world and age, the Church of Jesus Christ is both the sign and foretaste of the Kingdom present, indwelt by the Holy Spirit, the pledge of the full inheritance. The Church is now authorized to proclaim and demonstrate the victory of Christ over Satan and the curse as his agent and deputy. Mission proclaims that God is presently reasserting his rule over his universe in Jesus Christ, and through his agent, the Church.

Resources and Bibliographies

If you are interested in pursuing some of the ideas of *The Vision and Biblical Foundation for Christian Mission*, you might want to give these books a try:

> Costas, Orlando E. Christ *Outside the Gate: Mission Beyond Christendom.* Maryknoll, NY: Orbis Books, 1982.
>
> Curtis, Brent, and John Eldredge. *The Sacred Romance: Drawing Closer to the Heart of God.* Nashville: Nelson Books, 1997.
>
> Jones, E. Stanley. *Is the Kingdom of God Realism?* New York: Abingdon-Cokesbury, 1940.
>
> Newbigin, Lesslie. *Sign of the Kingdom.* Grand Rapids: Eerdmans, 1980.
>
> Yoder, John Howard. *The Politics of Jesus.* Grand Rapids: Eerdmans, 1972.

Ministry Connections

Ask God the Holy Spirit to help you so meditate on the motifs covered in this lesson that you may find real and practical ministry connections in your own life and ministry. Select one or more key themes and ideas to think about and pray for throughout this next week, and be open to the Spirit's leading about specific ways you can better understand and apply the meaning of these motifs to your teaching, preaching, and testimony.

Counseling and Prayer

Seek the Lord together with your classmates in prayer for one another and the things God has revealed in this material. Also, make a commitment to spend extended times of prayer with the Lord, both alone and if possible with others during the week. Extended time of prayer is key to the application of truth and the transformation of one's life before the Lord. E. M. Bounds makes this point plain:

> While many private prayers, in the nature of things, must be short; while public prayers, as a rule, ought to be short and condensed; while there is ample room for and value put on ejaculatory prayer – yet in our private communions with God time is a feature essential to its value. Much time spent with God is the secret of all successful praying. Prayer which is felt as a mighty force is the mediate or immediate product of much time spent with God. Our short prayers owe their point and efficiency to the long ones that have preceded them. The short prevailing prayer cannot be prayed by one who has not prevailed with God in a mightier struggle of long continuance. Jacob's victory of faith could not have been gained without that all-night wrestling. God's acquaintance is not made by pop calls. God does not bestow his

gifts on the casual or hasty comers and goers. Much with God alone is the secret of knowing him and of influence with him. He yields to the persistency of a faith that knows him. He bestows his richest gifts upon those who declare their desire for and appreciation of those gifts by the constancy as well as earnestness of their importunity. Christ, who in this as well as other things is our Example, spent many whole nights in prayer. His custom was to pray much. He had his habitual place to pray. Many long seasons of praying make up his history and character. Paul prayed day and night. It took time from very important interests for Daniel to pray three times a day. David's morning, noon, and night praying were doubtless on many occasions very protracted. While we have no specific account of the time these Bible saints spent in prayer, yet the indications are that they consumed much time in prayer, and on some occasions long seasons of praying was their custom.

~ E. M. Bounds. *Power Through Prayer.* (electronic ed.). Oak Harbor, WA: Logos Research Systems, 1999.

Make a commitment throughout this unit to pray long over your own heart, the requests of your fellow students, and open prayers to the Lord about his leading and these truths in your life.

ASSIGNMENTS

Scripture Memory Matthew 28.18-20

Reading Assignment To prepare for class, please visit **www.tumi.org/books** to find next week's reading assignment, or ask your Mentor.

Other Assignments Read the assigned reading and summarize each reading with no more than a paragraph or two for each. In this summary please give your best understanding of what you think was the main point in each of the readings. Do not be overly concerned about giving detail; simply write out what you consider to be the main point discussed in that section of the book. Please bring these summaries to class next week. (Please see the "Reading Completion Sheet" on page 16.)

Looking Forward to the Next Lesson

Our next lesson, *Evangelism and Spiritual Warfare: The Binding of the Strong Man*, shows that through the life, death, and resurrection of Jesus Christ, believers are delivered from Satan's dominion, as well as from the effects of the Curse through the power of the Spirit. Evangelism is proclaiming God's deliverance through Jesus Christ to the entire world in the power of the Holy Spirit. Our Lord Jesus desires that we bear much fruit to the glory and praise of God (John 15.8-16). May the Lord bless your study of his Word so you can join the harvest workers in gathering the fruit of the Lord's own salvation, to the Father's glory!

Please see the following resources in *Picturing Theology: An A-Z Collection of TUMI's Key Diagrams, Charts, Graphics, and Articles*:

- *Five Views of the Relationship between Christ and Culture*, page 138
- *Jesus and the Poor*, page 197
- *Substitute Centers to a Christ-Centered Vision*, page 408
- *Story: The Crux of Revelation*, page 402
- *Theology of Christus Victor*, page 457

Evangelism and Spiritual Warfare
Spiritual Warfare – Binding of the Strong Man

Lesson Objectives

Welcome in the strong name of Jesus Christ! After your reading, study, discussion, and application of the materials in this lesson, you will be able to:

- Demonstrate from the Bible that salvation essentially is God's deliverance of humankind and creation through the power of the Spirit from the power and effects of sin, from Satan's dominion and tyranny and the fear of death, as well as from the effects of the Curse and sin.

- Communicate clearly how evangelism is proclaiming God's promised and prophesied deliverance through Jesus Christ to the entire world in the power of the Holy Spirit.

Devotion

Like Us to Deliver Us

Heb. 2.14-15 – Since therefore the children share in flesh and blood, he himself likewise partook of the same things, that through death he might destroy the one who has the power of death, that is, the devil, [15] and deliver all those who through fear of death were subject to lifelong slavery.

Perhaps no thought in Scripture can compare to the unusual humility of our Lord Jesus in his willingness to become like us to deliver us. This text suggests that the Lord Jesus, in his great humiliation and obedience to the Father in the Incarnation, shared in our very essence, that is, our flesh and blood in order that he might through death destroy the one who has the power of death over humankind, the devil. We will never know the depth of humility and self-forgetfulness involved in this supreme act of kindness and grace toward us. Because of the bondage that we endured due to our own sinfulness, our Lord determined to become like us, to share our weakness, to partake of the very same things we do, in order that he might break death's stranglehold on us, and liberate us for the Lord's own purpose and our new destiny. Let no one think that their own struggle or pain is unique or is in some way so extreme or rare that not even the Lord fully comprehends their hurt. This text lays to rest all thoughts that we have regarding the uniqueness of our struggle. Jesus himself became just like us in order that he might deliver us who, our whole lives long, lay under the power of sin and its inevitable result, death. Praise to the One who was willing to share in our being in order to break our very own bondage.

Nicene Creed and Prayer

After reciting and/or singing the Nicene Creed (located in the Appendix), pray the following prayer:

> O God, whose blessed Son came into the world that he might destroy the works of the devil and make us children of God and heirs of eternal life: Grant that, having this hope, we may purify ourselves as he is pure, that, when he comes again with power and great glory, we may be made like him in his eternal and glorious kingdom; where he lives and reigns with you and the Holy Spirit, one God, for ever and ever. Amen.
>
> ~ Presbyterian Church (USA). *Book of Common Worship.* Louisville, KY: Westminister/John Knox Press, 1993. p. 236.

Scripture Memorization Review

Review with a partner, write out and/or recite the text for last class session's assigned memory verse: Matthew 28.18-20.

Assignments Due

Turn in your summary of the reading assignment for last week, that is, your brief response and explanation of the main points that the authors were seeking to make in the assigned reading (Reading Completion Sheet).

 CONTACT

"Why Do Bad Things Happen to Good People?"

 One evening, a little child was looking at the local news with her folks. In listening to the reports, the station told the story of a young boy who was accidentally killed by a motorist who lost control of their car on the ice, striking the young person, who died from the injuries shortly after. Later that night, filled with curiosity and questions about the incident, the little girl asked her believing mother, "Mama, you remember the story we heard about earlier, the little boy hit and killed by the car? Why did that happen? Why do things like that happen to people, even to people who haven't done anything wrong? Can't God stop things like that from happening? Why do bad things happen to good people?" How would you answer this little girl's question if you were her parent?

"There Is No Devil."

 In a conversation at work, during lunch hour, a mild argument broke out in the lunch room between two fellow employees. In discussing the events of 9-11, the horrific destruction of the Trade Towers in New York City, one employee claimed that this event and others like it are the work of evil people who simply are tools of the devil. The devil's lies are at the root of all evil in the world. The other employee rejected this idea, saying that evil is the result of bad choices of individuals and has nothing to do with any kind of demonic or satanic involvement. Blaming things on the devil, she said, is just an excuse for not taking personal responsibility for one's own actions. Seeming to get nowhere in their debate, they turn to you and ask your opinion. What would you say about this issue to them?

"What Can You Promise Me?"

 In sharing his faith with a friend at school, a young disciple of Jesus laid out an outline of the good news of God's salvation through Jesus Christ. He explained who Jesus was, why he came to earth and had to die, and what God promises to those who receive Jesus as Lord and believe that God raised him from the dead. After listening quietly for awhile to this witness of the Gospel, the young seeker said, "That's well and good, but I am not sure if the thought of eternal life and salvation and such is all that helpful to me now. I'm broke, I lost my job two days ago, and rent is due in two weeks. I failed my midterm in English, and my girlfriend and I are struggling. I just don't see how believing in Jesus will affect my life at all. I want to go to heaven when I die, but what about today, what about right now? What can you promise me, how will my life change if I say "yes!" to Jesus today? Will it make any real difference in my life today at all?" How might the young disciple answer this question?

Spiritual Warfare: Binding of the Strong Man

Rev. Dr. Don L. Davis

CONTENT

Summary

Salvation is God's deliverance from the devil and liberation from the effects of the Fall, i.e., from sin and its dominion. Evangelism is the declaration of the good news of this deliverance and salvation from Satan and sin which God has accomplished for us in the person of Jesus Christ.

Our objective for this lesson, *Spiritual Warfare: Binding of the Strong Man*, is to enable you to see that:

- The Bible teaches that salvation is God's deliverance of humankind and creation from the power of the devil and the effects of sin.

- Through faith in the person of Jesus Christ, those who believe can be delivered from Satan's dominion and from his tyranny (his deception and oppression) and the fear of death.

- The salvation of God in Christ also delivers those who believe from the effects of the Curse and sin through the power of the Spirit.

- Evangelism is the declaration of God's promised and prophesied deliverance through Jesus Christ to the entire world in the power of the Holy Spirit.

Video Outline

I. Salvation Is Deliverance from the Power of the Devil.

A. The purpose of the incarnation: to destroy the works of the devil

1. Appeared to destroy the devil's works, 1 John 3.8

2. Jesus disarmed the rulers and authorities, Col. 2.15.

3. Shared our nature to destroy the devil who had the power of death, Heb. 2.14

B. The *protoevangelium*: the first telling of the Gospel, Gen. 3.15

1. Enmity between the serpent and the woman

2. Hostility between the serpent's offspring and the woman's "Seed"

3. Bruising of the woman's offspring's heel, the crushing of the serpent's head

   a. Acts 2.23-24

   b. Rom. 16.20

   c. Eph. 4.8

   d. Rev. 12.7-8

C. The means: the life, death, and resurrection of Jesus Christ

   1. His *life*: the incarnation of the glory of the Father, John 1.14-18

   2. His *righteousness*: the representation of the second Adam for a new humanity, Rom. 5.17-19

   3. His *death*: the penalty paid for humankind's disobedience, Rom. 5.6-9

   4. His *resurrection*: the surety of God's forgiveness and grace

      a. 2 Cor. 13.4

      b. Eph. 1.19-23

II. Salvation as Deliverance from Sin and its Effects

A. Deliverance from the *penalty of sin*: Christ's substitutionary sacrifice for sin

1. 1 Pet. 3.18

2. Eph. 2.16-18

3. Heb. 9.26-28

B. Deliverance from the *personage of sin*: freedom from Satan and demonic oppression

1. 2 Cor. 2.14

2. 1 John 4.4

3. 1 John 5.19

4. 1 Cor. 2.12

5. Eph. 6.12

C. Deliverance from the *power of sin*: the outpouring of the Holy Spirit in this age

1. Eph. 1.13-14

2. Rom. 8.14-16

3. 2 Cor. 1.22

4. Eph. 4.30

D. Deliverance from the *presence of sin*: from the in-breaking to the consummation of the Kingdom

1. 1 Thess. 5.23-24

2. 1 Cor. 1.8-9

3. Eph. 5.26-27

4. Phil. 2.15-16

5. 1 Thess. 3.13

6. Jude 1.24

III. Evangelism: Declaring the Good News of This Deliverance and Salvation to Those Who Need to Hear God's Message of Deliverance in Jesus Christ

A. The *objective* side of evangelism: understanding exactly what God accomplished for creation and humankind in his work on the cross (the Good News)

1. Apostolicity of evangelism (the apostolic tradition), 1 Cor. 15.3-8

2. Forbidden to tamper with the Good News itself, Gal. 1.8-9

B. The *subjective* side of evangelism: making the message of the Good News plain to every people in their own language and culture

1. What we believe and confess, Rom. 10.8-13

2. The necessity of a messenger, Rom. 10.14-15

Conclusion

- Salvation is God's deliverance of humankind and creation from the power of the devil and the effects of sin.

- Through faith in Jesus Christ, believers are delivered from Satan's dominion and deception.

- God's deliverance in Christ also liberates believers from the effects of the Curse and sin through the power of the Spirit.

- Evangelism is the declaration of God's promised and prophesied deliverance through Jesus Christ to the entire world in the power of the Holy Spirit.

Student Questions and Response

The following questions were designed to help you review the material in the video. Recognizing the intimate connection between evangelism, salvation, and deliverance will greatly affect the way in which you both understand and practice biblical ministry to the lost. Be clear and concise in your answers, and where possible, support with Scripture!

1. According to the Scriptures, what precisely was the reason that Jesus came into the world? How did Jesus' death on the cross disarm the principalities and powers in their tyranny over us?

2. What is the *protoevangelium* and why is it so important for our understanding of evangelism as proclaiming the message of *God's deliverance* from satanic oppression?

3. What role does Jesus' life play in the destruction of the enemy? Be specific.

4. How did the death of Jesus accomplish for humankind its deliverance from the power of the devil, especially our fear of death and the bondage we suffer from that fear?

5. In what way does Jesus' resurrection provide us with confidence that the deliverance he won actually is accepted by God?

6. What does Scripture teach regarding Jesus' death as the sufficient penalty for our sin?

7. Why do believers never have to fear satanic domination again? What did Jesus' death and resurrection do to Satan for humankind?

8. How does the Holy Spirit guarantee us, in this age, that we are no longer under the power of sin?

9. At what point will we who believe finally be delivered from the very presence of sin?

10. Explain how evangelism is the declaration of the good news of God's deliverance from Satan and sin to those who do not believe.

CONNECTION

Summary of Key Concepts

This lesson focuses upon the foundational concepts which undergird our understanding of evangelism and spiritual warfare. Evangelism does not begin with what we do in our lives and testimonies with the lost; it began centuries ago when the devil and the first human pair rebelled against God's righteous rule. In seeking to live independent of God's authority and provision, the universe was thrown into spiritual chaos and darkness. Now, the universe is in spiritual war with God who promised to send to us a Deliverer who would crush the head of the serpent and deliver his people from their sins. Jesus Christ is that Deliverer! Understanding these basic critical points is essential in order to know just what evangelism seeks to do and what God does when those who are lost believe the good news of the Gospel.

- The Bible teaches that salvation is God's deliverance of humankind and creation from the power of the devil and the effects of sin.

- Through Jesus Christ, those who believe are delivered from Satan's dominion and tyranny (his deception and oppression) and the fear of death.

- The salvation of God in Christ also delivers those who believe from the effects of the Curse and sin through the power of the Spirit.

- Evangelism is the declaration of God's promised and prophesied deliverance through Jesus Christ to the entire world in the power of the Holy Spirit.

Student Application and Implications

Now is the time for you to discuss with your fellow students your questions about the spiritual conflict which has occurred as a result of the Fall, and salvation as deliverance from the devil and sin. These concepts lie at the heart of all discussion about ministry, evangelism, and spiritual liberation. What particular questions do you have in light of the material you have just studied? Maybe some of the questions below might help you form your own, more specific and critical questions.

- Why is it important to affirm right from the beginning that the Fall, the Curse, and all the effects of sin resulted from our rebellion and not from God's creation?

- In what way is it possible for us to describe all the evil down through human history as a result of both *satanic* influence and *human* choice, refusing to live under God's righteous rule?

- In light of what we know about the bondage that creation and humankind suffer as a result of sin, why is Jesus the only one who can bring deliverance to us? Support your answer with Scripture.

- Is it fair for God to hold the entire human race accountable for the sin committed by Adam and Eve? What is the relationship of *your sinning to their fall*?

- How does understanding salvation as deliverance from wicked powers influence the way we think about sharing the Good News in evangelism? What should we expect when people accept the good news of salvation in Christ?

- How does the Christian *live out victoriously* the deliverance that Jesus won for them on the cross? If a believer is not living in the freedom of Christ, how might we explain what is going on in their particular situation?

Demonic Deception Versus Personal Responsibility

In counseling a family who just had a loved one run into problems with the law and the courts, the issue comes up from one family member regarding the influence of the devil in this loved one's life. She believes with all her heart that the devil's deception and influence are at the heart of what has happened to their loved one. Only demonic influence could explain his swift turn, his accepting such terrible friends, and his involvement in crime and violence. Other family members reject that view, saying that the loved one knew what was right, but decided to ignore the good teaching at home and go the route of his less-instructed friends from the neighborhood. How would you explain to this family the relationship between the devil's deception in our lives and our own personal choices to do wrong as the cause of our personal sin?

Don't Expect Change Right Away

In a meeting before a community survey/door to door campaign, a member of the elders offers a word of encouragement to the workers before they leave the church. In asking them not to be discouraged, he suggests that we ought to share the Gospel with our neighbors, praying for God's working in their lives, but that we ought not be too expectant regarding change in their lives right away. Even if they say yes to Christ, moral change requires much time and effort. Some of the workers reject this view, saying that we can expect dramatic change every time someone accepts Jesus as Lord and Savior. What is the right/best/most biblical answer for this discussion?

It's Not Our Fault

In discussing with some young men on the corner about the Good News and salvation, one of the young men rejects the idea that the neighborhood is in its tough condition because of our sin. He suggests, "For years, this country treated people who were not white as second class, not letting us vote, or work, or participate in the larger society. We didn't ask for this neighborhood, and no one in it, if they could vote on the matter, would want to live in a neighborhood where our people aren't safe, well-fed and clothed, with good jobs and nice things like everybody else. I don't care what you say! It is not our fault that things are like this. The society has never treated us right – they are the ones who have made us like this!" How would you answer this viewpoint?

Where's the Beef?

After studying the entire biblical idea of salvation as deliverance, one of the students in class raises an important question. "What kind of victory can we promise to people who have been living their lives for decades doing all kinds of illegal and immoral things? I have worked for years in a substance abuse program where we have shared the Lord with the participants, and many people have indicated that they have believed in Christ. Still, even after they make the profession, they continue to shoot drugs, gamble, engage in all kinds of things that I know don't please the Lord. How can we say that salvation is deliverance when so many people who claim to be saved aren't living lives full of liberation and freedom?" How would you explain these facts?

Restatement of the Lesson's Thesis

Although God created the universe good and free, it fell into darkness and chaos as a result of the disobedience of the devil and the first human pair, Adam and Eve. As a result of this Fall, demonic powers were unleashed into the universe, all of creation was placed under a Curse and made subject to bondage and corruption, and humankind was made subject to selfishness, suffering, and death. Now through the death and resurrection of Jesus Christ, God's deliverance has come to us over the devil and the effects of sin. In Jesus we have been delivered from the penalty of sin, are being delivered from the person (i.e., the devil) and the power of sin by the Holy Spirit, and soon will be delivered from the presence of sin at Jesus' Second Coming. Evangelism is declaring this deliverance through the good news of the Gospel of Christ.

Resources and Bibliographies

If you are interested in pursuing some of the ideas of *Spiritual Warfare: Binding of the Strong Man*, you might want to give these books a try:

Billheimer, Paul. *Destined for the Throne*. Minneapolis: Bethany House, 1975.

Epp, Theodore H. *The Believer's Spiritual Warfare*. Lincoln: Back to the Bible, 1973.

Hayford, Jack W. (Executive Editor). *Answering the Call to Evangelism* (Spirit-Filled Life Kingdom Dynamics Study Guides). Nashville: Thomson Nelson Publishers, 1995.

Ministry Connections

Now is the time to try to isolate a principle or concept that can help you in your own particular ministry situation. Survey the various ideas, concepts, and truths that have been introduced in this lesson, and concentrate upon one insight that you will think about and pray for throughout this next week. What specific thought has the Holy Spirit impressed upon your heart regarding evangelism, spiritual warfare, and your own particular call to evangelism in your community? What particular situation or circumstance comes to mind when you think about how God has promised deliverance for those who believe the Good News? How does God want your own thinking to change in light of the truths that you have heard with your fellow students this week? Ask the Lord to give you wisdom as you pray and meditate on this lesson topic and the truth that the Spirit has impressed you with in this study.

Counseling and Prayer

Pray specifically that the Lord would give you his insight and understanding as you seek to understand evangelism against the backdrop of salvation as deliverance from the power of the devil and from sin and its effects. Ask God to increase your faith for results, to give you new insight into the Gospel as the very power of God unto salvation for all who believe (i.e., Romans 1.16). Ask for the Spirit's anointing as you share the Good News that the very delivering power of God might show itself in the lives of those with whom you share, even as that same power continues to transform your own life in Christ.

ASSIGNMENTS

Scripture Memory

Ephesians 2.8-10

Reading Assignment

To prepare for class, please visit *www.tumi.org/books* to find next week's reading assignment, or ask your Mentor.

Other Assignments

Again, make certain that you read the assignments above, and as last week, write a brief summary for them and bring these summaries to class next week. (Please see the "Reading Completion Sheet" on page 16.)

Also, now is the time to begin to think about the character of your ministry project, as well as decide what passage of Scripture you will select for your exegetical project. Do not delay in determining either your ministry or exegetical project. The sooner you select, the more time you will have to prepare!

Looking Forward to the Next Lesson

In our next lesson, *Focus on Reproduction: Church Growth – Reproducing in Number and Quality*, we survey Jesus' call to make disciples of all nations, to Evangelize, as well as to affirm that radical discipleship is proven in Christian community. Jesus has called us to evangelize the lost, equip new disciples to live the Christian life, and to empower his Church to reproduce itself, all for the glory of God. May his Spirit grant you the power and desire to make disciples where you live, and so multiply his Church, to the glory of his great name!

FOR FURTHER STUDY

Please see the following resources in *Picturing Theology: An A-Z Collection of TUMI's Key Diagrams, Charts, Graphics, and Articles*:

- *Receptivity Scale*, page 355
- *Translating the Story of God*, page 505
- *Thirty-Three Blessings in Christ*, page 480
- *Christus Victor: An Integrated Vision for the Christian Life*, page 43
- *Relationship of Cost and Effectiveness in Disciple-Making Endeavors*, page 356

Focus on Reproduction
Church Growth – Reproducing in Number and Quality

Lesson Objectives

Welcome in the strong name of Jesus Christ! After your reading, study, discussion, and application of the materials in this lesson, you will be able to:

- Demonstrate from the Bible the way in which radical discipleship is produced and authenticated in Christian community.

- Articulate the three integrated steps of urban church planting: evangelizing the lost, equipping the new disciples to live the Christian life in the context of Christian community – the Church, and empowering the leaders and the community to reproduce itself and associate with other like-minded churches.

- Highlight the ten critical principles drawn from a church planting model from Acts, and apply them to your own church planting efforts in the city.

Devotion

We Must Obey God Rather Than Men

Acts 5.27-32 – And when they had brought them, they set them before the council. And the high priest questioned them, [28] saying, "We strictly charged you not to teach in this name, yet here you have filled Jerusalem with your teaching, and you intend to bring this man's blood upon us." [29] But Peter and the apostles answered, "We must obey God rather than men. [30] The God of our fathers raised Jesus, whom you killed by hanging him on a tree. [31] God exalted him at his right hand as Leader and Savior, to give repentance to Israel and forgiveness of sins. [32] And we are witnesses to these things, and so is the Holy Spirit, whom God has given to those who obey him."

By whose authority do we have any right to talk to those who do not believe in the "outlandish" claims of Jesus of Nazareth? In a day of political correctness and at a time when religious intolerance is producing horrific acts of violence and terrorism, shouldn't all decent people sort of "simmer down," so to speak, and let everyone merely believe what they believe, without our interference or judgment? Is the time of sharing your faith for the purpose of persuading others to follow your view outmoded, outdated, and simply wrong?

The example of the Apostles is instructive for all men and women called to represent the interests and reputation of our risen Lord before others. In the face of horrible opposition and the threat of severe bodily harm if they continued to share the good news of Christ and his Kingdom, the Apostles remained unmoved. Peter and the Apostles are clear in the face of intimidation and threat: "We must obey God rather than men. The God of our fathers raised Jesus, whom you killed by hanging him on a tree. God exalted him at his right hand as Leader and Savior, to give repentance to Israel and forgiveness of sins. And we are witnesses to these things, and so is the Holy Spirit, whom God has given to those who obey him."

"We must obey God, rather than men." The Great Commission of our Lord, while given to the excited company of witnesses who heard the risen Lord's command to go into all the world and preach the Good News, is a generational command. Until the appearing of our Lord, every Christian generation goes forth into its own Jerusalems, Judeas, and Samarias with the Gospel of the Kingdom. All of us are responsible to share the Gospel to the ends of the earth. Nothing can detract us or intimidate us, for the very same Jesus of Nazareth crucified in Jerusalem so many centuries ago has been exalted. "The God of our fathers raised Jesus, whom you killed by hanging him on a tree. God exalted him at his right hand as Leader and Savior, to give repentance to Israel and forgiveness of sins." Exalted at the right hand of God as Leader and Savior, now repentance and forgiveness is preached to the entire world. To this, both the Apostles and the Holy Spirit testify.

What is the ground of our ministry? Why can we remain unmoved in the face of severe persecution and rejection? Why must we go, even if no one responds? Our God has exalted the Messiah to be Lord and Savior, and in obedience to his command, members of the Church have been going for centuries. Many have died, many have suffered, and many have been persecuted. But not one has been defeated. "God exalted him at his right hand as Leader and Savior . . ."(.) This great Commander will guide us until we die. Until then, we must obey God, rather than men.

Nicene Creed and Prayer

After reciting and/or singing the Nicene Creed (located in the Appendix), pray the following prayer:

> God, our heavenly Father, who revealed your love by sending your only Son into the world that all might live through him: grant that by the power of the Spirit your Church may fulfil the command to proclaim to all men the good news of Jesus Christ, and strengthen us in our resolution to work and witness for his kingdom, through Jesus Christ our Lord.
>
> ~ The Church of the Province of South Africa.
> *Minister's Book for Use With the Holy Eucharist and Morning and Evening Prayer.*
> Braamfontein: Publishing Department of the
> Church of the Province of South Africa. p. 114.

Scripture Memorization Review

Review with a partner, write out and/or recite the text for last class session's assigned memory verse: Ephesians 2.8-10.

Assignments Due

Turn in your summary of the reading assignment for last week, that is, your brief response and explanation of the main points that the authors were seeking to make in the assigned reading (Reading Completion Sheet).

Marketing and Godliness Do Mix

In a leader's meeting at a local urban church which was determined to grow, one of the head deacons commented that although their church is a godly church, it simply doesn't know how to market itself to those in the neighborhood. "Let's face it," he says, "the reason that many of the churches in the suburbs are growing is that they are constantly sharing their message and programs with others – they get the word out. And, what's good for the goose is good for the gander. If we want to grow as a church, we are going to have to get better marketing strategies. We can start small, but that's where we have to start. I believe, and you should too, that marketing and godliness do mix." Is this brother correct? What role does marketing play in growing the Church of Jesus Christ?

Not Ready Yet

 Hosea is a bright and wonderful new Christian in your church of twenty two years who expresses a deep passion to share the Good News with others. After service one morning you find him looking discouraged. When you ask what is going on, he says in a dejected way, "Oh, its about my feelings lately. Ever since I gave my heart to the Lord about two years ago, I have had this deep burden to be in the Lord's ministry. Not a day goes by without my heart being stirred about the lost. I can't sleep, I cry all the time; early in the morning I amup, pacing, asking the Lord to tell me what he wants me to do. I believe he has called me to the ministry. I shared my burden with Deacon Wilson, and he told me that I was not old enough in the Lord to be put in a position to share the Gospel with others. Not yet, at least. I needed more time in the Word and in the church to prepare myself. I know he is right, but this burden nearly consumes me. What should I do?" How would you answer Hosea?

The Church Turns People Off

 You hear of a new Bible study group formed by members of the church who are disgruntled with the way things are going in the church. While they don't intend to leave the church, nor lead a campaign to replace the pastor, they simply don't believe that the church is adequate to bring new converts in. The music is old-fashioned, the services are dry, and the people seem unfriendly. This group formed itself with the intent on being more inviting and appealing to new members. As one of its members recently said, "Our church loves the Lord and the Word, but it's got some problems. I fear that new people are going to find us too stiff and unattractive. We formed this church to bring in some excitement. The church turns people off, and we are going to help it out." What do you think about this member's opinion and the formation of the new group?

Church Growth: Reproducing in Number and Quality

How to Plant an Urban Church That Reproduces: An Overview

Rev. Dr. Don L. Davis

Summary

As disciples called to obey Christ's commission to go and make disciples of all nations, we know that radical discipleship is produced and authenticated only in Christian community. To plant churches is to fulfill the Great Commission, which involves three integrated steps: *Evangelizing* (winning the lost), *Equipping* (establishing new disciples in the Church), and *Empowering* (outfitting leaders and the church to reproduce itself in fellowship with other like-minded churches).

Our objective for this lesson, *How to Plant an Urban Church That Reproduces: An Overview*, is to enable you to see that:

- The Word of God teaches that radical discipleship is produced and authenticated only in the context of Christian community.

- To fulfill the Great Commission of the risen Lord Jesus we must plant healthy, Christ-honoring churches among all the peoples of the earth.

- Church planting is made up of three integrated steps of kingdom ministry.

- The first step is *Evangelize*, where we evangelize the lost by sharing in word and deed the good news of the Kingdom in Jesus Christ.

- The second step is *Equip*, which is establishing new disciples to live the Christian life in the context of Christian community – the Church.

- The third step is *Empower*, which involves resourcing and outfitting the leaders and the congregation of the newly formed church to reproduce itself and associate with other like-minded churches.

- Ten critical principles exist to guide us in our church planting efforts, which are drawn from the apostolic ministry in Acts, and can be readily applied to our own church planting efforts in the city.

- By *evangelizing* the lost, *equipping* new Christians to grow as disciples of Jesus, and *empowering* leaders and churches to reproduce, we can see dozens of solid, healthy churches planted throughout the cities of our nation and world.

Video Outline

Our work of ministry builds upon the Apostles' work. "The Twelve were chosen that they might be with Christ (Mark 3.14), and this personal association qualified them to act as his witnesses (Acts 1.8); they were from the first endowed with power over unclean spirits and diseases (Matt. 10.1), and this power was renewed and increased, in a more general form, when the promise of the Father (Luke 24.49) came upon them in the gift of the Holy Spirit (Acts 1.8); on their first mission they were sent forth to preach (Mark 3.14), and in the great commission they were instructed to teach all nations (Matt. 28.19). They thus received Christ's authority to evangelize at large. But they were also promised a more specific function as judges and rulers of God's people (Matt. 19.28; Luke 22.29-30), with power to bind and to loose (Matt. 18.18), to remit and to retain sins (John 20.23)."

~ D. R. W. Wood. New Bible Dictionary. 3rd ed. Downers Grove, IL: InterVarsity Press, 1996. p. 202.

I. **Evangelize: Share the Good News of Christ and His Kingdom in the Community.**

Mark 16.15-18 – And he said to them, "Go into all the world and proclaim the gospel to the whole creation. [16] Whoever believes and is baptized will be saved, but whoever does not believe will be condemned. [17] And these signs will accompany those who believe: in my name they will cast out demons; they will speak in new tongues; [18] they will pick up serpents with their hands; and if they drink any deadly poison, it will not hurt them; they will lay their hands on the sick, and they will recover."

A. Importance of Evangelism in reproducing urban churches

1. Evangelism is the *centerpiece* of all Christian mission and outreach; the Good News is the power of God to salvation to all who believe, Rom. 1.6-17.

2. No church or church plant that refuses to work tirelessly in sharing the Gospel will be dynamic or healthy.

3. Demonstrating both the power of the Spirit as well as proclaiming the Word of God is essential for effective disciple-making in urban communities.

   a. Signs and wonders of the Holy Spirit, Rom. 15.18-20 – "For I will not venture to speak of anything except what Christ has accomplished through me to bring the Gentiles to obedience – by word and deed, [19] by the power of signs and wonders, by the power of the Spirit of God – so that from Jerusalem and all the way around to Illyricum I have fulfilled the ministry of the Gospel of Christ; [20] and thus I make it my ambition to preach the Gospel, not where Christ has already been named, lest I build on someone else's foundation"

b. Good works which reveal the power of the Kingdom, Matt. 5.13-16

  c. Clear, bold presentations of the good news of the grace of God, Gal. 3.1ff.; 1 Thess. 1.5ff.

B. Keys to *Evangelizing the Lost*

  1. Evangelism is *being a herald: it is boldly declaring through word and deed that Jesus is the Messiah, the risen Lord of the Kingdom!*

  2. A boldness to engage neighbors with the lifestyle and witness of the Gospel

  3. A willingness to befriend and serve the community where God has placed you

  4. A focused, unbroken intercessory team that undergirds all the efforts with fervent, faith-filled prayer

C. Stage One: Prepare – *lay the initial foundation for responsible mission and outreach through your prayer, your team, your selection of your target area, and your understanding of the context.*

  1. Key texts

    a. Luke 24.46-49

    b. Matt. 28.19-20

2. Basic principle: spend the appropriate time seeking the mind of the Lord and preparing yourselves before you enter into the community to begin your work.

3. Form a church-plant team.

4. Pray.

5. Select a target area and population.

6. Do demographic and ethnographic studies.

D. Stage Two: Launch – *in the name of Jesus, enter into the community to learn, to serve, and to witness of the good news of Christ and his Kingdom in your target area.*

1. Key texts

   a. Acts 1.8

   b. Gal. 2.7-10

2. Basic principles: filled with the Holy Spirit, with knowledge of one another and the people and place to whom God has called them, the team goes forth into the community serving and witnessing in the name of Jesus.

3. Recruit and train volunteers.

4. Conduct evangelistic events and door-to-door evangelism.

II. Equip: Gather the New Disciples into an Assembly and Grow Them to Maturity.

Eph. 4.11-16 – And he gave the apostles, the prophets, the evangelists, the pastors and teachers, [12] to equip the saints for the work of ministry, for building up the body of Christ, [13] until we all attain to the unity of the faith and of the knowledge of the Son of God, to mature manhood, to the measure of the stature of the fullness of Christ, [14] so that we may no longer be children, tossed to and fro by the waves and carried about by every wind of doctrine, by human cunning, by craftiness in deceitful schemes. [15] Rather, speaking the truth in love, we are to grow up in every way into him who is the head, into Christ, [16] from whom the whole body, joined and held together by every joint with which it is equipped, when each part is working properly, makes the body grow so that it builds itself up in love.

A. Importance of *Equipping* in reproducing urban churches

1. The goal is *discipleship*, not conversion, Matt. 28.18-20.

2. Believers grow only as their gifts function together under the direction of the Holy Spirit.

   a. 1 Cor. 12.3-11

   b. 1 Pet. 4.10-11

   c. Rom. 12.3-8

   d. Eph. 4.9-16

3. The Jesus movement is a *communal commitment and journey*, not an individual religion.

4. No relationship to God is sustainable without the body of Christ.

B. Keys to *Equipping believers*

1. Equipping is *parenthood: raising spiritual children to maturity.*

2. Form deep convictions of its importance and place in reproduction.

3. Develop a clear plan on how to proceed.

4. Cultivate a flexible approach that allows the members to meet their own needs through solid leadership and the functioning of the gifts of the Spirit.

C. Stage Three: Assemble – *gather the new converts and small groups together to form a local assembly, announcing to the community the presence of a new Christ-centered fellowship in the neighborhood.*

1. Key texts

a. Acts 2.41-47

b. Heb. 10.24-25

2. Basic principle: new and immature believers must gather together as a local assembly to ensure their protection, feeding, fellowship, and care.

3. Form cell groups, Bible studies, etc. to follow up new believers, to continue evangelism, and to identify and train emerging leaders.

4. Announce the birth of a new church to the neighborhood and meet regularly for public worship, instruction and fellowship.

D. Stage Four: Nurture – *through small groups and individual discipleship, strengthen the disciples of Jesus in the basics of the Christian life, Christian community, and church growth.*

1. Key texts

    a. 1 Thess. 2.5-9

    b. 1 Cor. 4.14-15

2. Basic principle: through small groups and individual friendships, corporate worship, and solid teaching and fellowship, new believers are nurtured and equipped to live as disciples of Jesus in the body of Christ.

3. Develop individual and group discipleship.

4. Fill key roles in the church: identify and use spiritual gifts.

III. Empower: Commission Leaders for the Church and Train Them to Reproduce.

Acts 20.28 – Pay careful attention to yourselves and to all the flock, in which the Holy Spirit has made you overseers, to care for the church of God, which he obtained with his own blood.

Acts 20.32 – And now I commend you to God and to the word of his grace, which is able to build you up and to give you the inheritance among all those who are sanctified.

A. Importance of *Empowerment* in reproducing urban churches

1. Reproduction is largely a matter of *laying the right foundation* for the church's ongoing growth and development.

2. Empowerment is *investment*; it involves providing the growing church with all the tools that it needs in order to "take the baton" and continue on the journey.

3. To define empowerment in terms of abandonment is to ensure that it will never go further than its bitterness against those who started the effort.

4. The Holy Spirit must show you who plant the church the difference between *avoiding harmful dependence* and *being stingy and patronizing*.

B. Keys to *Empowering churches to reproduce*

1. Empowerment is investment: identifying, investing in, and releasing leaders to accomplish their own God-given dreams and tasks in the Lord.

    a. Investing in *people*

    b. Investing in *structures*

c. Investing in *facilities*

d. Investing in *relationships*

2. Seek the mind of the Spirit as to what the best times and means are to turn the church's affairs over to its leaders.

3. Challenge the assembly from the very beginning that *reproduction*, not *survival*, is the goal of the kingdom activity there.

4. Celebrate the church's growth and its right to *fall on its own face for God!*

C. Transition

1. Key texts

a. Titus 1.4-5

b. Acts 14.21-23

2. Basic principle: transferring authority, leadership, and direction over to the leaders and congregation of the church in order that they may continue to reproduce, and associate with other like-minded assemblies for fellowship and challenge

3. Transfer leadership to indigenous leaders so they become self-governing, self-supporting and self-reproducing (appoint elders and pastors).

4. Finalize decisions about denominational or other affiliations.

5. Commission the church.

6. Foster association with World Impact and other urban churches for fellowship, support and mission ministry.

IV. The Pauline Cycle: Hesselgrave's Model of Planting Churches Cross-Culturally

Pauline Precedents from Acts: The Pauline Cycle (The "Pauline Cycle" terminology and stages are taken from David J. Hesselgrave, *Planting Churches Cross-Culturally*. 2nd ed. [Grand Rapids: Baker Book House, 2000]).

A. The importance of Acts in cross-cultural missions

1. The Apostles were the *first cross-cultural urban missionaries.*

2. The churches of the cities of Asia minor were *urban cross-cultural church plants.*

3. The epistles from the Apostles were the *first urban follow-up materials.*

B. The steps to cross-cultural church planting (*note: see how our three principles of "Evangelize, Equip, and Empower" correspond to Hesselgrave's steps*)

1. Missionaries Commissioned: Acts 13.1-4; 15.39-40; Gal. 1.15-16

2. Audience Contacted: Acts 13.14-16; 14.1; 16.13-15; 17.16-19

3. Gospel Communicated: Acts 13.17-41; 16.31; Rom. 10.9-14; 2 Tim. 2.8

4. Hearers Converted: Acts 13.48; 16.14-15; 20.21; 26.20; 1 Thess. 1.9-10

5. Believers Congregated: Acts 13.43; 19.9; Rom. 16.4-5; 1 Cor. 14.26

6. Faith Confirmed: Acts 14.21-22; 15.41; Rom 16.17; Col. 1.28; 2 Thess. 2.15; 1 Tim. 1.3

7. Leadership Consecrated: Acts 14.23; 2 Tim. 2.2; Titus 1.5

8. Believers Commended: Acts 14.23; 16.40; 21.32 (2 Tim. 4.9 and Titus 3.12 by implication)

9. Relationships Continued: Acts 15.36; 18.23; 1 Cor. 16.5; Eph. 6.21-22; Col. 4.7-8

10. Sending Churches Convened: Acts 14.26-27; 15.1-4

C. Ten Principles of cross-cultural urban church planting

1. *Jesus is Lord.* (Matt. 9.37-38) All church plant activity is made effective and fruitful under the watch care and power of the Lord Jesus, who himself is the Lord of the harvest.

2. *Evangelize, Equip, and Empower unreached people to reach people.* (1 Thess. 1.6-8) Our goal in reaching others for Christ is not only for solid conversion but also for dynamic multiplication; those who are reached must be trained to reach others as well.

3. *Be inclusive: whosoever will may come.* (Rom. 10.12) No strategy should forbid any person or group from entering into the Kingdom through Jesus Christ by faith.

4. *Be culturally neutral: come just as you are.* (Col. 3.11) The Gospel places no demands on any seeker to change their culture as a prerequisite for coming to Jesus; they may come just as they are.

5. *Avoid a fortress mentality.* (Acts 1.8) The goal of missions is not to create an impregnable castle in the midst of an unsaved community, but a dynamic outpost of the Kingdom which launches a witness for Jesus within and unto the very borders of their world.

6. *Continue to evangelize to avoid stagnation.* (Rom. 1.16-17) Keep looking to new horizons with the vision of the Great Commission in mind; foster an environment of aggressive witness for Christ.

7. *Cross racial, class, gender, and language barriers.* (1 Cor. 9.19-22) Use your freedom in Christ to find new, credible ways to communicate the kingdom message to those farthest from the cultural spectrum of the traditional church.

8. *Respect the dominance of the receiving culture.* (Acts 15.23-29) Allow the Holy Spirit to incarnate the vision and the ethics of the Kingdom of God in the words, language, customs, styles, and experience of those who have embraced Jesus as their Lord.

9. *Avoid dependence.* (Eph. 4.11-16) Neither patronize nor be overly stingy towards the growing congregation; do not underestimate the power of the Spirit in the midst of even the smallest Christian community to accomplish God's work in their community.

10. *Think reproducibility.* (2 Tim. 2.2; Phil. 1.18) In every activity and project you initiate, think in terms of equipping others to do the same by maintaining an open mind regarding the means and ends of your missionary endeavors.

V. Last Word: The Fastest, Most Productive, and Most Biblical Method of World Evangelization and Discipleship Is to Plant Churches Cross-Culturally!

Conclusion

- Planting churches in obedience to the Great Commission of Christ involves three basic stages: *Evangelize, Equip,* and *Empower.*

- As we *evangelize* the lost, we share the Good News with those who have not heard of God's saving work in Jesus.

- We *equip* new disciples to live the Christian life by laying a foundation for solid Christian community for years to come.

- We *empower* leaders and the church for independence, helping them to reproduce themselves while associating with other like-minded churches.

Student Questions and Response

The following questions were designed to help you review the material in the video. The Great Commission of the Lord Jesus means that we are called to go to all nations making disciples in his name. We fulfill the Great Commission as we plant healthy, viable churches among the various people groups of the world. We accomplish this through *Evangelizing, Equipping,* and *Empowering.* Your ability to understand and apply these principles can be all the difference in ministering effectively in urban poor communities, so your ability to understand

and articulate them is important. Answer the questions thoroughly, and always support your thinking with Scripture.

1. Why can it be said that "evangelism is the centerpiece of all Christian mission and outreach?" Why is merely demonstrating the Gospel in good deeds not entirely sufficient to kingdom ministry?

2. What role did signs and wonders of the Holy Spirit play in the ministry of the apostles in testifying to the grace of God? What role can or should they play in our work today in the city?

3. What precisely is the Gospel that we are called to bear witness to in our ministry? How did your lesson summarize the church planting process through the acrostic PLANT? What do the letters refer to?

4. What is the definition of the "Prepare" step of church planting in the *Evangelism* stage? Correspondingly, what is the meaning of the "Launch" phase of church planting in the *Evangelism* stage? What is included in each, and what are the kinds of activities associated with each of these stages?

5. Why is equipping new Christians in the faith such a critical step in all true disciple making? What role does the local church play in the discipling of the new convert to Christ? What are the keys to equipping believers to live the Christian life?

6. Explain the "Assemble" and "Nurture" phases of church planting in urban ministry, and correlate how these phases enables us to *Equip* new believers to grow in Christ. How are they the same, how do they differ, and what is involved in each?

7. Why is it important for churches to constantly seek to reproduce themselves through continued evangelism and equipping of others? What is the relationship between spiritual health and spiritual fruit?

8. Explain the "Transition" phase of *Empowerment*. How is empowerment essentially an "investment" in the leadership and membership of the new church?

9. What are the three "selfs" of the "Transition" phase of urban church planting? Outline briefly Hesselgrave's model of planting churches cross-culturally. How do the three-self understanding, in the Hesselgrave model, and the three E's of church planting connect to one another?

10. Summarize briefly the ten principles of cross-cultural church planting. Do you agree with the statement that "the fastest, most productive, and most biblical method of world evangelization and discipleship is to plant churches cross-culturally?" Explain your answer.

CONNECTION

Summary of Key Concepts

This lesson focuses upon providing you with a general overview of the critical theology, methodology, and perspective in doing effective urban ministry. In order to be most effective in advancing the Kingdom of God in the city, we as his called servants must understand carefully and precisely what God is doing in the world through the proclamation of the Gospel. The Father has exalted Jesus to his right hand as Lord and Savior, and now, through the Spirit, the Gospel is bring proclaimed throughout the earth. As we plant healthy, viable churches of Jesus Christ in the city through evangelism, equipping, and empowerment we can see men and women, boys and girls be converted, grow, and become fruitful witnesses of the Kingdom of Christ where they live, play, and work.

- In every phase and dimension of mission, teaching, preaching, and outreach, we must appeal to our Lord Jesus for aid and direction, for he alone can enable us to win souls and plant churches in the city.

- The Great Commission of Christ is a call to go and make disciples of the nations, and this radical discipleship cannot be produced and proven valid apart from the Christian community.

- An effective church planting strategy can be summarized in the PLANT acrostic: prepare, launch, assemble, nurture, and transition. These phases are included within three integrated stages: evangelizing the lost, equipping the new disciples to live the Christian life in the church, and empowering the leaders and the community to reproduce itself and associate with other like-minded churches.

- The principles of cross-cultural church planting underwrite our efforts to minister among the poor in the city. Drawn from the apostles' experience outlined in Acts, these principles make plain the critical insights of effective urban ministry. They include affirming that Jesus is Lord, the challenge to evangelize, equip, and empower unreached people to reach people, and the need to be inclusive, culturally neutral, and to cross racial, class, gender, and language barriers to make the Gospel of the Kingdom plain to those who we seek to reach.

Student Application and Implications

Now is the time for you to discuss with your fellow students your questions about church growth and reproduction. To grapple with these concepts, we must seek the integrated nature of effective urban ministry. We evangelize with a mind to equip the new believers in the faith, and equip with a commitment to empower these same growing Christians to share their faith with others. As you reflect on these stages and ideas, what particular questions have come to mind? Explore your own questions, as you reflect on those below.

- Why is the teaching regarding the lordship of Christ so extremely foundational for any valid perspective of ministry or outreach of the Gospel? What is your understanding and application of this important doctrine in your life today? Explain.

- Have you sensed from the Lord a call to minister the Gospel? How and in what way? If you have sensed such a call, when did you first realize that he had called you to such a ministry?

- How would you describe your ability to trust in the lordship of Christ during times of difficulty, persecution, and trouble? Are you a worrier, that is, do you fret over the various dimensions of your life and ministry? How might an application of the doctrine of Christ help you overcome your fears and anxieties in these areas?

- What about the PLANT process seems most clear to you? What in the acrostic seems least clear? Have you ever considered the possibility that God might want you to be involved in planting new churches for him? Why or why not?

- Discuss the truthfulness and biblical validity of the following statement: "The fastest, most productive, and most biblical method of world evangelization and discipleship is to plant churches cross-culturally." Do you agree with this statement? Why or why not?

- Of the three broad areas of urban ministry (*Evangelize*, *Equip*, and *Empower*), which do you feel most drawn to and gifted to do? Are you part of a fellowship that emphasizes these principles in a practical way in your worship, life, and fellowship together?

- Do you feel comfortable in crossing barriers (class, race, gender, language, etc.) in sharing the good news of Christ and his Kingdom with others?

- How burdened are you to share the Gospel with your family, friends, and coworkers? What is the greatest obstacle for you to overcome in being a better witness for Christ among those with whom you live and work?

- Which of the ten cross-cultural principles most directly affects and influences your life situation right now? How might you apply this principle more directly in your own life and ministry today?

CASE STUDIES

Giving People a Little More Incentive

(Adapted from a true story) One church, in an effort to get more people interested and involved in their growing church, determined to give visitors a little more incentive to come to their Sunday services. The church began to advertise to the public that every Sunday after service they would be conducting a raffle where the lucky winner could win as much as $800! When asked about the advisability of such a tactic, those involved said, "Why shouldn't we use any means at our disposal to lure and woo people to a service that will not merely promise a handful of dollars but the eternal treasures of life in Jesus Christ?" Not only was the raffle successful, increasing the number of worshipers in the service, it has emboldened the church to think of even bigger and better "lures" to get the lost to come hear the Good News. What is right or wrong in such an approach to church growth?

God Is in This

Without the authorization of any parent church or ministry, a dear couple determined to follow through on a burden they had had for some time. In an act of courage and faith, they began a Bible study with an intent to plant a church that would be self-sufficient and godly. God has blessed their effort; in less than two years they have grown to a robust congregation of 300 active members, all who love the Lord and the "first family" of the pastor with their whole hearts. A gentle strife has been brewing lately, because a group feels more and more that the authority of the pastor and his wife seem almost absolute and dictatorial; nothing can be done or decided in the church without their involvement and endorsement. Some are suggesting that this goes against the teaching of the Bible on the lordship of Jesus, who is the Church's one true and only head. If the church asked you to give a teaching on this, how would you advise them to apply the lordship of Jesus to their situation?

Let's Start Our Own Service

 In a growing but small urban church, the young people are completely frustrated with the traditional congregational services. Although the pastor's teaching is fresh and edifying, and the believers in the church are loving and caring, the styles embraced in the services are so traditional and old fashioned that many of the young people coming to the church feel left out and alienated. The pastor, affirming our freedom in Christ, wants the young people to start their own service. His argument is clear: "Since the Gospel can overcome any barrier of culture or class or race, there is no reason why we can't overcome barriers of custom, music, and tradition, too." Some think this kind of teaching will lead to a compromise of the Gospel, and soon the leadership team will begin to discuss this possibility. How would you advise the leadership team to approach this issue in the church?

Charity Begins at Home

 The senior pastor has been in ongoing discussion with the leaders of the church about a new proposal that is causing much discussion throughout the church. Rather than moving to a larger building outside of the "needy neighborhood" where the church has been for the last ten years, the pastor wants to stay. His proposal is not to go to a bigger building, but rather equip members of the church to go and plant another church in the same neighborhood. The pastor, explaining the power of church planting to win new disciples to Christ, affirms his belief that no method is more biblical or faster. Those on the other side, while not rejecting church planting, want to have a strong, central church that can be better able to plant new churches if the "mother church" is strong. After all, they argue, charity should begin at home. If you were the associate pastor of the church, how would you seek to resolve the brewing conflict over methods?

Restatement of the Lesson's Thesis

The most foundational theological concept that grounds all of our understanding of evangelism, discipleship, and church planting in the city is the lordship of Jesus Christ. Because Jesus has been exalted to the Father's right hand as risen Lord and anointed Messiah, he now holds the position of head over all things, not only to the Church but also to the advance of the Kingdom in the world, as Lord of the harvest. Every dimension of ministry is subject to his direction and power.

The Great Commission of Christ is a call to go and make disciples of the nations, and this radical discipleship cannot be produced and proven valid apart from the Christian community. We can summarize that process for church planting in the PLANT acrostic: prepare, launch, assemble, nurture, and transition. Three stages connect these phases: evangelizing the lost, equipping new disciples to live the Christian life in the Church, and empowering leaders and the congregation to reproduce itself and associate with other like-minded churches.

The wisdom of the principles drawn from the apostles' experience outlined in Acts provide us with critical insights for effective urban ministry. They include affirming that Jesus is Lord, the challenge to evangelize, equip, and empower unreached people to reach people, and the need to be inclusive, culturally neutral, and to cross racial, class, gender, and language barriers to make the Gospel of the Kingdom plain to those whom we seek to reach.

Resources and Bibliographies

If you are interested in pursuing some of the ideas of *Church Growth: Reproducing in Number and Quality*, you might want to give these books a try:

Ellul, Jacques. *The Presence of the Kingdom*. New York: Seabury Press, 1967.

Garrison, David. *Church Planting Movements*. Bangalore, India: WIGTake Resources, 2004.

Hopler, Thom. *A World of Difference*. Downers Grove, IL: InterVarsity Press, 1981.

Pippert, Rebecca Manley. *Out of the Saltshaker and Into the World*. Downers Grove, IL: InterVarsity Press, 1979.

Ministry Connections

Now is your time to address the meaning of these doctrinal and theological insights to your own personal life situation as well as to your own very real practical ministry connection. Think in terms of what you want to meditate on, reconsider, and pray for throughout this upcoming week.

Specifically, what does it appear that the Holy Spirit is stirring within you as a result of your reflection, study, and discussion on the nature of the lordship of Christ, the Great Commission to go and make disciples of all the nations, and your own contribution to that? In what way do you feel called to contribute today to the call to make disciples of Jesus, in your family, in your church, in the neighborhood, or on the job? Do you sense a more formal calling to the Gospel ministry in your life, in other words, has or is God calling you to make the ministry your full time vocation? With whom might you share this desire and burden? What specifically have you done so far to articulate your burden to your pastor and spiritual leaders, to your husband or wife, to your friends and relatives? How might you personally give time, talent, or treasure to the mission of planting churches, both in your community, through your church, or even overseas? Is God calling you to consider a change in your employment, your schedule or life direction to pursue something more in sync and in line with presenting the Gospel to the lost?

If God is not suggesting these kinds of changes to you, how might you so apply these teachings to your life so you can become a more effective disciple maker for the Lord Jesus? Is the Holy Spirit placing a particular situation on your mind regarding how you might apply this teaching in your life today? Think prayerfully about these and related questions, and ask the Spirit to make plain to you his challenges for you to consider and respond to on this lesson topic.

Counseling and Prayer

As we seek our part in this great work of fulfilling the Great Commission, it will be necessary for us to be prayerful, even practicing the discipline of fasting and meditation in order to give God the opportunity to speak to our hearts more clearly. Make sure that you ask your mentor and colleagues to pray for specific leading and direction in your life as you pursue more and more practical ways in which you can join this grand effort to make Jesus known in all the places which have yet to hear of his loving grace and coming Kingdom. Set aside time to pray specifically to the Lord for guidance and wisdom as you pursue your calling under Christ to advance his Kingdom in the place and position where you are now. Be open to a new journey and a new future, even as you yield to the leading of the Spirit on these issues.

ASSIGNMENTS

Scripture Memory

Ephesians 6.10-13

Reading Assignment

To prepare for class, please visit *www.tumi.org/books* to find next week's reading assignment, or ask your Mentor.

LESSON 3 | FOCUS ON REPRODUCTION: CHURCH GROWTH / 387

Other Assignments

As usual you ought to come with your reading assignment sheet containing your summary of the reading material for the week. Also, you must have selected the text for your exegetical project and turn in your proposal for your ministry project.

Looking Forward to the Next Lesson

Our final lesson, *Doing Justice and Loving Mercy: Let Justice Roll Down – The Vision and Theology of the Kingdom*, focuses on the *imago Dei* (i.e., the image of God) in Scripture. We will see the uniqueness of humankind, and explore its implications for viewing all individuals, families, peoples, and nations as precious and irreplaceable. In a world torn by violence, cruelty, and injustice, we desperately need representatives of the Kingdom who can demonstrate both the justice and mercy of our Lord Jesus Christ. Only the Church can reveal the righteousness, unity, and grace of the Kingdom of God in the midst of a world torn by malice, vengeance, and disunity. Only in Christ can we pursue a peace that is authentic and that will last. Until our Lord returns, we are called to display his righteousness in the earth. May God richly bless you in every way as you refresh your memory of our call to demonstrate justice and love mercy, in the Church and in the world, to the glory of God.

FOR FURTHER STUDY

Please see the following resources in *Picturing Theology: An A-Z Collection of TUMI's Key Diagrams, Charts, Graphics, and Articles*:

- *Apostolic Band*, page 5
- *The Oikos Factor: Spheres of Relationship and Influence*, page 304
- *Overview of Church Plant Planning Phases*, page 312
- *Paul's Team Members*, page 316
- *That We May Be One*, page 426

Doing Justice and Loving Mercy
Let Justice Roll Down – The Vision and Theology of the Kingdom

Lesson Objectives

Welcome in the strong name of Jesus Christ! After your reading, study, discussion, and application of the materials in this lesson, you will be able to:

- Explain carefully and precisely the image of God and its basis in the teachings of the Bible.

- Lay out the ways in which the Scriptures portray humankind as unique and precious because of God's special gift of creation, forming human beings in his own image and likeness.

- List the reasons why we ought to view all individuals, families, peoples, and nations as precious and irreplaceable.

- Detail the theological implications of the teaching regarding the *imago Dei*, especially how this high view of humankind justifies our best and most dedicated effort at the preservation and care for human life, wherever it exists and wherever we find people in distress.

Devotion

Am I My Brother's Keeper?

Gen. 4.1-16 – Now Adam knew Eve his wife, and she conceived and bore Cain, saying, "I have gotten a man with the help of the Lord." [2] And again, she bore his brother Abel. Now Abel was a keeper of sheep, and Cain a worker of the ground. [3] In the course of time Cain brought to the Lord an offering of the fruit of the ground, [4] and Abel also brought of the firstborn of his flock and of their fat portions. And the Lord had regard for Abel and his offering, [5] but for Cain and his offering he had no regard. So Cain was very angry, and his face fell. [6] The Lord said to Cain, "Why are you angry, and why has your face fallen? [7] If you do well, will you not be accepted? And if you do not do well, sin is crouching at the door. Its desire is for you, but you must rule over it." [8] Cain spoke to Abel his brother. And when they were in the field, Cain rose up against his brother Abel and killed him. [9] Then the Lord said to Cain, "Where is Abel your brother?" He said, "I do not know; am I my brother's keeper?" [10] And the Lord said, "What have you done?

> The voice of your brother's blood is crying to me from the ground. [11] And now you are cursed from the ground, which has opened its mouth to receive your brother's blood from your hand. [12] When you work the ground, it shall no longer yield to you its strength. You shall be a fugitive and a wanderer on the earth." [13] Cain said to the Lord, "My punishment is greater than I can bear. [14] Behold, you have driven me today away from the ground, and from your face I shall be hidden. I shall be a fugitive and a wanderer on the earth, and whoever finds me will kill me." [15] Then the Lord said to him, "Not so! If anyone kills Cain, vengeance shall be taken on him sevenfold." And the Lord put a mark on Cain, lest any who found him should attack him. [16] Then Cain went away from the presence of the Lord and settled in the land of Nod, east of Eden.

What is ultimately our responsibility for the well-being of others, whether they are friends, family, neighbor or stranger, alien or kinsman, enemy or beloved? It appears in all of us that there is an inclination to only love those who are "near by," those people whom we count as friends, or immediate family. Why ought we to sacrifice our precious few resources and opportunities on behalf of people we either don't know well, on those who are inclined to waste our good will or abuse our kindness, or worse yet, on those who actually and indeed hate us? Ultimately, who is the neighbor that we are called to love even as ourselves (cf. Lev. 19.18)?

Genesis 4 contains one of the great but tragic episodes of the entire Scriptures. Occurring on the heels of the great Fall of the first human pain whose voluntary and unfortunate rebellion produced the curse and death on humankind, we see tangibly one of its results. Alienation. Jealousy. Hatred and malice, which lead to violent murder and justification. While this story appears on the surface to be about the conflict between two brothers, upon a closer look we see greater meaning. In this story of conflict between Cain and Abel in fact the prophecy of Genesis 3.15 is concretely played out: the seed of the woman meets the seed of the serpent. Cain yields to the evil that crouches at the door, brutally murders his very own brother because of jealousy and malice, is cursed, and becomes the original creator of the godless city and its godless society. This way of rejecting God's will, of hating those who in fact keep it, is referred to in the New Testament as the "way of Cain" (Jude 11), or as "sin against one's brother" (1 John 3.12, 15). All in all, this story reveals the kind of profound and cancerous lack of trust and obedience to the Lord which results in a dangerous envy of God's own people. This envy is deadly, and leads to violence, murder, alienation, and finally to the very judgment of God himself.

In this text, the brothers Cain and Abel are contrasted and played against one another, with the entire passage above contrasting them in every way. Cain is shown as a person whose work, as one commentator puts it, "lines him up with the curse," one who works the ground, (cf. Gen. 4.2; cf. 3.17). Abel, on the other hand, appears as a keeper of sheep, worships God through the sacrifice of the flock, a form of worship which foreshadows the great sacrifice of our Lord Jesus Christ. According to the Apostle John, Abel's act of offering sacrifice in worship was righteous, while Cain's works were evil (1 John 3.12). We know that the heart of the sacrifice was the offering of the gift in faith, without which it is impossible to please God (Heb. 11.6).

Instead of learning the kind of sacrifice that would please God, Cain's lack of trust in God is shown in his reaction to God's rejection of his fruit offering. Cain became angry, so much so that he refused to listen even to God's own advice (4.6-7). God's counsel was telling and specific: if in fact Cain would do what was right and therefore please God, his situation would be well. However, sin was crouching like a predatory beast ready to overcome him if he refused the counsel and surrendered to his dark discouragement. Sin desired him but he could master it.

Cain refused the good counsel of God and murdered his brother. Rather than admit any wrong, he denied his responsibility for his brother. "Am I my brother's keeper?" Here is the clear image of a heart that is dead and dark, that can hate his brother so much that he rejects all responsibility for his welfare, and even kill him, and feel no remorse for it. Here, in bold relief, is the modern problem – that rebellion against God creates an inevitable alienation with our brothers, and ultimately, if left unchecked, can lead to murder and curse. God is gracious even in judgment, protecting Cain in his banishment with a mark or sign that would deter those seeking to avenge Abel's murder. Even in this, the rebellious Cain defies God's punishment of wandering and instead builds the first city in the land of Nod (meaning "wandering"), east of Eden (v. 16).

The lessons for us are clear as we begin our study. Our relationship to God and relationship to others are deeply interconnected and affecting; no one can claim a deep walk with God and hate their brother (1 John 4.20-21), and if we do love God, we will sacrifice on behalf of our brothers and sisters (1 John 3.14ff.). We are in fact our brothers (and our sisters!) keepers, called to care for one another, and not consume one another in our comparisons, jealousies, hatreds, and violence. To be intimate with the God and Father of our Lord Jesus Christ is to care deeply for others, for God is love. The one claiming to know God who does not love, does not know God at all (1 John 4.7-8).

For those of us serving Christ in the city we must embrace this truth with all our hearts. A vital, growing, intimate walk with God will always express itself in specific, particular, and consistent acts of love and mercy to our brothers and sisters, our neighbors, and even our enemies. Are we our brother's keeper? Certainly, yes, if in fact we have been redeemed in the blood of Jesus Christ. Listen to the Apostle John's commentary on Cain and Abel:

> 1 John 3.11-15 – For this is the message that you have heard from the beginning, that we should love one another. [12] We should not be like Cain, who was of the evil one and murdered his brother. And why did he murder him? Because his own deeds were evil and his brother's righteous. [13] Do not be surprised, brothers, that the world hates you. [14] We know that we have passed out of death into life, because we love the brothers. Whoever does not love abides in death. [15] Everyone who hates his brother is a murderer, and you know that no murderer has eternal life abiding in him.

Let us embrace the new commandment of our Lord, to love one another. Indeed, we are truly our brother's keeper.

Nicene Creed and Prayer

After reciting and/or singing the Nicene Creed (located in the Appendix), pray the following prayer:

> Holy God, you confound the world's wisdom in giving your kingdom to the lowly and the pure in heart. Give us such a hunger and thirst for justice and perseverance in striving for peace, that by our words and deeds the world may see the promise of your kingdom, revealed in Jesus Christ our Lord, who lives and reigns with you in the unity of the Holy Spirit, one God, forever and ever. Amen.
>
> ~ Presbyterian Church (U.S.A.) and Cumberland Presbyterian Church. The Theology and Worship Ministry Unit. *Book of Common Worship*. Louisville, Ky.: Westminster/John Knox Press, 1993. p. 209.

Scripture Memorization Review

Review with a partner, write out and/or recite the text for last class session's assigned memory verse: Ephesians 6.10-13.

Assignments Due

Turn in your summary of the reading assignment for last week, that is, your brief response and explanation of the main points that the authors were seeking to make in the assigned reading (Reading Completion Sheet).

CONTACT

Family First, Always

1. In a discussion in an adult Sunday School class, several students are discussing the "order of loves" that the Christian is called to represent. Are we to love our marriages and family members first, in a way that is different, prior to, and better than the other loves that we have. Some argued that the love commandment implies that we are to love all people sacrificially, even our enemies. Others read the text to suggest that we are to do good to all people, but especially to the members of the household of God (cf. Gal. 6.10). What is your understanding of the various orders of love the disciple of Jesus is called to demonstrate to others? Are we to love different people in different degrees, or are we called to love everyone the same?

Humanism Is a Bad Word

2. In the late twentieth century a number of Christian scholars began to discuss the idea of Christian humanism, an idea that human beings, all of them, are made in the image of God and therefore are deserving of basic human rights that we must protect and defend. While some evangelical Christian leaders embraced this vision, many others rejected it as both compromise and a kind of first step toward universalism. Humanists, they argued, center their thinking and explanation of the highest of creation on *human life*, as if it were the end of all things. This is patently unchristian; God almighty, his sovereign purpose and will, are in fact the end of all things. On the other side, Christian humanists contend that salvation proves the uniqueness and wonder of human life to God; he gave his only Son to redeem his creation, especially his human creation. What do you think of the validity of the concept of Christian humanism? Is it actually possible to be both a *Christian* and a *humanist*?

Human Life Begins at Creation, not the Fall

3. Many lament the fact that a number of Protestant theologies on human life seem to put all of their emphasis on the Fall, that tragic event of the voluntary rebellion against the will of God committed by Adam and Eve which spiraled the creation into curse and chaos. The first statements of humankind, however, do not begin with the Fall, but with creation, where God made humankind in his own image, beautiful, creative, and free. What difference does it make if you base your fundamental thinking about humankind on the *creation of humankind* rather than on the *fall of humankind*? How ought we, in our theological discussions, to

understand the importance of both of these foundational realities when describing the nature and purpose of humanity in the world?

Let Justice Roll Down: The Vision and Theology of the Kingdom

The Image of God as Basis for Social Concern and Action

Rev. Dr. Don L. Davis

Summary

The ground for doing justice and loving mercy among the poor in the city is the affirmation of the *imago Dei* in every boy, girl, woman, and man. Every person is worthy of care because they share in God's unmatched, unique, and irreplaceable *imago Dei*. Because all are made in God's image, all humankind is unique and precious. This image constitutes the reason why we ought to do justice and love mercy among all individuals, families, peoples, and nations on earth. Each of them as bearers of the *imago Dei* are to be considered as precious and irreplaceable.

Our objective for this lesson, *The Image of God as Basis for Social Concern and Action*, is to enable you to see that:

- A good working definition of the *imago Dei* (i.e., image of God) in Scripture, is "The unique condition of all human beings that they are made like God and therefore are worthy of our respect, protection, and care."

- The affirmation of humankind being created in the image of God is a *unique affirmation*, no other creature or angels are said to have been created in the image of God.

- While the precise manner in which humankind is created in God's image is not explicitly stated in Scripture, evidence exists to suggest that human beings share in corresponding traits of God's own person, namely, our personality, our reason, our ability to choose, and our moral capacity.

- The fact that humankind was made in the *imago Dei* suggests that all human beings share this image; all human beings, regardless of their individual or communal state, are therefore unique, precious, and priceless *in and of themselves*.

- The biblical implications of the *imago Dei* in humankind transforms our understanding of human persons. They are created in God's own image, crowned with glory and honor, are fearfully and wonderfully made, and are providentially nourished by God. As such, human beings have been made the objects of God's unmerited, unconditional favor and grace, and he identifies with the struggles, needs, and burdens of even the most vulnerable human beings on earth.

- Human beings, regardless of their background, can be so transformed and renewed as to become partakers of the divine nature through faith in Jesus Christ. While those who reject Christ do not share in this renewal of the image of God, they still share God's likeness *as human beings*.

- The ground for doing justice and loving mercy among the poor in the city is the affirmation of the *imago Dei* in every boy, girl, woman, and man. Every person is worthy of care because they share in God's unmatched, unique, and irreplaceable *imago Dei*.

Video Outline

I. The *Imago Dei*: Humankind Shares in the Likeness of God.

A. Definition of the *imago Dei*

1. "The unique condition of all human beings that they are made like God and therefore are worthy of our respect, protection, and care"

2. Genesis 1.26-28 as the seminal text dealing with humankind sharing God's image and likeness

   Gen. 1.26-28 – Then God said, "Let us make man in our image, after our likeness. And let them have dominion over the fish of the sea and over the birds of the heavens and over the livestock and over all the earth and over every creeping thing that creeps on the earth." [27] So God created man in his own image, in the image of God He created him; male and female He created them. [28] And God blessed them. And God said to them, "Be fruitful and multiply and fill the earth and subdue it and have dominion over the fish of the sea and over the birds of the heavens and over every living thing that moves on the earth."

a. A *unique* affirmation: no other living creatures are said to have been created in God's image.

b. Some argue that *angels* share in this image (because of their participation in *moral righteousness*).

c. No Scripture supports this view of angels being made in the *imago Dei*.

d. Creatures have their being *from* God, human beings have their being *in* God (cf. Acts 17.28-29).

3. Humankind became a living being: Gen. 2.7.

a. A previous living creature did not *become* one who came to share God's image.

b. The image of God did not *evolve* from a lower form of life.

c. The moment, the instant man and woman became human beings, they were the image of God, both male and female, Gen. 1.27.

B. Biblical usage of the term *image of God*

1. Biblical references

a. Gen. 5.1

b. Gen. 9.6

c. 1 Cor. 11.7

d. James 3.9

2. References regarding our *recreation*

a. Eph. 4.24

b. Col. 3.10

C. What precisely is the *image of God* in humankind?

1. Humankind made from *the dust of the ground*: our kinship with the earth, Gen. 2.7

   a. We have a kinship with *the products and resources of the earth*: we need air, water, and food in order to survive.

   b. Our constitutions and functions are *similar to other creatures which depend on the earth* for their lives and existence.

   c. The image of God *is not* rooted in our physical nature and kinship with the earth.

2. The image of God viewed from the perspective of our *personality and spirituality*

   a. Our *personality*: we share with God a sense of our own self-consciousness.

b. Our *rationality*: we share with God self-consciousness and reason.

c. Our *will*: we share with God the ability to choose.

d. Our *moral capacity*: we share with God a moral sensibility.

D. The preciousness of humankind: all human beings share in the *imago Dei*.

1. All humankind shares in this image: there are no distinctions among human beings regarding the image of God, Acts 17.26.

2. This image is foundational to understanding God's relationship to humankind, and human beings response to each other, James 3.9.

3. We are bad off because of the curse, but human beings are unique and precious, because of creation.

II. The Implications of the Imago Dei in Humankind: the Remarkable Workmanship of Human Beings

A. Human beings are created in *the image of God*.

Gen. 1. 26-28 – Then God said, "Let us make man in our image, after our likeness. And let them have dominion over the fish of the sea and over the birds of the heavens and over the livestock and over all the earth and over every creeping thing that creeps on the earth." [27] So God created man in his own image, in the image of God he created him; male and female he created them. [28] And God blessed them. And God said to them, "Be fruitful and multiply and fill the earth and subdue it and have dominion over the fish of the sea and over the birds of the heavens and over every living thing that moves on the earth."

1. Made in the very image of God (all other beings made by God but not in his own image)

2. Granted dominion over all creation

3. Exalted status and position given to humankind as they were created male and female

4. Given the mandate to be fruitful and multiply

5. Implication: *Every human being, despite their social status or condition, is created in the image of God, a reflection of the divine mind and person, an instance of God's own magnificent imagination and creative power.*

B. Human beings are crowned with glory and honor.

Ps. 8.3-7 – When I look at your heavens, the work of your fingers, the moon and the stars, which you have set in place, [4] what is man that you are mindful of him, and the son of man that you care for him? [5] Yet you have made him a little lower than the heavenly beings and crowned him with glory and honor. [6] You have given him dominion over the works of your hands; you have put all things under his feet, [7] all sheep and oxen, and also the beasts of the field.

1. Made a *little lower than the angels*

2. Crowned with glory and honor

3. Granted dominion over the works of the Lord's hands

4. All things placed under humankind's feet

5. This is an allusion to the dominion of Messiah Jesus, cf. Ps. 110.1; 1 Cor. 15.24-28; Eph. 1.22; Heb. 2.8.

6. Implication: *All human beings, regardless of their histories or behaviors, have been created just a little lower than the angels, crowned by God with glory, honor, and dominion.*

C. Human beings are fearfully and wonderfully made.

Ps. 139.13-16 – For you formed my inward parts; you knitted me together in my mother's womb. [14] I praise you, for I am fearfully and wonderfully made. Wonderful are your works; my soul knows it very well. [15] My frame was not hidden from you, when I was being made in secret, intricately woven in the depths of the earth. [16] Your eyes saw my unformed substance; in your book were written, every one of them, the days that were formed for me, when as yet there were none of them.

1. Formed in every way (physically and spiritually) by the genius and brilliance of Almighty God

2. Crafted by God's own special craftsmanship and care

3. From cradle to casket: God's personal design lies upon every human life.

4. God's sovereignty touches and impacts the days of every human being.

5. Implication: *Every human being is the product of God's divine genius and workmanship, fearfully and wonderfully created by him as a unique and infinitely precious being.*

D. Human life is abundantly nourished and providentially supplied by God.

> Ps. 104.13-24 – From your lofty abode you water the mountains; the earth is satisfied with the fruit of your work. [14] You cause the grass to grow for the livestock and plants for man to cultivate, that he may bring forth food from the earth [15] and wine to gladden the heart of man, oil to make his face shine and bread to strengthen man's heart. [16] The trees of the LORD are watered abundantly, the cedars of Lebanon that he planted. [17] In them the birds build their nests; the stork has her home in the fir trees. [18] The high mountains are for the wild goats; the rocks are a refuge for the rock badgers. [19] He made the moon to mark the seasons; the sun knows its time for setting. [20] You make darkness, and it is night, when all the beasts of the forest creep about. [21] The young lions roar for their prey, seeking their food from God. [22] When the sun rises, they steal away and lie down in their dens. [23] Man goes out to his work and to his labor until the evening. [24] O LORD, how manifold are your works! In wisdom have you made them all; the earth is full of your creatures.

1. The abundance of the earth is provided for through God's generous providential care.

2. God is the operative cause of every good and perfect gift enjoyed by human beings everywhere, James 1.17.

3. The earth and its supply is resourced by God's hands for all the inhabitants on the earth.

4. The earth is the Lord's, and is full of his possessions.

5. Implications: *All of the bounty and nutrients that sustains human life everywhere is given by God without respect of persons or favor, Matt. 5.44-45.*

E. Human beings are the objects of God's unmerited, unconditional favor and grace.

John 3.16-17 – For God so loved the world, that he gave his only Son, that whoever believes in him should not perish but have eternal life. [17] For God did not send his Son into the world to condemn the world, but in order that the world might be saved through him.

1. God loved without qualification or partiality everyone in the entire world, living, dead, and yet unborn.

    a. 2 Cor. 5.19

    b. 1 John 4.9-10

    c. Luke 12.7

2. The value of God's love is shown in the sacrifice of his only Son for each and every single soul, Matt. 18.14.

3. God did not send his Son to condemn, but to save all those in the world.

4. Implication: *God's unlimited and unbounded favor rests on every human being, though they may be unaware of it.*

F. God identifies with the struggles, needs, and burdens of the most vulnerable and hurting among us.

Ps. 146.5-9 – Blessed is he whose help is the God of Jacob, whose hope is in the Lord his God, [6] who made heaven and earth, the sea, and all that is in them, who keeps faith forever; [7] who executes justice for the oppressed, who gives food to the hungry. The Lord sets the prisoners free; [8] the Lord opens the eyes of the blind. The Lord lifts up those who are bowed down; the Lord loves the righteous. [9] The Lord watches over the sojourners; he upholds the widow and the fatherless, but the way of the wicked he brings to ruin.

1. God is burdened for human beings everywhere who are oppressed, hungry, and abused.

2. The Lord actively involves himself in the justice of those who are hurting, i.e., those who are blind and bowed down.

3. The Lord is aware of the cause of all those who are refugees, widows, orphans, and powerless.

4. Religion in its purest practice before God involves caring for the needs of those most vulnerable and least able to defend and protect themselves among us, James 1.27.

5. Implication: *The God of Jacob is fundamentally a God who identifies with the hurting, the poor, and the oppressed.*

G. Human beings can be so transformed and renewed as to become partakers of the divine nature.

2 Pet. 1.2-4 – May grace and peace be multiplied to you in the knowledge of God and of Jesus our Lord. [3] His divine power has granted to us all things that pertain to life and godliness, through the knowledge of him who called us to his own glory and excellence, [4] by which he has granted to us his precious and very great promises, so that through them you may become partakers of the divine nature, having escaped from the corruption that is in the world because of sinful desire.

1. Through Christ, believers have been given all things that pertain to life and godliness, 2 Pet. 1.3.

2. God has called the saved to his glory and virtue.

3. Through God's exceedingly great and precious promises, we may become partakers of God's very own nature.

4. The believing have escaped the corruption that is resident in the world, which is activated by lust.

    a. Gal. 1.3-4

    b. 1 John 5.4-5

    c. 1 John 5.19-20

5. When Christ returns for his own, we who believe will come to share in his very own glory and image.

    a. 1 John 3.2

    b. Ps. 17.15

    c. Rom. 8.29

    d. 1 Cor. 15.49

    e. Phil. 3.21

6. Implication: *Humankind, once redeemed, is capable of the unimaginable: we can actually partake of the divine nature, indwelt by God himself, sharing in his life and glory.*

III. The Implications of the *Imago Dei* for Urban Ministry

A. Through faith in Jesus Christ, we are re-created in the image of God.

1. Biblical citations

   a. Eph. 4.24

   b. Col. 3.10

2. We are created in righteousness and true holiness, destined to be conformed to the image of Jesus Christ, Rom. 8.29.

3. As the fall affected the image of God in humankind in a way of corruption and death, so salvation results in renewal of the image after the likeness of Jesus Christ himself.

   a. Jesus is the one who shares uniquely in God's image, 2 Cor. 4.4; Col. 1.15; Heb. 1.3.

   b. Jesus is the last Adam, the pattern of a new humanity to come, Rom. 8.29.

   c. The image of Jesus Christ is being formed in the Christian by the Holy Spirit, 2 Cor. 3.18; cf. Eph. 4.24; Col. 3.10.

B. Though unbelievers do not share in this renewal of the image of God, they still share in the very likeness of God.

1. Human life is therefore unique, irreplaceable, and precious.

2. Doing justice and loving mercy, even toward those who do not know Christ, is both mandated and necessary.

3. Each human being is priceless and worthy to be loved, protected, and cared for.

C. The *imago Dei* in every human being is the ground of our doing justice and loving mercy.

1. *Refuse to endorse, therefore*, any escapist or conformist notions of the world, asking God to give you grace to re-engage the world as being one who is in it, but not of it.

2. *Affirm the uniqueness and preciousness of human life*, at all levels, unborn, infants and children, the elderly.

3. *Allow the biblical view* of God as creator and humankind made in the image of God to reinterpret your "theological anthropology" (i.e., the doctrine of humanity) to conform you to the Bible's high and wondrous view of human beings.

4. *Reject any conflicts* between social justice, loving mercy, and evangelization.

    a. Recognize their common source and goal.

    b. Understand how they both affirm God as *creator* and *ruler* of the world.

    c. *Refuse to dichotomize* (to split and separate, to create a conflict between) evangelism and social justice; they are both required to provide a full understanding of God and his Gospel.

5. See every person and every opportunity to care for them through the lens of each person sharing in God's unmatched, unique, and irreplaceable *imago Dei*.

   a. To see a human being is to see something infinitely precious.

   b. To see a broken human being is to see the Lord Jesus himself, Matt. 25.34-40.

Conclusion

- A biblical understanding of the *imago Dei* in human beings grounds and informs our commitment to love, cherish, and protect human beings, wherever we find them and whatever their lot.

- Every person is worthy of care because they share in God's unmatched, unique, and irreplaceable *imago Dei*.

Student Questions and Response

The following questions were designed to help you review the material in the video. In this lesson we saw how the ground and basis for our executing justice and demonstrating mercy among the poor in the city is our commitment to the biblical affirmation of the *imago Dei* in every boy, girl, woman, and man. Every human being, regardless or race, background, or culture, is worthy of our care because they share in God's unmatched, unique, and irreplaceable *imago Dei*. Each human person and all human groups are unique and precious. Each are bearers of the *imago Dei* and are to be considered as precious and irreplaceable. Explore these concepts through the questions below, and support your own arguments with Scripture.

1. What is the definition of the "image of God" (*imago Dei*) given in the lesson? In what ways is this affirmation of the image of God in human beings both a *unique* affirmation as well as a *special* one?

2. Do the Scriptures offer us an explicit definition of the image of God mentioned in Genesis 1 in humankind? What are some of the traits mentioned of God that we know human beings to also share?

3. How does the biblical teaching express the fact that all humankind was made in the *imago Dei*? Are there any human beings who, for some reason, no longer share this image? Do even the most rebellious and irreligious human beings, regardless of their individual or communal state, share in the imago Dei? What is the biblical evidence for your answer?

4. In light of the *imago Dei*, what are some of the ways in which the Word of God describes the implications of the *imago Dei* in humankind? How ought these various implications transform our understanding of human persons, even those we find distasteful or obnoxious?

5. How do the Scriptures describe God's inclinations and feelings toward those who are poor, oppressed, and broken? What are the implications for this in understanding the poor as *special* objects of God's unmerited, unconditional favor and grace? Explain your answer with Scripture.

6. What is the significance of the fact that human beings, regardless of their background, can be so transformed and renewed as to become partakers of the divine nature through faith in Jesus Christ? Can all human beings come to share this new nature?

7. What can be said of those who reject the offer of God's grace in Christ – do they still share God's likeness as human beings? Explain.

8. In light of the insights above, what would you consider to be the fundamental ground for doing justice and loving mercy among the poor in the city? How does this ground inform us of the worthiness of each person in the city, regardless of the character of their lives and histories?

CONNECTION

Summary of Key Concepts

This lesson focuses upon the theology and vision of the Kingdom, both in terms of God as our creator who is concerned about the world and those who live within it. We also considered the power of the image of God in every person, and how that image serves as the ground for doing justice and loving mercy among the poor in the city. Although Christians have traditionally taken differing positions in regards to the Church's relationship to the world, we must engage it. The Church is both the locus and agent of the Kingdom of God *in the world but not of it*. The God and Father of our Lord Jesus is a God of nature, creation, and justice, as well as a God of salvation, covenant, and justification. In addition, we saw in this lesson how the ground for doing justice and loving mercy among the poor in the city is the affirmation of the *imago Dei* in every boy, girl, woman, and man. Every person is worthy of care because they share in God's unmatched, unique, and irreplaceable *imago Dei*. Review these and related concepts in their listing below.

- A good working definition of the *imago Dei* (i.e., image of God) in Scripture is "The unique condition of all human beings that they are made like God and therefore are worthy of our respect, protection, and care."

- The affirmation of humankind being created in the image of God is a *unique affirmation*, no other creatures or angels are said to have been created in the image of God.

- While the precise manner in which humankind is created in God's image is not explicitly stated in Scripture, evidence exists to suggest that human beings share in corresponding traits of God's own person, namely, our personality, our reason, our ability to choose, and our moral capacity.

- The fact that humankind was made in the *imago Dei* suggests that all human beings share this image; all human beings, regardless of their individual or communal state, are therefore unique, precious, and priceless *in and of themselves*.

- The biblical implications of the *imago Dei* in humankind transforms our understanding of human persons. They are created in God's own image, crowned with glory and honor, are fearfully and wonderfully made, and are providentially nourished by God. As such, human beings have been made the objects of God's unmerited, unconditional favor and grace, and he identifies with the struggles, needs, and burdens of even the most vulnerable human beings on earth.

- Human beings, regardless of their background, can be so transformed and renewed as to become partakers of the divine nature through faith in Jesus Christ. While those who reject Christ do not share in this renewal of the image of God, they still share God's likeness *as human beings*.

- The ground for doing justice and loving mercy among the poor in the city is the affirmation of the *imago Dei* in every boy, girl, woman, and man. Every person is worthy of care because they share in God's unmatched, unique, and irreplaceable *imago Dei*.

Student Application and Implications

Now is the time for you to discuss with your fellow students your questions about the theology of doing justice and loving mercy, and getting to the heart of the meaning of the *imago Dei* for doing ministry in the city. It is clear that we must lay a proper theological foundation before we can truly explore the various dimensions and elements of compassion ministries in the Church. As a disciple of Jesus and an emerging Christian leader, you need to master these ideas, and explore the implications of them for your own life and ministry. Here is your opportunity to consider with your fellow students your own particular questions regarding the theology of justice and *imago Dei* ideas covered in the lesson. The questions below may help you explore your own, more specific questions about the material.

- Is it possible to believe that God is both *creator* and *maker* of the heavens and the earth and not also believe that God is concerned about the world and those who live within it? Explain your answer.

- Is the concept of world as *kosmos* a negative or positive concept in Scripture, or both (cf. John 3.16 with 1 John 2.15-17)? How do we know that God loves the inhabitants of the world but that he is against the world system?

- Of all the views covered in the lesson about the relationship of the Church to the world, which one makes the most sense to you so far in your studies?

- Does a serious theological problem exist if we view *the Church* as the agent of the Kingdom and not the *Holy Spirit* as the agent? What is the role of the Holy Spirit in the Church as the people of God represent the Kingdom in the world?

- Does it weaken what we believe if we try to correct our theology by saying that God is the God of all nature as well as the God of salvation, the God of creation as well as the God of covenant, and the God of justice as well as the God of justification? Explain.

- We defined the *imago Dei* (i.e., image of God) in Scripture as "the unique condition of all human beings that they are made like God and therefore worthy of our respect, protection, and care." Are even the most vicious, cruel, and hurtful people made in God's image, too?

- Doesn't it go against what we know about God to say that he has a special concern for the poor and oppressed? If that is so, how are we to understand passages like Matthew 25 and the "least of these, my brethren" our Lord spoke of?

- If all human beings are made in the *imago Dei*, how can we dare to put any human beings to death, whether in capital punishment or criminal justice or war? Does the *imago Dei* suggest that no human life ought ever to be taken under any circumstances? Explain your answer.

- Why do you think that many Christians advocate positions about people which seem to go against the biblical implications of the *imago Dei* in humankind? Under what circumstances (if any) can we justify treating other human beings as our *enemies*? Explain.

- What if I have grown up *disliking a particular race or group*. Is it possible to tolerate any prejudice or bigotry and still claim to be partakers of the divine nature through faith in Jesus Christ?

- How might affirming the *imago Dei* in every boy, girl, woman, and man in a group you do not appreciate transform your ideas and feelings toward them? What if affirming the truth about them doesn't lead to changed feelings about them – what next?

CASE STUDIES

Taking These Matters a Little Too Far

1. A huge discussion now rages in the church on a recent elder's decision to start a Men's Home focused on ex-prisoners, and helping them matriculate back into society. One of the members of the church with the vision, burden, and expertise to start such a ministry, shared his burden with the elders, and over nine months they researched his burden and determined it to be valid and within the mission of the church. A growing group in the church, however, were skeptical of the validity of this idea from the start. How would they be able to guarantee the safety of many of the church members with these men now so visible in the services and activities of the church? Some of the men had sex-offender backgrounds, and many young families have expressed their dismay and concern about the presence of such individuals in the church body. Others argued strongly that the grace of God can transform, and that all human beings, regardless of background, can be changed by the grace of God in Christ. The prospect of starting this ministry has created rumors about wholesale departure from the church if they continue on with the idea. If you were senior pastor in such a congregation, how would you approach this ministry, especially in light of the insights covered in this lesson on the church, the *imago Dei*, and the church as the locus and agent of the Kingdom of God? Explain your answer.

Studying War No More

 In light of the many skirmishes, battles, armed conflicts, and all out combats being waged in many parts of the world today, we as Christians must come to understand our view regarding war and violence. If God is a God of justification by faith and justice, too, then, it may be possible to talk about wars and conflicts that are justified. Throughout Church history, godly, sincere, and biblical Christians have disagreed on the validity of war to settle disputes, of Christians serving in war, even of Christians in the military. The lines are typically drawn very clearly. One side argues unequivocally that Christians are forbidden to kill others, since human beings, *all of them*, are precious in the sight of God, made in his image. Others argue, that the powers that exist do so by the authority of God, and numerous texts exhort the Christian to honor the king, submit to the reigning powers, and serve the governing institutions with deference and honor. How far are we as believers to take this teaching about the *imago Dei* when it comes to serving in a branch of armed services in a country? Can we affirm the *imago Dei* and still serve in the military, in a capacity that will require you to take human life?

The *Imago Dei* and Capital Punishment

 One of the living controversies among many Christian communities is the issue of capital punishment. Many believers hold the position today that since all human beings are made in the *imago Dei*, we are forbidden to put any human being to death, even if that person has been proven to be guilty of the capital crime that brought the punishment of death upon them. Others, quoting the same texts, believe that for the state to deter evil and institute justice, capital punishment is both necessary and helpful. They claim that it not only inflicts justice on the perpetrator of the crime, it also serves as a reminder for others of the consequences of similar criminal behavior. What do you say regarding the legitimacy of the capital punishment, and the affirmation that all human beings (even guilty ones) are made in the *imago Dei*? Should it make a difference in what we think about capital punishment?

Give Me Time, I'm Still Growing

 While few would contest the clear biblical injunction to love others as Christ loved us as the identifying sign of all true discipleship (John 13.34-35), many do argue about the *ways in which* that love ought to be shown, as well as *when it needs to be shown*. A new Christian who had been socialized his entire life to hate people of a particular race was not strictly exhorted to change his feelings and ideas towards them. His conversion and faith in Jesus Christ seemed in every way to be both sincere and authentic, but his ongoing suspicion, hatred, and distrust of others of another race lingered on for months, and the new convert did not hide his disdain and disgust for "those people." While some believed that his lingering attitude was a sign of his failure to convert, others viewed the residue of his past as merely an area for him to grow. All newborn babes in Christ, they argued will have areas in their lives that require time to put off the old man, be renewed in the spirit of their minds, and put on the new man created after God in the image of true holiness and righteousness (cf. Eph. 4.20ff.). What do you think of this situation – is failure to love in this case a situation of normal Christian growth, or a sign of a failure to repent? How might the leaders in such a situation find out which one it really was?

Restatement of the Lesson's Thesis

As *creator* and *maker* of the earth, our God is concerned about the world and those who live within it. Traditionally, Christian communities have taken various positions to the world, including withdrawal from it, living in tension with it, or accepting responsibility to transform it. The Church is both the locus and agent of the Kingdom of God *in the world but not of it*. As such, the Church affirms that God is the God of all nature as well as the God of salvation, the God of creation as well as the God of covenant, and the God of justice as well as the God of justification. In its own ministry as the representative of the Kingdom of God, the Church is called to display and announce freedom to the world, called to express God's wholeness in the world, and stand for God's justice throughout the world.

The ground for doing justice and loving mercy among the poor in the city is the affirmation of the *imago Dei* in every boy, girl, woman, and man. Every person is worthy of care because they share in God's unmatched, unique, and irreplaceable *imago Dei*. Because all are made in God's image, all humankind is unique and precious. This image constitutes the reason why we ought to do justice and love mercy among all individuals, families, peoples, and nations on earth. Each of them as bearers of the *imago Dei* are to be considered as precious and irreplaceable.

Resources and Bibliographies

If you are interested in pursuing some of the ideas of *Let Justice Roll Down: The Vision and Theology of the Kingdom*, you might want to give these books a try:

> Cone, James. *The God of The Oppressed.* New York: Seabury Press, 1975.
>
> Conn, Harvie. *Evangelism: Doing Justice and Preaching Grace.* Grand Rapids: Zondervan, 1982.
>
> Fletcher, William M. *The Second Greatest Commandment: A Call to A Personal and Corporate Life of Caring.* Colorado Springs: NavPress, 1983.
>
> Kirk, Andrew. *The Good News of the Kingdom Coming: The Marriage of Evangelism and Social Responsibility.* Downers Grove, IL: InterVarsity Press, 1983.

Ministry Connections

This section is a specific opportunity for you to seek the leading of the Holy Spirit as to your own particular application of the material in the lesson. This ability to listen and follow the prompting of the Holy Spirit is significant in all study, dialogue, and submission. Here now is your chance to discover through meditation and prayer a correlation of this high theology to a real practical ministry connection in your life. The scope of this application could be today, this week, this month, or even throughout the year. All of this depends on what you need to know and what the Holy Spirit *wants you to apply in your life and ministry*.

Therefore, take some time to wait before the Lord and listen to the Holy Spirit in open prayer. What does he seem to be suggesting to you regarding your own understanding of the importance of justice and mercy in your life, in your preaching and teaching, in your ministry at church, with your neighbors? Does the Lord bring a particular person, situation, or encounter to mind that he wants you to respond to him in light of the teaching in this lesson? Does the Holy Spirit seem to be moving you to change something in your life and ministry, or perhaps begin or initiate something? The promise is sure from the Word of God: the blessing comes to the person who simply does not hear the Word, but does it (James 1.22-25). Be open to the Spirit as you explore the various implications of this teaching for your own life and ministry.

LESSON 4 | DOING JUSTICE AND LOVING MERCY: LET JUSTICE ROLL DOWN / 415

Counseling and Prayer

The power of prayer is critical to our development as disciples of Christ and leaders of the Church. Learning to share requests with your fellow students and leaders will enhance every phase of your growth in Christ. Of course, no one can read your mind; you will need to be open and transparent about the ways in which you will be seeking the Lord's grace to apply and relate these truths to your own walk and ministry. Moreover, your instructors are more than willing to provide you with counsel, advice, and insight into particular issues and circumstances that you may be facing. Be open to receive the counsel of your leaders as you address the various challenges you are facing today, and be sure to ask your fellow students to lift you up in prayer as seek to make the truths you mined in this lesson your very own treasure.

Remember the words of our Lord when he instructs on the power of prayer:

> Matt. 7.7-11 – Ask, and it will be given to you; seek, and you will find; knock, and it will be opened to you. [8] For everyone who asks receives, and the one who seeks finds, and to the one who knocks it will be opened. [9] Or which one of you, if his son asks him for bread, will give him a stone? [10] Or if he asks for a fish, will give him a serpent? [11] If you then, who are evil, know how to give good gifts to your children, how much more will your Father who is in heaven give good things to those who ask him!

With this encouragement in mind, ask the Lord to provide you with keen insight into the meaning of the truths here, as well as opportunity and energy to respond promptly and obediently to the Word of God for your own life. Share requests with your fellow students, and pray for one another. The prayer of the righteous is a powerful thing, indeed (James 5.16)!

ASSIGNMENTS

Scripture Memory: Amos 5.20-24

Reading Assignment: To prepare for class, please visit *www.tumi.org/books* to find next week's reading assignment, or ask your Mentor.

Other Assignments

Your ministry project and your exegetical project should now be outlined, determined, and accepted by your instructor. Make sure that you plan ahead, so you will not be late in turning in your assignments.

As You Complete This Final Lesson

Congratulations on completing the Cornerstone Curriculum! It is our prayer that the training you received through these sixteen lessons equips you to glorify God by serving Christ and his Church. If you are wondering what to do next, we recommend looking at our MAP Course (see page 425). The Ministry Assessment Program (MAP) is an excellent tool to help you discern with your leaders how you can best serve in the body of Christ.

The Urban Ministry Institute also offers a full catalog of courses and resources to further equip you for ministry. If you are interested in finding out more visit *www.tumientree.com*.

FOR FURTHER STUDY

Please see the following resources in *Picturing Theology: An A-Z Collection of TUMI's Key Diagrams, Charts, Graphics, and Articles*:

- *Authentic Freedom in Jesus Christ*, page 15
- *Culture, Not Color: Interaction of Class, Culture, and Race*, page 64
- *Empowering People for Freedom, Wholeness, and Justice*, page 90
- *Five Views of the Relationship between Christ and Culture*, page 138
- *Theology of the Church in Kingdom Perspective*, page 477

Appendix

419 Appendix 1: The Nicene Creed

421 Appendix 2: List of Core Documents and Charts from *Picturing Theology*

APPENDIX 1
The Nicene Creed

We believe in one God,   *(Deut. 6.4-5; Mark 12.29; 1 Cor. 8.6)*
    the Father Almighty,   *(Gen. 17.1; Dan. 4.35; Matt. 6.9; Eph. 4.6; Rev. 1.8)*
    Maker of heaven and earth   *(Gen 1.1; Isa. 40.28; Rev. 10.6)*
    and of all things visible and invisible.   *(Ps. 148; Rom. 11.36; Rev. 4.11)*

We believe in one Lord Jesus Christ, the only Begotten Son of God, begotten of the Father before all ages, God from God, Light from Light, True God from True God, begotten not created, of the same essence as the Father,
    (John 1.1-2; 3.18; 8.58; 14.9-10; 20.28; Col. 1.15, 17; Heb. 1.3-6)
    through whom all things were made.   *(John 1.3; Col. 1.16)*

Who for us men and for our salvation came down from heaven and was incarnate by the Holy Spirit and the virgin Mary and became human.
    (Matt. 1.20-23; John 1.14; 6.38; Luke 19.10)
    Who for us too, was crucified under Pontius Pilate, suffered, and was buried.
    (Matt. 27.1-2; Mark 15.24-39, 43-47; Acts 13.29; Rom. 5.8; Heb. 2.10; 13.12)
    The third day he rose again according to the Scriptures,
    (Mark 16.5-7; Luke 24.6-8; Acts 1.3; Rom. 6.9; 10.9; 2 Tim. 2.8)
    ascended into heaven, and is seated at the right hand of the Father.
    (Mark 16.19; Eph. 1.19-20)
    He will come again in glory to judge the living and the dead, and his Kingdom will have no end.
    (Isa. 9.7; Matt. 24.30; John 5.22; Acts 1.11; 17.31; Rom. 14.9; 2 Cor. 5.10; 2 Tim. 4.1)

We believe in the Holy Spirit, the Lord and life-giver,
    (Gen. 1.1-2; Job 33.4; Ps. 104.30; 139.7-8; Luke 4.18-19; John 3.5-6; Acts 1.1-2; 1 Cor. 2.11; Rev. 3.22)
    who proceeds from the Father and the Son,   *(John 14.16-18, 26; 15.26; 20.22)*
    who together with the Father and Son is worshiped and glorified,
    (Isa. 6.3; Matt. 28.19; 2 Cor. 13.14; Rev. 4.8)
    who spoke by the prophets.
    (Num. 11.29; Mic. 3.8; Acts 2.17-18; 2 Pet. 1.21)

We believe in one holy, catholic, and apostolic Church.
    (Matt. 16.18; Eph. 5.25-28; 1 Cor. 1.2; 10.17; 1 Tim. 3.15; Rev. 7.9)

We acknowledge one baptism for the forgiveness of sin,
    (Acts 22.16; 1 Pet. 3.21; Eph. 4.4-5)
    And we look for the resurrection of the dead and the life of the age to come.
    (Isa. 11.6-10; Mic. 4.1-7; Luke 18.29-30; Rev. 21.1-5; 21.22-22.5)
    Amen.

Memory Verses

The Father	Rev. 4.11 (ESV) – Worthy are you, our Lord and God, to receive glory and honor and power, for you created all things, and by your will they existed and were created.
The Son	John 1.1 (ESV) – In the beginning was the Word, and the Word was with God, and the Word was God.
The Son's Mission	1 Cor. 15.3-5 (ESV) – For what I received I passed on to you as of first importance: that Christ died for our sins according to the Scriptures, that he was buried, that he was raised on the third day according to the Scriptures, and that he appeared to Peter, and then to the Twelve.
The Holy Spirit	Rom. 8.11 (ESV) – If the Spirit of him who raised Jesus from the dead dwells in you, he who raised Christ Jesus from the dead will also give life to your mortal bodies through his Spirit who dwells in you.
The Church	1 Pet. 2.9 (ESV) – But you are a chosen race, a royal priesthood, a holy nation, a people for his own possession, that you may proclaim the excellencies of him who called you out of darkness into his marvelous light.
Our Hope	1 Thess. 4.16-17 (ESV) – For the Lord himself will descend from heaven with a cry of command, with the voice of an archangel, and with the sound of the trumpet of God. And the dead in Christ will rise first. Then we who are alive, who are left, will be caught up together with them in the clouds to meet the Lord in the air, and so we will always be with the Lord.

APPENDIX 2
List of Core Documents and Charts from *Picturing Theology*

Davis, Cornett, and Allsman. *Picturing Theology: An A-Z Collection of TUMI's Key Diagrams, Charts, Graphics, and Articles.* Wichita, KS: TUMI Press, 2019.

The following items from your supplementary text, *Picturing Theology: An A-Z Collection of TUMI's Key Diagrams, Charts, Graphics, and Articles* are excellent resources for all of your Cornerstone Curriculum studies.

Title	*Picturing Theology* Page #
We Believe: Confession of the Nicene Creed (Common Meter)	523
We Believe: Confession of the Nicene Creed (8.7.8.7 meter)	524
The Story of God: Our Sacred Roots	401
The Theology of *Christus Victor*: A Christ-Centered Biblical Motif for Integrating and Renewing the Urban Church	457
Christus Victor: An Integrated Vision for the Christian Life and Witness	43
Old Testament Witness to Christ and His Kingdom	307
Summary Outline of the Scriptures	416
From Before to Beyond Time: The Plan of God and Human History	141
There Is a River: Identifying the Streams of a Revitalized Authentic Christian Community in the City	479
A Schematic for a Theology of the Kingdom and the Church	376
Living in the Already and the Not Yet Kingdom	261
Jesus of Nazareth: The Presence of the Future	204
Traditions: *Paradosis*	497
Documenting Your Work: A Guide to Help You Give Credit Where Credit Is Due	81
The Three-Step Model	486

Ministry Assessment Program

425 MAP Process: Diploma Students

427 C3-303 Ministry Assessment Project:
Agreement to Supervised Ministry Plan

428 Course Instruction Plan: C3-303 Ministry Assessment Project

441 Outline for First Interview with
Academic Advisor, Student, and Pastoral Supervisor

443 Outline for Final Interview with
Academic Advisor, Student, and Pastoral Supervisor

MAP Process
Diploma Students

The MAP (Ministry Assessment Program) course and process enables students to reflect on their gifts and calling in ministry, and determine the types of training they need to seek out in order to properly prepare for their future ministry directions. We desire to empower our TUMI students to minister effectively within their own church, with the leaders of their tradition and denomination. In our view, advanced ministry training should be integrated with the student's calling and service within their congregation's ministry vision.

The process is as follows:

Host initial MAP Course Meeting

- Host meeting for those qualified for and interested in MAP course.

- Print out *MAP Course Instruction Plan (CIP)* for each student, review instruction plan together, and answer any questions related to the course. All students must purchase their own textbooks.

- Assign Academic Advisor to students for this course (student preferences should weigh heavily in the final decision).

- Communicate due date for *Philosophy of Ministry Paper.*

Communicate with the Student's Pastoral Supervisor

- Send a *letter to the student's pastor* on their behalf, alone with a copy to the student.

- The student should then contact their pastor, informing them of the course requirements. If the pastor agrees to participate, then set up initial meeting for the Pastoral Supervisor, Academic Advisor, and student.

- The student will write *Philosophy of Ministry Paper*, sending copy to their Pastoral Supervisor and Academic Advisor.

- Coordinate the date of the first Interview with the Student, Pastoral Advisor, and Academic Advisor.

Host First Meeting with Pastoral Supervisor, Student, and Academic Advisor

- The Academic Advisor will lead this meeting, following the *Outline for First Interview.*

- Give a copy of the MAP CIP to the Pastoral Supervisor.

- Explain to student and their Pastoral Supervisor the next step: completion of the ministry plan. The student and Pastoral Supervisor ought to discuss regularly progress of this work to finalize the assignment details.

- Set target date for Ministry Plan completion, i.e., when given to Academic Advisor and Pastoral Supervisor.

- Set tentative date for next meeting with Pastoral Supervisor and student.

Host Second Meeting with Pastoral Supervisor, Student, and Academic Advisor

- The Academic Advisor will lead this meeting following the *Outline for Final Interview.*

- Collect the student's Reading Papers.

- Collect the student's Defense of the Nicene Creed Paper.

- Sign the *Agreement to Supervised Ministry Plan paper* (Student, Pastoral Supervisor, and Academic Advisor) and attach it to the Academic Advisor's copy of the ministry plan.

- Set date for meeting with the student to recite Nicene Creed to Academic Advisor (word for word).

- Set tentative date for Student to meet with Pastoral Supervisor to review *Questions for Supervised Ministry Meetings.*

C3-303 Ministry Assessment Project
Agreement to Supervised Ministry Plan

We agree that _____ will complete

Name of Student

the attached ministry plan as written, or with the following changes

(see below). The student will intern and/or serve in their supervised

ministry according to the plan at _____.

Name of Church or Ministry

The ministry assignment will conclude on _____.

Date

Changes to Supervised Ministry Plan (if needed):

_____ _____
Student (Name)   Date

_____ _____
Pastoral Supervisor (Name)   Date

_____ _____
Academic Advisor (Name)   Date

Course Instruction Plan
C3-303 Ministry Assessment Project

Credit Hours: 3 credits
Department: Christian Ministry

I. Course Description and Objectives

This course is designed to help students reflect on their gifts and calling in ministry, to help them determine the types of training they need to seek out in order to properly prepare for their future ministry directions, and to help students work with their own church or denominational leaders to ensure that this training is integrated with their congregation's ministry vision.

After taking this course, each student should be able to:

- Clearly explain their calling to ministry and their vision for future ministry.

- Identify the core theological principles of church, ministry and leadership that will guide their development in ministry.

- Explain how their spiritual gifts shape their ministry.

- Recognize the areas that they will seek further training in and use this to shape their Ministerial Studies Diploma program.

- Develop a pastorally approved plan for a supervised ministry experience within their congregation or denomination.

II. Books and Materials

Cothen, Joe H. and Jerry N. Barlow. *Equipped for Good Work: A Guide for Pastors*. Rev. ed. Gretna, LA: Pelican Publishing, 2002.

Sanders, J. Oswald. *Spiritual Leadership: Principles of Excellence for Every Believer*. Rev. ed. Chicago: Moody Press, 1984.

Schmitt, Harley H. *Many Gifts, One Lord*. Fairfax, VA: Xulon Press, 2002.

III. Course Requirements

Summary of Grade Categories and Weights

1) Meetings with Advisor or Mentor 10%

2) Readings Summaries 15%

3) Philosophy of Ministry Paper 20%

4) Doctrinal Summary Review 20%

5) Nicene Creed Memorization Project 20%

6) Ministry Plan (to be shared with ministry leader or pastoral supervisor) . . . <u>15%</u>

                                                                                100 pts

Grade Requirements

Initial Meetings with Your Advisor or Mentor

You will be required to meet with your faculty advisor or mentor to discuss the various assignments you will need to fulfill to complete the MAP course. These assignments will include your completion of the Readings summaries, your Philosophy of Ministry paper, a short Doctrinal Summary Review, the Nicene Creed Memorization Project, and the creation of a Ministry Plan that you will share with your ministry leader or pastoral supervisor.

Our desire is that you share your plan for the next phase of your ministry with your leader. Your pastoral supervisor will normally be your senior pastor or a leader appointed by your senior pastor. If you are a senior pastor, you might select either a) a denominational supervisor, [for example, a Bishop, a District Superintendent, etc.], or b) another trusted pastor from the community who has more experience then the student and who is willing to invest in their ministry development.

Readings Summaries (See Appendix One)

The readings and the "readings papers" are designed to help you to select the key principles for ministry from each reading and make applications to your own ministry situation. These are due at the last meeting with your academic advisor and pastoral supervisor.

Philosophy of Ministry Paper (See Appendix Two)
The Philosophy of Ministry paper offers you an opportunity to reflect upon your call to ministry, your ministry experiences, your spiritual gifts, your goals for the future, and the areas in which you may need further training and investment.

Doctrinal Summary Review
In order to be an effective minister of the Gospel, you must be able to defend the key tenets of the apostolic faith, summarized in the themes of systematic theology. You will need to write a paragraph for each of the following key doctrines of the Christian faith: the doctrine of the Word of God, the doctrine of God (including the Trinity), the doctrine of Christ, the doctrine of the Holy Spirit, the doctrine of angels, the doctrine of salvation, the doctrine the church, the doctrine of the Kingdom, and the doctrine of last things. This is not meant to be a weighty theological treatise; you are only required to write your best understanding of the key ideas and truths associated with each theme. Cite Scripture references where necessary, and concentrate upon the *central teachings* of each theme.

Nicene Creed Memorization Project (See Appendix Three)
In order to fulfill the requirements of the MAP course, you will need to write out (or recite) the Nicene Creed clause-by-clause, along with the biblical references attached to each clause. You will also need to memorize the Scripture verses that are listed in the right column that represent a key passage for each clause. The Nicene Creed is perhaps the most significant theological doctrinal statement in the history of the Church, and represents a concise and compelling summary of the apostolic doctrine. Written in the 4th century, it has stood the test of time, serving as the ground for confirmation of faith to ordination to the Gospel ministry. Please set as your goal to memorize the Creed and the corresponding references and Scripture texts verbatim (word-for-word). In order to pass the course, you cannot make more than ten total errors.

Ministry Plan and Dialogue with Pastoral Supervisor (See Appendix Four)
Your final course requirement includes your draft of a ministry plan which you will prepare, and review with your ministry leader or pastoral supervisor. The goal of this dialogue is to get the counsel, input, and assessment of your future desires for ministry in order that you may discover new opportunities and challenges for your ongoing developing ministry. After your dialogue with your pastoral supervisor, you must provide copies of your final plan to both your pastoral supervisor and your advisor or mentor.

Appendix One: Readings Summaries

1. Theology of Leadership

Read *Spiritual Leadership: Principles of Excellence for Every Believer* by J. Oswald Sanders and then:

a. Answer the study questions located at the end of the book on pages 167-179. (These can be done after each chapter for maximum effectiveness.)

b. After you have completed these study questions, please also answer the following questions, "What was the most important insight you gained from the book?" and "How do you want this to affect the way in which you minister to others?"

2. Theology of Ministry

Read *Equipped for Good Work: A Guide for Pastors* by Joe H. Cothen and Jerry N. Barlow and then write a brief paper that answers these questions:

a. What is the best way to describe the purpose of pastoral ministry? (Defend your answer).

b. Choose one of the following aspects of pastoral ministry (preaching and teaching, evangelism, leadership of worship, baptism and Lord's Supper, or helper of the sick, hurting and bereaved) and explain what the pastor's most important responsibilities are in this area and what preparation is needed to do them well.

c. "What was the most important insight you gained from the book?"

d. "As a Christian leader called into pastoral ministry, how do you want the truths in this book to affect the way in which you minister to others?" **OR** "As a Christian leader who has not been called into a pastoral form of ministry, what are the ways in which the insights from this book should affect the way you minister to others?"

3. **Theology of Spiritual Gifts**

   Read *Many Gifts, One Lord* by Harley H. Schmitt and then write a brief paper that answers these questions:

   a. What is the definition of "spiritual gifts" as you understand the term? (Use Scripture to support your definition.)

   b. What is the relationship between "spiritual gifts" and "the grace of God"?

   c. What is the relationship between the "fruit of the Spirit" and the "gifts of the Spirit?"

   d. Are there areas of disagreement that you (or your church) would have with the way Rev. Schmitt understands spiritual gifts and their use in this reading? If so, what are these and how would you define and defend those differences?

   e. What spiritual gifts do you use in your ministry? How have you discovered these gifts?

   f. Are you ministering primarily in your areas of giftedness? If so, how do you know? If not, how can you take steps toward doing this?

   g. How do you make sure that your gifts are being placed at the service of your congregation rather than simply being used as a means for individual fulfillment?

   h. "What was the most important insight you gained from the book?" and "How do you want this to affect the way in which you minister to others?"

Appendix Two: Philosophy of Ministry Paper

Write a paper that helps you to make clear to yourself and others your own calling to ministry and the ways in which you have and will prepare yourself to fulfill your calling. To help you do this, we are asking you to create this paper by answering the following series of questions.

Section One: Calling

1. How did God call you into your current ministry?*

    a. What are your current ministry responsibilities?

    b. Are there any people or events that God especially used to lead you into this ministry?

    c. Is there a specific Scripture verse or passage that God used in leading you toward ministry?

    d. How has your church's pastoral leadership confirmed your calling?

2. How would you define the calling that is on your life?

    a. What are burdens, passions, and desires that God has placed in your heart as a leader?

    b. What spiritual gifts do you use in your ministry and how did you discover these gifts?

    c. How has you calling been made more clear over time?

    d. How are you presently living out this calling?

    e. What convictions has living out your calling produced in your life?

    f. If you had to define what you have been called to do in only one sentence, how would you communicate it?

3. What is your vision for future ministry?

    a. What dreams do you have about how you would like to see God use you in the future?

    b. What barriers stand between you and fully living out your calling?

    c. What kinds of ministry have you been particularly fruitful or effective in so far and what does this say about future ministry directions?

* By *ministry*, we do not mean only *pastoral ministry*. If God has called you to recognized leadership in any area of church life or outreach whether lay or pastoral, we believe this assessment process will be of value to both you and your church.

d. How will you make sure that your ministry development is firmly rooted in your church congregation, has the support of your church's leaders, and places the needs of the church community above your own individual needs?

Section Two: Preparation

4. How has God already prepared you to fulfill your calling?

    a. What people, experiences, and/or formal training have prepared you for ministry so far?

    b. What are the key things you have learned through the things discussed above?

5. What are the life experiences and training courses that you will need to fulfill your vision for future ministry?

    a. What "gaps" are there in your preparation for ministry?

    b. What are the things you most want to learn in order to be better prepared?

    c. What existing TUMI courses do you most need to take?

    d. What new courses would you like to see TUMI offer in the upcoming sessions?

    e. What independent studies and/or supervised internships might be helpful?

    f. What possibilities would you like to explore with your pastor for seeing how your church or denominational leadership can invest in your preparation for leadership?

Appendix Three: The Nicene Creed

We believe in one God,   *(Deut. 6.4-5; Mark 12.29; 1 Cor. 8.6)*
    the Father Almighty,   *(Gen. 17.1; Dan. 4.35; Matt. 6.9; Eph. 4.6; Rev. 1.8)*
    Maker of heaven and earth   *(Gen 1.1; Isa. 40.28; Rev. 10.6)*
    and of all things visible and invisible.   *(Ps. 148; Rom. 11.36; Rev. 4.11)*

We believe in one Lord Jesus Christ, the only Begotten Son of God, begotten of the Father before all ages, God from God, Light from Light, True God from True God, begotten not created, of the same essence as the Father,
    (John 1.1-2; 3.18; 8.58; 14.9-10; 20.28; Col. 1.15, 17; Heb. 1.3-6)
    through whom all things were made.   *(John 1.3; Col. 1.16)*

Who for us men and for our salvation came down from heaven and was incarnate by the Holy Spirit and the virgin Mary and became human.
    (Matt. 1.20-23; John 1.14; 6.38; Luke 19.10)
    Who for us too, was crucified under Pontius Pilate, suffered, and was buried.
    (Matt. 27.1-2; Mark 15.24-39, 43-47; Acts 13.29; Rom. 5.8; Heb. 2.10; 13.12)
    The third day he rose again according to the Scriptures,
    (Mark 16.5-7; Luke 24.6-8; Acts 1.3; Rom. 6.9; 10.9; 2 Tim. 2.8)
    ascended into heaven, and is seated at the right hand of the Father.
    (Mark 16.19; Eph. 1.19-20)
    He will come again in glory to judge the living and the dead, and his Kingdom will have no end.
    (Isa. 9.7; Matt. 24.30; John 5.22; Acts 1.11; 17.31; Rom. 14.9; 2 Cor. 5.10; 2 Tim. 4.1)

We believe in the Holy Spirit, the Lord and life-giver,
    (Gen. 1.1-2; Job 33.4; Ps. 104.30; 139.7-8; Luke 4.18-19; John 3.5-6; Acts 1.1-2; 1 Cor. 2.11; Rev. 3.22)
    who proceeds from the Father and the Son,   *(John 14.16-18, 26; 15.26; 20.22)*
    who together with the Father and Son is worshiped and glorified,
    (Isa. 6.3; Matt. 28.19; 2 Cor. 13.14; Rev. 4.8)
    who spoke by the prophets.
    (Num. 11.29; Mic. 3.8; Acts 2.17-18; 2 Pet. 1.21)

We believe in one holy, catholic, and apostolic Church.
    (Matt. 16.18; Eph. 5.25-28; 1 Cor. 1.2; 10.17; 1 Tim. 3.15; Rev. 7.9)

We acknowledge one baptism for the forgiveness of sin,
    (Acts 22.16; 1 Pet. 3.21; Eph. 4.4-5)
    And we look for the resurrection of the dead and the life of the age to come.
    (Isa. 11.6-10; Mic. 4.1-7; Luke 18.29-30; Rev. 21.1-5; 21.22-22.5)
    Amen.

Memory Verses

The Father — Rev. 4.11 (ESV) – Worthy are you, our Lord and God, to receive glory and honor and power, for you created all things, and by your will they existed and were created.

The Son — John 1.1 (ESV) – In the beginning was the Word, and the Word was with God, and the Word was God.

The Son's Mission — 1 Cor. 15.3-5 (ESV) – For what I received I passed on to you as of first importance: that Christ died for our sins according to the Scriptures, that he was buried, that he was raised on the third day according to the Scriptures, and that he appeared to Peter, and then to the Twelve.

The Holy Spirit — Rom. 8.11 (ESV) – If the Spirit of him who raised Jesus from the dead dwells in you, he who raised Christ Jesus from the dead will also give life to your mortal bodies through his Spirit who dwells in you.

The Church — 1 Pet. 2.9 (ESV) – But you are a chosen race, a royal priesthood, a holy nation, a people for his own possession, that you may proclaim the excellencies of him who called you out of darkness into his marvelous light.

Our Hope — 1 Thess. 4.16-17 (ESV) – For the Lord himself will descend from heaven with a cry of command, with the voice of an archangel, and with the sound of the trumpet of God. And the dead in Christ will rise first. Then we who are alive, who are left, will be caught up together with them in the clouds to meet the Lord in the air, and so we will always be with the Lord.

Appendix Four: Ministry Plan

The heart of man plans his way, but the Lord establishes his steps.

~ Proverbs 16.9 (ESV)

Based upon the insight gained from your readings, Philosophy of Ministry papers and Doctrinal Summary Reviews, and your initial meeting with your advisor, you will be required to draft a plan which summarizes your future desires for ministry. These questions are designed to help you understand and articulate, as best you can, the next steps in your own preparation for ministry, in the area you believe God has called you to serve. Answer the following questions as honestly as possible, and be prepared to share your reasoning for your answers with your pastoral supervisor and advisor.

1. **What Are My Ministry Goals?**

    a. Write a vision statement that describes what you want to accomplish in ministry. George Barna says that "Vision for ministry is a reflection of what God wants to accomplish through you to build His Kingdom" and defines vision statements as "a clear mental image of a preferable future imparted by God to his chosen servants" that is "based upon an accurate understanding of God, self, and circumstances."* *Therefore, your vision statement should say clearly and concisely what you want to do and accomplish in ministry.* This statement should take seriously both what you believe God has placed in your own heart and also the input of your pastoral supervisor.

    b. Using the insights gained in your Philosophy of Ministry paper, write out:

    - At least three short-term ministry goals (things that you will try and accomplish in the next six months to one year)

    - At least three longer-term ministry goals (things that you will try to accomplish in the next two to five years).

    These goals should help you make progress toward what you wrote in your vision statement. They may include both:

    - *Spiritual development goals* (ways that you want to grow in classic spiritual disciplines [prayer, fasting, Scripture reading and memorization, etc.] or ways in which you want to grow in spiritual maturity)

* George Barna, *The Power of Vision: How You Can Capture and Apply God's Vision for Your Ministry*, (Ventura, CA: Regal Books, 1992), pp. 28-29.

*Taken from Gary Pearson, "Designing a Learning Covenant," in *Experiencing Ministry Supervision*, William T. Pyle and Mary Alice Seals, eds., (Nashville: Broadman and Holman Publishers, 1995), p. 60.

- *Ministry skills goals* (ways that you want to increase your experience and competency in performing ministry tasks).

Note: Good goals are SMART.
    S – Specific (an observable behavior if possible)
    M – Measurable (how many, how long)
    A – Attainable (with the resources available)
    R – Relevant (to your vocational goal or personal growth)
    T – Trackable (by what dates)*

2. What Theological and Ministry Course Work Should I Concentrate On?

Using the insights gained in your Philosophy of Ministry paper, write down the types of courses that you most want to take in order to meet your short-term and long-term ministry goals.

3. How Do I Master My Denominational (or Congregational) Distinctives?

The theological courses at TUMI are designed to help you understand and defend the major doctrines of the Christian faith as summarized by the Nicene Creed. This training focuses on what all Christians share in common in their understanding of the faith. However, your ministry will occur as part of a denomination (or independent congregation) that has specific doctrinal distinctives and ministry practices that distinguish your church from other Christian groups. You need to develop a plan of reading or other instruction that will help you to learn the distinctive doctrines and practices of your congregation and the Scriptural principles that support them.

4. What Supervised Ministry Will I Undertake?

a. What supervised ministry will I do on behalf of my church?

b. How long will this supervised assignment last?

c. Will my pastoral supervisor give direct supervision of this ministry or will another person be assigned to oversee my progress?

d. How often will I meet with my pastoral supervisor or the person they designate?

e. What will these meeting times include? (See Appendix Five)

f. How will I show that I am applying the principles learned from the readings papers to my ministry experience?

Appendix Five: Questions for Supervised Ministry Meetings

Please give this form to your ministry leader or pastoral supervisor

The following questions are offered as a primer to encourage open and honest communication between you as pastoral supervisor and the TUMI student. In order to fulfill the requirements for our Ministry Assessment Project course, the student is responsible to discuss with you the challenges and opportunities connected to their service in their current position in the church, as well as their future goals for ministry. We offer these questions to assist you in helping the student understand their gifts, opportunities, and calling as they consider their future service in the church.

Note: Please feel free to draft your own questions as you discuss with the student their fitness and availability for ministry.

1. How much time are you presently giving to this area of service – weekly, monthly, etc.? How much of this time is preparation and how much is direct service?

2. What are your current ministry roles and responsibilities in connection to this assignment?

3. What are your feelings about, and current reaction to this area of service? Are there any areas of discouragement or frustration? Are there any conflicts that need to be resolved? Explain.

4. How are those being served responding to the efforts and care of you and others in this service area? Explain.

5. How are you and your co-workers getting along and relating in your current assignment? What insights about leadership and teamwork are you receiving from this experience?

6. What would you say are your three greatest challenges for you at this moment in this service?

7. What is the most significant or rewarding thing that happened through your ministry since we last talked?

8. How would you describe your three most important lessons learned since we last met to discuss your assignment?

9. Does this area of service and outreach line up well with your gifts and ministry skills? If yes, how so? If not, why not?

10. What particular ideas are you having about your personal ministry calling as you have served the church in this area?

11. How is your reading and writing for your class assignments affecting the way you see your ministry at church?

12. What kind of training or input do you feel you need in order to serve with greater excellence in this particular arena of outreach?

13. What kinds of theological or biblical questions are surfacing for you at this time in this ministry?

14. What progress are you making in mastering our denominational (or congregational) doctrinal distinctives and/or administrative policies? Is there anything that needs to be clarified?

15. What are two areas of growth that you intend to focus upon before our next oversight and evaluation meeting?

16. Is there anything else that you need me to help you with?

Outline for First Interview
With Academic Advisor, Student, and Pastoral Supervisor

1. Welcome the Pastoral Supervisor and the student and share your own sense of encouragement and expectation about the value of this process. Explain the *Ministerial Studies Diploma* and stress that it assumes that the central responsibility for training is through the pastors of the local church. *Give the Pastoral Supervisor a copy of the Course Instruction Plan.* (Note: Remind the student to take notes on everything the Pastoral Supervisor shares since they are to take it into account in creating their ministry plan).

2. Ask the student to share briefly how they would define what their long-term goals in ministry are and what types of training they feel they need to achieve those goals.

3. Ask the Pastoral Supervisor whether they have any comment on the student's *Philosophy of Ministry Paper*. After these comments have been shared and discussed, ask the supervisor to define what kind of leadership roles they envision for the student and what kind of ministries they would like to see them involved in.

4. Ask the student and the Pastoral Supervisor to reflect on the spiritual gifts they believe the student exercises in the church.

5. Ask the student to talk about the types of supervised ministry that would like to be involved in and what that might look like.

6. Ask the Pastoral Supervisor to talk about the type of ministry assignments they could put the student in that would benefit both the student and the church. (Give the Pastoral Supervisor a copy of the supervisory styles handout sheet and suggest that they use it as a resource when talking to the student about the way the ministry assignment will be supervised. Stress that the form their supervision takes is entirely up to them and that the sheet is only for the purpose of stimulating ideas).

7. Ask how the Pastoral Supervisor whether there are any ways they would recommend for the student to master their denominational or congregational distinctives.

8. End the meeting with the following instructions and reminders:

   a. The next step for the student is to complete the ministry plan. Set a suggested target date for completion. Emphasize to the student that they will have to meet and talk with the pastoral supervisor as this is being prepared in order to finalize the assignment details.

   b. Set a tentative date for the second meeting. Remind the student that copies of the ministry plan will need to be sent to the Academic Advisor and Pastoral Supervisor before the next meeting.

   c. Remind the student that they will need to turn in their *Reading Papers* and their *Defense of the Nicene Creed Paper* at your next meeting.

   d. Ask the student and the supervisor whether they have any further questions.

   e. Close by praying for the student and the Pastoral Supervisor.

Outline for Final Interview
With Academic Advisor, Student, and Pastoral Supervisor

1. Welcome the student and the Pastoral Supervisor and thank them for coming.

2. Remind the student that experience without reflection is not education. Make sure they understand that they are to use the readings papers and the meetings with their Pastoral Supervisor to reflect on the ministry experience they are having and in order to improve the way the approach and perform ministry tasks.

3. Ask the Pastoral Supervisor whether they have read the ministry plan and whether they have any questions about it.

4. Ask the student whether there is any question in his/her mind about any part of the plan they have proposed, especially regarding the details of the supervised ministry assignment and its supervision.

5. Ask the student to summarize the most important things they learned from this process. Expand the discussion by asking them the following questions:

    a. How has your calling been changed, clarified, or confirmed?

    b. Are there any things that you would change in your *Philosophy of Ministry Paper* or *Ministry Plan* if you were to rewrite them after having this experience?

    c. What did the readings contribute to your understanding of ministry?

    d. Do you have any new short or long term goals in light of what you have learned?

6. Ask the Pastoral Supervisor what they learned about the student and what they believe God may be saying or doing in the student's life and ministry calling. *Are there any next steps the Pastoral Supervisor would like to suggest for the student?*

7. Invite the Pastoral Supervisor, the student, and yourself to sign the "Agreement to Supervised Ministry Plan" paper and attach it to the academic advisors copy of the Ministry Plan. (If the plan needs to be amended in light of questions raised during the interview, check the appropriate box on the form and attach it to the amended copy when it become available.)

8. Collect the student's *Reading Papers* and their *Defense of the Nicene Creed Paper.*

9. Set date for meeting with the student to recite Nicene Creed to Academic Advisor (word-for-word).

10. Set tentative date for Student to meet with Pastoral Supervisor to review *Questions for Supervised Ministry Meetings.*

11. Conclude with a brief time of prayer. Thank the pastoral supervisor and the student, and encourage them about how God is using them to build his Kingdom.

CPSIA information can be obtained
at www.ICGtesting.com
Printed in the USA
LVHW011725020123
736212LV00008B/479